Ulithi Atoll, Micronesia

Recalling the Past, Reaffirming the Future

ULITHI ATOLL, MICRONESIA:

Recalling the Past, Reaffirming the Future

Rebecca A. Stephenson and Mary L. Spencer
Editors

Distributed by University of Guam Press

Frist published in 2019 in Mangilao, Guam by Rebecca A. Stephenson and Mary L. Spencer
in partnership with University of Guam Press.
Re-published with a new cover in 2024 by University of Guam Press.

University of Guam Press
Richard F. Taitano Micronesian Area Research Center (MARC)

303 University Drive, UOG Station
Mangilao, Guam 96923-9000
(671) 735-2153/4
www.uogpress.com

ISBN: 9781878453969 (hardback)
ISBN: 9781878453976 (paperback)
ISBN: 9781878453990 (library ebook)
ISBN: 9781878453983 (trade ebook)

Library of Congress Catalog Number: 2018902476

In Part 2, the chapter authored by Joliene G. Hasugulayag, entitled "Ulithi, Yap: Navigating
the Seas of Cultural Tradition and Change", is copyrighted material that has been slightly
updated and reprinted with permission from the National Association of Social Workers, Inc.
It originally appeared with the same title as Chapter 5 in the NASW book:

Ofahengaue Vakalahi, H.F., & Talai Godinet, M. (2014). *Transnational Pacific
Islander Americans and Social Work: Dancing to the Beat of a Different Drum*, pp. 91-106.
Washington,
DC: NASW.

Book design by Mary Castro
Original (2019) cover design by Ron Castro
Second (2024) cover design by Ralph Eurich Patacsil

Dedicated to the people of Ulithi Atoll

The editors and authors extend their sincere thanks to all who have made financial gifts to support the publication of

Ulithi Atoll, Micronesia:
Recalling the Past, Reaffirming the Future

*For their significant contributions,
we wish to acknowledge the following donors:*

**Matson Foundation
Hagatña, Guam**
Bernie Valencia, Vice President/General Manager for Guam/Micronesia
Phil Santos, Account Executive
Gloria Propst Perez, Executive Assistant, Guam/Micronesia

**College of Liberal Arts & Social Sciences
University of Guam
Mangilao, Guam**
Dr. James D. Sellmann, Dean

**Nancy L. Stephenson
Hawaii Island, HI**
Physician Relations, Medtronic Inc., Minneapolis, MN (Retired)

**Paul Dahlquist, Ph.D.
Hawaii Island, HI**
Lyman Museum and Mission House, Hilo, HI (Retired)

Thanks are also due to:
**The University of Guam Endowment Foundation
and Katrina Perez, who coordinated donations**

Contents

List of Maps viii

List of Tables ix

List of Figures x

Acknowledgements xvii

Historical Overview and Introduction 3
    Mary L. Spencer and Rebecca A. Stephenson

Part 1: Encountering Ulithi -
    A University of Guam Field School in Cultural Anthropology 45
        Field Report: Discovering Aspects of Life, Culture, and Environment on
            Ulithi Atoll 47
            Rebecca A. Stephenson
        Material Culture of Ulithi: A Fusion of Past and Present 56
            Shawn Holstrum
        Catching Flying-Fish in Ulithi Atoll: A Study of Gorges 64
            Yosihiko H. Sinoto
        Notes on Some Traditional and Contemporary Ulithian Economics 73
            Melvin D. Cruz
        A Tale of Two Islands: Being Disabled in the Western Pacific, Perspectives
            from Guam and Ulithi 84
            Rebecca A. Stephenson and Eulalia J. Harui-Walsh
        Resources in Print Concerning Ulithi Atoll 97
            Deborah Piscusa Bratt with Rebecca A. Stephenson

Part 2: Culture, Economics, Learning, and Life Challenges in Ulithi 111
        Ulithi, Yap: Navigating the Seas of Cultural Tradition and Change 113
            Joliene G. Hasugulayag
        My Parents Named Me Joshua 129
            Joshua D. Walsh
        Lava Lava: Hallmark of Ulithian Culture 139
            Eulalia J. Harui-Walsh with Rebecca A. Stephenson
        Economic Well-being in a Subsistence Economy: Production, Marketing, and
            Micro-finance on Yap Proper and Falalop Islet, Ulithi, Yap State 152
            Ann Ames
        Field Notes from Ulithi 167
            Todd Ames
        Glimpses of Ulithian and Other Yap Outer Island Learning Traditions for
            Children 184
            Mary L. Spencer
        Ulithi: Physical Environment Bibliography 215
            Harley I. Manner

Afterword 238

Index 243

List of Maps

1. Ulithi Atoll in the Western Pacific and close up of Ulithi Atoll 2
2. Other island entities near Ulithi Atoll 5

List of Tables

Historical Overview and Introduction
  Mary L. Spencer and Rebecca A. Stephenson
    1. Western Caroline Company's 30 Year Land Lease Property in Ulithi
       (effective January 15, 1913)..9
    2. Islander Population in Angaur, Palau, and Place of Birth (1925) 15
    3. Total Population of Ulithi and Distribution across Islands in 1920
       and 1925 15
    4. Islander Population in Ulithi and their places of Birth (1930)...........................16

Part 1 Encountering Ulithi - A University of Guam Field School in Cultural Anthropology
  Catching Flying-Fish at Ulithi Atoll: A Study of Gorges
    Yosihiko H. Sinoto
    1. Measurements (mm) of Gorges...66
  Notes on Some Traditional and Contemporary Ulithian Economics
    Melvin D. Cruz
    1. Goods found in Ulithi stores 80

Part 2 Culture, Economics, Learning, and Life Challenges in Ulithi
  Economic Well-being in a Subsistence Economy: Production, Marketing, and
       Micro-finance on Yap Proper and Falalop Islet, Ulithi, Yap State
    Ann Ames
    1. Methods of data collection and analysis 155
    2. A listing of the species found in the gardens and agroforests of three
       Ulithi households..164

List of Figures

Historical Overview and Introduction
Mary L. Spencer and Rebecca A. Stephenson

1. Ulithi Atoll 3
2. Johann Kubary (left) who studied the tattoos of Ulithi people, and (right) a full body tattoo that Kubary observed on a Mogmog man 6
3. George Thilenius, Coordinator of the Südsee Expedition for anthropological research of 1908 – 1910 in Ulithi and other Micronesian and Melanesian locations 6
4. Chancellor Otto von Bismarck of Germany 7
5. King Alfonso XIII of Spain 7
6. Ulithi women in 1935 during the Japanese colonial period. The man on the left is probably a Nan'yo Boeki employee. The man to his right may be Sionji Kiikazy and the man in the rear with a cap and in uniform is possibly a naval officer 12
7. Islander laborers at the Angaur phosphate mining station in late 1910s 16
8. September 1935 postcard from Tangruis of Mogmog while he worked on Angaur...17
9. The Japanese Navy's aerial photographs of Asor, Falalop, and Sorlen islands in Ulithi Atoll; the first aerial photos in their history (altitude of 500 meters from seaplane carrier *Wakamiya*, 1921) 19
10. A weather sub-station – *bunshitsu* – like the one built in Asor, Ulithi. The same substation structure was constructed in Pagan Island in the pre-war northern Mariana Islands, and Woleai, another outer island of Yap 19
11. The man sitting, on the right, may be a weather station employee in Asor in the 1930s. The man with the hat is probably Tanaka Jun'ichi, a kogakko teacher, and the woman on the left may be his wife 21
12. A Japanese school on Yap Proper with Micronesian students. The Japanese words shown in the framed display over the chalk board are (left to right): "diligence, sincerity, stand up" 21
13. Ulithi Chief Ueg and other Ulithians meet US Navy Admiral Carleton Wright, and his Navy companions in 1946 25
14. Ulithian outrigger canoes at Asor Island, Ulithi Atoll during World War II, August 1945. Parts of the secret US base on Ulithi are shown along the shore 27
15. US ships in anchorage at Ulithi Atoll, December 1944 27
16. Mogmog Island was used as a recreational area for the US sailors, as shown here ...28
17. Harry S. Truman, US President from 1945 – 1953, during the end of WWII and the postwar period when the United Nations was established and the Trust Territory of the Pacific Islands was created 29
18. John F. Kennedy, US President from 1961 – 1963, who established the Peace Corps, lifted the travel and security restrictions on Micronesia, shifted Trust Territory administration from military to civilian control, and doubled the TTPI budget in order to support economic, educational, and health progress 29
19. Ulithi Men's Council with King Ueg (center, row 1), Mogmog, Ulithi, 1948 30
20. Swearing-in of the first Congress of Micronesia, c1965 31
21. Yap Governor John Mangefel and Lieutenant Governor Hilary Tacheliol of Ulithi visit Ulithi in 1979 32

22. Hilary Tacheliol, 2009 33
23. Rosa Huffer Tacheliol, 2016 33
24. William Lessa, anthropologist and author of research on Ulithi and other Micronesian cultural matters 34
25. William Alkire, an American anthropologist and author of the widely read book, *Peoples and Cultures of the Pacific*, which includes a section on Yap and the outer islands of Yap. Shown here on Lamotrek in 1962 34
26. Young Micronesian priests posing with Bishop Neylon at the ordination of Fr. John Hagileiram in 1985; (from left) Fr. Nick Rahoy, Fr. Apollo Thall, Bishop Neylon, Fr. John Hagileiram, Fr. Julio Angkel 35

Part 1 Encountering Ulithi - A University of Guam Field School in Cultural Anthropology

Field Report: Discovering Aspects of Life, Culture, and Environment on Ulithi Atoll
Rebecca A. Stephenson

1. Field school participants, faculty, and UOG administrator: Shawn Holstrum, Deborah Piscusa Bratt, Melvin Cruz, Rebecca Stephenson (Team Leader), Remington Rose Crossley, (Dean, College of Arts and Sciences), Eulalia Harui-Walsh (Co-Team Leader), and Edward Mendiola, Jr. 48
2. The regional field trip ship stopping at Ulithi to deliver vital supplies and to exchange disembarking Ulithi passengers with newly boarding passengers headed to Yap and beyond 51
3. Outer Island High School, Falalop, Ulithi: Young women graduates, 1992 52
4. Outer Island High School, Falalop, Ulithi: Young men graduates, 1992 53
5. Outer Island High School, Falalop, Ulithi: Families enjoy watching students do a traditional dance at the graduation event, 1992 53
6. John B. Rulmal, Sr., the Yap State Governor's Representative in Ulithi, who ensured that the needs of the members of the UOG Ulithi Field School Team were fulfilled 54

Material Culture of Ulithi: A Fusion of Past and Present
Shawn Holstrum Davis

1. Group preparation of seafood, with Dr. Stephenson (right) observing......................57
2. Family prepares baskets of seeded breadfruit and other foods for a large gathering 57

Catching Flying-Fish at Ulithi Atoll: A Study of Gorges
Yosihiko H. Sinoto

1. Fishing gorges, related method and materials 65
2. Coconut eyes plugged with pieces of wood to secure the leaders onto which bent type gorges are attached...67
3. Bent type gorges: a. Angular type; b. Notched type; c. Concave type; d. Manufacturing stage of gorges by chipping. Scale 1/1..67
4. a. Stick gorge with coconut and fish meat; b., c., d. Movement of the gorge when swallowed and points at which gorge may lodge....................................68
5. Mechanism of gorges to catch flying fish: a. Width; b. Height; c. Angle; d. Angles for 68 complete and incomplete gorges combined 69
6. Yosihiko Sinoto discussing fishing gorges with Ulithi fishing expert 69

7. Open mouth of a flying fish. Height of the mouth is 21 mm 70
8. Fish dangling 70
9. Close up of hook with only one point protruding...70

Notes on Some Traditional and Contemporary Ulithian Economics
Melvin D. Cruz

1. Exterior and interior views of one of Ulithi's "Mom and Pop" stores, 1992 74
2. Exterior and interior views of a second of Ulithi's "Mom and Pop" stores, 1992 75
3. Exterior and interior views of a third "Mom and Pop" store in Ulithi, 1992 75
4. A Mobile Gas Station, Falalop, Ulithi, 1992 76
5. A laundromat, Falalop, Ulithi, 1992 78
6. Philip Nery, one of the Ulithi leaders 83

Resources in Print Concerning Ulithi Atoll
Deborah Piscusa Bratt with Rebecca A. Stephenson

1. Philip Nery and his daughter Shirley of Ulithi Atoll 97
2. Ulithi home compound with WWII bomb artifact..98
3. A Ulithian teenager helps prepare a meal that is cooking over a fire in
   the family compound 99
4. A pre-adolescent Ulithian girl prepares a dried pandanus leaf for weaving.............100
5. Mariano John Laimoh, Editor of the *English-Ulithian Dictionary I*.
   Born in Asor and often working in Falalop, Ulithi Atoll, Mariano is a Ulithian
   linguist. He has also authored children's books for the Yap State Education
   Enterprising Department that are used in Ulithi, Fais, Sorol, and Ngulu.................102
6. Ulithi men and adolescent boys rest and converse in a canoe house on
   Ulithi Atoll 103
7. Ulithi boys collect green coconuts and remove the outer husk, in preparation
   for drinking or grating 104
8. Two Ulithi women engaged in the preparation of threads on the *maliel* spool
   apparatus (left) for weaving a lava lava, on a *thur* (top right) on which a
   lava lava weaving project is already underway. The woman on the right
   is likely mentoring the young woman on the left on how to weave *(faesiu)*............105
9. Teenage girls on Ulithi Atoll prepare leis of orange *hulu* flowers *(Cordia
   subcordata)* for a celebration 106
10. Young girl playing with her dog in her family compound....................................107
11. Example of a fresh water catchment on Ulithi, reported by Stephenson, 1984........108
12. John Rulmal, Jr. ("Junior") with his classmates, waiting for his men's
    group to begin to dance on Graduation Day, 1992 109

Part 2 Culture, Economics, Learning, and Life Challenges in Ulithi

Ulithi, Yap: Navigating the Seas of Cultural Tradition and Change
Joliene G. Hasugulayag

1. Joliene Hasugulayag, MSW, LSW, author..115
2. Author with family members..116
3. Author's childhood in Ulithi Atoll..117
4. Author and husband Derwin's wedding day on Ulithi 118

My Parents Named Me Joshua
Joshua Depmar Walsh

1. Joshua Walsh with his two boys, Elijah Depmethou Walsh and
   Jeremiah Harui Walsh 130
2. Joshua and brother John with their families 131
3. Joshua Walsh in the FSM Supreme Court room in Palikir 132
4. Eulalia Harui and Jack Walsh's wedding party, 1979 136

Lava Lava: Hallmark of Ulithian Culture
Eulalia J. Harui-Walsh with Rebecca A. Stephenson

1. Linda Ylmarag and her *maliel*, where she prepares the threads *(chow)*
   for the loom *(thur)* 141
2. Ulithi lava lava No. 1, a *peg* lava lava by Carmen Haduemog................144
3. Ulithi lava lava No. 2, *ilotal gulfoy*, by Lourdes Ydwechog 145
4. Ulithi lava lava No. 3, *marub*, by Carmen Haduemog 145
5. Ulithi lava lava No. 4, *dorol satawal*, by Maria Pemadaw.......................146
6. Ulithi lava lava No. 5, *dorol satawal*, by Carmen Haduemog..................146
7. Ulithi lava lava No. 6. *peg rang*, by Maria Rosogmar 147
8. Ulithi *pad chig* thread lava lava, No. 7, green, woven by Maria Rosogmar 147
9. Ulithi *pad chig* thread lava lava, No. 8, purple, woven by Linda Ylmarag.............147
10. Ulithi *pad chig* thread lava lava, No. 9, *dololtad*, "color of the ocean,"
    woven by Alberta Ului Dipwek 148
11. Ulithi *pad chig* thread lava lava, No. 10, pink, woven by Alberta Ului Dipwek......148

**Economic Well-being in a Subsistence Economy: Production, Marketing, and
Micro-finance on Yap Proper and Falalop Islet, Ulithi, Yap State**
Ann Ames

1. Maria Luhudul and Emanual Hadhomar, both provided outstanding
   assistance and insights to the research on Ulithi 152
2. Positive factors to production and marketing 161
3. General store on Ulithi that is most often open 162

Field Notes from Ulithi
Todd Ames

1. Falalop from the air 168
2. Research team..169
3. Healthy taro pit with Harley Manner..170
4. Falalop garden with H. Manner, A. Ames, and D. Rolmar........................170
5. Store goods 171
6. Stakeholders meeting...173
7. Chief Yach of Falalop with Derwin Rolmar 174
8. *Wa* builders 175
9. Ulithian *wa* detail..176
10. Hiro Kurashina, Todd Ames, Becky Stephenson, and Jan Ames at the
    wedding on Asor 177
11. Wedding on Asor 177
12. Wedding party on Asor...179
13. Effects of salt water intrusion 180

14. Farmer shows dying taro pit 181
15. Blighted breadfruit..181
16. Shoreline erosion 182
17. Women dancing on Falalop 183

Glimpses of Ulithian and Other Yap Outer Island Learning Traditions for Children
Mary L. Spencer

1. Falalop Island, Ulithi Atoll, Dec 7, 2004, 10° 01' 01.96" N, 139° 47'
   24.40" E, elev 6m 185
2. One of my 1985 Ulithi UOG classes with Yap Outer Island educators...................186
3. Another of my 1985 Ulithi UOG classs with Yap Outer Island educators 186
4. Sampling of Ulithi children's activities at varying ages, by girls and boys,
   and in varying contexts, including some visiting children from other Yap
   Outer Island 188
5. Ulithi families and children maneuver their boats to ferry out to a ship
   that has anchored briefly off shore to supply the island 189
6. Ulithi children's drawings...191
7. Ulithian language picture books 197
8. Course students explore the cognitive development and learning styles of local
   children of different ages through the use of Piagetian conservation tasks..............198
9. In a private home, a child (left) begins the creation of an intricately woven
   traditional flower *mwarmwar*, closely observing and practicing her mother's expert
   work (right). Earlier, the mother dispatched several children with instructions
   for picking the correct flowers and greenery 201
10. Men take an active role in teaching children in both private and
    community settings..203
11. A Ulithian women's village cooking circle, in which children of varying
    ages observe, pitch in, and occasionally receive requests or suggestions 205
12. Traditional skills observed in 1985 continued in 2010............................207

Ulithi Physical Environment Bibliography
Harley I. Manner

1. Harley Manner discusses survey with Ulithi men at research gathering in 2010.....215
2. Derwin Rolmar and Ulithi men discuss environmental research survey in
   a 2010 study visit..216
3. Ulithi gardener examines newly planted and mulched taro plants in one
   of the concrete tanks, 1990 217
4. William H. Alkire, Department of Anthropology, University of Victoria,
   British Columbia, Canada. Dr. Alkire wrote one of the most widely read
   books on the people and cultures of Micronesia, and also conducted research
   on specific principles of societal organization in the Outer Islands of Yap 220
5. Ann Ames discusses environmental survey with Ulithi woman at
   community meeting, 2010 221
6. Todd Ames, Derwin Rolmar, and Ulithi man discuss environmental and
   food production matters after 2010 workshop..221
7. Chandra Legdesog of Ulithi is a Master of Arts graduate student in the
   Micronesian Studies Program at the University of Guam. She is active in
   research on climate change in the Micronesian region and also participates in

federally funded health research and treatment.Her environmental research explores the perceptions of Ulithians about climate change phenomenon, and their cultural and life style adaptations to these phenomenon 222

8. Isadore Dyen, was a Professor of Linguistics at Yale University, and was one of the original members of the small research team that the US Navy placed on Romonum Island in Chuuk State immediately after WWII hostilities ceased..223

9. Samuel H. Elbert is the linguist who developed the Ulithi-English word lists for the US Navy immediately after World War II. These formed the basis for many other Ulithi language activities such as work with Peace Corps Volunteers. He may be known even more widely for co-authoring the Hawaiian-English Dictionary with Mary Kawena Pukui. He also published articles and books on Hawaiian folklore 224

10. Renowned island botanist F. Raymond Fosberg who worked at the Smithsonian Institution, documenting and creating an archive of plant materials from the Micronesian region. He is credited with playing a significant role in the development of coral reef and island studies. (1908 – 1993)..224

11. Ward H. Goodenough, at 90 years of age, one of the original Yale University members of the anthropology team sent to Micronesia immediately after World War II by the US Navy's Coordinated Investigations of Micronesia (CIMA) 225

12. Father Francis X. Hezel, author of multiple books on the history of Micronesia. Father Hezel has also conducted original research on important issues such as the high rate of suicide among Micronesian teens and young adults, and census studies 226

13. William Lessa, a UCLA anthropologist who conducted extensive field work on Ulithi, working with Ulithians to describe their way of life, as well as contemporary challenges presented to them in events such as typhoons...228

14. Marianna Chim, a Falalop Ulithi woman, reviews a report of environmental research conducted on Ulithi and in her garden by the Ames, Ames, Manner, and Rolmar team, 2010 230

15. Marie-Helene Sachet, preeminent botanist with the Smithsonian Institution, and curator in the Department of Botany, National Museum of Natural History. She was particularly dedicated to collecting, organizing, and disseminating research and information on the botany of islands (1922 – 1986) 232

16. Anthony M. Solomon conducted a major study and report for President John F. Kennedy regarding the status, development and needs of the Trust Territory of the Pacific Islands (TTPI) 233

17. Navy physician Marshall Wees being taken on a turtle hunt by Ulithian youth during his WWII assignment to Fassarai..........................236

18. King Ueg of Ulithi...236

19. Robert Yangerluo of Woleai, receiving the Presidential Thesis Award for Outstanding Thesis at the University of Guam. His research

explored political and socioeconomic land issues for outer islanders
of Yap. Yangerluo received the Master of Arts degree in Micronesian
Studies in 2012 and is now a faculty member at the College of Micronesia,
Yap State. Robert Yangerluo also worked as a Research Associate with
University of Guam faculty, Todd Ames, Ann Ames, and Harley Manner.
His work in Yap Proper served as the foundation for the later work
presented in their respective chapters in Part 2 of this book 237

20. In 1983, while conducting a Fresh Water Resources field project in Ulithi
for Dr. Steven J. Winter at WERI, University of Guam, Dr. Rebecca
Stephenson was able to view this large traditional structure on Fassarai
that featured a high gabled roof. Note also the elevated airplane pontoon
on the left that was used as a rainwater catchment device 237

ACKNOWLEDGEMENTS

The authors and editors extend their deepest appreciation to the following individuals and organizations for sharing their resources and knowledge during our preparation of this book. This included assistance in locating or providing photographs; in locating representatives or owners of key photographs; and in obtaining reprint permission for photographs:

Hilary Tacheliol, Ulithi

Rosa Huffer Tacheliol, Ulithi

Julius Chosemal, Ulithi

Wakako Higuchi, Guam, personal collection, Guam

Doug Herman, *Pacific Worlds* website, Baltimore, MD

George Underwood, personal collection

Fr. Francis X. Hezel, S.J.

Stuart Dawrs, Senior Librarian, Pacific Collection, Hamilton Library, University of Hawai'i-Manoa

Museum of New Zealand *Te Papa Tongarewa*

Nancy E. Levine, Professor of Anthropology, Chair of the Anthropology Department, University of California, Los Angeles

Stephen Acabado, Assistant Professor of Anthropology, Anthropology Department, University of California, Los Angeles

Smithsonian Institution, Washington, DC

Atoll Research Bulletin, Smithsonian Institution

U.S. National Archives and Records Administration, Still Picture Branch

Macmillan/Holt Rinehart & Winston

Wikipedia Foundation, Inc.

Office of Public Information, Department of Defense and the Photographic Library, Bureau of Aeronautics

Vidalino Staley Raatior, Educational Consultant, Web Designer

Craig R. Elevitch, Agroforestry Net Inc, Holualoa, HI

William Alkire, Department of Anthropology, University of Victoria, Canada

Chandra Legdesog, University of Guam, Micronesian Studies Program

Pamela Legdesog, Pacific Resources for Education and Learning (PREL)

Micronesian Seminar

Wanderling.tripod.co

Alamy Limited, United Kingdom

Other information on photography in this book is provided in the *Afterword*.

Special thanks are due to the scholars, co-authors, designers, and distribution specialists who were particularly generous with their time and knowledge as they provided advice, review, photography, book design, cover art, and revision assistance: Hiro Kurashina, Wakako Higuchi, Harley I. Manner, Ann Ames, Todd Ames, Joliene Hasugulayag, Josede Figirliyong, Dana Figirliyong, Joshua

D. Walsh, Mary Castro, Ron Castro, Susan Biolchino, Jessie Rosario, Monique Carriveau Storie, and Victoria Lola Leon Guerrero.

Our heartfelt affection and deepest respect will always be associated with three colleagues who contributed to the book, but who are no longer with us: Eulalia J. Harui-Walsh, Yosihiko H. Sinoto, and George Underwood.

ULITHI ATOLL, MICRONESIA:

Recalling the Past, Reaffirming the Future

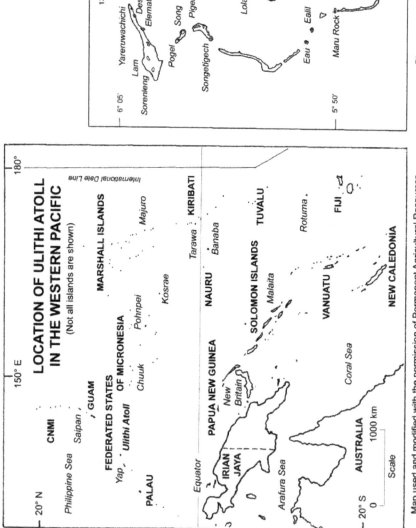

Placenames and map of Ulithi Atoll from Bryan, Jr. (1971).

Cartography by Harley I. Manner, 2017.

Map used and modified with the permission of Permanent Agricultural Resources.

Map 1. Ulithi Atoll in the Western Pacific and close up of Ulithi Atoll.

HISTORICAL OVERVIEW AND INTRODUCTION

Mary L. Spencer and Rebecca A. Stephenson

The larger populated islets in Ulithi Atoll have been described in the literature as including Mogmog, Asor, Falalop, and Fasserai, and sometimes Lossau.[1] Ulithi Atoll's population numbered 514 in 1960 and 773 in 2000 (Wikipedia, 2017a), with the majority of the residents residing on Mogmog, Falalop, and Fassarai. To the east of the atoll are two protected and uninhabited islands, the Turtle Islands of Giil'ab and Yaaor, owned by a Falalop family (Pacific Worlds, 2017a, p. 5). Sorol Atoll is also considered part of Ulithi. It is a coral atoll located 93 miles south of Ulithi Atoll (Wikipedia, 2017b). Sorol is not currently inhabited due to tidal wave damage and lack of infrastructure (C. Legdesog, 2017). As late as the 2000 census, 215 people were reportedly living there. Now, Sorol people continue to visit their atoll in order to access its agricultural and ocean-based food resources.

Figure 1. Ulithi Atoll. (© Alamy Stock Photo)

Fais Island and Ulithi Atoll have a close association, in terms of a shared origin in their mythology (Rubinstein, 1979, pp. 18 – 22), and in terms of their interactional and governmental associations. Fais is a raised coral island lying 54 miles southeast of Ulithi Atoll, and had a population of 215 people according to the 2000 census (Wikipedia, 2017c). Fais is a separate legislative district of the Yap State Government. The Yap State Constitution specifies that Ulithi Atoll, Fais

---

[1] Readers should be aware that the written form of the Ulithi language has been undergoing some linguistic modifications and they may encounter spelling changes for these atoll and islet names. Pacific Worlds (Wikipedia, 2017a) provides a comparative list of old/new names: Mogmog/Mwagmwog; Asor/Yasor; Falalop/Fl'aalop; Losiap/L'oosiyep; Fasserai or Fatherai/Fedraey; Sorlen/Sohl'oay; Potangeras/Potoangroas.

Island, Sorol Atoll, and Ngulu Atoll comprise the second election district, and shall have one member. The Constitution defines the roles of traditional leaders and traditions via two councils: The Council of Tamol in which Ulithi and Fais are both represented by the same member, and the Council of Pilung for Yap Islands Proper (FSMlaw, 2017).

The Ulithian language is used by people of Ulithi Atoll, Sorol, and Fais. Ngulu, which is 65 miles south-southwest of Yap, is also a separate legislative district and was reported by the 2000 census to have a population of 26 people (Wikipedia, 2017d). They reportedly use both Yapese and Ulithian languages and perhaps their own dialects as well (Pacific Worlds, 2017a, p. 7).

The origins of the people of Ulithi remains an open question. William Lessa, the foremost academic scholar to date who has conducted field research in Ulithi, suggested that the people may have come from the Asian west, but with contacts terminated long, long ago (1966, p. 8). But he also emphasized Ulithi's connections with people of the Micronesian islands east of Ulithi, citing cultural similarities and the fact that the Ulithian language and the languages of those islands are mutually intelligible — a finding documented by other researchers (e.g., Ellis, S. J., 2012).

European Contact and Control

The period preceding Ulithi's contact by European explorers is estimated to have endured until the early 1500s, when ships of Portugal, Spain, and Germany only very occasionally touched the lives of Ulithians (summarized here from Lessa, 1966, pp. 5 – 8). Some historians report the possibility that a Portuguese captain, Diogo da Rocha, visited Ulithi in 1525, and that a Spanish explorer, Ruy Lopez de Villalobos, sighted Ulithi in 1543. Spanish voyager, Don Bernardo de Egui y Zabalaga, arrived at Ulithi in 1712 and invited some of the islanders on board his ship.

There is a tendency for outside scholars to assume that prior to these European contacts the people of Ulithi and other islands in the region were isolated. However, as the deeply established navigational knowledge of these islanders at the time of European contact attests, men and women of their islands had long been actively exploring the Pacific world. From these voyages, Ulithi seafarers brought home important economic materials, developed a knowledge of multiple lands and cultures, learned about living among people different from themselves, and established many diplomatic relationships in the Pacific.[2]

In 1721, a Woleaian canoe was sighted off the eastern coast of Guam (Barratt, 1988, pp. 20 – 24). In route to Ulithi, it had become lost in a storm. After landing, the 11 men, 7 women, and 6 children peacefully collected coconuts, met Padre Muscati, and offered items from their own islands. Two days later, a second canoe

---

[2] Barratt (1988, pp. 67) asserts that "a principal characteristic of the natives of Oceania may be considered to be constant cheerfulness," referring especially to their music, singing, dancing, and public "concerts." He describes how these are interwoven with planning and preparations for navigational activities. Could the development of these qualities be interpreted as learning the correct social behavior so useful in public and even international interactions?

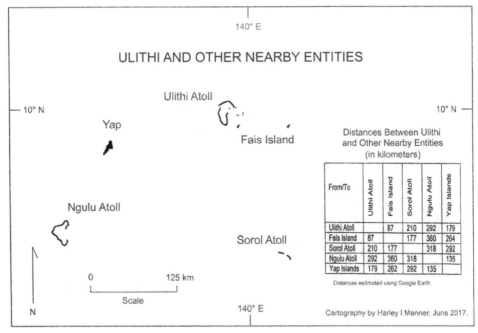

Map 2. Other island entities near Ulithi Atoll.

from that original 6-canoe flotilla landed on a western Guam shore with 4 men, 1 woman, and 1 child, and were taken to Umatac to meet Governor Sanchez and Padre Juan Antonio Cantova, both of whom were Spanish. Through interpreters, the Woleaians indicated that they knew of Guam and its "rulers." Padre Cantova stayed with them and learned language and geography from them throughout their 8-month visit. Based on these lessons, Cantova created a regional map that was used by European ship captains for many years.

These interactions with people from islands south of Ulithi encouraged Padre Cantova to persistently strive toward a visit to the Caroline Islands, a goal he and Padre Victor Walter finally realized in 1731 when they sailed to Ulithi via the Philippines. Cantova stayed on Ulithi for several months during which he baptized 127 children and counseled islanders in religious matters. After Cantova sent Father Victor Walter back to Guam, Cantova was killed, reportedly because news had reached Ulithi that the Spanish on Guam had mistreated some Ulithi seamen. Walter later sailed from Guam to the Philippines, and returned to Ulithi two years later.

In 1823, nearly a century after Padre Cantova's time on Ulithi, English Captain John MacKenzie sighted the islands of Ulithi and had some peaceful interactions with islanders (Lessa, 1966, p. 7). In his 1826-29 voyage, Russian explorer Fedor Petrowitsch Litke visited multiple Caroline islands, reportedly including Ulithi. He later recorded complimentary comments about Ulithians. Brief contacts were made by French and other Spanish visitors prior to the period of European commercial trade in the western Pacific.

In the 1870s, a blend of international commercial and anthropological interest in Ulithi drew Johann Kubary to Ulithi (Vincent and Viti, 1973, p. 109). He was a Polish trader and ethnologist who worked with the Godeffroy Trading Company of Hamburg, Germany. While in Ulithi he made observations of tattooing (Figure 2) (Wikipedia, 2017e). These studies were augmented when Georg

 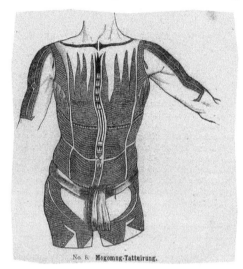

No. 8. Mogomug-Tattuirung.

Figure 2. Johann Kubary (left) who studied the tattoos of Ulithi people, and (right) a full body tattoo that Kubary observed on a Mogmog man.

Christian Thilenius (Figure 3), a German physician and anthropologist, organized the famous Südsee Expedition of Micronesia and Melanesia (Wikipedia, 2017f).[3] The respected expedition team collected 15,000 objects and artifacts in the South Pacific, which they brought back to Hamburg – enough to fill 23 books with descriptions, illustrations, and photographs (Damm, 1938). Added to the sporadic visits of these scholars was the presence of Germans such as Alfred Tetens and Irish-American David O'Keefe on nearby Yap (Lessa, 1966, pp. 6 – 7).[4, 5] In 1869, Tetens established the first trading post of J. C. Godeffrey & Sons on Yap, which conducted commercial interactions with Ulithi over the years. In addition to this enterprise, Tetens engaged in historical and ethnographic studies, co-authoring a book with Edward Gräffe: *The Caroline islands of Yap or Quap*

Figure 3. George Thilenius, Coordinator of the Südsee Expedition for anthropological research of 1908-1910 in Ulithi and other Micronesian and Melanesian locations.

[3] Other members included Friedrich Fülleborn, Augustin Krämer, Paul Hambrüch, Otto Reche, Ernst Sarfert, and Wilhelm Müller-Wismar.

[4] See the book, *His Majesty O'Keefe* (1950), by Klingman & Green, for a fictionalized account of O'Keefe's life in Yap and other parts of the world.

[5] Also see Pacific Worlds' online *Chronology for Yap and Ulithi* (Wikipedia, 2017b).

Figure 4. Chancellor Otto von Bismarck of Germany

according to the reports of Alfred Tetens and Johann Kubary (c1870).

Life in Ulithi may have been calmer before the German and Spanish outsiders began competing for influence and control of the atoll. But there was a spirit of expansionism in European countries that was fueled by hopes of finding precious ores and jewels, economic resources such as copra, and the international prestige that came from the exploration. Germany and Spain had both been active in colonizing various Pacific countries throughout the 1800s. German Chancellor Otto von Bismarck had been involved in trade in the Marshall Islands and the Caroline Islands earlier in the century (Figure 4) (Wikipedia, 2017g). When Spain failed to create actual governments in these areas, Bismarck annexed the Caroline Islands in 1885. The Spanish-American war began in 1898. By the time Spain lost the war, Spain's royal house was declining. King Alfonso XII died in 1885. His wife, Maria Christine of Austria, ruled as the Regent until their son, Alfonso XIII could take over in 1898 (Figure 5) (Wikipedia, 2017h). After the US defeated Spain in 1898, Spain sold the Carolines, the Palaus, and all of the Mariana Islands except Guam to Germany for $5,000,000 (See Sanchez, 1987, pp. 70 – 75, regarding Guam). But Germany's control of Ulithi was also a brief arrangement.

Figure 5. King Alfonso XIII of Spain

Japanese Contact and Administration

To date, little has been written about life on Ulithi during the long and eventful Japanese period in Ulithi from 1914 to 1944. With Wakako Higuchi's original contributions to this section (Higuchi, 2017) and her additional permission to quote from her recent paper (2017) on the Japanese Administration during these years, we are able to shed more light on this history.[6] The full range of Japanese relationships with Ulithi extends from the beginning of the 1900s through US occupation

---

[6] Quotations from Wakako Higuchi are based on: Higuchi, W. (July 2017). *Draft working paper: Ulithi during the Japanese Administration, 1914-1944.* This includes figures, tables, and photographs from her personal collection. Higuchi's paper is her original work written on the basis of numerous Japanese archival materials that have never been published in the past.

of the Atoll, which commenced in 1944. Higuchi suggests that these relationships can be divided into eight historical periods and key events, as follows:

1907-1914: The Japanese company, *Nan'yo Boeki*, expanded to Micronesia but had no contacts with Ulithians.

1914: The Japanese Navy occupied German Micronesia.

1918 – 1922: Japan's military administration headquarters, *Minseibu* (Civil Administration Department) was established to administer the affairs of the civilian islanders. Ulithi became part of the Yap Administrative District.

1914 – 1943: Ulithiian phosphate mining involvements.

1935: Japan withdrew from the League of Nations. The Japanese Navy declared that Japan would continue administering the South Seas Islands, including Ulithi.

1937: The Japanese Navy began airfield construction in the South Sea Islands for military use.

1941 – 1944: Japan declared war against the United States, Great Britain, and Holland. The Japanese Navy and Army were dispatched throughout Micronesia.

1944: The Palau and Yap districts were attacked by US air raids, followed by US occupation of Ulithi.

1907 – 1914

Ulithians had a history of at least some minor early contacts with the Japanese during both the Spanish and the German periods when *Nan'yo Boeki* (also known as the South Sea Trading Company or *Nanbo)* expanded to western Micronesia (pre-1900s and 1906 – 1907). On August 14, 1906, German Governor Fritz prohibited the Yap Islanders from selling coconuts and copra to foreigners, including the Japanese. On April 22, 1907, this order also became effective for the islanders of Woleai, Ifaluk, Sorol, and Ulithi. Die West-Karolinen-Gesellschaft, m.b.H. was established in 1912, and Deutsche Jaluit-Gesellschaft was granted a 30 year lease of German land on Yap.

1914 – 1918

In 1914, the Japanese Navy occupied German Micronesia and began military administration over the South Sea Islands. They named Micronesia: *Nan'yo Gunto.* A special land combat unit *(tokubetsu rikusentai),* on board the military ship *Satsuma*, landed on Yap at 10:00 am on October 7, 1914 and Germany surrendered without a fight. The Japanese unit reported: "There was nothing unusual about Europeans and the islanders. It seems the islanders are welcoming us." (Higuchi, 2017). The Navy's Palau Garrison Unit *(shubitai)*, and the Yap Detachment *(bunkentai),* guarded the island. Yap was made a part of the Palau Civil

Administration District *(Palau Minsei-ku)*. Eight employees of *Nan'yo Boeki* were on island. On October 8, 10 island chiefs were called and informed that Japan's Imperial Navy occupied Yap (Higuchi, 2017). This included the entire Yap sector. Yap was part of the Palau Garrison's purview (Peattie, 1988, p. 62; p. 64). Japan physically occupied the major outer islands of Yap during this period, meaning only Falalop, Ifaluk, Lamotrek, Woleai, Yauar, and Sorol, a list which includes two Ulithi islands – Falalop and Sorol. Table 1 reveals some of the details of the Japanese government holdings (all of which were leased to Nanyo Boeki) on Ulithi as a result of this occupation. The Ulithi civilian population at that time was probably 400 or fewer people.

Table 1. Western Caroline Company's 30 Year Land Lease Property in Ulithi (Effective January 15, 1913).[7]

Leased Land or Village (hectare)	Leased Land or Village (hectare)
Sogoroi (12.2 ha)	Song (7.4)
Etsusol (28 ha)	Pigelelei (0.5 ha)
Mangejang (12.2 ha)	Sorenleng (8.7 ha)
Feitabul (13.2 ha)	Lam (8.5 ha)
Pugerlug (0.5 ha)	Elemot (3.0 ha)
Pig (2.0 ha)	Pau (Eu) (11.4 ha)
Eau (1.5 ha)	Bulbul (1.0 ha)
Songetigech (1.5 ha)	Roshieppu (13.3 ha)
Elipig (2.6 ha)	Yaru (3.0 ha)
Pigelelet (9.4 ha)	Gielap (2.0 ha)
	Total: 566 Hectares[8]

1918 – 1922

Nan'yo Boeki submitted a report to the Japanese Navy in 1917 that stated: "…the Ulithi archipelago and its German state properties were leased to the Western Caroline Company but there was nothing which suggested the German company had previously *developed* Ulithi's resources." Thus, Japan's *Nan'yo Boeki* appears to be the first foreign company to attempt to develop coconut plantations in Ulithi.

Nan'yo Boeki concluded that, "…if proper agricultural methods are introduced (by the company) to the islanders, five times more coconuts could be harvested."[9] According to the survey, there were 3,850 coconut trees (725 acres) in Asor and 1,200 coconut trees in Soren (217 acres).

Some information is available on the Japanese administration's educational goals and activities for Ulithi youth. An office employee of *Nan'yo Boeki's*

---

[7] Source: *Nishi Caroline Kaisha oyobi Higashi Caroline Kaisha ni taisura tokkyo meirei narabini shoyuchi oyobi soshakuchi no seishitsu* in Rinji Nan'yo Gunto Bobitai Shireibu, *Nan'yo shoto ni kansuru chosa no ken.*

[8] The size specification of each parcel of the leased lands was determined by survey and confirmed and approved by Baumert (Secretary of the German government), Yansen (Jaluit Company), and Scott (agent of Okif Company) in September 1911.

[8] "Nishi Caroline gunto rito shoto jicchi chosasho" in "Rin-Nan-Bo minsei-rei, Rin-Nan-Bo minmei 859-go no 2, tochi kashisage ni kansuru ken ha go sengi ai nasu" in Shisetsu Keiei 2-tome (6) (January 26, 1917), NIDS.

Ulithi sub-branch, Masaoka Tamizo, was authorized by the Yap *Minseibu* office to perform teaching duties in Ulithi. It was reported that as of 1918, the number of Ulithian students who were taught at the school (*gakko*) was 24 (13 female students; 11 male students).[10] A 1920 military ship report stated that a *Nan'yo Boeki* Ulithi sub-branch employee was teaching elementary Japanese language and arithmetic in Asor and Falalop. Reportedly, the Japanese expectation was that children whom they considered to be performing well would attend *hoshu-ka* (a supplementary course) of the *Tomin Gakko* (Islanders' School) in Yap.[11] Also, in 1918 the Navy commander issued a civil administrative order, *Nan'yo Gunto Tomin Gakko Kisoku* (rules for the Islanders' School in the South Seas Islands). This may have been the impetus for the beginning of schooling in Ulithi. Article 1 of the rules stated that the purpose of school was to "…have the islander children be receptive to *koon* (Imperial favor), and teach Japanese language to give moral training as well as ordinary knowledge and skills necessary to daily life (Higuchi, 2017). The rules allowed consideration of the conditions on each island; e.g., the people's customs and conventions. Based on these considerations, it was decided to teach reading and writing of *katakana* characters, counting up to 20, and addition, subtraction, multiplication, and division. However, since the teacher was a *Nan'yo Boeki* employee stationed in Asor with part time teaching duties, he had to devote most of his time to being a copra trader. Much of his time would have been dedicated to furthering the *Nan'yo Boeki* interests during occupation, which included: 1) supervision of the occupied German properties (later, control and management of the state owned land); and 2) influencing the islanders to recognize and accept that Ulithi was now under Japanese rule.

In February of 1919, Administrative Vice-Minister of the Japanese Navy, Tochinai Sojiro, submitted a statement to Secretary of the Cabinet, Takahashi Koi, expressing the preferences of a group of village chiefs in Micronesia for Japanese rule. A separate version of the declaration had been prepared for each islander chief. The appropriate version of the document was signed by islander village chiefs separately in Ponape, Jaluit, Truk, Saipan, Rota, Palau, Angaur, and Yap (including a Chamorro leader on Yap). All of their statements were sent by the Extraordinary South Seas Islands Defense Corps Commander, Nagata Taijiro in Truk to Tochinai in Tokyo on January 25, 1919. This happened to coincide with the timing of the Paris Peace Conference where allocations of the occupied German territories were to be decided by the Allies at meetings beginning on January 18, 1919. Yap's version stated:

> "We heard that the Allies *had* a great victory in the war in Europe and concluded a cease-fire agreement. It will not be long before a peace treaty is signed. We, the islanders, declare that we generally hope the South Seas Islands fall into the occupier Japan's hands.

---

[10] "Keibikan moushitsugi jiko, Gunkan Yodo" in "Gunkan Yodo nan'yo Shoto jokyo shirabe (1), 1921.

[11] "Gunkan Yodo junko shisatsu hokoku, Rinji Nan'yo Gunto Bobitai Shireikan, Nozaki Kojuro" (August 23, 1920).

In the time of *the* German period, the islanders were treated as low-grade people and we could not stand up in every respect *to* the authorities' oppression even during copra trading. Taking this opportunity, we express our intense desire for freedom from German domination and *that* our islands are integrated into Japanese territory. December 23, 1918, Tereg, Tamangin, Falan, Fanouai, Wamoon, Garangamau, Taman, Figir, Zarangan, and Aijn. A separate document in Chamorro language is submitted by Antonio."

While meeting in Geneva in 1921, in accordance with Article 22 of the Covenant of the League of Nations (1920), which formed the *mandate system* (a post-war approach to protecting colonies of the larger parties to a war), the League Council recognized the Japanese mandate. Japanese administration of Ulithi, according to the 1920 "Mandate for the German Possessions in the Pacific Ocean lying North of the Equator," was delegated to the Japanese Navy. In 1922, the Japanese Navy's responsibilities to administer and conduct civil affairs were transferred to the *Nan'yocho* (the South Seas Bureau, a civilian government agency). A Director was appointed to administer *Nan'yocho's* affairs (Peattie, 1988, p68). After the 1922 establishment of *Nan'yocho*, the *Nan'yo Boeki's* local branch employee continued to stay and assist with administrative work in Ulithi until March 1944.

Soon after occupation of the German territory, the Japanese navy declared that the three values of the South Sea Islands for Japan were: 1) military value; 2) industrial value; and 3) value as a southward expansion base. Ulithi's military value was remarkably important at the national level because of its location. Yap (with which Ulithi has had a long history of cultural association) and Ulithi are located between Saipan (the closest island to Japanese water), and Palau, the southern most advance base relative to the Dutch Indies and New Guinea. Also, Yap was a station on the East-West line of the South Seas positions linking Palau, Yap, and Jaluit in the Marshall Islands. But there was no natural harbor in Yap that was suitable for anchoring a fleet. The Japanese Navy considered Ulithi Atoll as a possible fleet base, similar to that of Woleai. The Japanese Navy battleship *Kasuga* studied the pros and cons in 1921. They reported that there were few unknown reefs between Hammarin channel and Mangejang Islands, that ships could pass through the Towachi channel in Ulithi, and that the east and west channels were convenient for ship entrance and exit. Ulithi was deemed to be the most ideal location west of Truk for atoll entry and exit. It was believed that many ships and fleets could anchor there and that ships could be quickly re-supplied in Ulithi.[12] The Japanese Navy built a light buoy at Mangejang Island in Ulithi. The *Kasuga* conducted extensive aerial surveys of the western Caroline vicinity, seeking potential sites for seaplane bases, trying to identify possible mines in the ocean, and strategically installing searchlights, wireless communication, and radar. The leadership reportedly considered Ulithian needs as well. The following cautionary statement was

---

[12] "Honkan no deiri seshi suido oyobi fukin no jokyo" in "Hokoku shorui teishutsu no ken, Dai-ni kengai kantai shireikan Yoshida Seifu (April 4, 1921), in *"Gunkan Kasuga Nan'yo Gunto junko hokoku."*

included in a communication from the *Kasuga*: "Stationing land flying corps on these islands needs to be carefully considered because of limited size of flatlands, difficulties of removing coconut trees, *and because* both will divest islanders' *of* staple food."[13]

Figure 6. Ulithi women in 1935 during the Japanese colonial period. The man on the left is probably a Nan'yo Boeki employee. The man to his right may be Sionji Kiikazy and the man in the rear with a cap and in uniform is possibly a naval officer.[14] *(© Wakako Higuchi Personal Photo Collection, 2017)*

In the early years of the 1920s, there were other reports from the Japanese Navy leadership in Ulithi and Yap regarding living conditions of the Islanders. On Asor, *Nan'yo Boeki* unsuccessfully attempted to breed pigs. They also tried to improve the sanitary conditions of the islands by addressing the mosquito and fly problem and by cleaning roads and villages. The military ship *Yodo* reported on Ulithians in 1921, saying: "Islanders in Falalop and Asor have cheerful spirit, desire to save, ability of economy." Although they felt that the islanders in Mogmog, Fassarai, and Lossau were less industrious, they reported that they liked fishing and that fish was their staple food. The Japanese observers explained that the chief who controlled Ulithi lived on the island of Mogmog and that he was the subject of the high chief in Yap. Men were required to pay an annual poll tax of 3 yen to the Japanese administration, which was actually paid in copra. The children of Ulithi rarely attended a *kogakko* (public school) in Yap and almost no

---

[13] "Taisho 10-nen ichi-gatsu jugo-nichi, do san-gatsu sanju-nichi, Gunkan Kasuga Nan'yo Gunto junko chu, hikoki ni kansuru kenkyu hokoku" (April 4, 1921), in "Hokoku shori teishutsu no ken, Dai-ni Knegai Kantai Shireikan Yoshida Seifu," in "Gunkan Kasuga Nan'yo Gunto junko hokoku."

[14] Saionji, a grandson of Genro (a senior statesman) Saianji Kinmochi and a part-time officer of the Foreign Affairs Ministry, made an on-site inspection of the South Sea Islands in February 1935 to write a report for the League. He probably stopped over at Ulithi via the Yamashiro-Maru on the way to Truk from Palau. This Oxford graduate later became an advisor of Prime Minister Konoe Fuminaro.

one understood the Japanese language. There was no medical facility on Ulithi. Housing and sanitation were judged to be in need of improvement, and it was reported that many had a skin disease. Asor reportedly had a large cistern, but it was not considered suitable for drinking water. In spite of periodic reports of this type, actual contact between islanders and the Japanese on the island was reported to be very limited.

In 1921, the *Shoriki* patrol ship reported that another problem on Ulithi was the shortage of farming labor: "The Ulithians planted potatoes but had a poor harvest. Their food was mainly coconuts and breadfruits but these are not enough. Therefore, they live on *hinatasou* (or *portulacacae*, the low growing nutritious succulent *purslane*)[15] boiled with coconut molasses."[16] When considering the reasons for food shortages, the authors mentioned: The smaller number of males compared to females, leading to a shortage of farming labor; the reluctance of inhabitants to engage in farm work; and the disproportionately large amount of government land (as established by the former German company) relative to the smaller size of private lands. This condition led to the small copra output, which was not even sufficient for the islanders' needs. Similarly, the islander needs had not been met in the *Nan'yo Boeki* pig breeding experiment.

1914 – 1943

Japanese phosphate mining activities affecting the people of Ulithi Atoll and nearby Fais Island spanned several of the periods of our analysis; therefore, we have placed the discussion of this period near the time of its beginning. The authority's mining and labor recruitment activities had extensive impacts on the lives of the Ulithi miners as well as on their families and the entire Ulithi community complex. Mining occurred in Angaur (or Ngeaur),[17] Palau, and also on Fais Island. In this section, evidence is presented primarily on the mining activities in Angaur. An historical summary of the Fais mine was provided by Rubinstein (1979, pp 27 – 29), in which he indicated that the people of Fais did not participate in the mining work on their island that was conducted between August 1937 and May 1944. Rather, he estimates that 600 workers from Okinawa, Yap, and other outer islands of Yap were brought to Fais by the Japanese for the mining enterprise. He explained how mining on nearby Fais caused serious and long lasting negative impacts to the environment and to human subsistence living patterns because, "…the entire center of the island was stripped of soil, which left barren 36% of the land surface of Fais, the richest and most fertile third of the island."

---

[15] Higuchi identifies *hinatasou* (or *hinatagusa*) as a plant belonging to the family Portulacaceae. Manner explains that within this family, Fosberg, Sachet, and Oliver (1979, p. 74) list two species *(Portulaca australis* Endl and *Portulaca oleracea* var. *granulato-stellulata* v. Poelln.) each found on Ulithi Atoll. Both of these species, also known as purslane or pigweed, are edible either raw or cooked. Both species range from being common to abundant, and are spontaneous herbaceous plants on all islands and can be found in open spaces, paths, and agroforest gardens.

[16] "Keibikan moushitsugi jiko, Gunkan Yodo" in "Gunkan Yodo Nan'yo Shoto jokyo shirabe (1), 1921.

[17] A new spelling system has been created for the language of Palau in which the name Palau is spelled Belau, and the name Angaur is spelled Ngeaur (McManus, S. J., Josephs, L. S., and Emesiochel, M. (1977).

Angaur, the site of two other open pit phosphate mines, is a small 3 square mile island in the Republic of Palau, and is located 432 miles southwest of Ulithi (Google Earth, 2017). Waters surrounding Angaur are well known to mariners for being rough and dangerous. The Germans began mining phosphate on Angaur during their occupation in 1909. The Japanese government purchased the mining rights and all facilities and machines from the German company in 1914, and conducted mining there under the name of *Nan'yo Keiei Kumiai* (South Sea Management Union Company). Later, the Japanese Navy managed it directly. All management was transferred to the *Nan'yocho* after 1922. Japan depended on phosphate imports in order to make phosphorus fertilizer. The mines on Angaur were finally closed by the Americans in 1954 (Thyssen, 1988).

An artifact on Angaur from German times that remains even today is the presence of macaque monkeys (Marsh-Kautz, Leon Gulibert, & Wheatley, 2003; Marsh-Kautz & Wheatley, 2004; Wheatley, Stephenson, Kurashina, & Marsh-Kautz, 2004). Macaques were brought to Anguar from Indonesia by Germans during their 1909 – 1914 governance of Micronesia. So it is likely that Ulithians who worked in the mines became familiar with this species that is found nowhere else in Micronesia. According to several researchers, the macaques were hunted by mine workers for sport, consumption, medicinal purposes, or as pets, practices that were continued through the US war period on Angaur (Poirier & Smith, 1974, p. 265; Marsh-Kautz & Singeo, 1999; Marsh-Kautz & Wheatley, 2004, p. 147). Other artifacts of the Ulithian experience on Anguar may have developed because of opportunities to share music and dance with other miners, including Chinese, Chamorros, Filipinos, and Micronesians from many different islands, such as local Palauans. Hezel (1995) and Hanlon (1998) have both described parts of this history. The Ouchacha website (2017) provides a musical analysis of these collaborations.

The Japanese transfer of Ulithi workers to Angaur was considered to be part of the Japanese *dekasegi* policy, in which Ulithians were expected to work away from home. The colonial theory was that islanders would be encouraged to become migrant workers in other islands in order to maintain a balance in Ulithi between the food supply and the demand for it. In addition to Angaur, some Ulithians were sent to Weno Island in Chuuk. Table 2 displays the home-island distribution of islanders placed in Angaur in 1925. According to some sources,[18] during the Japanese navy administration period of 1914 – 1922, the inhabitants of islands "west of Truk Islands" were "nearly forced to subscribe mining laborers, boys, and others to Angaur to do physical work," with village chiefs being paid a commission of 30 *sen* for each laborer. For outer islanders the term of employment was about one year.[19] Direct and indirect evidence of Ulithi labor in the mines is provided in several tables below. We believe the data in Table 2 includes Ulithians with others in the Yap district.

---

[18] "Keibikan moushitsugi jiko, Gunkan Yodo" in "Gunkan Yodo Nan'yo Shoto jokyo shirabe (1), 1921.

[19] In fieldwork in Puluwat, Chuuk in 1988, co-editor Mary Spencer documented interviews in which an elder Puluwatese navigator explained his experience working for the Japanese in Angaur.

Table 2. Islander Population in Angaur, Palau, and Place of Birth (1925)

	Total (789)		Saipan (53)		Palau (345)		Yap (229)		Chuuk (136)	
	M	F	M	F	M	F	M	F	M	F
Kita-Mura	230	602	24	29	121	140	33	5	30	0
							5%			
Minami-mura	372	0	0	0	75	0	191	0	106	0
							52%			

Source: *Nan'yocho, Nan'yo Gunto Tosei chosa hokoku*, Tisho 14-nen (Palau, 1925), pp. 110 – 111.
M = Male, F = Female. Kita-mura = North Village, Minami-mura = South Village

Table 2 shows that a group of Yapese laborers (combined with an unknown number of Ulithians) worked at both the northern and the southern mining sites in Angaur, Palau in 1925 and were second in population size only to Palauans.

Table 3. Total Population of Ulithi and Distribution across Islands in 1920 and 1925

Island	Subtotal (Islanders)	Houses	Male (Islanders)	Female (Islanders)	Island Population 1920	1925
Asor	56	12	23	33	-	62
Mogmog	133	37	57	70	-	142
Lossau	35	0	14	21	-	35
Fassarai	78	21	35	43	-	80
Falalop	149	46	57	92	-	183
Total	449	440	184	265	448	505

Source: *Nan'yocho, Nan'yo Gunto tosei chosasho, dai ni-kan tomin-hen* (1930), pp. 6 – 7.

The presence of male workers relative to female workers was much greater for Chuuk and Yap, but almost evenly distributed for Saipan and Palau. Only five women in the Yap category were reported and all were at the north village. The presence of female *dekasegi* at mine sites begs the question, "What were their activities there?"

Table 3 documents total Ulithi population size in 1920 (448) and 1925 (505), as well as population and housing subtotals for individual Ulithi islands. Table 4 provides 1930 population data as well as place of birth information. Table 4 shows a 1930 total population somewhat lower than 1925, rather than the expectation of a rising population due to additional births. This 56 person decline could be associated with placements of Ulithians in the Angaur mines or in other assignments.

One of Higuchi's (2017a) most significant findings regarding this period is revealed by the population data in Table 4. When the percent of women and men during this time are compared for each Ulithi island separately, and also for Ulithi as a whole, we see an alarming discrepancy between the numbers and percentages of males and females in the 1930 data. Of a total Ulithi population of 449 people, 41% were male and 59% were female. The negative difference for males varies

Table 4. Islander population in Ulithi and their places of birth (1930)

Island	Subtotal		Born in own village/island		Born in the Yap District		Born in Another District	
	Male	Female	Male	Female	Male	Female	Male	Female
Asor	23	33	18	27	4	5	1	1
Mogmog	57	76	54	71	2	4	1	1
Lossau	14	21	13	21	1	0	0	0
Fassarai	33	43	29	43	4	0	0	0
Falalop	57	92	44	82	13	9	0	1
Total	184	265	158	244	24	18	2	3
	Islander Population				Present Address Yap District		Present Address Palau District*	
Ulithians	211	261			188	261	22	0

Source: *Nan'yocho, Nan'yo Gunto tosei chosasho, dai ni-kan tomin-hen* (1930), pp. 486 – 487, pp. 550 – 551.
* Three males were born in the Jaluit district.

across the five Ulithi islands cited: -14% for Mogmog and Fassarai; -18% for Asor; -20% for Lossau; and -24% for Falalop, with Falalop the most severely affected. This imbalance between males and females raises questions about both causes and effects. Why were there so many fewer males than expected at this time, and what happened to them? Are the answers related to the Japanese *dekasegi* policy; and if so, what are the details? How were the lives of women and children affected, not only by the numerical difference, but also by the emotional impact on individuals and the functioning of families and communities?

Higuchi's historical research on the Angaur lives of Ulithians has also brought to light several photographs of interest. In Figure 7 below, a postcard photo from the very early phosphate mining years in Angaur during Japanese military admin- istration shows islander laborers lined up at the mining station (c. late 1910s).

The medical needs of workers at the Angaur mines were provided for by the Navy clinic and later by the *Nan'yocho* Angaur clinic. Higu- chi reports that at first the clinic provided medical treatment to the islanders for free, and then later began charging fees. How- ever, because the islanders' economic resources were very

Figure 7. Islander laborers at the Angaur phosphate mining station in late 1910s. *(© Wakako Higuchi personal collection.)*

low, the charges were minimal. In June and July of 1920, dengue spread among the islander laborers. The number of islander inpatients (c. 1932) was 15 in ordinary rooms, and 4 in isolation rooms.[20]

On the back of a postcard from Higuchi's collection (Figure 8), apparently from the 1930s, a Ulithian miner wrote a message in Japanese characters (which, according to Higuchi, are well formed *katakana* and *kanji* characters, but not written by a Japanese person). He identified himself as Tangruis from Mogmog island, and gave his address as "a dormitory at Angaur Phosphate Mining Station." He was a Kogakko graduate, and worked for Angaur for a number of years.

He wrote:

> The dancing we will show you from this time is from Magmog, Oleai, and Fais islanders. When we play we are happy. It might not be as good as expected, but we are pleased to have this opportunity to show it to the Japanese guests who came from the mainland. Please be patient for a while to see the dancing. [Magmog shima], Tangruis, Mogmog Island, Outer Island of Yap, South Seas.

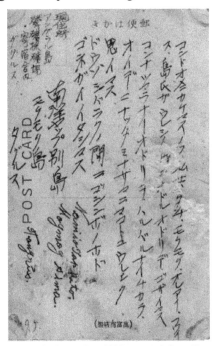

Figure 8. September 1935 postcard from Tangruis of Mogmog while on Angaur. *(© Wakako Higuchi personal collection.)*

An important disincentive to the recruitment and retention of islanders for the Angaur phosphate mines was the irregular and sometimes complete lack of transportation back to Ulithi after the miners' terms of service were completed. Higuchi relates a 1920 report from patrol ship *Shoriki*, in which the head of the Navy's Angaur Mining Station requested that 14 Woleaian and 8 Mogmog *dekasegi* workers be returned home via the *Shoriki*. They all disembarked in Woleai and the Mogmog islanders then had to take a *Nan'yo Boeki* schooner to Ulithi from there. The *Shoriki* report stated:

> Soon after they saw the lee of Woleai, they expressed their indescribable happiness. Japanese police patrolman Fukushima on Woleai reported that the islanders who the mining station and other Japanese had recruited were not allowed to return to their home even after their term ended, for reasons of "no transportation to return home." Their families had been waiting for their return for years but sometimes "tragedy" (e.g., their family member's death), or "comedy" (e.g., adultery) happened.[21]

[20] "Angaur Iin gaikyo" (cir. 1932) in Yanaihara Tadao Bunko shokuminchi kankei shiryo, Ryukyu Daigaku Fuzoku Toshokan.

[21] Nan'yo Gunto keibi junko chu no shoken, Mogami kancho Takeuchi Yasukichi. (April 17, 1920) In: Junko shisatsu kokai hokoku, (9), senji shorui maki 28, Nan'yo Gunto kankei 13, shohokoku 3) (1920).

According to these sources, the claim of "no transportation to return" was not a valid reason. The company needed proficient mining workers. As the islanders who labored in the mines did not go back to their island, other islanders in their atoll began to refuse to go to *dekasegi*. And South Seas Bureau patrolmen "had to force" the islanders to accept that they must leave for Angaur. At the time of the islanders' departure, they and their families, "…cried loudly and sobbed with grief," according to the report. Although the mining and government authorities insisted that there was no way to solve the transportation problems, eventually the *Nishi Caroline-maru* ship that had been abandoned on Yap was repaired to "…remove islanders' negative impression…" and relieve their concerns.

1935

At this point in the Japanese occupation and administration of Ulithi and other parts of Micronesia, priorities became increasingly apparent for technological and strategic planning, as well as for development. The year of 1935 began with food and recovery concerns in Ulithi due to a major typhoon that had caused great damage the month before. The first *Nan'yocho* seaplane, *Shirohato*, made a test flight on May 9, 1935. Its course began in Palau and proceeded through several touchdowns and take-offs over two days, finally landing in Ulithi after having made strategic photographs throughout the voyage. Higuchi explains that this successful flight was regarded as one of the epoch-making events for the Navy's progress in seaplane technology, and that it was aimed at both commercial and military uses of seaplanes in the South Sea Islands.

1937

Across Micronesia, military development under the Japanese Navy's supervision began in earnest in January 1937. It was at this point that they abandoned the Washington Disarmament Treaty and Japan's withdrawal from the London Disarmament Conference became effective.[22] In preparation for the new period of the non-disarmament treaty in the Western Pacific, the Navy cooperated with the *Nan'yocho*, to make a 10-year total development plan for the South Sea Islands, focusing on Saipan, Palau, and Pohnpei. It went into effect in FY1936 (April 1936 – March 1939).[23] According to this plan, the *Nan'yocho* Meteorological Observatory, Ulithi sub-branch, was built in Asor in March 1937: "Because the South Seas Islands is the origin of typhoons, *and because* ocean transportation and communication between islands is rapidly increasing, and *also because* irregular air services began." Two Japanese assistant observers were stationed there. An azimuth finder station was built in Ulithi in FY 1937, which was transferred to the Navy from the *Nan'yocho* in December 1938. A higher-ranking assistant technician was then assigned.[24]

---

[22] See Higuchi, W. (2013). The Japanese administration of Guam, 1941 – 1944: A study of occupation and integration policies, with Japanese oral histories. North Carolina: McFarland & Company, Inc.

[23] See Higuchi, 2017a.

[24] Nan'yocho koku jigyo no gaiyo" in "Takumu Daiji seigi Nan'yocho Kishodai kansei seitei no ken" (July 8, 1938.)

N
W   E
S

Asor Island

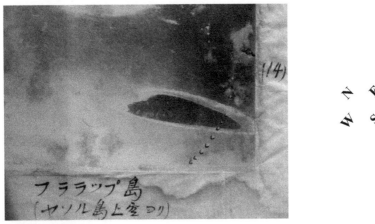

N
W   E
S

Falalop Island

N
W   E
S

Sorlen Island

Figure 9. The Japanese Navy's aerial photographs of Asor, Falalop, and Sorlen islands in Ulithi Atoll; the first aerial photos in their history (altitude of 500 meters from seaplane carrier *Wakamiya*, 1921). *(Source: Yamaguchi Yoji personal collection/Japan Institute of Pacific Studies; © Wakako Higuchi, personal collection.)*

Figure 10. A weather sub-station – *bunshitsu* – like the one built in Asor, Ulithi. The same substation structure was constructed in Pagan Island in the pre-war northern Mariana Islands, and Woleai, another outer island of Yap.

Throughout this period, the Japanese representatives were concerned with the manner in which Ulithi could support Japanese military plans with regard to weather, water, food supplies, and agricultural conditions. For example:

> "There is a rainwater cistern of 20 tons, belonging to the Nan-yo'cho, made of concrete, next to the oil storage in Asor. The weather station workers are using the water now. There is one well in the islanders' village but it is not suitable for drinking because of hygiene concerns and shortage of water."

> "There is no water supply pipe or other water facilities. It is necessary to transport water in containers and canoes to ships and airplanes."[25]

In the 1930s, the *Palau-Maru* and the *Saipan-Maru*, 5,000 – 8,000 ton ships, operated between Yokohama and Palau via Saipan and Yap. It was very rarely that these ships called at Ulithi Atoll, but occasional visits allowed administrators to check on a variety of issues. Yamano Yukichi, a high ranking South Seas Bureau officer, was one of the passengers on the ship. He wrote: "Islanders' canoes came out *to* the sea and rowed around the ship. I asked the islanders for a ride." It seemed to be an honor to have a South Seas Bureau officer ride in their canoes. The weather substation was only 200 meters from a pier. There were no Japanese women on the island.

Higuchi points out that besides the water supply, serious problems with the food supply also had to be addressed. Until the weather sub-station was established, a *Nan'yo Boeki* employee was the only permanently stationed employee at Ulithi. There was no power. Quoting related reports:

> It was "…impossible to have many Japanese station workers" in Ulithi because of lack of food. During the construction of the weather sub-station, the food for 12 workers was all shipped from the mainland Japan via Yap. It took 30-days to ship potatoes from Japan to Ulithi and the Navy planned to store them on the island for 20 days. The food supply for islanders consisted only of taro planted in a patch of *500 tsubo (1,653.9 square meters)* in Asor, 100 chickens, and 6 pigs" (believed to refer to Asor only). If some staff are permanently stationed at Ulithi all food would need to be shipped from Japan. It is not impossible to plant some vegetables near their housing area, but it will be very difficult"[26]

A 1937 survey of the 450 Ulithi inhabitants by the *Juni Sentai* (12th squadron) led to the further understanding of needs and supplies, information which was important to military plans. In addition, repeated surveys were conducted in eight different Ulithi islets to document the number of coconut trees and the copra production in 1917 and 1935. In Asor there were 3,850 coconut trees in 1917 compared to 6,529 in 1935. Copra production was reported to have increased from 10 to 88 tons per year by fiscal year 1935.

---

[25] Dai Juni Sentai Shireibu, "Showa juni-nendo Dai Juni Sentai heiyo chosa hokoku, Dai yon, shigen hokyu kankei (1937).

[26] Dai Juni Sentai Shireibu, "Showa juni-nendo Dai juni Sentai heiyo chosa hokoku, Dai-yon Shigen hokyu kankei (1937).

Figure 11. The man sitting, on the right, may be a weather station employee in Asor in the 1930s. The man with the hat is probably Tanaka Jun'ichi, a kogakko teacher, and the woman on the left may be his wife *(© Wakako Higuchi Personal Photo Collection, 2017).*

The education of select Ulithian youth was on the minds of Japanese colonial officials. Higuchi (2017) reports that at least some Ulithian children attended Japanese public school, known as *kogakko*, on Yap Proper (e.g., Figure 12). It is not possible to definitively identify which, if any, of the children in the photo are from Ulithi. The students in the photo below may be from multiple islands. As American military members discovered after landing in Ulithi in 1944, a cadre of youth were fluent in both Ulithian and Japanese, evidence of their sustained interactions with the Japanese before or during the war. Wees (1950, p. 16) reported that this was because some of them "had been forced through a course of training on Yap." King Ueg of Ulithi appointed one of these individuals, Hatae, to serve as an interpreter for Dr. Wees as the doctor provided medical care to the Ulithi people living on Fassarai near the

Figure 12. A Japanese school on Yap Proper with Micronesian students. The Japanese words shown in the framed display over the chalk board are (left to right): "diligence, sincerity, stand up." *(Palau: Nan'yo Gunto Bunka Kyokai and Nan'yo Kyokai Nan'yo Gunto-shibu, 1938, p. 93.)*

end of the US military occupation of Ulithi. Wees used his old Japanese-English dictionary to mediate the process. He would point to an English term, for which Hatae could read the adjacent Japanese equivalent (indicating Hatae's literacy). This process allowed the two of them to negotiate meaning across the languages.

1941 – 1944

During this period, the Japanese Navy technically occupied Ulithi Atoll. However, it appears that the *Nan'yocho* did not generally have officers stationed in Ulithi; instead, they made field visits for specific tasks such as conducting a population census or recruiting laborers. In some cases a Japanese employee of *Nan'yo Boeki* for the Ulithi sub-branch office would have instructions given to the islanders by a Yapese *junkei* (assistant patrolman), who was always a graduate of the *kogakko* (the school in Yap). The *junkei* also acted as a language and cultural interpreter between the Japanese administrator and the islander community. Higuchi found that the South Seas Bureau's directory of October 1943 listed one Ulithian patrolman, a *junkei* named Fugiri, who worked at the Ulithi *Chuzaisho* (residential police box) with a monthly wage of 41 yen. This was an admirable salary, placing him above the 31 yen salary of the lowest-ranked *yatoi* – or Japanese government employee. Believing that there were no Japanese administrators in Ulithi at that time, Higuchi suggests that Fugiri's role was that of an administrative assistant. Higuchi also reports documentation showing that in 1944 approximately 10 personnel from the Japanese Naval Guard Unit *(keibitai)* landed on Ulithi Atoll as well as on Fais for the purpose of conducting meteorological observations and vigilance for the US enemy. However, they withdrew from Ulithi because communication was cut off.

As the war situation worsened in 1943, the South Seas Bureau's administrative structure was reorganized and unified with the Navy in October 1943. This process integrated the Yap District Branch Office into the *Seibu-shicho* (Western District Branch headquarters in Palau), and converted to wartime military administration.

Compared to Palau and Saipan, Yap was defenseless until February 1944 when the 205 *Setsuei tai* (Naval Construction Battalion) landed to build an airfield on Yap. The islanders, including Ulithians, were mobilized (probably from Angaur) to join the construction. On May 10, 1944, three months after the construction began, the 22nd Naval Air Squadron landed on Yap with 50 planes. On the next day, the 46th Naval Guard Unit arrived on Yap. It was July 9, 1944 when the Independent Mixed 49th Brigade landed to defend the airfield, led by Captain Eto Daihachi.

Higuchi's research discovered the following description of what occurred on Ulithi in the first quarter of 1944:[27]

---

[27] Dai 30 Konkyochitai Dai-ichi Kihou-maru, "Showa 19-nen 5-gatsu 4-kkui, Tokusetsu kanshitei. Dai-ichi Kihou-maru sento shoho, showa 19-na 3-gatsu 31-nichi, Nishi Caroline homen taikasen (May 4, 1944).

As ordered by the 30th Base Force commander, the *Dai-ichi Kihou-maru*, a special picket boat, anchored at the Ulithi berth (near Asor island) at 8:37 am on March 31, 1944. By 9:00 am they had completed their discharge of supplies. At 10:20 am, a roaring sound was heard in the sky. At almost this same time, six US fleet fighters were seen at 4,500 meters (14,764 feet) altitude. They bombed the ship and the Ulithi weather sub-station. At 10:21 am, five more US planes (11 in total) appeared. The ship was attacked, a communication room was hit, and a receiver was broken. The Ulithi weather sub-station was hit and set afire. At 10:24 am, a Japanese machine gun member was killed and three others were injured. At 10:36 am, four Japanese anti-submarine depth bombs were dumped into the ocean. At 10:37 am, the US attack and resulting fire became more serious. At 12:10 pm, the ship hit a reef near the Ulithi island of Yogoroporapu. The dead and wounded were landed on the island. Arms and ammunitions were unloaded. A machine gun position was built at the western part of Sorlen Island. At 12:35 the wounded were moved to a tent there. At 13:37, four Japanese airplanes passed toward the northeast. After March 31, the dead were buried. A fuel tank had also been hit and 16 tons of fuel were lost. At the end of this episode, 8 Japanese were injured and 5 died, from a total of 22.

Japan withdrew from Ulithi, although US-occupied Ulithi was later counterattacked by a corps *(hikotai)* of Japanese planes.[28]

The Japanese sowed mines in the waterway and left Ulithi for Yap. On September 23, the US landed on Ulithi. "In September 1944, the deserted atoll of Ulithi, northeast of Yap, had been occupied by the Americans without resistance," (Peattie, 1988, p. 297).

1945

The last Japanese garrison in Micronesia to go down fighting was an eight-man detachment of the *(Japanese)* Navy's Special Landing Party that was exterminated in brief and fatal combat to defend Fais Island, southeast of Ulithi, in January 1945 (Peattie, 1988, p. 297)."

The historical briefs provided above for the Japanese period in Ulithi have only afforded us brief glances into the lives of Ulithians during this particularly tumultuous period. From the early visits and trading experiences that Ulithians had with the Japanese during the Spanish and German periods, continuing through

---

[28] This group of Japanese planes are also termed, *tokko*, a special attack unit of Japanese aviators conducting kamikaze attacks in World War II (Wikipedia, 8/14/17). See Stern's description of a Japanese naval attempt to carry out a major attack on American warships anchored at Ulithi after Japan's withdrawal from the atoll in September 1944 (2010). Masami Jinno (2000) also wrote about the special attack plans and the book was reviewed and supplemented in an online article, *Kamikaze Images*, 2017: "Only two *Ginga* bombers hit targets at Ulithi Atoll. ...one plane struck the air carrier *Randolph* about 100 feet forward from the stern... Another plane crashed into Ulithi's Sorlen Island, where the pilot may have mistaken it for an aircraft carrier in the darkness." The Sorlen crash caused two deaths with 6 others wounded. Most of the original 24 *Ginga* bombers are believed to have crashed into the sea. Three of the bodies of the Japanese bombers were recovered from the Randolph. Author Masami Jinno visited Ulithi to conduct research and reports that the bodies of five crewmembers of the bombing expedition on the *Randolph* and Sorlen Island were buried by Americans on Falalop Island, Ulithi Atoll.

the rare but controlling activities of the Japanese commercial and early military preparation activities, there were few Japanese citizens actually in residence on Ulithi. However, for almost the entire period of occupation (1914 – 1944) Ulithians experienced increasing Japanese domination. Key among these pressures were demands for substantial numbers of Ulithians to go to the phosphate mines in Angaur, sometimes with their promised return postponed for many months. Japanese supervision of Ulithi agriculture appears to have increased yields. Still, food shortages persisted for the Ulithians. Finally, Ulithians observed and were impacted by the experience of full blown Japanese war preparations, military troop presence, and fighting between the Americans and the Japanese on and surrounding Ulithi atoll proper and its outlying islands and atolls. At this point, no Ulithian in residence could escape danger, anxiety, hunger, and cessation of normalcy.

Because much about this important period in Ulithi life is still unknown or unrecorded, future researchers – particularly those with language and culture skills, and with familial associations – have a broad canvas on which to develop further research. What caused, and what were the effects of the substantial male-female discrepancies recorded in the 1930 Japanese census of Ulithi? What more can be said about the Angaur phosphate mining experiences of Ulithians, or of the nearby Fais community's experience with phosphate mining on their island? How do the families left at home on Ulithi, as well as the Ulithians who went to Angaur, remember these times? Since both women and men participated in the mining experience on Angaur, are there descriptions available of their varied experiences? How did the traditional land and property holdings in the Ulithi territory, and activities on them, evolve and change throughout the Japanese period? What more can be said to describe the schooling experiences and the healthcare arrangements for Ulithians that the Japanese agencies created? How did traditional chiefly and lineage based authorities operate – or were they altered – during this period? Is it still possible to obtain descriptions from elder Ulithians, or from those who have received their stories, about the many facets of life during the Japanese period? One excellent example of creative work of this type is the dance song composed after the war on nearby Fais Island by Halamar and others from Faliyow village (collected, recorded, and annotated by D. Rubinstein, in Falgout, Poyer, & Carucci, 2008, pp. 228 – 238).

US Occupation of Ulithi

The Japanese Mandate faded in 1944 during the final chapters of World War II in the Pacific. Japanese forces left Ulithi at that point, presumably to concentrate their resources on areas they considered to be of greater strategic value, and necessary to their roles in battles such as those in the Yap mainland, Palau, and eventually in the Philippines and Okinawa. Peattie (1988, pp. 279-280) explains that by summer 1944 atolls relatively near Ulithi became the subject of US bombing (e.g., Woleai, Ifaluk, Puluwat, and Pulusuk). Poyer, Falgout, and Carucci (2001, pp. 157 – 158) advise that the far western atolls experienced few if any US attacks, although accidents occurred occasionally. However, Woleai was intensely targeted by US and even Australian air raids, while Ifaluk "was occasionally attacked."

Everything changed in 1944 when the American military established a secret advance military base in Ulithi (Poyer, Falgout, Carucci, 2001; Falgout, Power, Carucci, 2008). The US Navy removed the Ulithians from their traditional island homes and villages and relocated them to the island of Fassarai (Wees, 1950, p. 6). An estimated one million servicemen passed through the atoll that year as the USA prepared to invade the Philippines and Japan. In December 1944, Navy doctor Marshall Wees was sent to Fassarai, Ulithi for six months to review and address the health and medical needs of the island population. His book on the extraordinary experiences that he and the Ulithians shared during that period provides the deepest and best documented look we are likely to have of that important time of change. While he was there he largely succeeded in reducing the widespread suffering of the Ulithians from yaws to a small cluster of those who needed continuing treatment. In addition, it appears that he and his American assistant collaborated well with Ulithian King Ueg, Catholic priest – Father Norton, and many youth and adults as they worked to acquire resources from the Navy that improved the community's well being and capacity for further development.

When the military left Ulithi, the US put in place a long-range radio navigation station (LORAC) that operated within Ulithi Atoll for nearly a decade. Hezel

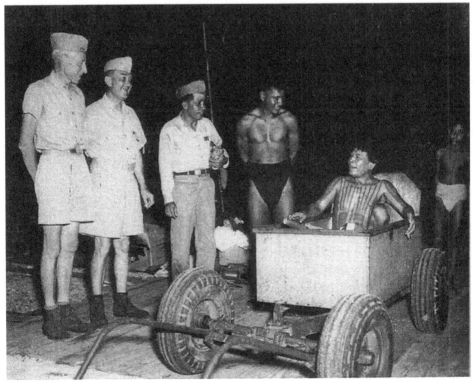

Figure 13. Ulithi Chief Ueg and other Ulithians meet US Navy Admiral Carleton Wright and his Navy companions in 1946.

(1995, pp. 252 – 253) described the transition in Ulithi that occurred at the end of the war:

> …the atolls that had been major bases during the Allied sweep westward in 1944 now served no purpose. Enewetak, the US advance base in the early months of the counteroffensive, was used as a base against the Japanese-held islands in the Marshalls for a time, but after the war it was all but forgotten. Ulithi, the atoll that replaced Enewetak as the forward base for the last year of the war, was abandoned by the US Navy. In its heyday it had been a center of intense naval activity: hundreds of warships rode at anchor there on any given day, and thousands of sailors and marines lined up on shore for their beer and cokes. Then, at the end of the war the navy summarily left. The four hundred military tents were destroyed, the fuel dump set on fire, and the landing craft sunk by gunfire. The huge machine shop that once performed ship repairs was crated and sent to China. The Ulithians, who had been relocated on the islet of Fasserai when the navy first moved in, were given most of the cast-off military clothing as they took possession of their atoll once again.

Postwar in Ulithi and Micronesia

Perhaps in the future, Ulithians themselves will tell the stories that they and their elders have retained regarding the end of World War II and postwar times on their atoll, as well as tales about Ulithians' new experiences with the US, and in association with other entities of Micronesia and the world. It was a time when all of the leaders of Micronesia were part of a complex international debate and planning process that led to the redesign, both internally and externally, of governance and of inter-island affiliations and distinctions. There was a reckoning of economic opportunities and rights, and assertion of long-term islander rights and responsibilities at home and in the world. Micronesian leadership undertook this momentous work within the membranes of their respective traditional cultures and languages, while simultaneously coping with US and international efforts to shift the balance to American, European, or Asian cultural bases.

One way to look into the postwar process is to explore the American side of the matter. Readers will find that this particular history has been well articulated by Hezel and other academic scholars (e.g., Hezel, 1995, pp. 254-365; Petersen, 1999), some of which is summarized here. The full story includes events that occurred during and after the war. US President Franklin D. Roosevelt issued Executive Order 8683 (1941) that required that travel to and from Guam be severely restricted, a condition that would be applied in the future by US President Harry S. Truman to the entire Micronesian region. Very important to the postwar changes that would affect Ulithi and the Micronesian Region in general is the fact that the United Nations was chartered in 1945. The charter had a trustee system that was designed to support formerly colonized peoples on the road to independence. In

Figure 14. Ulithian outrigger canoes at Asor Island, Ulithi Atoll during World War II, August 1945. Parts of the secret US base on Ulithi are shown along the shore. *(US National Archives and Records Administration.)*

Figure 15. US ships in anchorage at Ulithi Atoll, December 1944. *(US National Archives and Records Administration.)*

Figure 16. Mogmog Island was used as a recreational area for the US sailors, as shown here. *(This photo was personally contributed for use in this book by US Navy veteran George Underwood, third from left, with cigarette, who served on Ulithi.)*

spite of fierce internal arguments, a US trusteeship for Micronesia was created on July 19, 1947, known as the Trust Territory of the Pacific Islands. As part of this arrangement, the US Navy, under President Harry S. Truman, continued to administer the region, but with an ever-growing roster of administrators, social scientists, and local principals of schools. For example, between 1947 and 1949, teams of anthropologists and other scientists conducted field research all over Micronesia for the Coordinated Investigations of Micronesia. A team of 42 social scientists, including William Lessa, the finest scholar to date to work in Ulithi, was among them. Micronesian culture and language colleagues were essential to this undertaking. Truman also issued Executive Orders 10265 in 1951, 10408 in 1952, and 10470 in 1953 (summarized in Federal Register, 1954, pp. 267-269), which severely restricted and closely monitored circulation in, out of, and around the Trust Territory and Guam. Through these executive orders, the Secretary of the Interior was charged with the administration of the Marshall Islands, the Caroline Islands, and Rota Island in the northern Mariana Islands. The Navy was charged with administering all of the other Mariana Islands.

John F. Kennedy was US President from 1961 to 1963. During his brief presidency he did a number of things to promote the progress of Ulithi and Micronesia. He established the Peace Corps. He issued Executive Order 11045 which lifted the travel and security restrictions on Micronesia and Guam (Kennedy, 1962a, b, c), and he shifted Trust Territory administration from military to civilian control. Recognizing the great needs for resources in Micronesia, President Kennedy doubled the TTPI budget for economic, educational, and health development.

Figure 17. Harry S. Truman, US President from 1945 to 1953, during the end of WWII and the postwar period when the United Nations was established and the Trust Territory of the Pacific Islands was created.

Figure 18. John F. Kennedy, US President from 1961 to 1963, who established the Peace Corps, lifted the travel and security restrictions on Micronesia, shifted Trust Territory administration from military to civilian control, and doubled the TTPI budget in order to support economic, educational, and health progress.

Organizing Governance. Hezel (1995) reports that in Yap, traditional practices re-emerged. Although an American administrative structure was being created, the hereditary chiefly structure operated on a parallel track. Elections of new municipal leaders began in 1947 and other leaders were appointed on the basis of lineage. In Yap, the Counsel of Chiefs continued the work it had begun in German times. In the 1950s two bodies were charged with maintaining the cultural traditions: The Counsel of Chiefs and a group of elected officials, both of which were advisory up to the mid-1950s. At the end of the 1950s, Yap had a separate traditional Council of Chiefs, and also a legislature. For the region, there was a high commissioner of the Trust Territory of the Pacific Islands. The Trust Territory headquarters began operations in 1954 in Quonset huts on the grounds of Guam's only hotel. Their work was augmented by units set up in Wach Micronesian district. In 1961, a "Council of Micronesia" was established for the entire Trust Territory, later renamed the "Congress of Micronesia."

Disaster and change in the 1960s. On November 30, 1960, Ulithi Atoll began the decade with a disastrous concussion from Category 4 Typhoon Ophelia (Lessa, W. A., 1964; Wikipedia, 2017k). A similarly harmful typhoon had struck Ulithi in 1907, and weather threats were a familiar concern to the residents. Nevertheless, Ophelia's impacts seemed different from the earlier events because of her severity and because she hastened multiple technological interventions from the

Figure 19. Ulithi Men's Council with King Ueg (center, row 1), Mogmog, Ulithi, 1948. *(Lessa, 1966, p. xii).*

US. Ophelia even changed the way the Ulithi people ate and the roles of women and youth. Lessa (1964, pp. 14 – 15) estimated that tremendous damage was done to structures, with the total loss of one-fourth, severe damage to an additional one-half, with one-fourth remaining habitable, and: "All the council houses, except a small one on Lossau, and all the menstrual houses, dispensaries, and schools were lost." The concrete Coast Guard Station and the two concrete Catholic Churches survived (Lessa, 1964, pp. 9, 27), but 300 feet of the runway was swept into the ocean.

The strafing of food trees, inundation of taro patches by salt water, and the loss or severe damage to over two-thirds of the outrigger canoes used for subsistence fishing could have led to widespread starvation of Ulithi families had they not had the continuing rain as a source of fresh water and also the arrival of emergency assistance. The damage or loss suffered because of the loss of taro patches, and breadfruit and coconut trees, accelerated the dietary shifts that had begun during the American military presence in Ulithi Atoll, especially when canned and dried food supplies were abandoned as the military left. After the typhoon, Ulithi people appreciated the canned goods, sugar, flour, and coffee when these were brought in by the government. Ulithians began immediately to undertake the recovery. This time their preference was for rectangular homes made of concrete, rather than the traditional form made with wood and natural fiber materials. Clothing choices were altered, with both women and men increasingly using fabric top coverings, as chiefly permission allowed. Hats became popular and barefootedness increasingly gave way to zories when these reached the Ulithi islands from off-island travelers. Women's roles began to incorporate a great deal of nontraditional and cash-producing work, especially in the manufacture of copra and the gathering of trochus shells. Women increasingly shared the heavy work of digging, chopping, carrying, and the endless cleanup and reconstruction of their ravaged islands, both as individuals and members of work teams (Lessa, 1964, pp. 33 – 34).

Lessa reports that the traditional internal political and leadership structure of Ulithi Atoll was also changed by Typhoon Ophelia (Lessa, 1964, pp. 37 – 39). Most apparent was that the strong and well-reasoned behavior of the younger men during and after the storm had enhanced their roles in the community and their measure by the elders. In the traditional councils of elders, the younger men began to speak up, while still maintaining their traditional respectful demeanor. In addition, Lessa estimated that the authority of reigning King Malefich had declined. But front and center in the traditional context of Ulithi was its symbolic role as child to parent Yap. Yap did not forget its reciprocal duties to Ulithi in this time of need. A month after the storm, the ship *M/V Erroll* arrived in Ulithi's lagoon to deliver 200 baskets of taro, yams, and Polynesian chestnuts from the people of Gagil Village, Yap.

Beyond Ulithi shores, other forces were at work that would affect the Atoll (see Hezel, 1995, on "Micronesia Remade," pp. 297 – 367). In 1962, US President John F. Kennedy signed the National Security Action Memorandum No 145. This document detailed a "New Policy for the US Trust Territory of the Pacific Islands," recognizing Micronesia's needs for an "accelerated program of political, economic, and social development" (Kennedy, 1962). Also in 1962, the US Department of Interior established headquarters in Saipan for its administration of Micronesia. A US interagency task force was created to monitor and motivate development in Micronesia. The goal was to create a permanent relationship between Micronesia

Figure 20. Swearing-in of the first Congress of Micronesia, c1965. *(Trust Territory of the Pacific Islands Photo Collection, University of Hawaii-Manoa Library).*

Figure 21. Yap Governor John Mangefel and Lieutenant Governor Hilary Tacheliol of Ulithi visit Ulithi in 1979. *(Trust Territory of the Pacific Islands Photo Collection, University of Hawaii-Manoa Library).*

and the US. The famous "Solomon Report" (Solomon, 1963) was issued, detailing an early analysis of a US-centered approach to this goal. With President Kennedy's assassination in November 1963, US planning for Micronesia was rattled. However, substantial US federal funds were invested in the region, one benefit of which was the construction of schools in Ulithi and other districts. In 1966, the first 395 Peace Corps volunteers were placed in Micronesia, growing to 940 volunteers two years later.

In 1964 the Congress of Micronesia was established by US Secretarial Order 2882 and held its first session in July 1965. As long as it did not create conflicts with US treaties, laws, or executive orders, it was allowed to make its own laws, and it began by asking the United Nations for technical assistance. It held a territory wide election for the Congress of Micronesia. Rugulumar, a Ulithian teacher, became a long time member of the new Congress. In 1967, the political leaders of the Micronesian region began to prepare for independence by forming a Status Commission, and the following year reported that there would be four options: Independence; free association or a protectorate; integration with a nation as a commonwealth or territory; or to continue as a trust territory. Yap joined with Kosrae, Pohnpei, and Chuuk to negotiate as a team with the US, while the Northern Marianas split off to form a commonwealth with the US. The US agreed to negotiate separately with Palau and the Marshall Islands. Thus, the four-state outline of the Federated States of Micronesia (FSM) was formed and the Trust Territory of the Pacific Islands functions were decentralized across the four proposed nations.

Reaching major governance goals in the 1970s and 1980s. In 1975, Tosiwo Nakayama was inaugurated as President of the FSM. John Mangefel became the Governor of Yap State and Hilary Tacheliol of Ulithi became Lieutenant Governor. In 1982, seven years later, the FSM Compact was signed. Ulithi finally obtained independence as part of Yap State within the newly constituted Federated States of Micronesia (FSM) in 1986. FSM gained full authority over its internal and external affairs and became entirely self-governing. It would rely on the US only for financial assistance. In return, the US became responsible for FSM's defense and security.

Figure 22. Hilary Tacheliol (left), 2009, was the first Neighboring Islander to graduate from St. Mary's Mission School in Yap District, and later the first to graduate from Xavier High School in Chuuk. Further, he was the first from the Neighboring Islands to earn a BA degree from the University of Guam. Following leadership roles in the TTPI administration, Mr. Tacheliol served as Yap State's first Lieutenant Governor of the Federated States of Micronesia from 1980 – 1987. He is the retired chair of the Council of Tamol, which is the prestigious body composed of traditional leaders of Yap Neighboring Islands. He extended this leadership through his role as the Chief of Mogmog, which is the Paramount Chief of Yap Neighboring Islands. He was also with the FSM Development Bank for 24 years and still serves as a Board Member of the Yap Cooperative Association and Waab Companies. Mr. Tacheliol is married to Rosa Huffer Tacheliol (see *Figure 23* below). (Program cover, 9th Annual Pacific Region Investment Conference, Asia Pacific Association for Fiduciary Studies, 2009.)

Figure 23. Rosa Huffer Tacheliol, 2016, originally from the Guam Chamorro community, has been a major figure in Ulithi Atoll and Yap State educational growth and development. In the mid-1980s, she provided educator training and technical assistance throughout the Micronesian region via the US Department of Education's Bilingual Education Assistance Center, Project BEAM, which was directed by Dr. Robert Underwood at the University of Guam. Following this, she provided volunteer teaching to the St. Mary's Elementary School's English classes in Colonia, Yap for two years; followed by serving as Curriculum Coordinator at the Yap State Department of Education. She then served as a faculty member of the College of Micronesia, Yap Campus, until her appointment as Director of the Yap State Department of Education from 2006 to 2007.

The establishment of the Federated States of Micronesia ended 100 years of foreign rule over Ulithi and its companion FSM islands.

Leaders of the new FSM State of Yap created a State Constitution and declared it the supreme law of the State. It was amended in 2004 (Yap State, Federated States of Micronesia, 2004). Article III (FSMlaw, 2004) defines the roles of traditional leaders and traditions by establishing a Council of Pilung (relative to Yap Islands Proper) and a Council of Tamol (relative to the Yap Outer Islands, which includes Ulithi) to perform functions that concern tradition and custom.

Research on culture and language. Even before the war had ended, the US Navy and faculty from some of America's most prestigious universities (e.g., Harvard and Yale) were planning research on the languages, cultures, and environments of Micronesia (e.g. Goodenough, 1951). They felt that establishing these foundations of knowledge was an essential step to bringing quality to the work the US would be able to perform with these communities following the end of the war. Under the auspices of the US Navy, the Office of Naval Research, later the Pacific Science Board of the National Academy of Sciences, and the Coordinated Investigation of Micronesian Anthropology (CIMA), anthropologist William Lessa visited Ulithi in 1947, 1948-49, 1960, and 1961 (Lessa, 1950a,b,c; 1961a,b; 1962; 1964; 1966; 1977; Lessa and Lay, 1953; Lessa and Meyers, 1962). While there, he worked closely with Ulithian mentors (e.g., Melchethal) to understand

and describe what he called their *Design for Living* (1966). Lessa's trip to Ulithi in 1960 was made expressly for the purpose of observing effects of the US TTPI activities within the atoll. Within one year, he returned to document and analyze the impact of Typhoon Ophelia and how the people of Ulithi adjusted and accommodated to the physical, psychological, and social changes that the disaster had imposed on them (1964).

Figure 24. William Lessa, anthropologist and author of research on Ulithi and other Micronesian cultural matters.

William H. Alkire, another of the post-war American anthropologists who conducted research in Micronesia, contributed an important analysis of life and culture within the outer islands of Yap in *Peoples and Cultures of the Pacific* (1977), one of the most widely read early general textbooks concerning Pacific Islanders. Many people of Ulithi will remember the American Peace Corps workers who joined their efforts to enlarge and improve Ulithi schools in the late 1960s and early 1970s. Readers may enjoy perusing the websites dedicated to memories of these times; e.g., Microbuds: Peace Corps Volunteers in Micronesia (www.microbuds.com). Other volunteers continue to contribute to the development of language and educational resources for Ulithi; e.g., Habele Outer Island Education Fund, which has published a hard cover print version of a Ulithian dictionary and periodically awards scholarships (Mellen & Hancock, 2010; http://habele.org/).

Figure 25. William Alkire, an American anthropologist and author of the widely read book, *Peoples and Cultures of the Pacific*, which includes a section on Yap and the outer islands of Yap. Shown here on Lamotrek in 1962.

The Balance Tips.

As the American colonial period waned, indigenous people throughout Micronesia sought and created opportunities for self-directed educational and professional advancement. One outstanding example is the Outer Islands High School (OIHS), located on Falalop Island, Ulithi. OIHS has provided secondary education within the context of a boarding school for students from all of the outer islands in Yap State, under the leadership of teachers and administrators hailing from many of these islands themselves. Many post-colonial Ulithians have engaged in post-secondary

Figure 26. Young Micronesian priests posing with Bishop Neylon at the ordination of Fr. John Hagileiram in 1985; (from left) Fr. Nick Rahoy, Fr. Apollo Thall, Bishop Neylon, Fr. John Hagileiram, Fr. Julio Angkel *(Micronesian Seminar, 2003).*

education opportunities at a variety of colleges and universities within the Pacific Region and also abroad, preparing themselves for a wide array of professional roles that have been of great benefit to their families, their home islands, Yap State, and the entire FSM.

The opening of opportunities to Ulithians and Yapese for leadership in the Catholic Church was another example of goals for indigenization being realized.[29] Father F. X. Hezel has written about this process (1991; 2003): In 1975, six Yapese men were the first to be ordained as deacons. In 1977, John Rulmal was raised to the diaconate and Nicholas Rahoy from Ulithi was the first person from the Yap area to be ordained a priest. Amando Samo, originally of Moch Island, Chuuk was ordained a few months later to serve as a Priest of the Caroline Islands. During the 1980s, Fr. Apollo Thal from Yap Proper was ordained. In 1985, Father John Hagileiram of Eauripik was ordained.

A Closer and More Recent Look: Purposes of this Book

In the chapters of this publication, the reader will become acquainted with the research and writing of a number of contemporary Ulithi academic scholars, working within the context of research teams or independently. Other authors of this volume share research endeavors that were undertaken with, and extensively supported by, the care and participation of members of the Ulithi community. In some cases, the reported research highlights connections with other places in Micronesia or with citizens of other outer islands of Yap who are living in Ulithi.

---

[29] See the online Micronesian Seminar article by Father Francis X. Hezel on this subject: The Catholic Church in Yap http://www.micsem.org/pubs/books/catholic/yap/

Part 1

The remainder of this publication is divided into two parts. Part 1 consists of six chapters and includes reports on the 1992 University of Guam (UOG) Ulithi Field School in Cultural Anthropology. There were eight participants on the project team, five of them being UOG undergraduate students. The project was co-directed by Dr. Rebecca A. Stephenson and Eulalia J. Harui-Walsh, an indigenous Ulithi scholar, both of whom were representing the University of Guam. Senior scientist, Dr. Yosihiko H. Sinoto, of the Bernice P. Bishop Museum in Honolulu, Hawaii, completed the faculty team. In the first chapter of Part 1, Stephenson explains processes of the UOG Field School and overviews the research results. This is followed by a chapter in which Shawn H. Davis presents her study of the material culture associated with Ulithi fishing enterprises. In a related empirical study in Chapter 3, Sinoto explores the evidence for catching flying fish in Ulithi Atoll via the technology of gorges. In the following chapter, Melvin D. Cruz documents and interprets aspects of traditional and contemporary Ulithian economics. Stephenson and Harui-Walsh then shift the research focus to their comparative study of the experiences of disability and the contextual response to disability in two islands of the Micronesian region, namely Ulithi and Guam. Part 1 is concluded with a bibliography of resources in print concerning Ulithi Atoll, compiled by Deborah Piscusa-Bratt and Stephenson.

Altogether, the University of Guam team sought to engage Ulithi culture and society via on-site field studies in cultural anthropology that included traditional and contemporary economics, subsistence practices, aspects of expressive culture such as chanting and dancing, fishing technologies, material culture with special reference to the sea, and the Atoll's approach to the phenomenon of disability and those who experience disability. This project serves as a model of a university "capstone" course; that is, a course that engages experienced students in activities that integrate their diverse previous educational experiences. It is worthy of replication on Ulithi or elsewhere in Micronesia.

Part 2

Part 2 of the book consists of seven chapters, written by a variety of scholars including three indigenous Ulithian authors. The first chapter was written by a social worker and University of Guam faculty member, Joliene G. Hasugulayag, and the second was provided by a Guam attorney, Joshua Depmar Walsh. The third chapter was written by Eulalia J. Harui-Walsh – anthropologist, expert Ulithi artist, and social worker.

In Hasugulayag's Part 2 chapter, she describes the Atoll of Ulithi, and explains several important aspects of Ulithi culture and customs. She brings valued perspectives to this information by sharing the results of her interviews with several prominent and respected Ulithi leaders; e.g., J. Figirliyong and T. Guiormog. Hasugulayag posits that three elements serve as the foundation of Ulithian cultural practices: relationship to land; relationships within the family context; and relationships within the community context. For the first of these, she discusses the *role of land*, which includes the reefs and surrounding waters; subsistence living and sustainability; and the work of the *Palus Wolfulu* (land navigator). In the section on *relationships in family context,* she explains the classic Ulithian family structure; the nature and dynamics of authority; expectations for and interrelationships among brothers, sisters, and first cousins of the opposite sex; and adoption practices. She places another frame on Ulithi life in her discussion of *relationships in the community context* (social structure; gender roles; and reciprocity), and concludes with a section on *foreign influences in Ulithi culture.* These influences include World War II, the Trust Territory of the Pacific Islands, western education, cable television, and the Compact of Free Association. Following this is a section on *migration*. In an important statement of professional guidance, Hasugulayag cited factors that must be part of social work practices undertaken with people of Ulithi, especially in migration settings: the strength of the family; the impact of gender roles; respect for authority; and the importance of acknowledging the positive contributions made by Ulithians who have migrated to the US. She concludes with a consideration of the *meaning of civilization,* both within and beyond Ulithi.

In his chapter, Joshua Walsh opens a window onto the life of a son whose mother, Eulalia Dolomog Harui-Walsh, was a native daughter of Fassarai in Ulithi, and whose father, Jack Walsh, was an American professor and scholar. In his chapter, readers will learn how he has combined his dual heritage in every aspect of his life. He shares how he finds Ulithi every day in the mirror and how his understanding of the importance of conflict resolution and cooperation, so essential to his mother's culture of origin, is important to his work as a lawyer to resolve the conflicts of his clients. Moreover, as he finds himself jetting overseas to meet legal obligations, aboard an American aircraft – his *wa* [vessel] of the moment – he prepares to apply his father's tool of choice, the rhetoric of the English language, as a means to sincerely serve his clients.

The reader will find that the chapter written by Eulalia Harui-Walsh and Rebecca Stephenson offers a rare first-hand commentary on the history and cultural aspects of the creation and use of the lava lava textiles of Ulithi. As the ubiquitous article of clothing for women of these outer islands, the lava lava has a long history of significant cultural symbolism, economic, and political values. The lava lava is a tool for displaying respect, conducting negotiations, and conferring honors. To the individual woman weaver, it is an activity of gratifying expression concerning artistic knowledge and skill. A rich heritage of mother to daughter transfer of knowledge is necessary for preparing the materials, stringing the loom, and performing the actual weaving that occurs in this part of Micronesia. Some of this unique heritage can be gleaned even now via structured observation of chants and songs performed by the children of weaving women. Harui-Walsh describes the ceremonial uses of lava lavas and their traditional roles in significant island and interisland social interactions. She describes a classification system for lava lavas based on the selection of the weaving fiber and design, and explains the social giving system for distributing lava lavas of different quality. She then provides historical comments on the notable weavers of each type of lava lava. In addition, Harui-Walsh's commentary is keyed to the exhibition of lava lavas from Ulithi that can be found in the material culture collection of Te Papa Tongarewa, the National Museum of New Zealand in Wellington, as these were exhibited there in the early 1990s.

Next, this publication provides a collection of four analyses conducted on Ulithi over approximately 30 years (1985 – 2016). Ann Ames shares her recent research on marketing and micro-finance in Ulithi, as part of her larger research program in Yap State. She offers implications for future economic directions in Ulithi. Her work in Ulithi is part of a larger research program in Micronesia that focuses on marketing initiatives, micro-finance, and economic indicators. Based on her interviews with local Ulithian food producers, opinion leaders, and officials, she was able to identify fundamental issues regarding production, marketing, and the situation with raw resources, management training and support, access to capital, export and local market issues, climate change, and cultural economies.

This is followed by a chapter written by Dr. Todd Ames, who describes his research experiences on Ulithi Atoll through the lenses of his field notes and his camera. The photographs accompanying his text provide an intimate window onto the contemporary physical and social environment of Falalop and onto a special event held on Asor.

Then, Spencer describes and supplies supportive images of the learning traditions of children and families of Ulithi and of other Yap Outer Islands. She recounts the insights provided with regard to culture and cross-cultural child development during her 1985 summer teaching experiences in Ulithi for the University of Guam and the Yap State Department of Education. Her students included teachers and administrators of the Yap State Department of Education, who originated from Ulithi Atoll as well as from most of the other outer islands of Yap. Her daily companions were the families of Falalop Island. As a result of observing and collecting information within Ulithi about topics such as socialization to literacy, child-parent interactions regarding gendered behavior, and the interrelationships of language, culture, and education, she identified research inquiries that have inspired her research ever since.

Part 2 of this book concludes with an extensive annotated bibliography compiled by geographer Harley I. Manner, that includes an emphasis on environmental and ecological matters. In his chapter, Manner cites resources across a century of research and commentary on or relevant to Ulithi. The authors hope that this bibliography will be useful to current and future Ulithians who seek to read what has been known and reported about their Atoll over time. Armed with these references, Ulithians will be in a position to strategically access, select, and deselect earlier notions for relevance and accuracy – as baselines, or as heuristic sign posts.

The Authors' Intentions.

This research collection is intended to bring new attention to Ulithi Atoll by sharing a body of research studies mostly unreported in readily available sources concerning Ulithi. These studies have been undertaken by University of Guam faculty and students, as well as other scholars of Micronesia. Where appropriate, these writings link to older extant literature that is widely available. Of particular interest is the extensive field research conducted in Ulithi by William Lessa (e.g., 1964, 1966), with the guidance and assistance of indigenous Ulithian mentors. There are opportunities in some chapters to compare and contrast observations and analyses concerning Ulithi with those found in American and other Micronesian venues. Each chapter in this volume draws readers directly into the research process employed to examine distinct questions, including those regarding culture and society, life science, agriculture, the economy, child development, and artistic activities within Ulithi Atoll. Significantly, this book can project the voices and views of indigenous Ulithian residents, as well as educators and researchers who include Ulithi in their study areas. This approach forecasts, promotes, and encourages the likely prominence that indigenous Pacific Islanders will take up within the continuing and future conduct and interpretation of academic research occurring within their islands of origin.

From the earliest writing efforts that have led to the preparation of this book, the authors have intended their priority audience to be the Ulithians. None of the research presented would have been possible without the generous and extensive contributions of the families of Ulithi Atoll. We wanted to ensure that the results of our collaborated endeavors are in their hands, to use or not to use as they deem desirable and appropriate. Speaking for the editors of this volume, let it be said that the emergence of outstanding scholars and professionals from Ulithi and throughout Micronesia is a source of great pleasure and admiration for us. We look forward to their continuing meritorious works and to the health and happiness of all.

References

Alkire, W. H. (1977). *An introduction to the peoples and cultures of Micronesia, second edition.* Menlo Park, CA: Cummings Publishing Co.

Barratt, G. (1988). *Carolinean contacts with the islands of the Marianas: The European record.* Saipan, CNMI: The Micronesian Archaeological Survey, Division of Historic Preservation, Department of Community and Cultural Affairs, info@cnmihpo.net

Bates, Marston, & Abbott, D. P. (1958). *Ifaluk: Portrait of a coral island.* London: Museum Press. (207)

Boyer, D. S. (1967). Micronesia: The Americanization of Eden. *National Geographic, May,* 702 – 744.

Bryan, E. H. Jr. (1971). *Guide to place names in the Trust Territory of the Pacific Islands.* (Car.41, Ulithi Atoll). Honolulu: Pacific Science Information Center, Bernice P. Bishop Museum.

Burrows, E. G. & Spiro, M. E. (1957). *An atoll culture: Ethnography of Ifaluk in the central Carolines.* New Haven, CT: Human Relations Area Files. (204).

Damm, H. (1938). Zentralkarolinen: Ifaluk, Aurepik, Faraulip, Sorol, Mogmog. Based on the notes of Paul Hambruch and Ernst Sarfert. In G. Thilenius, (Ed.), *Ergebnisse der Südsee-Expedition, 1908 – 1910. II. Ethnographie, B. Mikronesien, Band 10, Halband 2*, 1 – 379. Hamburg: Friederichsen, De Gruyter and Co.

Ellis, S. J. (2012). *Saipan Carolinian, one Chuukic language blended from many (Unpublished doctoral dissertation).* University of Hawaiʻi, Honolulu, HI. (Retrieved from http://www.ling.hawaii.edu/graduate/Dissertations/JimEllisFinal)

Falgout, S., Poyer, L., & Carucci, L. M. (2008). *Memories of war: Micronesians in the Pacific War.* Honolulu, HI: University of Hawaiʻi Press.

Federal Register. (1954). *Code of federal regulations, Title 32, Parts 700 to 799, revised,* pp. 267 – 269. Washington, DC: Federal Register Division, National Archives and Records Service, General Services Administration. Retrieved 6/11/17. https://bookstore.gpo.gov/products/sku/869-082-00132-1?ctid=190

Fosberg, F. R., Sachet, M.-H., and Oliver, R. (1979). A geographical checklist of the Micronesian Dicotyledonae. *Micronesica*, 15(1-2), 41 – 295.

FSMlaw. (2017). YSC, Title 5. Traditional leaders & traditions, Chapter 1. Councils of traditional leaders. Retrieved 10/19/17: http://www.fsmlaw.org/yap/code/title05/T05_Ch01.htm

Goodenough, W. H. (1951; 1978). *Property, kin, and community on Truk.* Hamden, CN: Archon Books.

Google Earth. (2017). Angaur, Palau. Retrieved 8/15/17 at: https://www.google.com/maps/place/Ngeaur+Island/@6.9942205,134.1632203,10.8z/data=!4m5!3m4!1s0x32d441adc17fcded:0x9b07d92fb7653753!8m2!3d6.909223!4d134.1387934

Hanlon, D. (1998). *Remaking Micronesia: Discourses over development in a Pacific Territory, 1944-1982.* Honolulu, HI: University of Hawaiʻi Press.

Hezel, F. X. (1991). *The Catholic Church in Micronesia: Historical essays on the Catholic Church in the Caroline-Marshall Islands.* Chicago, IL: Loyola University Press.

Hezel, F. X. (1995). *Strangers in their own land, a century of colonial rule in the Caroline and Marshall Islands.* Honolulu, HI: University of Hawaiʻi Press.

Hezel, F. X. (2003). The Catholic Church in Micronesia: The Catholic Church in Yap. Micronesian Seminar. Retrieved 6/12/17. http://www.micsem.org/pubs/books/catholic/yap/

Higuchi, W. (2013). The Japanese administration of Guam, 1941 – 1944: A study of occupation and integration policies, with Japanese oral histories. North Carolina: McFarland & Company, Inc.

Higuchi, W. (2017a). Draft working paper: *Ulithi during the Japanese Administration, 1914 – 1944.*

Higuchi, W. (2017b). Extensive professional communications from July through November, 2017, based on Dr. Higuchi's Japanese history archives.

Jinno, Masami. (2007). *Azusa tokubetsu koi gekitai: Bakugekiki ginga sanzenkiro no koi seki.* Toì"kyoì": Koì"jinsha

Johnson, Robert H. (September 19, 1961). *Memorandum for Mr. Arthur Schlesinger, Jr., The White House. Subject: US Trust Territories.* Boston, MA: John F. Kennedy Presidential Library.

Kamikaze Images (book review) (n.d.). *Azusa tokubetsu kougekitai (Azusa special attack unit).* Retrieved 10/21/17: http://www.kamikazeimages.net/books/Japanese/azusa/index.htm

Kennedy, J. F. (April 18, 1962a). *National security action memorandum no. 145: New Policy for the U.S. Trust Territory of the Pacific Islands.* Boston, MA: John F. Kennedy Presidential Library.

Kennedy, J. F. (August 21, 1962b). *Executive Order 11045: Discontinuing the Guam Island Naval Defensive Sea Area and Guam Island Naval Airspace Reservation.* Boston, MA: John F. Kennedy Presidential Library.

Kennedy, J. F. (August 23, 1962c). *The White House, Statement of the President, Office of the White House Press Secretary* (Resending 1941 Executive Order 8683 which established the Guam Naval and Airspace Reservation). Boston, MA: John F. Kennedy Presidential Library.

Kiste, R. C. & Marshall, M. (Eds.) (1999). *American anthropology in Micronesia, an assessment.* Honolulu, HI: University of Hawai'i Press.

Klingman, L. & Green, G. (1950). *His majesty O'Keefe.* NY: Charles Scribner's Sons.

Legdesog, C. (2017). Personal communication regarding Damm photographs and current population and social use of Sorol Atoll.

Lessa, W. A. (1950a). *The ethnography of Ulithi Atoll. Final CIMA Report, No. 28.* Washington, D.C.: Pacific Science Board and National Research Council.

Lessa, W. A. (1950b). The place of Ulithi in the Yap empire. *Society for Applied Anthropology,* 16 – 18.

Lessa, W. A. (1950c). Ulithi and the outer native world. *American Anthropologist, 52,* 27 – 52.

Lessa, W. A. (1961a). Sorcery on Ifaluk. *American Anthropologist, 63*(4), 817 – 820.

Lessa, W. A. (1961b). Tales from Ulithi Atoll. *University of California, Folklore Studies, 13,* 1 – 493.

Lessa, W. A. (1962). An evaluation of early descriptions of Carolinian culture. *Ethnohistory,* 9(4), 313 – 403.

Lessa, W. A. (1964). The social effects of typhoon Ophelia (1960) on Ulithi. *Micronesica,* 1(1), 1 – 47.

Lessa, W. A. (1966). *Ulithi: A Micronesian design for living.* (1 – 118). NY: Holt, Rinehart, & Winston, Inc.

Lessa, W. A. (1977). Traditional uses of the vascular plants of Ulithi Atoll, with comparative notes. *Micronesica,* 13/2, 129 – 190.

Lessa, W. A. & Lay, T. (1953). The somatology of Ulithi Atoll. *American Journal of Physical Anthropology, 11,* 405 – 412.

Lessa, W. A. & Meyers, G. C. (1962). Population dynamics of an atoll community. *Population Studies, 15,* 244 – 257.

Marsh-Kautz, K. G., & Singeo, Y. (1999). *Ngeaur community perceptions of their island's mongkii (Macaca fascicularis): An island under siege.* Report prepared for the community of Ngeaur. Privately circulated.

Marsh-Kautz, K. G., Gulibert, L., & Wheatley, B. P. (2003). Connecting local and international: Exploring the pressing *Mongkii* (Monkey) issues of Ngeaur, *Beluu er a* Belau (Angaur, Republic of Palau. In Lan-Hung Nora Chiang, J. Lidstone, & R. A. Stephenson (Eds.) *The challenges of globalization: Cultures in transition in the Pacific-Asia region.* Lanham, MD: University Press of America, Inc.

McManus, S. J., Josephs, L. S., & Emesiochl, M. (1977). *Palauan-English Dictionary.* Honolulu: University of Hawaii Press.

Mellen & Hancock. (2010). *Ulithian-English dictionary.* Columbia, South Carolina: Habele. Retrieved 4/27/17. http//habele.org/

Microbuds: *Peace Corps Volunteers in Micronesia; Yap, the Outer Islands and Beyond.* Retrieved 4/29/17. http://www.microbuds.com/

Micronesian Seminar. (2017). *The Catholic church in Yap.* Retrieved 4/29/17. http://www.micsem.org/pubs/books/catholic/yap/

Ouchacha. (2017). Musings on Palauan cha-cha and other musical forms: Phosphate mining on Angaur. http://www.ouchacha.wordpress.com/2016/09/15/

phosphaate-mining-on-angaur/Posted on September 15, 2016 by jimgeselbracht. Retrieved 8/11/17.

Pacific Worlds. (2017a). *Orientation to Ulithi.* Retrieved 6/11/17. http://www.pacificworlds. com/yap/home/oriented.cfm#turtleisles

Pacific Worlds. (2017b). *Chronology for Yap and Ulithi.* Retrieved 2/18/17. http://www. pacificworlds.com/yap/memories/chronol.cfm.

Peattie, M. R. (1988). *Nan'yo, the rise and fall of the Japanese in Micronesia, 1885 – 1945.* Honolulu, HI: University of Hawaii Press.

Petersen, G. (1999). Politics in postwar Micronesia. In R. Kiste & M. Marshall (Eds.), *American Anthropology in Micronesia, An Assessment* (pp.145 – 195). Honolulu, HI: University of Hawaii Press.

Poirier, F. E., & Smith, E. O. (1974). Crab-eating macaques (Macaca fascicularis) of Angaur Island, Palau, Micronesia, *Folia Primatologia, 22,* 258 – 306.

Poyer, L., Falgout, S., & Carucci, L. M. (2001). *The typhoon of war: Micronesian experiences of the Pacific war.* Honolulu, HI: University of Hawai'i Press. (157 – 158).

Roosevelt, F. D. (1941). Executive Order 8683: Establishing naval defensive sea areas around and naval airspace reservations over the islands of Rose, Tutuila, and Guam. Retrieved 6/11/17. http://www.presidency.ucsb.edu/ws/?pid=60881

Rubinstein, D. H. (1979). An ethnography of Micronesian childhood: Contexts of socialization of Fais Island (Doctoral dissertation). Stanford University, Palo Alto, CA.

Rubinstein, D. H. (n.d.). Oral literature: A song text from Fais Island. Unpublished manuscript in the files of the author. In S. Falgout, L. Poyer, & L. M. Carucci. (2008). *Memories of war: Micronesians in the Pacific War.* Honolulu, HI: University of Hawaii Press.

Sanchez, P. C. (c1987). *The history of our island.* Agaña, Guam: Sanchez Publishing House, (70 – 75).

Solomon, A. M. (1963). National Security Action Memorandum No. 243, Survey Mission to the Trust Territory of the Pacific Islands. Washington, DC: The White House.

Stern, R. C. (2010). *Fire from the sky: Surviving the kamikaze threat.* Barnsley, England (S70 2AS): Seaforth Publishing.

Tetens, A. & Gräffe, (c1870). *The Caroline islands of Yap or Guap according to the reports of Alfred Tetens and Johann Kubary.* (Die Carolineninsel Yap oder Guap nach den Mittheilungen von Alfred Tetens und Johann Kubary.) New Haven, Conn: Microform Reprint.

Thyssen, M. (1988). *A guidebook to the Palau Islands.* Palau: Champion Service & Trading PTE Ltd.

United Nations. Trusteeship Council. (1961). *Report of the United Nations Visiting Mission to the Trust Territory of the Pacific Islands. Supplement 20 Official Records.* Twenty-seventh Session, June 1-July 19. NY: United Nations.

United States. (1963). *Report by the United States Government Survey Mission to the Trust Territory of the Pacific Islands ("Solomon Report"). Summary and two volumes.* Honolulu, HI: University of Hawai'i, Hamilton Library, Hawaiian and Pacific Collection. Retrieved 6/13/17. https://evols.library.manoa.hawaii.edu/handle/10524/18931

United States Strategic Bombing Survey (USSBS). (1946). *The campaigns of the Pacific War.* Washington, DC: Naval Analysis Division. (206).

Vincent, J. M. & Viti, C. (1973). *Micronesia's yesterday.* Saipan: Trust Territory Department of Education.

Wees, M. P. (1950). *King-doctor of Ulithi.* 1-128. NY: The Macmillan Company.

Wheatley, B., Stephenson, R., Kurashina, H., & Marsh-Kautz, K. G. (1999). The effects of hunting on the Longtailed Macaques of Ngeaur Island, Palau. In P. Dolhinow & A. Fuentes (Eds.), *The nonhuman primates.* California: Mayfield Publishing Company.

Wheatley, B., Stephenson, R., Kurashina, H., & Marsh-Kautz, K. G. (c 2002). *The University of Guam Field School in Anthropology field report: Ngeaur, Belau, Micronesia.*

Wheatley, B., Stephenson, R., Kurashina, H., & Marsh-Kautz, K. G. (2002). A cultural primatological study of *Macaca fascicularis* on Ngeaur Island, Republic of Palau. In A. Fuentes & L. Wolf (Eds.), *Primates face to face: The conservation implications of human-nonhuman primate interconnections* (pp. 240 – 253). Cambridge: Cambridge University Press.

Wikipedia. (2017a). *Ulithi population.* Retrieved 3/3/17. https://en.wikipedia.org/wiki/Ulithi

Wikipedia. (2017b). *Sorol.* Retrieved 6/5/17. https://en.wikipedia.org/wiki/Sorol

Wikipedia. (2017c). *Fais Island.* Retrieved 6/11/17. https://en.wikipedia.org/wiki/Fais Island

Wikipedia. (2017d). *Ngulu Atoll.* Retrieved 6/11/17. https://en.wikipedia.org/wiki/Ngulu_Atoll

Wikipedia. (2017e). *Johann Kubary image results.* Retrieved 5/3/17. https://images.search.yahoo.com/search/images;_ylt=A0SO8xuqMwpZgjMA8XpXNyoA;_ylu=X3oDMTByNWU4cGh1BGNvbG8DZ3ExBHBvcwMxBHZ0aWQD-BHNlYwNzYw--?p=Johann+Kubary&fr=yfp-t

Wikipedia. (2017f). *Georg Christian Thilenius.* Retrieved 5/3/17. https://images.search.yahoo.com/search/images;_ylt=A0SO80sFOApZGNwAi5pXNyoA;_ylu=X3oDMTByNWU4cGh1BGNvbG8DZ3ExBHBvcwMxBHZ0aWQD-BHNlYwNzYw--?p=Georg+Christian+Thilenius&fr=yfp-t

Wikipedia. (2017g). *Otto Von Bismarck.* Retrieved 5/3/17. https://en.wikipedia.org/wiki/Otto_von_Bismarck

Wikipedia. (2017h). *King XIII of Spain.* Retrieved 5/3/17. https://en.wikipedia.org/wiki/Alfonso_XIII_of_Spain

Wikipedia (2017i). *Treaty of Versailles.* Retrieved 4/26/17: https://en.wikipedia.org/wiki/Treaty_of_Versailles

Wikipedia (2017k). *Typhoon Ophelia.* Retrieved 4/27/17: https://en.wikipedia.org/wiki/Typhoon_Ophelia

Wikipedia (2017l). *tokko,* Retrieved 8/14/17: https://en.wikipedia.org/wiki/Tokko

Yap State, Federated States of Micronesia. (2004). *The constitution of the State of Yap.* Retrieved 10/19/17: http://www.fsmlaw.org/yap/constitution/entire.htm

PART 1: ENCOUNTERING ULITHI – A UNIVERSITY OF GUAM FIELD SCHOOL IN CULTURAL ANTHROPOLOGY

Field Report: Discovering Aspects of Life, Culture, and Environment on Ulithi Atoll

Rebecca A. Stephenson

The mission of the University of Guam (UOG) addresses the opportunities and imperatives of serving the entire Micronesian region, which includes Yap and the Outer Islands of Yap through teaching, research, and service. UOG's Anthropology Program embodies this mission through multiple objectives, including those that focus on historical, cultural, economic, linguistic, and biological heritage. More specifically, anthropology study at UOG addresses cultural change, globalization, regional studies, social problems, identity, and language, to name a few focal points. These topics could be applied to any part of the world. In the work examined in Part I of this book, an anthropological study was conducted in Ulithi Atoll, an outer island of Yap State, Federated States of Micronesia, with the permission of Ulithian authorities and the participation of multiple individuals and families in Ulithi.

The comprehensive research approach adopted for this project was the *field study* – an approach that requires researchers to be present for an extended period of time in the location of interest, while they live and learn about the destination community, primarily from the people of the community. The *field school* curricular strategy used in the project requires that students and faculty engage in course lessons and activities *in situ*; i.e., after they have traveled to the study site – in this case, a distant and unfamiliar community. The students in the Ulithi Field School were advanced undergraduate students who, as a group, brought multiple academic major studies to the project.

A project such as this may also be called a *capstone course* because it is intended to provide a focused opportunity for students to integrate their individual selections of college courses, combining theory and application. Often, this opportunity may be provided while they are also studying in a setting that is new and different to them and perhaps beyond their typical comfort zone. The result for individual students may be powerful. In courses similar to the one reported upon here, student feedback summaries often include the statement: "It has changed my life." One salient reason for describing the Ulithi Field School experience in these pages is that it serves as an example that may be helpful to other university faculty and students as they plan their own capstone courses using the field study approach.[1]

The University of Guam Field School in Cultural Anthropology, as reported in the chapters of Part I of this book, was conducted at Ulithi Atoll in the Caroline Islands, Yap State, Federated States of Micronesia, beginning in late May, 1992. The field team was comprised of five UOG students and three anthropology fac-

---

[1] The Ulithi Field School concepts may be kept in mind while considering other ideas and examples of capstone courses from Hauhart and Grahe (2015) and other sources.

Figure 1. Field school participants, faculty, and UOG administrator: Shawn Holstrum, Deborah Piscusa Bratt, Melvin Cruz, Rebecca Stephenson (Team Leader), Remington Rose Crossley (Dean, College of Arts and Sciences), Eulalia Harui-Walsh (Co-Team Leader), and Edward Mendiola, Jr.

ulty: Dr. Rebecca A. Stephenson, Professor of Anthropology, University of Guam, and Field School Leader; Eulalia J. Harui-Walsh, M.A. in Anthropology, Social Worker at Guam Memorial Hospital, Co-Team Leader, with the personal history of having been born and raised on Fassarai Island, Ulithi Atoll; and Dr. Yosihiko H. Sinoto, Archaeologist, Kenneth P. Emory Chair of Anthropology at the Bernice Pauahi Bishop Museum, Honolulu, Hawaii, Ulithi Field School Advisor and Senior Scientist. The UOG Field School students were: Deborah Piscusa Bratt, B.A. Degree Candidate in Anthropology; Melvin Cruz, B.A. Degree Candidate in Business; Shawn Holstrum, B.A. Degree Candidate in Anthropology; Edward Mendiola, Jr., B.A Degree Candidate in Math; and Joanne Scherfel, B.A. Degree Candidate in Anthropology.

Along with various group activities, each member of the Ulithi Field School team, including the two team leaders and the senior scientist, conducted an individual field research project during the team's stay in Ulithi. Aspects of Ulithian culture and society studied by the members of the group included traditional and contemporary economics, subsistence practices, expressive culture such as chanting and dancing, artistic culture including the weaving of lava lava, fishing technologies, material culture, especially with reference to the sea, the culture of childhood and youth, and the concept of disability and the disabled in Ulithi.

Project team members conducted reference research for their individual projects at the UOG Richard Flores Taitano Micronesian Area Research Center and at the UOG Robert F. Kennedy Library on campus prior to departing for Ulithi.

While in Ulithi, team members collected hands-on original data for their projects especially utilizing the field methodology of participant-observation. Upon returning to Guam, team members began to analyze their research findings. Final research papers of Stephenson, Harui-Walsh, Sinoto, Holstrum, Cruz, Mendiola, and Piscusa Bratt are presented below.

Design and Scope

The University of Guam's Ulithi Field School in Anthropology was designed during Spring Semester 1992 to meet several carefully defined needs. First, it seemed highly desirable for UOG students to gain direct "outside the classroom" experiences with peoples and cultures of the Western Pacific region in the context of their Anthropology studies. Second, UOG students could greatly benefit from the opportunity to conduct hands-on field research in anthropology and to collect original field data. Finally, UOG students could then be further empowered to prepare the data they had collected in a written format.

The Ulithi Field School was designed to begin with a preparatory training period at the university. A time frame of 15 hours was settled upon for the on-campus training, for which each student enrolled in the field school could earn 1 hour of UOG credit.

The time frame of the off-campus Field School was designed to allow the group to have a one-day field exploration and overnight stay on the island of Yap while en route to Ulithi. The purpose of the interim stay in Yap was to enhance the group's focus and readiness to engage the chosen field site, Ulithi Atoll. Likewise, this would give the group a chance to experience something of a transition to Micronesian culture, within a setting where team members could still enjoy some of the amenities taken for granted within daily life on Guam. In Yap, this included overland transportation by bus, western-style food served in a restaurant, beverages such as Coca Cola served cold with ice, and an overnight stay in a small western style hotel. The short stay in Yap was designed to mitigate the likely aspects of culture shock that would be experienced by Field School team members upon their entry into Ulithi.

Then, all participants traveled as a group via a small aircraft from the airport in Yap to Falalop, the main island within Ulithi Atoll. Upon arrival, each member of the Field School team was introduced to his or her local host family. Each of the host families had indicated their willingness in advance to provide board and room for their houseguest, to serve as daily companions for their guest, and to facilitate their guest in the course of gathering data for his or her research project in Ulithi. Host families received a stipend from this project for their willingness to participate. Especially because of the sincere caring and guidance we received from our host families, our team members were able to glean significant, informed, and meaningful perspectives of everyday life in Ulithi Atoll during our stay there.

Preparation for the Project

While on the UOG campus, the Ulithi Field School team members met daily in the conference room at the Richard Flores Taitano Micronesian Area Research Center on campus during the training period. Academic materials in the MARC collection concerning Yap state in the Federated States of Micronesia, with particular reference to Ulithi Atoll, were read and discussed. Proposed field projects were defined. The methodology of the field projects in Ulithi highlighted the classic methodologies of Anthropology, i.e., formal interviews, informal interviews, and participant-observation.

Dr. Yosihiko H. Sinoto of the Bernice P. Bishop Museum in Honolulu, Hawaii, joined the group on-site in Ulithi. He advised the students and the field school leaders together as a team, and likewise worked with team members on an individual basis. He shared thoughtful ideas and insights with the Field School team based on his many years of conducting scholarly research in the Pacific Region (as reported in: Sinoto with Aramata, 2016). Dr. Sinoto also went fishing with the local men in Ulithi. In doing so, he sought to add to his profound knowledge of classic and contemporary fishing practices in the Pacific region. Dr. Sinoto has generously contributed an academic paper to this publication.

Interim Visit to Yap

The Ulithi Field School team members left Guam at 7:40 A.M. on Wednesday, May 27, 1992, via Continental Airlines for Yap. Upon arrival in Yap, the group traveled on a pre-arranged tour bus to the ESA Hotel in Colonia, the commercial and governmental center of Yap. After checking in at the hotel, the tour of Yap for the group continued. The team visited and photographed the iconic *faluw* (men's house) and *rai* (stone money) in the "stone money bank" at Balabat village in Rull. Colorful FSM postage stamps were purchased at the Post Office in Colonia, as well as finely constructed handicrafts at the Yap Women's Association. The last stop of the day was the Bechiyal Cultural Center located at Map Village. Members of the group hiked overland from where the bus was required to park in order to view the unique buildings and grounds of the Cultural Center. Team members photographed and video-taped the localities with the expressed permission of local residents. That evening, the group dined at the ESA Hotel and then took a walking tour of the Colonia town area.

On Thursday, May 28, the UOG team returned via the tour bus to the Yap Airport for departure via Pacific Mission Aviation (PMA) to Ulithi Atoll. Team members lent a hand to a novel task, that of helping to push the small aircraft out of its hanger before departure. The aircraft's close-to-ground-level positioning during the flight gave team members astonishing vistas to contemplate. Excitement mounted as the small islets of Ulithi came into view, positioned here and there at the edge of Ulithi's lagoon, which at approximately 212 square miles is one of the largest lagoons in the world. Ulithi Atoll appeared to be a beautiful necklace lying on the sea ahead. The mid-morning PMA flight from Yap deposited the UOG team at Falalop Island in Ulithi by noon.

The Field Experience: Residence in Ulithi

The University of Guam Field School team members arrived in Falalop, Ulithi on Thursday, May 28, 1992. Designated host families waited near the Ulithi airstrip. After team members disembarked from the aircraft, introductions were made concerning key persons in the Ulithian community, along with welcoming remarks. Then team members dispersed in the company of their new host family members.

In the days that followed, UOG team members were on-task with their individual field research projects. Frequent project team meetings were held to make sure that all were on track. Many team members had the opportunity to travel via small watercraft with their host families across the lagoon to other islands in Ulithi Atoll, including the islands of Asor, Mogmog, and Fassarai. Dusk frequently found team members at the concrete airstrip that bisects the island of Falalop, enjoying the cool night breezes, and viewing the astonishing starry sky overhead with their Ulithian family members and new Ulithian friends.

Figure 2. The regional field trip ship stopping at Ulithi to deliver vital supplies and to exchange disembarking Ulithi passengers with newly boarding passengers headed to Yap and beyond.

Members of the UOG Ulithi Field team were especially fortunate to be able to attend the Graduation at Outer Islands High School on Falalop on June 3. Seventy-three young men and women from Ulithi Atoll and from many of the outer islands in the Caroline archipelago comprised the senior class. The slow and solemn march of the Outer Islands High School graduates was unforgettable. They proceeded one by one across the graduation stage with the shores of Ulithi lagoon providing the backdrop, and lively music provided by the USA Navy Band who came from Guam to entertain. Stirring speeches were offered by many constituents, and the Guam team joined the joyful receiving line to congratulate the new graduates at the end of the ceremony. UOG team members placed lei-style garlands that the group had made from local materials and pieces of wrapped candy around the neck of each graduate at this time. A number of other special activities, including the Graduation at the Elementary School on Falalop, and the Graduation at the Junior High School on Mogmog, happened while the UOG team was in residence in Ulithi. The team was kindly invited to attend. UOG team members observed community food preparations, extraordinary community dancing and singing, and many other cultural activities during treasured everyday hands-on experiences of life in Ulithi Atoll.

Figure 3. Outer Island High School, Falalop, Ulithi: Young women graduates, 1992.

Project Summary

Members of the University of Guam Field Team in Anthropology returned to Guam on June 5, 1992, after a brief stopover to change planes in Yap. For members of the UOG team, the Field School in Anthropology provided unique individual and group experiences in anthropological field research in the central Caroline Islands of Micronesia. Likewise, team members enjoyed the opportunity to meet and begin to get to know the people of Ulithi Atoll.

The UOG team presented research findings from the Ulithi Project in the Seminar Series of the Richard Flores Taitano Micronesian Area Research Center at the University of Guam on April 21, 1993. The team presentation was entitled: "Ulithi: Traditional Perspectives and Modern Life." The UOG Field School in Anthropology in Ulithi was also highlighted in a front-page story in Guam's *Pacific Daily News* (Whaley,1993).

Figure 4. Outer Island High School, Falalop, Ulithi: Young men graduates, 1992.

Figure 5. Outer Island High School, Falalop, Ulithi: Families enjoy watching students do a traditional dance at the Graduation event, 1992.

Reflections and Acknowledgements

Spelling systems of the indigenous languages of Micronesia have been undergoing a process of change since the 1970s. Reflecting the time of the field study, the authors adopted the classic orthography utilized for Ulithian place names and other common words appearing in print at that time, in Summer 1992. We are mindful of other publications that utilize the spelling of Ulithian words that appears to be closer to the contemporary articulation of these place names by Micronesian language speakers (e.g., Fassarai? Fatharai? Federey?), and also that new dictionaries have appeared in recent years (e.g., Laimoh, 2002). These will undoubtedly be important sources for future studies of Ulithi.

Figure 6. John B. Rulmal, Sr., the Yap State Governor's Representative in Ulithi, who ensured that the needs of the members of the UOG Ulithi Field School team were fulfilled. *(RDK Herman, Pacific Worlds, 2017.)*

At the University of Guam at the time that this Field School was undertaken, Dean of the College of Arts and Sciences, Dr. Remington Rose-Crossley was instrumental in proposing the project at the outset and in making sure that the project progressed from university desktops to the on-site field location in Ulithi Atoll. Mr. John Rulmal, the Yap State Governor's Representative in Ulithi, expertly and graciously assisted the UOG team with all of the logistical needs. Mr. James Nelson of Continental Airlines provided the UOG students with subsidies for the airplane tickets from Guam to Yap and return. On Guam, additional people who provided assistance to the team as it prepared to depart for Ulithi included Dr. John Walsh, Mr. Josede Figirliong, Mrs. Dana Figirliong, Mr. Louis Rama, Mrs. Joanne Rama, and others. In Ulithi, the host families provided meals and lodging for team members in their homes, looked after their guests, reassured team members, and offered singular and profound insights into Ulithian ways of living. The team is deeply grateful to all of them for their many kindnesses, and for welcoming team members into their homes in Ulithi and into their lives with such great enthusiasm. Finally, the UOG Ulithi Field School project leaders wish to formally acknowledge the University of Guam students who chose to become team members of this hands-on project in Cultural Anthropology. Any errors of facts or points of view that appear in these research papers are the writers' own errors, and not those of the many people who generously offered their assistance in the course of the UOG Field School in Cultural Anthropology held in Ulithi Atoll, Yap State, Federated States of Micronesia, in Summer 1992.

References

Hauhart, R. C. & Grahe, J. E. (2015). *Designing and teaching undergraduate capstone courses.* San Francisco: Jossey Bass.

Laimoh, M. (2002). *English-Ulithian dictionary 1.* Colonia, Yap State, FSM: Yap State Enterprising Department (SEED).

Pacific Worlds. (November 18, 2017). *War claims money.* http://www.pacificworlds.com/yap/ memories/ warclaim.cfm

Sinoto, Y. with Aramata, H. (2016). *Curve of the hook: Yosihiko Sinoto: An archaeologist in Polynesia.* Honolulu, HI: University of Hawai'i Press.

Whaley, F. (May 10, 1993). Living lab: UOG students take classroom to Ulithi. Guam: *Pacific Daily News, Vol 24*(No. 98).

MATERIAL CULTURE OF ULITHI:
A FUSION OF PAST AND PRESENT

Shawn Holstrum

This paper is primarily concerned with the material culture of Ulithi, focusing especially on fishing technology and practices. Material culture in Ulithi today appears to represent a blend of traditional and modern technology and materials. In Ulithi Atoll, traditional activities today are often undertaken with the aid of modern tools and materials. For example, metal blades are hafted onto traditionally shaped, hand crafted adze handles. For food preparation, bananas and other fruits are pounded with the traditional stone pounder. Yet, inside the house, rice is prepared in the electric rice cooker.

With the continued increase in westernization and modernization, many Ulithian elders are becoming concerned that the traditional cultural ways will be lost entirely. Ulithian children do not appear to be learning the old songs and crafts. Ulithian women often take on non-traditional roles in the community.

Partly in an effort to circumscribe or fight this loss of culture, new curricula has been introduced into the Outer Islands High School (OIHS) on Falalop Island in Ulithi Atoll, that guides the students during instruction of some of the traditional crafts. Mr. Joseph Tawag is the Cultural Teacher at OIHS. Much of my time in the field in Ulithi was spent with Tawag while he demonstrated the manufacture of three different types of fishing gear which are made from locally available materials, but using modern tools. Additional information was gleaned from conversation with Father Nick, the Catholic priest, who expressed a deep concern for the changing culture on Ulithi.

Cultural Context

Ulithi continues to undergo westernization. As is seen in other papers in this volume, the western concept of money is becoming an integral part of society and daily life in Ulithi. Using modern western tools and technology can often make daily tasks less strenuous and less time consuming. Also, modern equipment can be more effective, or at least it is thought to be, than the traditional equipment. For example, Tawag noted that those who use modern fishing line and other modern equipment catch more fish than those using traditional gear. Fish are such an important staple in an atoll community's diet that it is logical that fishermen would prefer to use the more effective, modern equipment.

One unfortunate result of the reliance on modern fishing equipment is that there does not seem to be any local motivation to learn the craft of fishhook manufacture. Consequently, a cultural tradition and technology may become lost. Father Nick expressed his concern that the young people of Ulithi are no longer interested in preserving Ulithian culture. He feels that the students in Tawag's classes may only learn the traditions in order to pass a test. Then, as soon as the test is over,

Figure 1. Group preparation of seafood, with Dr. Stephenson (right) observing. *(Photograph by Hiro Kurashina, 1983.)*

Figure 2. Family prepares baskets of seeded breadfruit and other foods for a large gathering. *(Photograph by Hiro Kurashina, 1983.)*

they may forget all of what they have learned. Ulithian elders possess a wealth of knowledge, but it is at risk of being lost soon.

Another consequence of the preference for more effective modern tools in Ulithi is the transference to a cash based economy. As early as the 1970s, "almost every family [had] at least one member employed as a teacher, health aide, or government worker, and this gives some purchasing power" (Walsh, 1979, p. 20). But means of generating monetary income is quite limited in Ulithi. Many of the young men are leaving the atoll to make money. Many work on Yap, but it is becoming more common for Ulithians to travel to Guam, or even Hawaii and the United States mainland, in search of a cash income. Some of those who leave send money home, but some do not. The loss of Ulithi's youth may have a harsh impact on Ulithian culture in years to come.

Siala Fetah! Let's go Fishing!

Traditionally, only the men of Ulithi were allowed to go out on the ocean to fish. If a woman was present, a man could not even throw a fishing line in the water. In fact, Ulithi traditionally was among the most restrictive of cultures in Oceania, allowing women to participate only in "reef gleaning... (which) involves walking along the reef probing with a stick, or simply with the bare hands, for octopus, shellfish, echinoderms, crabs, and other invertebrates" (Chapman, 1987, pp. 268 – 269).

When cultural anthropologist William A. Lessa visited Ulithi, first in the 1940s and later in the 1960s, he noted the importance of seafood in the Ulithian diet. He observed a variety of marine exploitation techniques, including net catch methods both from canoes and on the reef, hook and line fishing, traps, weirs, fish clubbing, and occasional spearfishing (Lessa, 1986, pp. 14 – 15). He noted that "the importance of fishing is attested to by the number of taboos surrounding the fisherman and his techniques, as well as the folklore accounting for the origin of fishing itself" (Lessa, 1986, p. 15).

The westernizing influences in Ulithi are not only changing the material culture. Father Nick reflected that many of the traditional taboos in Ulithi concerning fishing rights and practices are no longer being observed. Women now sometimes fish in the boats with the men. There are situations where women may fish from the shore. Sometimes, out of necessity, women are now learning to drive motorboats. This gives women access to the deeper water, hence the opportunity for them to learn and practice new fishing techniques.

Not everyone is comfortable with the changes happening in Ulithi. Some of the older men are offended by the behavior of Ulithian women today. Deeply seated in Ulithian culture is the concept of the "ideal traditional woman ... [who] ... knows her place" (Harui-Walsh, 1985, p. 35). Among other subservient behaviors required of women, it has been critical that Ulithian women adhere strictly to all taboos. Therefore, women disregarding the fishing taboo is an unacceptable concept to those who still adhere to the strict cultural codes. The rift between the "ideal woman of Ulithi" and the modern Ulithian woman, reported by Harui-Walsh in 1985, continues to grow.

Modern Manufacture of Traditional Fishhooks in Ulithi

In a section discussing methods of food procurement, Lessa (1986, p. 14) briefly mentioned various types of hook and line fishing techniques practiced in Ulithi. In this section, I will elaborate on three types of fishhooks, with some notes on their disbursement throughout Micronesia. Discussion is included concerning the modern method of manufacture used to make these fishhooks.

One-piece fishhook. The first type of fishhook Tawag made was a one-piece fishhook, "usually made of tortoise shell or coconut shell, or nowadays steel" (Lessa, 1986, p. 14). Craib notes that there is "no mention of marine shell or bone used as a source material" (1980, p. 25) for such one-piece fishhooks in Ulithi. The predominance of turtle shell for one-piece fishhook manufacture is consistent with fishhooks in most Micronesian islands, with the exception of the Mariana Islands, Nukuoro, and Kapingamarangi (Anell, 1955, pp. 92 – 95).

For the Mariana Islands, mention is made of turtle shell fishhooks in the ethnographic and historic literature. But according to Anell (1955, p.92), "No such hooks have been found in connection with the excavations, and it is, moreover, pointed out that turtle shell suitable for the purpose is very rare here." The fish-hooks recovered from archaeological excavation from the Mariana Islands were manufactured from pearl shell. On Nukuoro and Kapingamarangi, one-piece fish-hooks were manufactured from both pearl shell and turtle shell (Anell, 1955, p. 94).

The specimen that Tawag prepared was manufactured from turtle shell *(bochol wol)*. The specimen has a straight shank with the point forming an approx-imately 45-degree angle to the shank. The tip of the point bends upward, to lie parallel with the shank. There is a perforation in the top of the shank for the line attachment. A hackle of chicken feathers was attached near the top of the shank, below the perforation.

Gorge. A gorge is "a straight stick of bone or wood pointed at both ends, the line being attached in the middle" (Anell, 1955, p. 72). A gorge is designed to be swallowed whole with "the bait and (when) tension was applied to the line, the gorge turned sideways and lodged in the stomach or throat" (Johannes, 1981, p. 15).

The specific gorge that Tawag made was manufactured from coconut shell and exhibited an obtuse angle bend. It was baited with a piece of coconut meat, and attached to a coconut shell float. This type of fishing devise is also known in Palau and the Mariana Islands (Anell, 1955, pp. 72 – 73; Amesbury, Cushing, and Sakamoto, 1986, p. 7). The flying fish caught were then used as bait to catch larger pelagic fish. An advantage of the gorge is that it is relatively easy to manufacture, and a number of these devices can be set at one time.

The coconut shell gorge that Tawag made is known on Ulithi as *chi*. The first step in the manufacturing process was to cut a square tab out of a dry coconut shell, i.e., the interior shell immediately surrounding the coconut meat. Tawag used a metal handsaw to do this. The tab was then cut into a V shape with the saw. A metal file was used to thin the legs and grind them to sharp points. The coconut fiber line *(tarah)* was tied to the apex of the gorge. Tawag explained that the line was then attached to a coconut shell used for a float, which is set from a canoe *(wal fulyatch),* and used for catching flying fish *(mangar).*

Compound fishhook. The particular type of compound fishhook made by Tawag is known on Ulithi as *pa*. It is designed for trolling, used to catch tuna and other large pelagic fish. Anell (1955) calls this type of compound fishhook a "bonito spinner." He divides them into two basic categories: 1) those whose line attaches to the top of the shank only, and 2) those whose line extends down to the point. Fishhooks of the first type tend to be found in eastern Micronesia. The lure and point both are usually manufactured from pearl shell. Turtle shell, although not unheard of, "is less frequent" according to Anell. The points from this type of fishhook generally show "no indication of any base-projection," and "the angle between the point and the lure is very obtuse, in fact almost a right-angle" (Anell, 1955, p. 153).

The fishhook made by Tawag is of the second type. Anell explained that this type of spinner, used in Polynesia and in the western Carolines:

> …differs in especially one essential respect from the types described above, viz, that the line, after having been fastened secondarily to the top of the lure, is always drawn down along the inside of the same to the point-base (1955, p. 156).

These fishhooks may be further divided "according to the projection of the base," and "with reference to the way in which the line is attached."

Tawag's fishhook, the point of which is manufactured from turtle shell, is in essence shaped like a small fishhook with the basal projection reaching almost halfway up the lure. The line loops through a perforation drilled in the top of the basal projection. Anell affirms that this type of bonito spinner is known from "the central Carolines as far westwards as Yap," as well as from western Polynesia (1955, p. 156). Anell seems to refer to this variety of fishhook as a Samoan type (Anell, 1955, p. 156 – 160). The most common material used for the point is turtle shell.

The actual fishing technique used with this "Samoan type" fishhook referred to in Anell is almost identical to the account related by Tawag. The line is attached to a short pole. The pole is held by a fisherman in a canoe (or possibly in a motor boat today). Tuna, mahi, wahoo, and other fish can be caught with this type of hook. When the fish bites, a sudden jerk is given to the pole, which yanks the fish from the water into the boat in a single motion.

Tawag used a portion of a large pearl shell, which was stored in a shed, to manufacture the fishhook lure. The Ulithian name for this shell is *sar*. He mentioned that this type of shell is no longer common in the waters surrounding the atoll. A metal hacksaw was used to make the initial triangular shaped tab. Using a metal file, the top of the lure was rounded, and the bottom was narrowed to a point. The rough, opaque back of the shell was filed off to reveal the shiny, brown toned pearly interior.

The point of the composite fishhook was manufactured from turtle shell. Using the hand saw, Tawag cut out a V shaped tab. The metal file was used to grind the specimen into the characteristic fishhook form. A single perforation was drilled in the top of the basal projection. The point was lashed to the lower end of the shank, and then the line was attached as specified above. The final step was to attach a hackle of chicken feathers to the sides of the point.

Sennit. The line that Tawag used on all of the fishhooks was manufactured from coconut fiber. Hibiscus fiber is also sometimes used. Tawag explained that large batches of fibers are prepared by boiling, drying in the sun, and then are stored for later use.

Sennit is made by twisting fibers together into a cord. The ends of the fibers are placed to overlap and then twisted together to achieve the desired length of cord. These cords of fibers are then twisted together to make a thicker rope. The process continues until the desired length, strength, and thickness of rope is achieved.

To twist the fibers, Tawag rolls them back and forth along his leg. He picks up the new bunch of fibers in the backward motion. The process is not time consuming for the thickness of line needed for fishing gear.

Tawag's tool kit. Tawag demonstrated a mastery of both modern and traditional tools and raw materials. His most prominent tool was his adze. It was comprised of a metal blade hafted to a traditionally shaped, hand crafted handle. He often carried this adze about with him. Since Craib's 1980 report indicated the presence of *Tridacna* adzes in Ulithi, it would be expected to see metal blades replace their shell counterpart.

Tawag uses his adze to made a variety of "Ulithian souvenirs," so to speak. To the delight of Peace Corps workers, Tawag has made forks, spoons, and cups out of dried coconut shell. He has also made a sort of decorative sword out of locally available wood.

Bypassing the need for an elaborate workroom and clamps, Tawag often worked in the sheltered area outside his home during my observations. Using his feet as clamps, he showed tremendous confidence in the use of metal cutting devises, even though the slightest slip could cost him a toe.

Many of the tools Tawag needed could be found in the gravel on which he sat. For instance, Tawag did not need to use sandpaper to smooth the wood when making a sword. He grabbed a glass shard that was lying on the ground behind him. The shard proved highly efficient to achieve a finely polished finish on the rough surface. The shard was casually tossed aside after use. In past times, perhaps, the same technique was used with lithic flakes littering the ground.

The final Ulithian tool to be discussed in this paper is the drill. Tawag utilized both a modern, hand-powered drill, and the traditional style drill using a metal bit. The traditional drill consists basically of a stick with some type of sharp bit lashed to one end, and a cord attached to the other end. The cord is wrapped around the stick.

By pulling downwards on the cord's handle, the cord is pulled straight, thus rotating the stick and the bit. When the momentum of the rotating stick causes the cord to again become wrapped around the stick, the operator raises the handle to allow the cord to coil around the stick. He pulls down again on the handle to start the drill spinning in the opposite direction.

Looking Toward the Future

Ulithi is no longer an isolated piece of land in the middle of the Pacific Ocean. Because of the growing reliance on western goods, there is a continuing demand for opportunities to generate monetary income. The attention of the younger Ulithians seems to be oriented toward obtaining western goods, rather than preserving the Ulithian culture. But there are still Ulithian elders who hold the knowledge of the ancient ways.

Today, there is talk about the possibility of opening Ulithi Atoll to tourism. As I have demonstrated in this paper, changes in outward appearances may have far-reaching impact on the culture of Ulithi. Perhaps there is a way to incorporate a revival of traditional tools and culture with the growing interest in bringing tourism to the atoll. What is needed is a mind set focused toward the total ecological system of the land and the people. Sustainable development in Ulithi should incorporate the traditions, values, and beliefs of the Ulithian people.

Acknowledgements

I gratefully acknowledge the generosity bestowed on me by my host family during my stay in Ulithi (I never ate so well in all my life), with special thanks and a heartfelt hello to Cassie. I also thank Tawag for his willingness to demonstrate the manufacture of fishhooks, donating so much time and patience, and to note that they are truly beautiful specimens. Thanks also to all of the people of Ulithi, for allowing us into your homes, and into your lives.

I am thankful for the love and support of my fellow students and advisors, without whom I would not have survived my culture shock. And finally, I give all of the usual thanks to the University of Guam and our other funding sources, for making this Field School in Cultural Anthropology possible.

References

Amesbury, S. S., Cushing, F. A., and Sakamoto, R. K. (1986). *Fishing on Guam, Guide to the Coastal Resources of Guam, 3, Marine Laboratory Contribution #225*. Mangilao, Guam: University of Guam, UOG Press.

Anell, B. (1955). Contribution to the history of fishing in the southern seas, *Studia Ethno-graphica Upsaliensia, IX, Uppsala, Vol 9, pp 29 – 41. http://www.friendsoftobi.org/tobithings/fishing/anell1955.pdf*

Chapman, M. D. (1987). Women's Fishing in Oceania, *Human Ecology, 15(3).*

Craib, J. L., Figiriliyong, J., & Price, S. T. (1980). *Archaeological Survey of Ulithi Atoll, Western Caroline Islands.* Presented to Historic Preservation Program, Micronesian Archaeological Survey, Trust Territory of the Pacific Islands, at the meeting of the Pacific Studies Institute, Agana, Guam.

Harui-Walsh, E. J. (1985). *Status and roles of island women in the context of cultural change in Ulithi.* (Master of Arts Thesis in Behavioral Science.) Mangilao, Guam: University of Guam.

Johannes, R.E. (1981). *Words of the lagoon: Fishing and marine lore in the Palau District of Micronesia.* Berkeley, CA: University of California Press.

Lessa, W. A. (1986). *Ulithi: A Micronesian design for living, revised edition.* Long Grove, Ill: Waveland Press, Inc.

Walsh, J. A. (1979, March-April). Language and change in Ulithi. *The New Pacific,* pp 20 – 21. (Reprinted in Walsh, J. A. (2013). *Ulithi: A Micronesian Anthology,* pp. 83 – 87. Guam: J. A. Walsh.)

Additional References on Fishing in Oceania

Bell, D., Specht, J., and Ham, D. (1986). Beyond the Reef: Compound Fishhooks in the Solomon Islands. In A. Anderson (Ed.), Traditional fishing in the Pacific: Ethnograph-ical and archaeological papers, 15th Pacific Science Congress. *Pacific anthropological records #37.* Honolulu: Department of Anthropology, Bernice P. Bishop Museum.

Emory, K. P., Bonk, W. J., and Sinoto, Y. H. (1968). Hawaiian archaeology: Fishhooks. Ber-nice P. *Bishop Museum special publication #47.* Honolulu, HI: Bishop Museum Press.

Masse, W. B. (1986). A millennium of fishing in the Palau Islands, Micronesia. In A. Anderson (Ed.), *Traditional fishing in the Pacific: Ethnographical and archaeological papers, 15th Pacific Science Congress. Pacific anthropological records #37.* Hono-lulu, HI: Department of Anthropology, Bernice P. Bishop Museum.

Nason, J. D. (1975). The effects of social change on marine technology in a Pacific atoll community. In R. W. Caasteel and G. I. Quimby (Eds.), *Maritime adaptations of the Pacific.* The Hague, Paris: Mouton Publishers.

Pollock, N. J. (1975). The risks of dietary change: A Pacific atoll example. In R. W. Caas-teel and G. I. Quimby (Eds.), *Maritime adaptations of the Pacific.* The Hague, Paris: Mouton Publishers.

Severance, Craig J. (1986). Traditional fishing strategies on Losap Atoll: Ethnographic reconstruction and the problems of innovation and adaptation. In A. Anderson (Ed.), *Traditional fishing in the Pacific: Ethnographical and archaeological Papers, 15th Pacific Science Congress.* Pacific anthropological records #37. Honolulu, HI: Depart-ment of Anthropology, Bernice P. Bishop Museum.

CATCHING FLYING-FISH IN ULITHI ATOLL:
A STUDY OF GORGES

Yosihiko H. Sinoto

Before the Nikko Hotel was built in Gognga Cove (Gun Beach) in Tumon on Guam, the Micronesian Area Research Center (MARC) at the University of Guam and the Department of Anthropology at the Bishop Museum of Honolulu surveyed and excavated sites in 1987 – 88 (Kurashina, 1988). From these excavations a number of fishhooks were uncovered with other portable artifacts. Dr. Hiro Kurashina of MARC, the Principal Investigator of the project, invited me to examine the fishhook collections.

Of the 671 fishhooks recorded in these excavations, 409 are one-piece fishhooks, 241 are gorges, and 21 are composite hooks.[2] They represent a ratio of 61%, 36%, and 3% respectively. The unusually high percentage of gorges was especially interesting, since I have never encountered such a large volume of gorges during my many studies of fishhooks in Oceania. The Gognga Cove-Gun Beach site manifested an occupational span of 700 years between A.D. 900 to 1600, and is culturally associated with the Latte Period of Guam prehistory.

In this paper, I will first describe the gorges from the Gognga Cove-Gun Beach Site, and then discuss the fundamental aspects of how flying-fish can be caught by using such gorges. In order to test replicas of the Gognga Cove gorges, I visited Ulithi Atoll in June 1992, by the kind invitation of Dr. Rebecca Stephenson, Anthropology Program, University of Guam. By some standards the fishing experiment in Ulithi might be considered a failure. However, it provided opportunities to expand our understanding. Subsequently, I was able to successfully demonstrate the most likely mechanism of how flying-fish can be caught by gorges during a visit to Tahiti.

Typology of Gorges

Two types of gorges are represented in the Pacific: The stick type and the bent type.

Stick Type

The material used is a straight stick, with sharpened ends of bone or wood (Figure 1a). These are called stick gorges, or eel gorges, and are distributed widely in the Pacific (Anell, 1955).

Bent Type

This type resembles a caret symbol with sharpened ends (Figure 1b). All of the gorges found from the Gognga Cove-Gun Beach site are of this type. The bent type from an archaeological context is so far known only from Micronesia (Erd-

---

[2] See Sinoto (1991) regarding the classification of fishhooks.

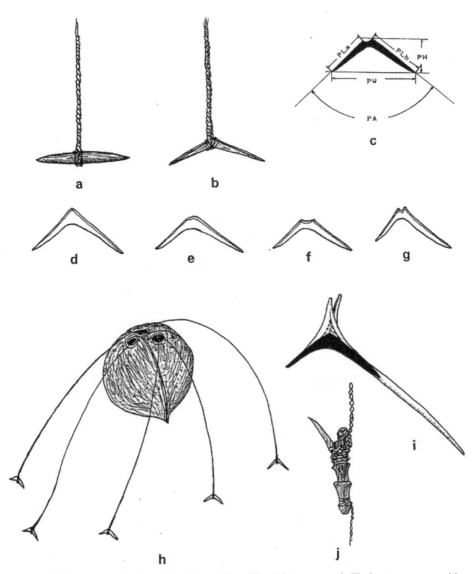

Figure 1. Fishing gorges, related method and materials: a. The stick type gorge; b. The bent type gorge; c. Measuring method of gorges; d. Angular type; e. Rounded type; f. Concave type; g. Notched type; h. A coconut float rig with several gorges. i. A puffer fish spine used for making gorges (darkened portion); j. Flying fishhook from the Yami Tribe, Taiwan (after Hsu). Scale: a, b, d-g, i, j, 1/1; and h, 1/3. Gorge width (PW); Gorge height (PH); Gorge Angle (PA).

land, 1912; Spoehr, 1957; Takayama & Egami, 1971; Thompson, 1945), except for one example recovered from excavations in Nukuhiva, Marquesas Islands in 1992 (Barry Rolett, Personal communication). I am greatly interested in the functional aspects of this type of gorge.

Description of the Bent Type Gorges from Guam

Of the total of 241 gorges, 149 are finished gorges either complete or fragmented, and 92 are unfinished gorges that cannot be used for further classifications.

Formal Classification of Bent Gorges

After careful examination of the bent type gorges, I classified them into four groups based on features at the bend: Angular (Figure 1d), round (Figure 1e), concave (Figure 1f), and notched (Figure 1g). These groups are easily distinguished, based on morphology. Whether or not all of these features were contemporary or represent a chronological sequence is not yet determined.

Measurements of the Bent Type Gorges

Among the finished gorges, 20 are complete and 48 are broken, but have measurable bend angles. Table 1 shows the measurements. The lengths of both points are not equal. One is shorter (PLa) than the other (PLb) (Figure 1g). The ratio of the length of both points is represented as PLb - PLa= ratio.

Raw Materials

All of the bent gorges from the Gognga Cove-Gun Beach Site are made of *Isognomon* sp. shells. These shells were readily available and were large enough for the manufacture of the bent type gorges.

Table 1. *Measurements (mm) of Gorges*

| | 20 Complete gorges | | | | 48 Incomplete | | 68 Combine | |
	Width (PW)	Height (PH)	Point Length (PLa)	(PLb)	Ratio	Angle (PA) (degree)	(PA)	(PA)
Minimum	25.0	10.0	15.0	17.0	1.13	67.0	67.0	67.0
Maximum	34.0	15.0	20.0	27.0	1.33	109.0	109.0	109.0
Mean	29.0	12.8	17.1	19.9	1.16	91.5	93.2	92.7

Manufacturing Method and Tools

For the preparation of preforms (tabs), stone, coral or shell like *terebra* could be used as tools. However, only branch coral (*Acropora* sp.) files have been identified from the site. All of the tabs observed were initially shaped by chipping, then all edges were ground using branch-coral abraders. However, the number of abraders found from the site are very small compared to the number of the gorges found.

Historical and Ethnological Accounts of Flying-Fish Catching

Today, catching flying-fish in many areas of the Pacific is done at night by net. Torches or kerosene lamps are used to attract flying-fish, and then scoop nets are used to catch the fish. It is clear from previous accounts that the bent type gorges were only used for catching flying-fish in the day-time. Based on historical accounts (e.g., Driver, 1989) and some ethnological studies (Kubary, 1892), it is certain that these types of gorges were used to catch flying-fish, but none of those accounts and studies tell how the gorges actually worked. The Fuller Collection Catalog includes fishing gear from Melanesia with gorges of the bent type

(Force & Force, 1971, p. 259) but a detailed description is lacking. According to Anell (1955), the gorges of Melanesia originated through historic influence from Micronesia.

Preparation for Fishing

At first, fishermen prepare several hooks by tying a foot-long leader made of sennet to each gorge, then a small stick of wood or bone is tied at the other end of the leader. They also prepare several coconut floats by extracting the copra from inside the nut. Three to five leaders are placed with the sticks into the eyes of a coconut float, then the holes are plugged with wooden plugs to secure the leaders (Figure 1h and Figure 2).

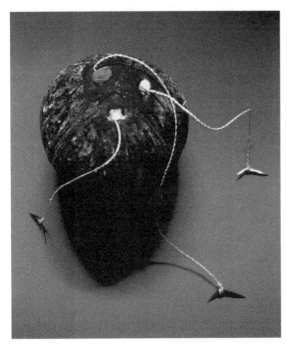

Figure 2. Coconut eyes plugged with pieces of wood to secure the leaders onto which bent type gorges are attached.

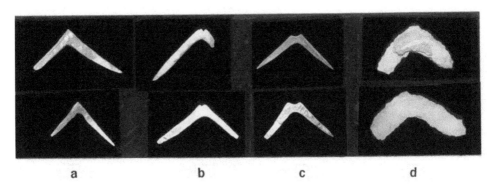

a   b   c   d

Figure 3. Bent type gorges: a. Angular type; b. Notched type; c. Concave type; d. Manufacturing stage of gorges by chipping. Scale 1/1.

Fishing

Upon reaching the fishing grounds by canoe, each fisherman places a small fish, a shrimp, or a piece of fish meat on one point of the gorge. Then a piece of copra is placed upon the other (Figure 4a). He releases several floats with hooks alongside his canoe (Driver 1989). According to Turbott (1950), in Kiribati and Tuvalu, fishermen use women's hair to tie the bait to gorges. Their gorges are the stick type. The float will signal when a fish bites. The fisherman then picks up the float with a fish or two.

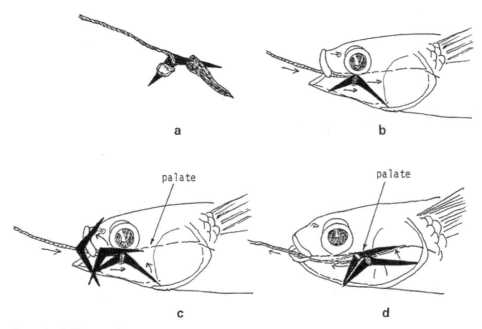

Figure 4. a. Stick gorge with coconut and fish meat; b., c., d. Movement of the gorge when swallowed and points at which gorge may lodge.

Experimental Use of Replica Gorges in Ulithi Atoll

It is hard to understand how the bent type gorges work to catch flying-fish, due to the shape of the gorges, which resembles *caret symbols*. They would seemingly easily slip out of the fishes' mouths. (See Figure 5 for physical characteristics of 68 gorges.) When I was invited to go to Ulithi Atoll by Dr. Rebecca Stephenson, I accepted because I heard that there were a couple of old fishermen who still remembered how to catch fish using gorges. I made several gorges using mother-of-pearl. They were similar in size to the gorges from the Gognga Cove assemblage on Guam. I arrived on Falalop Islet in Ulithi Atoll on May 29, and stayed until June 5, 1992.

On the islet I met two elderly men. One was Mr. Thomas Rolmar, who was known on the island as a good fisherman, and the other was a retired school teacher, Mr. Philip Nery. Both men said they knew about gorges. Mr. Nery informed me that the name of gorge in the island is *"chi."* This word also means "bone." The reason why the gorge was called *"chi"* is that the gorge was made from the bones

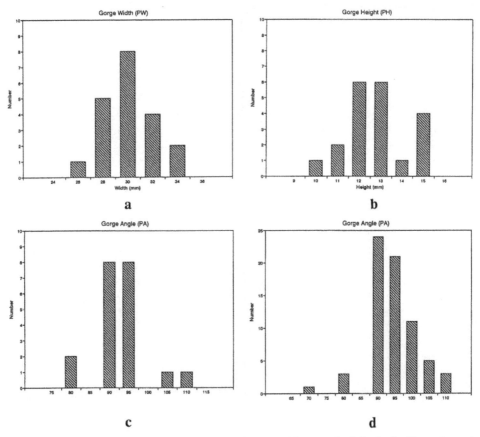

Figure 5. Mechanism of gorges to catch flying fish: a. Width; b. Height; c. Angle; d. Angles for 68 complete and incomplete gorges combined.

of fish, specifically the spines of the puffer fish *(Diondon hystrix)*. Their spines are naturally formed as bent gorges (Figures 1 – 4). The usual fishhooks are called *hoi*.

Mr. Rolmar agreed to take me fishing using gorges. His son-in-law, Mr. Moglith drove a boat and took us fishing. We spent nearly five hours at sea, but no fish were caught. We had good bites, and we let the line out. But, the gorge always slipped out of the fish's mouth. I knew that the gorges were for catching flying-fish in the day-time. If flying-fish can be caught, it should be possible to catch other fish as well, using gorges. Mr. Rolmar did not mention flying-fish at all. However, the fail-

Figure 6. Yosihiko Sinoto discussing fishing gorges with Ulithi fishing expert.

ure to catch any fish prompted some questions regarding the possible relationship between features of gorges (size and angle) and the size of fishes' mouths. I went fishing with other fisherman, but with no success.

By the time I left the island, I realized two things: (a) Even Mr. Rolmar never had his own experience in using the gorges for fishing, and (b) Gorges may work well only for flying-fish because of the effective relationship between the size and angle of gorges and the mouths of flying-fish. (Note the relationships shown in Figure 4).

Flying Fish and the Gorge, Island of Huahine, Society Islands, French Polynesia

On the Island of Huahine, Society Islands, French Polynesia, I was given a flying fish that was caught by a net at night. The total length of the fish was 312 mm. Its open mouth measures 21 mm high and 15 mm wide (Figure 7). The size of the gorge I used is 33 mm wide, 14 mm high, and the bend angle is 95 degrees.

I placed the gorge sideways and pushed it into the mouth of the flying fish (Figure 4). I pulled on the line and saw that the fish was dangling (Figure 8). Then I jerked on the line up and down, but the fish never came off. At first, only one point protruded from the mouth just behind the lip, and the other point was in the mouth (Figure 9), but eventually the other point also protruded and the gorge was secured firmly.

Figure 7. Open mouth of a flying fish. Height of the mouth is 21 mm.

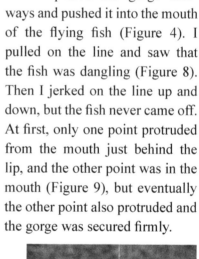

Figure 9. Close up of hook with only one point protruding.

Figure 8. Fish dangling.

Discussion

The foregoing experiment convinced me that the bent type gorges work, but I am still not sure if the gorges will work for other fish. If the gorges work specifically for flying-fish, the question is raised regarding why it was necessary for Micronesians to develop such a specialized hook. Another important question is whether or not the occupants of the Gognga Cove Beach site on Guam actually caught flying fish. Analysis of the midden collection should clarify this, but at present, pertinent data is unavailable.

Another interesting point is that, unlike bonito fishing gear that are basically the same throughout the Pacific, the types of flying-fish hooks are different from area to area. The best example is the flying-fish hooks of the Yami tribe on the Orchid (Lanyu) Island of Taiwan (Hsu, 1982). The hooks are made of wood and they have a general shape of ordinary one-piece hooks. However, they have two parts: shank and point. These two parts are tied together (Figure 1j). The mechanics of how a fish is caught on such a hook is easily understood.

The last task, as far as I am concerned, is to catch flying fish in the daytime using the bent type gorges. Probably the best place to do it is in Ulithi, where I heard, a large school of flying fish is always to be found. So I have a good excuse to return to Ulithi, and I hope it will not be too far away in the future.

Acknowledgements

I am grateful to both Drs. Rebecca Stephenson and Hiro Kurashina for inviting me to join their research group. Also Mr. Thomas Rolmar, Mr. Fernando Moglith, Mr. Philip Nery, and many other people on Ulithi Atoll who were so hospitable and made our stay so pleasant. It was quite an occasion to have an opportunity to observe the Graduation Ceremony at Outer Islands High School on Falalop. Mr. Eric Komori, Hawaii State Historic Preservation Office, Honolulu, prepared the gorge measurement statistics and the diagrams.

References

Amemiya, M. (1987). Bone, antler and tusk fishing gear in the Pan-East China Sea Region. Busshitsu Bunka (online database). *Journal of Material Culture, 48*, 1 – 26.

Anell, B. (1955). Contribution to the history of fishing in the South Seas. *Studia Ethnographica Upsaliensia, 9.* Uppsala, Sweden.

Driver, M. G. (1989). *The account of Fray Juan Pobre's residence in the Marianas 1606.* Mangilao, Guam: Micronesian Area Research Center, University of Guam.

Erdland, B. A. (1912). *Die Marshall-Insulaner. Leben und Sitte, Sinn und Religion eines Sudseevolkes. In Ethno-Anthropos Bibliotheek, Munster in Westf., Vol. 2.*

Force, R., & Force, M. (1971). *The Fuller collection of Pacific artifacts.* New York: Praeger Publishers.

Tsu, Y-C. (1982). *Yami fishing practices: Migratory fish.* Taipei: Southern Material Center, Inc.

Kubary, J. S. (1892). *Ethnographische Beitrage zur Kenntis des Karolinen Archipels.* Leiden: T.W.M. Trap.

Kurashina, H. (1988). *Hotel Nikko Guam archaeological testing in the general vicinity of locality Y at Gognga-Gun Beach, Tumon Bay, Guam.* Mangilao, Guam: Micronesian Area Research Center, University of Guam.

Li, K-C. (1983). *Report of archaeological investigations in the O-Luan-Pi Park at southern tip of Taiwan.* Taipei, Taiwan: National Taiwan University.

Sinoto, Y. H. (1991). Revised system for the classification and coding of Hawaiian fishhooks. *Bishop Museum Occasional Paper, 31,* 85 – 105.

Sinoto, Y. H., Aramata, H., Stewart, F., & Nagado, M. (2016). *Curve of the Hook: An Archaeologist in Polynesia.* Honolulu, HI: University of Hawai'i Press.

Spoehr, A. (1957). Marianas prehistory: Archaeological survey and excavation on Saipan, Tinian, and Rota. *Fieldana: Anthropology, 48.* Chicago.

Sun, W-H. (1969). Changpinian: A newly discovered pre-ceramic culture from the agglomerate caves on the east coast of Taiwan, *Ethnology of China, 9,* 1 – 27. Taipei.

Takayama, J., & Egami, T. (1971). Archaeology on Rota in the Marianas Islands. Preliminary report on the first excavation of the Latte site (M-1). *Report of Pacific Archaeological Survey, 1.* Hiratsuka: Tokai University.

Thompson, L. M. (1945). *The native culture of the Marianas Islands, Bulletin 185.* Honolulu: Bishop Museum.

Turbott, I.G. (1950). Fishing for flying fish in the Gilbert and Ellice Islands, *Journal of the Polynesian Society, 59* (4), 349 – 367.

Watanabe, M. (1974). *Fishing in the Jomon Period* (in Japanese), Kokegaku Sensho, 4. Tokyo: Yuzankaku.

Notes on Some Traditional and Contemporary Ulithian Economics

Melvin D. Cruz

This paper focuses on economic aspects of life in Ulithi Atoll. I will be focusing especially on the island of Falalop, since most of my research data was derived from there. However, this is not to say that some of the information in this paper would not apply to the other islands as well. This paper attempts to set forth the present everyday life of Ulithians with regard to economics, past to present day, extended family life with regard to generalized and balanced reciprocity, the impact of modernization, and the non-existence, at the present time (1992) of tourism.

Falalop is the largest of the four inhabited islands in Ulithi Atoll. The other three islands where people reside are Asor, Fassarai, and Mogmog. Since Falalop is the largest island, it is the only island capable of sustaining a runway that is long enough for a commuter aircraft. Small planes of Pacific Missionary Aviation (PMA) provide scheduled flights into Ulithi. Falalop may be described as the financial district of Ulithi and Falalop is the only island with considerable modern infrastructure such as electricity and plumbing. Although Falalop stands out in this way, one must not forget the more important, traditional side of Ulithi. That is the island of Mogmog, which is the paramount chief's island. On Mogmog, traditional values and traditional ways have been maintained. For example, on Falalop, Fassarai, and Asor, women can be seen wearing a blouse or T-shirt. But on Mogmog women are forbidden to wear such items of clothing and must therefore remain topless. In essence, any activity taking place on Falalop, Fassarai, or Asor that goes against the traditional values will not be seen on Mogmog. This is due to the respect given to the paramount chief by the people of Ulithi.

Background

In the late 1940s and early 1950s, availability of raw materials on Ulithi for material objects was limited to wood, shell, carapaces, coconut shell, sennit, and hibiscus bast. Although raw materials were limited it is uniquely surprising that tools and other devices were made. Kitchen artifacts too were crafted using traditional adzes, drills, and files. Some kitchen artifacts include scrapers, graters, grinders, knives, spoons, ladles, taro crushers, dishes, bowls, baskets, beakers, boxes, and hanging hooks. Prior to the introduction of flint and steel tools from European influence, local carpenters were able to construct good looms, fine houses, and superb canoes (Lessa, 1950, p. 12).

Subsistence activities of that period were restricted primarily to gardening and fishing, with little emphasis on the raising of domesticated animals. Gathering too was restricted primarily to reef fauna and the outgrowth of wild plants and trees. Some examples of food resources include coconuts; three types of aroids, Colocasia esculenta, or true taro, Cyrtosperma chamissonis, sometimes know as *elephant's ears,* and Alocasia macrorhiza, sometimes called by its Hawaiian name ape; and also sweet potatoes; breadfruit; bananas; fish; turtles; crabs; and lobsters (Lessa, 1950, pp. 13 – 14).

On November 30, 1960, Typhoon Ophelia collided with Ulithi leaving the islands virtually destroyed (Lessa, 1964). For the purposes of this paper, I will focus on the economic environment before and after the typhoon.

It was customary for goods to be distributed within Ulithi through gift and ritualistic exchange. Bartering outside of the atoll had been an ordinary practice. The emergence of cash came about during the Japanese administration, whereas the use of cash, then and after the war, was not practiced within the community except in the purchasing of a pig. Income was available through the sale of handicrafts and employment with American governmental and military units but primarily through the sale of copra. Non-indigenous goods such as rice, canned meats and fish, tools, textiles, kerosene, matches, flashlights, soap, dyes, fishline and fishhooks were in demand. In 1956, local stores were opened on Mogmog, Asor, Falalop, and Fassarai. This prompted the use of cash within the community (Lessa, 1964, pp. 30 – 31).

These stores were entirely destroyed by the typhoon. However, it was apparent that they had become inherent in the economic structure and that nothing could suppress their reappearance (Lessa, 1964, p. 31). The store concept came about from a prototype set up by a Navy medical officer who was residing on Fassarai in 1945. This prototype was devised to facilitate the selling of handicrafts to military personnel who visited there once a week. Subsequently, due to the opposition of the chief, attempts by the Trust Territory to encourage the maintenance of stores faltered. Following the death of the chief, attempts to establish stores were successful. The first to be opened was in 1954 on Mogmog. Afterwards, stores were opened up on the islands of Falalop, Asor, and Fassarai (Lessa, 1964, p. 31).

Figure 1. Exterior and interior views of one of Ulithi's "Mom and Pop" stores, 1992.

Figure 2. Exterior and interior views of a second of Ulithi's "Mom and Pop" stores, 1992.

The Ulithians' adaptation to the new cash economy organized a change in traditional values and patterns of exchange. One change in traditional values and patterns of exchange from the new cash economy was in the change in old work rhythms. All work activities required the people to use immense speed and energy owing to the desire for money.

Another change in traditional values and patterns of exchange inspired by the new cash economy was in the traditional roles of women. The most apparent change was the women's participation in the production of copra. Women participated in other cash-producing activities as well such as the fashioning of handicrafts for sale to the Yap Trading Company, the Coast Guard, and occasional visitors. This motivation was primarily due to the need to purchase trade goods, especially when items became available from the opening of the stores (Lessa, 1964, pp. 32 – 33).

Ulithi, therefore, had taken some steps toward a new economy prior to the typhoon. However, these changes apparently were accelerated by Typhoon Ophelia. Subsequent to the typhoon, changes within the community continued. Women performed work that was unaccustomed to them such as digging, chopping, hauling, and even carpentering.

Figure 3. Exterior and interior views of a third "Mom and Pop" store in Ulithi, 1992.

Communal labor which was once traditional was now being undertaken in innovative ways. Children participated in the labor for the first time, and were made to view it not only as obligatory but as a sport (Lessa, 1964, pp. 34 – 35).

Typhoon Ophelia, undoubtedly, did not hinder Ulithi's step towards a new economy; rather, it hastened it. This was apparent from the local spirit to restore their lands and reconstruct their homes as well as for their desire for a cash based economy.

Contemporary Ulithi

Ulithians in the early 1990s still depended in some ways on their traditional subsistence economy. Outboard motor boats replaced outrigger canoes, and were utilized for fishing as well as for transportation. Although modern technology has taken over, Ulithians still depend on the sea for food as well as for transportation. Food is also acquired from the land such as taro, breadfruit, coconuts, bananas and other vegetable foods. However, rice seems to have made its way into the daily Ulithian diet. Other imported goods are being consumed or utilized by Ulithians, and will be discussed in detail later in this paper. Basic land transportation in Ulithi is by foot; that is, by walking. This is adequate because the islands are small. In addition, there are usually three government vehicles, mainly pickup trucks, used on Falalop Island for various purposes.

Figure 4. A Mobile Gas Station, Falalop, Ulithi, 1992.

The extended family in Ulithi remains closely knit. This is especially so with regard to generalized and balanced reciprocity. Considering income, for example, family members who do not have paid employment or a steady income are mainly supported by other family members who do. For example, siblings who work provide items such as food, money, and other necessities to their parents and to other siblings who are unemployed. Likewise, assistance is provided to aunts, uncles, and cousins who are unemployed. Ulithians feel a sense of obligation to repay in some way or another the assistance given to them. For example, if a relative provided another relative with gas for the boat to go fishing, then some of whatever is caught is given to that relative from whom the gas was received.

On the other hand, if something is needed at a store but the individual has no money, he or she may take that merchandise and pay at a later time. Ulithians refer to this as *molfid*. The word has two meanings, the first being the previously mentioned and the second being a sin that has been committed against God. The use of this word only came about when the Jesuit missionaries settled in Ulithi and introduced Christianity. Nowadays, children and teenagers use this word jokingly, as when an individual takes something that does not belong to him or her. This might be a type of negative reciprocity because it may be that the individual does not have specific plans to pay the storekeeper for the merchandise that was taken.

As one can see by now, some types of modernization exist in Ulithi. Examples cited so far in this paper are the existence of outboard motorboats, pickup trucks, electricity and plumbing. However, there is more to Ulithi than meets the eye. Many of the houses on Ulithi in the early 1990s were constructed of either wood and corrugated iron, or of concrete, rather than in the traditional manner using coconut fronds. The men's and women's houses have been re-constructed using concrete, but with an attempt to keep some aspects of traditional architecture within the design. Institutions such as the local Catholic church and the local high school are also made of concrete and probably are the largest concrete structures on Falalop.

While on the subject of houses, I noticed one technological invention at the present time that no house apparently should be without. That is the television and videocassette recorder. There were few houses, though, on Falalop that have both a TV and VCR. One of the houses looked to me like a typical drive-in movie setting. But in this case, it was more of a sit-in movie. Those who were watching the movie were seated in the spot of their choice on the ground outside the house while watching the TV that was situated at a window within the house. There is no cable TV in Ulithi, so videos are watched instead. However, since there are no video rental outlets, I learned that the same movies are watched over and over again.

I noticed that Ulithians are very ingenious when it comes to recycling. The word recycle in this sense means that Ulithians are able to make continuing use of whatever is available. An example of this would be the rainwater catchment system. Ulithians were able to devise a rainwater catchment system by using an old run down building. Ulithi itself has no lakes or reservoirs; that is why this system was devised. The catchment system collects rainwater for the entire population of Falalop. However, I observed that some individual houses have constructed rainwater catchment systems for their private use, as well.

In Ulithi, some things that once had a particular purpose seem to have been transformed into something else that is used for an entirely different purpose. Some examples include the use of World War II bomb shells as part of a loom used for weaving lava lava, which is a skirt woven with hibiscus fiber, or nowadays with thread; the use of a plastic bucket as part of a commode; and the use of the top of a Corned Beef can as a peeler used to peel off the skins of breadfruit. Coconut shells were once used for this purpose.

There is an elementary school on each of the four inhabited islands in Ulithi. The island of Falalop is the only island to house a high school, Outer Islands High School. The school caters to students from all the islands in the Carolines outside of Yap Island Proper. Our Ulithi research group went to Ulithi at the right time to witness two graduation ceremonies on Falalop, one at the elementary school and the other at the high school. These ceremonies combined both traditional and modern elements. The students were dressed in traditional attire but primary colored cloth had also been incorporated into the attire. Also, the graduation was modern in the way that microphones, loud speakers, and keyboard synthesizers were used in the ceremony. I noticed the presence of military dignitaries at the Outer Islands High School graduation ceremony. One person in particular was Admiral Kristensen from Guam. According to an informant, the U.S. Navy representatives on Guam have been invited to take part in the high school graduation ceremony every year for the past ten years or so. I inquired if there was a significant reason for their presence. My informant mentioned that the Navy is invited every year as a gesture of appreciation for the support the Navy has given to Ulithi Atoll.

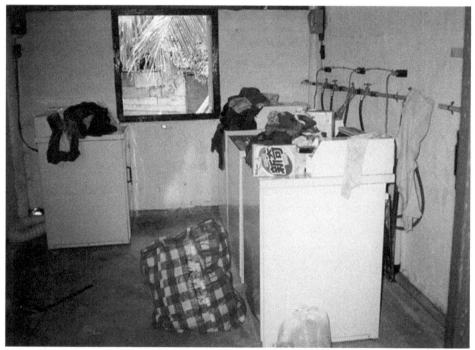

Figure 5. A laundromat, Falalop, Ulithi, 1992.

I was fortunate to witness a Head Start graduation on the island of Fassarai during my brief visit there. The types of food served after the graduation were much the same as on Falalop. The celebration foods included barbecued fish, turtle meat, chicken, boiled breadfruit, and bananas. It was divided between each family household. The food portions were plentiful, too. The portion I received was enough to feed myself and two other people. It seemed that there was enough food for everyone. Division of food is practiced on Falalop in the same manner. The drink that was served with the food was a mixture of Carnation brand condensed milk, water and some ice. This was the first time I encountered such a drink. One individual mentioned to me that this drink was utilized as a thirst quencher. Because of the milk's sugar content, the beverage replenishes energy as well. I noticed a slight variation in the pronunciation of words on Fassarai.

On Falalop in Ulithi, there are six "Mom and Pop" stores, one laundramat, one gas station and one Catholic church. The stores are rather like the ones on Guam but on a small scale basis. The Falalop stores sell a variety of goods, examples of which are listed in Table 1.

According to a local woman, supplies for the small stores usually arrive on the fieldtrip ship, the *Micro Spirit*. The only time supplies are shipped by aircraft is when the supplies are badly needed. The reason being is that freight expenses cost more to ship by plane than by boat. According to my informant, PMA flights are scheduled twice a week, on Mondays and Fridays. According to another informant, a local man who is a teacher, the field trip ship *Micro Spirit* usually arrives twice a month. However, there are no set dates for when the *Micro Spirit* is to arrive; therefore, sea transport is rather unpredictable. My informant mentioned that enough supplies are bought to last until the next shipment arrives because sometimes there is not enough money to purchase larger quantities. My informant mentioned that it is very difficult for a storekeeper to make a profit because of the way the extended family uses the store, and also because of high bills. The least a storekeeper could do would be to break even.

I asked my informant why it seemed difficult to find soft drinks on the island. He said that salt spray in the atmosphere settles on the cans which eventually builds up and creates holes in the cans. Also, soft drinks are considered a luxury rather than a necessity and the monies would be better spent on necessities. Based on my observations I suggest two additional reasons: 1) First, soft drinks are very popular among the children, creating a demand for this commodity that is many times greater than the supply; and 2) Space availability on the *Micro Spirit* is limited; so, priorities for shipping space favors necessities over than luxury goods.

As for the hours of operation of the stores, one storekeeper mentioned that his hours of operation are from 7 a.m. until 8 p.m. However, my observations suggest otherwise. It appeared to me that there are no set hours of operation for any of the six stores on Falalop. If the door of the store was closed and someone needed something, then the person minding the store or the owner will open the store for that customer. I found it very frustrating at first, but realized that it wasn't my place to tell local people how to run their businesses. I also realized that this is the way in which Ulithians have been running their businesses, and that no individual living there had any complaints about it.

Table 1. Goods found in Ulithi stores

Items with prices	No prices available
Winston cigarettes, $15.00/carton, $1.50/pack	Canned mackerel (15 oz. can)
Kool-Aid drink mix, $3.75/canister	Canned tuna (6 1/2 oz. can)
Spam luncheon meat (12 oz.), $2.55/can	Kim chee base
Black pepper, $2.45/canister	Crisco lard
Soy sauce (5 fl. oz.), $3.50/bottle	Tylenol (50 tablets/container)
Garlic salt, $4.85/canister	Excedrin (50 tablets/container)
Zippo lighter fluid, $3.30/can	Bufferin (50 tablets/container)
White vinegar, $2.50/bottle	Toshiba size "AA" batteries (4 in a pack)
Lipton tea bags, $ 2.95/box	Light bulbs (2 in a pack)
Salt, $1.20/bag	Dial bath soap
	Mosquito coils
	Charmin toilet tissue (4 rolls)
	Bounce fabric softener
	Downy fabric softener
	Wonderful laundry detergent
	Wesson vegetable oil
	Reynolds aluminum foil
	Pencils
	Dive mask
	Joy dish soap
	Juicy Fruit chewing gum
	Scotch transparent tape
	Barbecue sauce
	Navy biscuits
	Best Foods mayonnaise (32 fl. oz. jar)
	Peanut butter (28 oz. jar)
	Carnation Non-dairy creamer
	Black Flag insect spray
	Canned sardines (7 1/2 oz. can)
	Sapporo ichiban noodle soup
	Eggs (1 dozen/carton)

One piece of information that a prospective retailer might like to know is which are the "hottest" selling items. According to a majority of my informants, the "hottest" selling items in the store are cigarettes, sugar, coffee, rice, canned meats and fish, and soft drinks. For the most popular brand of cigarettes, Winston is number one among Ulithians. As for canned meats, canned mackerel would rank number one. Only one brand of rice is sold on Falalop and that is Calrose. I wasn't able to determine, however, what brand of coffee was purchased the most.

I previously mentioned that there is a laundromat on Falalop. The laundromat is owned by a local family. It has both washers and dryers. These machines are coin operated which means that there is a need to have access to cash. This is another situation in which those who have jobs with cash salaries, or who are able to share cash with family members, have the advantage of being able to use this convenience. There are no set hours of operation for the laundromat. What I learned was that the opening and closing of the laundromat coincides with the ocean tides. That is, when it is low tide then the laundro-mat will remain closed and when it is high tide then it will open. This is due to the fact that the water used for the washing machines is pumped up from a groundwater well. The depth of the water in the well is dependent upon the tidal conditions. When it is high tide the water level within the well rises, but when it is low tide the water level within the well recedes. Therefore, the pumps are only able to extract water from the well when it is high tide rather than low tide. Stephenson (1984) provided for additional information on fresh water resources in Ulithi in her earlier study.

Throughout my stay on Falalop, I never once saw the gas station open. Like the "Mom and Pop" stores, I believe that the gas station would open only when services are to be rendered. Gas is a major resource in Ulithi. As one Ulithian put it, "Boats are important to us like cars are important to you." This means that on Guam we depend on cars for transportation to get us from Point A to Point B. Ulithians depend on boats for their livelihood. Therefore, without gas, Ulithians would have difficulty securing their food supply.

Tourism per se did not exist on Ulithi at the time of this study.[3] One reason for this is that there were no hotels or restaurants on the atoll at the time of our study. But it is important to note that island chiefs and traditional leaders are currently studying the pros and cons of tourism with respect to its impact on modernization, westernization, and other consequences. It would be important to also mention that there exist diverse opinions among the Ulithian community on the issue of tourism within Ulithi. This subject is analyzed a little further in the discussion section below.

Discussion

Focusing on economics in small-scale societies, of which Ulithi is one, I noticed that it is much different than economics in large-scale societies. For example, in small-scale societies there is a sense of community. People share with one another. It is like an extended family, where if someone within the family needed help then everyone comes together to help that individual. However, in large-scale societies each person fends for himself or herself. However, it would be wise to mention that a sense of community can be formed within large-scale societies. People who share something in common can come together and support one another.

---

[3] See the description in Todd Ames's chapter in this book of tourism opportunities on Ulithi in 2008 at the Ulithi Adventure Lodge, owned and run by John Rulmal.

For example, those who share a common culture living away from their homeland in another place may come together to form an organization to keep that sense of community and support that they once shared back home.

Also, I mentioned earlier the idea of tourism within Ulithi. Considering the need for additional monies, tourism may or may not be the way to go. Residents and island leaders must perform an in-depth study of the pros and cons of tourism. They must also take into consideration the availability of resources within the atoll needed to sustain such an economy. If the idea is to have hotels on the atoll for the purpose of overnight stay then they must consider the availability of resources such as land and water. Land is a limited resource. Once it is used up then there is no way to make more land. With regard to the water situation, at the time this research was undertaken, the atoll was going through a major drought. Ulithi has no surface water such as streams and rivers; therefore, the atoll is totally dependent upon rainwater catchments and groundwater. The only possible alternative is to invest in water desalinization units which perform a process called reverse osmosis. This process removes the salt from sea water and transforms it into fresh water. This investment is costly but is probably the only alternative they have. Also, there must be adequate sewage treatment and disposal. Evidently, sewage could not be disposed of into the ground because such activity would contaminate the ground water. They must also take into consideration the availability of adequate power needed to sustain such developments as well as residential homes.

Besides overnight stay, there is the option of bringing in tourists on cruise ships for a one-day visit. In this way, there might not be a greater demand for such resources or infrastructure. One must also consider the effects between the Ulithian culture and the diverse cultures of the tourists. For example, some tourists may not be accustomed to seeing topless women or men in thu's. Likewise, Ulithians are unaccustomed to people gawking. Therefore, such cultural differences may impact Ulithian traditional practices.

Apparently, Ulithi has come a long way since the well-known publication written by William A. Lessa with respect to westernization, modernization, and technological changes. Traditional canoes have been replaced by outboard motor boats; traditional tools and equipment have been replaced by modern tools and equipment; homes and other structures are now being constructed with either wood and corrugated iron or concrete. Eventually, other traditional practices will be replaced with newer and better ways of performing those practices. In time, traditional practices may be only a memory, part of an exhibit, or just passing the time away. These changes may be positive but negative as well. Ulithians have to decide on the future of their island and of themselves. We, as outside researchers, can only make suggestions on what to do and what not to do. Ulithians themselves must make the final decisions. And once those decisions are made, it is very difficult to turn back. Ulithians can choose to learn from the mistakes of other island peoples, or can choose to learn from their own mistakes.

Acknowledgements

I would like to take this opportunity to personally thank Joe Figirliong, John A. Walsh, and Eulalia J. Harui-Walsh who provided the group with some background on the history, culture, and language of Ulithi in order to prepare us for our trip to Ulithi. I am appreciative of the people of Ulithi who helped in any way with this particular project, most especially Philip Nery, Sara, and Josef Taug. I would particularly like to thank Fernando and Linda Moglith who were my host family while I was in Ulithi and who also provided me with some information for this project. I would like to thank John Rulmal, the Governor's Representative, and his wife Terry. I personally thank Rebecca A. Stephenson and Eulalia J. Harui-Walsh, our University of Guam team leaders, for their guidance during our stay in Ulithi and also during the preparation of this paper. A great acknowledgement is extended to our research team members for supporting one another during our times of need in Ulithi. *Ho sa ha cheg cheg!* However, I hereby assume full responsibility for any fallacies within any of the information presented in this paper.

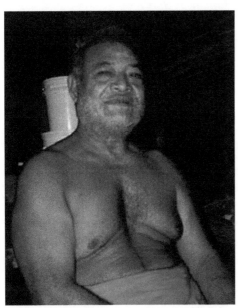

Figure 6. Philip Nery, one of the Ulithi leaders who was instrumental in making the lives of the Ulithi Field School students comfortable and productive, and who enhanced the quality of their work and cultural understanding. Mr. Nery was a teacher on Ulithi for 33 years and a resource on information about the authority system of chiefs in regional islands; e.g., the *mtaang* system *(RDK Pacific Worlds, http://pacificworlds.com/ yap/home/guides.cfm. Also see descriptions of other Ulithi leaders on the Pacific Worlds websites).*

References

Lessa, W. A. (1964). The social effects of typhoon Ophelia (1960) on Ulithi. *Micronesica 1(1),* 1 – 47.

Lessa, W. A. (1966). *Ulithi: A Micronesian design for living.* New York: Holt, Rinehart and Winston.

Pacific Worlds. (2017). *Guides to Ulithi.* http://www.pacificworlds.com/yap/home/ guides.cfm

Rama, Luis. (1993). Personal communication.

Stephenson, R. A. (1984). *A comparison of freshwater use customs on Ulithi Atoll with those of selected other Micronesian Atolls. Technical Report No. 51 (August).* University of Guam, Water and Energy Research Institute of the Western Pacific. Mangilao, Guam: WERI.

A TALE OF TWO ISLANDS:
BEING DISABLED IN THE WESTERN PACIFIC, PERSPECTIVES FROM GUAM AND ULITHI[4]

Rebecca A. Stephenson and Eulalia J. Harui-Walsh

This chapter discusses persons with disabilities in two Western Pacific Island communities, Guam and Ulithi. In general, the public on Guam is aware of the needs of people with disabilities, especially with regard to unmet needs of high priority. In Ulithi, in contrast, it was learned in this field study that persons who are disabled are incorporated into the life of the community in a matter-of-fact manner. The American model of activism on Guam regarding the rights of persons with disabilities is contrasted in this chapter with the Ulithian model, wherein the disabled "should not be treated differently from other people." Historical and present day contexts concerning disability are examined in both locations in this study, as well as some of the more significant needs of individuals with disabilities.

Guam

On Saturday, September 26, 1992, on Guam, a 25-year old mother of two children independently checked herself out of the Guam Department of Mental Health facility (a hospital operated by the Government of Guam), where she had been in residence. Shortly thereafter, she jumped to her death at a local scenic lookout, Two Lovers Point. A few days earlier, a 36-year old man with a disability in Ulithi Atoll asked members of his extended family to give him a knife. He sat among them while he carefully sharpened the knife. Then he walked to the nearby Men's House and slit his throat.

Persons with disabilities of various types reside on Guam and in Ulithi Atoll. It is clear that a notion of disability has long been present within Pacific Islands in socio-cultural contexts (e.g., Armstrong, 1991). This chapter attempts to assess what the present writers consider to be markedly different responses to disability in two island communities in the Western Pacific region.

With regard to the two individuals described above, the greatest concern expressed in the aftermath of the woman's suicide on Guam appears to have been a legal one. Family members of the woman questioned the Government of Guam policies that permit a person with a diagnosed mental instability to walk away from a treatment facility without her immediate family's knowledge. "Patients are in there (the mental health facility) because they can't perform in society what society calls for…," a family friend was quoted as saying in Guam's Pacific Daily News (Austin, 1992, pp. 1, 4). "For mental health patients to be released wherever they are held (but) not brought home is ironic." In the Ulithi situation, in marked contrast, the major matter of concern with reference to the man's suicide appears to have been a

---

[4] Originally prepared for the 1993 ASAO (Assocation for Social Anthropology in Oceania) Annual Meeting, Culture and Disability in the Pacific Symposium. Maureen H. Fitzgerald and Jocelyn Armstrong, Organizers. Kona, Hawaii, March 24 – 28.

customary one. Family members reportedly questioned themselves and each other as to appropriate role behaviors with regard to individuals who are disabled. They wondered aloud whether they might have been able to prevent the suicide that took place in their community: "Why was he given a knife, anyway?" "Because he asked for it." "But he is not entirely responsible for what he does." "We should have known better." "We should not have given him the knife in the first place."

Disability and Sociopolitical Considerations: Contemporary Guam

In Guam, an unincorporated territory of the USA located in the western Pacific region, the fact that some residents of Guam are disabled is not newsworthy as such.[5] Nonetheless, Guam's Pacific Daily News called the attention of its readership to the American with Disabilities Act in a highlighted article on July 27, 1992. The article began as follows:

> Guam became the first in the United States family to implement the Americans with Disabilities Act yesterday, meaning many of Guam's employers will feel those regulations today. The act prohibits private and public employers from discriminating against qualified people with disabilities during the initial application, hiring, firing and promotion procedures, according to a press release from acting Gov. Frank F. Blas...[6]
> (Daily News Staff, 1992c, 4).

The arrival of Typhoon Omar on Guam on August 24, 1992, impacted the island in many ways. Diverse urgent matters were in the news in the course of the typhoon recovery efforts, including Guam's people with special needs. Guam's grass-roots community organization known as the Western Pacific Association of the Disabled (WPAD) made major contributions to the Guam community. For example, WPAD insured that public transportation was provided for the island's persons with disabilities. In the wake of Typhoon Omar, WPAD personnel drove four vans, served an average of 100 home-style meals three times a day to people with disabilities or elderly people who could not transport themselves to shelters where hot meals were being served (Santos, 1992b, p. 5).

---

[5] In 1991, the month of October was deemed National Disabilities Awareness Month. Activities that took place on Guam for disabilities awareness included the following: Oct. 2 – a workshop entitled 'Employment of Individuals With Disabilities" conducted by the U.S. Navy; Oct. 4 – Nomination deadlines for the following "outstanding" awards: employee with a disability, supervisor of a person with a disability, trainee with a disability, trainer of a person with a disability, employer/organization; Oct. 5 – 12 – Displays and activities concerning disability at the Agaña Shopping Center and Micronesia Mall; Oct. 15 – 18 – "Visibility of an Individual With a Disability" Week. This awareness effort placed individuals with a disability in a work setting with an employer, community or government leader, for the mutual awareness exchange of both participating individuals; Oct. 19 – Micronesia Mall Fair, with public and private agencies on Guam providing information regarding services and programs available to individuals with disabilities; Oct. 30 – Lunch/Awards Presentation, for disabled employees, sponsored by the Government of Guam Credit Union.

[6] The PDN news article continued as follows: "Agencies and companies with more than 25 employees will be required to follow the new guidelines starting today. Smaller firms, those with fewer than 25 workers, have until July 1993 to comply. Some phases of the act, those covering transportation and public access for the disabled, were implemented in January of this year. The newest round of regulations focus on internal employment practices such as hiring and promotions. Critics have said the act is worded vaguely, leaving employers and employees confused about their rights and obligations. Briefly, the act defines a disabled person as one who has a physical or mental impairment that substantially limits one or more life activities, such as walking, talking, seeing and hearing. Such a person is protected by the act only if he or she is able to perform the essential functions of a job with or without reasonable accommodation. Those essential functions are defined by the employer. If the employee is capable of performing the essential functions, then the employer must be willing to make reasonable accommodations for the employee unless that duty would create undue hardships on the employer."

But WPAD'S transportation services became a political football in October 1992, some three weeks before Guam's Election Day on Nov. 3. Funds previously allotted to the WPAD transportation program were cut from the Government of Guam budget. The justification was that transportation services which can accommodate the disabled were also provided by Guam Mass Transit, and thus what WPAD had to offer was a duplication of efforts (Archibald, 1992, p. 3).

Persons with disabilities on Guam were incensed. Pat Botten, Director of the non-profit WPAD group, indicated she had at hand some 300 people willing to perform acts of civil disobedience, ranging from blocking Marine Drive to surrounding Government of Guam buildings if necessary, in order to protest the funding cut. Incumbent Senator Madeleine Bordallo, a long-time advocate for people with disabilities, swiftly introduced local legislation to re-appropriate $292,340 from the Government of Guam's general fund for WPAD's transportation services for people with disabilities (Pacific Daily News Staff, 1992b, p. 6).

The matter was apparently resolved. The day after Typhoon Brian on Guam, October 22, 1992, the *Pacific Daily News* announced that Guam's public bus system was once again fully operational. The announcement went on to note that the Paratransit system, a ride system for people with disabilities, was back on the road as of 5:30 A.M. (Pacific Daily News Staff, 1992a).

WPAD, in the course of its short existence on Guam, made a noticeable impact on the local community. For example, WPAD undertook a creative endeavor in July 1992 in the formation of a Tourist Enhancement Division within their organization, chaired by a Tourists' with Disabilities Director (Spiers, 1992, p. 28). The new division offered local tour companies transportation for the disabled. It could also offer the services of trained disabilities assistants to accompany tourists with disabilities during their stay on Guam. Each contract could be negotiated on a case-by-case basis. Funds generated were utilized to offset the operating expenses of the vans with drivers and to pay the disabilities assistants. Outright profits generated by the new division would be turned over to WPAD.

The inspiration for this new division of WPAD came about in Summer 1991, when a Guam-based tour company contacted WPAD. The company was anticipating the arrival of a group of tourists from a school for the disabled in Japan. Six of the group members would need wheelchairs. The tour company needed help. WPAD lent their assistance to the endeavor so successfully that the same group from Japan returned to Guam for a second holiday in Summer 1992. They were assisted by the same tour company which again subcontracted the assistance of WPAD.

John Peifer, the second vice president of WPAD on Guam, went on record indicating the variety of needs within the Guam community that WPAD could meet. "Recently one of our drivers picked up a young wheelchair-bound woman and took her to Pizza Hut for a party with her friends," Peifer stated by way of example. "We can provide that kind of custom service" (Spiers, 1992, p. 28).[7]

October 1992 on Guam was National Down's Syndrome Month. Guam's *Pacific Daily News*, in a feature article (Santos, 1992a, p. 3) pointed out that the only real difference between Down's children and other children is an extra chromosome. The article stated that most Down's children live normal or close-to-normal lives. But parents, it was stated, have to put up with ugly (sic) myths that surround the congenital disorder. Jessica Wilder, then President of the Guam Down's Syndrome Association, made the point that one of the most difficult aspects of having a Down's child of her own has been the myths typically associated with people who have Down's syndrome. "I hate the one about them being happy all the time," she offered by way of example. "That's not true. They're just like any other child. Down's syndrome two-year-olds have their temper tantrums; and Down's teen-agers have the same problems as regular teen-agers."

An additional matter on Guam involving persons with disabilities concerned the agency that would be contracted to pick up trash on the beach on Tumon Bay at regular intervals (Runquist, 1992, p. 5). Ron Smith, Executive Director of the Guam Vocational Training Center, Inc., made the point that his organization, which employs persons with disabilities along with other workers, held the previous contract and had done a satisfactory job. Smith felt his group should have been awarded the new contract. Joey Cepeda, General Manager for the Guam Visitors Bureau, responded that another group, Tropical Landscapers, submitted a lower bid and that Smith was not willing to renegotiate his group's bid. Smith acknowledged that the $300.00 bid of his group was necessary to make it worthwhile for his workers to do the job. Smith stated he doubted that Tropical Landscapers would do the same quality of work his group had done. Likewise, Smith doubted that his group would bid on another trash removal contract: "There's no respect for our efforts."

Disability and Culture: The Chamorros of Guam

Historical Context. An attempt to view the human history of disability on Guam dates back to pre-contact times. When Spanish explorers came to Guam, the first of them in 1521, they noted in writing that some Chamorros had disfiguring diseases such as elephantiasis. Jacques Arago (1823), the French artist with the Freycinet expedition, drew contact-era Chamorros who were unusual looking, having what appeared to be various bodily deformities. Pineda (in Driver, 1990) described an individual with a condition called *bubas*, possibly yaws. In examining the early Spanish documents concerning Guam, it can be noted that there were Chamorros at the time of contact who likely would have been described as disabled by both the Spaniards and the Chamorros.

---

[7] In October 1992, WPAD advertised in the *Pacific Daily News* for people willing to undergo basic health care training in order to act as tourist disabilities assistants and accompany disabled tourists around Guam. Duties would involve helping people in and out of wheelchairs, attending to their personal needs during the course of the tour, and also helping them have fun, such as taking them in the water at the beach or in the pool. People with previous experience as nurses' aides or home health care workers were especially invited to lend a hand, but such experience would not be required in advance.

Contemporary Context. In Topping et al.'s (1975) Chamorro-English Dictionary, the word "handicap" is not included in the English-to-Chamorro Finder List, but the word *disable* can be found *(yamak - break, destroy, impair, disable*, p. 247). Other words in English and Chamorro that may allude to disabilities include, for example, *harelip (a'pe', pire'*, p. 265), *abnormal (ti naturat - not natural*, p. 219), *cripple (makebebi*, p. 242), *crippled (kohu, nianko - to amputate, to cut off*, p. 242),[8] *blind (bachet - cannot see*, p. 229), *deaf (tangnga - cannot hear*, p. 244),[9] *deafness (tinangnga - hard of hearing*, p. 244), *dumb; stutterer; stupid, don't think (taktamuda, tattamudu*,[10] *uda* - feminine form, *udu* - masculine form, p. 250), and *crazy (a'baba' [baba* means bad], *o'duko', atmariao* (has no care for what anybody thinks), *kaduka* (f), *kaduku* (m), *kuka', loka, loku (crazy* as slang is *a'langa').* Older people on Guam might use the word *ke'yao* to mean to limp or to be loose jointed when walking. The term has a negative connotation, as if to downgrade a person's manner of locomotion (see also Jarrow and Rengiil 1991).

From the set of examples cited above, it can be seen that terms and concepts concerning disability exist within the Chamorro language. As the examples indicate, it appears that shades and connotations of meaning in an evaluative sense are attached to a number of the Chamorro words that address disability.

Public acknowledgement of disabilities can also be found in what Chamorros term, "better-known-as" family names on Guam. These are mostly descriptive references from long ago that were attached to particular local extended families. For example, one of the Chamorro "better-known-as" family names is *Cojo*, which means lame, or person with a limp. Disabilities on Guam, as noted above, include both physical and mental dimensions. People who have *lytico* and/or *bodig*, local neuromuscular diseases (e.g., Steele and Guzman, 1987; Stephenson and Chargualaf, 1989) may be among the most commonly known cases of disability on Guam. Some 100 individuals with these disorders were being assisted by the Guam Lytico and Bodig Association at the time of this field study (Custodio, 1992, p. 17). Clients aided by the Association likely received donations such as wheelchairs, commodes, shower chairs, hydraulic hospital beds, as well as adult diapers and milk, with these items being purchased at a fifty percent discount. At Christmas time, the Association distributed gifts to clients such as small refrigerators, televisions, microwave ovens, blenders, mattresses, electric fans, and air conditioners.

Yet, especially within the context of Chamorro culture on Guam, it may be that individuals with disabilities mostly stay at home. Testimonials attesting to this phenomenon within the Guam community can be collected here and there. Factors of shame within the context of Chamorro culture may be involved. Shame *(mamah'lao)* is a collective concept in Chamorro culture that might be used, for

---

[8] Older people on Guam may use the word *ke'yao* to mean to limp or to be loose jointed when walking. The term has a negative connotation, as if to downgrade a person's manner of locomotion. (Also, see Jarrow and Rengiil 1991).

[9] The words *bachet* and *tangnga* might be used by parents when children are not paying attention to them ["Are you blind?" "Are you deaf?"]. Children may also use the same words to tease each other.

[10] The Chamorro language at the time of this writing is not fully standardized in its orthography.

example, to assign blame to an entire kinship group for the situation of a single individual within the group. But for some Chamorro families, the appropriate emotion may be better described as pride. Some Chamorros may prefer to look after their own family members who are in need and may not seek or accept outside charitable assistance.

Disability on Guam: Reflections

Thompson's monograph (1947) is still the classic work that describes pre-war Guam. Guam over the years appears to be an increasingly complex sociocultural community. It is difficult to make a definitive description concerning the disabled on Guam in this writing. It is suggested that the contemporary Guam community is quite different from the classic Chamorro community described by Thompson. Contemporary Guam is an island community with varied ethnic representation within its resident population of some 160,000 people. Chamorros, Filipinos, Micronesians, state-siders, and many others have made Guam their place of permanent residence over the course of many years. It is likely there may be individuals with disabilities within all of the ethnic groups that reside on Guam. Future research might study the differentially abled people to be found within Guam's diverse ethnic communities. WPAD is the most visible organization on Guam at the time of this writing for the disabled. WPAD, however, appears to have chosen a particular posture, that of an American-model sociopolitical activist organization.[11]

Persons with disabilities residing on Guam face a mixture of advantages and disadvantages in their daily lives. The primary pluses seem to be legal and proprietary ones. Progress has included increased public awareness of people with disabilities; physical plant accommodations (e.g., parking spaces for the disabled; ramps; convenience accesses to public buildings); local press coverage via newspaper, radio, and television; and the like. But stumbling blocks include a lag in the provision of appropriate accommodations, disregard for existing accommodations, as well as general community attitudes. On Guam, especially because of the Americans with Disabilities Act, the attempt is to accommodate those with disabilities, to make sure that they have the same access and opportunities "as everyone else." But in attempting to do so, it may seem that persons with disabilities may be forced to be situated, in some situations, further apart from other people in Guam society.

Ulithi
Disability and Sociopolitical Considerations: Ulithi

In Ulithi Atoll in the Caroline Islands, four of the atoll's thirty-something small islands are currently inhabited by approximately 500 people. Lessa (1950, 1964, 1966) has published extensive ethnographic data on the lives of people in Ulithi. We encountered members of the Ulithian community while assisting with

---

[11] In 1993, the University of Guam established the federally funded Center for Excellence in Developmental Disabilities Education, Research, and Service (CEDDERS), which provides training, service, support, and research throughout Micronesia. Regional needs continue to be much greater than service resources can address.

an assessment of fresh water resource needs in Ulithi in the 1980s (Stephenson, 1984). In the course of conducting the Field School in Cultural Anthropology for the University of Guam in Ulithi beginning in May 1992, we talked with many people in Ulithi. Individuals with disabilities were not readily observable at first. Who are the disabled in Ulithi? What does it mean to be disabled in Ulithi Atoll? (For comparison, see Marshall (1991) concerning disability at Namoluk in the Federated States of Micronesia.) Ulithians interviewed by us in Ulithi Atoll in Summer 1992 offered the following examples for our consideration:

"B" cannot hear well. She lives on Mogmog, She's now about 12 years old. She had a hearing aid from Hawaii. It went bad. She had to stop going to school when her hearing aid went out. She can draw very well. She communicates with hand gestures.

"U" is middle-aged, living on Asor. She likes to wear dance fronds on her hands and feet. She sits down with you and asks you for cigarettes. If you tell her to go away, she will go. Just don't bother her. Sometimes she will be walking along and she will start yelling.

"K" is in his late 50s or early 60s. He might go in the water, take off his *thu*, and wrap his *thu* around the buoy that ties up the boat. Later on he will get out of the water, totally naked. He will take a clean *thu* out of his betelnut basket and slowly put it on, right in front of people. It's like he is in his own world. He doesn't seem to pay attention to who is around. At night, he might knock on doors or walls. He spends his time in the Men's House, lying about with the other men.

"F" on Falalop has problems with his hands. They are misshapen and have limited motion. Maybe he has arthritis. He can bait a fishhook, but he cannot drive his boat.

"B" is a deaf schoolboy living on Fassarai. You have to tap him on the shoulder to get his attention.

"T", a youth, has behavior problems. He lives on Falalop. His family has to chain him up. He's dangerous. He's young and strong; he might hurt somebody."

In short, disability in Ulithi Atoll can be described as clearly known and recognizable. Disabilities encompass both males and females of a variety of ages in the society. Both physical disabilities and mental disabling conditions can be described by Ulithians as occurring in their community. Later we became aware of individuals with disabilities in the course of this field research. But, at the time of this study, there were no visible accommodations for the disabled to be seen in Ulithi, no ramps, nor the like.

The Senator representing Ulithi in the Yap State Legislature who was interviewed for this study said no U.S.A. federal laws that he was aware of could apply to the disabled in Ulithi. He was not aware of laws or statutes that had been passed in Yap State or in the Federated States of Micronesia with reference to disability. The Senator was very interested to know details of the Americans with Disabilities Act, and the extent to which the Act had been implemented on Guam. He stated,

"We don't have that here in Ulithi. Also, I am not aware of that Act being a matter of attention in Yap at this time. However, in Yap, I am aware of parking spaces labeled for the handicapped."

Disability and Culture: Ulithians

Alkire (1992) effectively set forth the personal characteristics that an ideal person should possess in the Caroline Islands. Our field research revealed that humor appears to be indispensable with regard to people with disabilities in Ulithi (e.g., see also Peter, 1991). Ulithians have explained that they use humor with reference to people who have disabilities "to make them feel good, so they won't feel so awkward about their disabilities." Ulithians encourage everyone to take part in group activities, even if some persons perform in a differential fashion. In 1991, Rensel and Howard also commented on this situation for Rotuma. In Ulithi, this may include some teasing of those who behave differently. For example, a young woman who comes late to a group activity for women may be greeted as follows: "Ho, here comes the last canoe." The Ulithian inclusion principle may also involve self-deprecation. A woman on Falalop stated: "People call my husband and myself *buch*, crazy. That's the word they use on Asor for crazy people. Well, we are from that island. So, what's wrong with calling us that?"

A schoolteacher observed, "Disabled people can be accommodated very easily in this society. An old man in Fassarai lost the use of his legs. But he carved very well and people admired him for it. A blind man at Mogmog sits in the Men's House and you wouldn't even know he was blind. He just sits there, busy talking away with the other men like a sighted person. Physical handicaps here are just a detail, like being fat or thin." A middle-aged man had this to offer: "I can remember my uncle, because he was disabled. He could not use his legs. He put zories on his hands so that he could crawl about. He was very stubborn and did not let his disability stop him. He made a ladder so that he could climb up and get his tuba. People admired him very much for the way he went on with his life."

People with disabilities in Ulithi at the time of this field study mainly used energy and resourcefulness to get by. But community members were aware that persons with disabilities cannot always have their needs met. A teacher at Outer Islands High School explained: "About a year ago, we really wanted to accept a deaf Carolinian student in this school. She was very bright and we knew she could do the work academically. She would have been the first. But none of us know sign language. Our classes on campus are quite large; as you know. There are 71 seniors who are about to graduate this year. We have to move fast in our work with the students. We just didn't know how to make sure this young woman could keep up with the others. She did not force us to admit her. Had she persisted in seeking her admission to Outer Islands High School, maybe we would have found a way."

People in Ulithi recalled that American federal aid had been available to people with disabilities in the Caroline Islands in the past. A man explained, "When we had the Voc-Rehab money, a four-wheel drive vehicle was purchased for my father. It was very helpful for him to get about down on Fassarai. But then it broke down. It can't be fixed or replaced now, because there's no more Voc-Rehab money."

We sought local explanations as to how people might become disabled. Responses were varied. One young man stated with conviction that disabilities occur because of accidents, such as falling out of a coconut tree. Another man felt that disabilities might come about because of birth defects. A middle-aged woman offered thoughtfully, "If a woman tried to get rid of a pregnancy, like taking a lot of pills, being massaged, jumping up and down, the baby might be affected." In contrast to Alkire's (1992) study concerning Woleai and Lamotrek in the Caroline Islands, people we spoke to in Ulithi in Summer 1992 did not have much to say about ghosts in relation to disabilities. When asked if ghosts cause disabilities, people said that they did not know and that it did not concern them much. A middle-aged woman offered that people in Ulithi do not believe in ghosts or evil spirits as causal factors anymore, although, she reflected, "A long time ago, people believed disability came about as a curse on a family." An older man reminded us that Father Walter Cantova had greatly influenced the people of Ulithi during his four months there in 1731. He taught Ulithians that they could not practice magic and be faithful Catholics at the same time (see Driver, 1992, 170-173). When we said that beliefs in ghosts causing disabilities had been reported for Woleai and Lamotrek, Ulithi people responded, "Oh, well, we would expect that from people in those places." The primary articulated concerns of the Ulithians we spoke with about disability issues discussed ways in which to more effectively meet the needs of local people with disabilities (see also Fitzgerald, 1991).

It is our understanding that USA federal funding granted to Yap State via the Compact of Free Association had not been renewed for the disabled via Vocational Rehabilitation in the funding cycle in 1992, although the Head Start Program had been retained. "The Head Start Program helps us greatly," explained the local administrator of the program. "But we really need the funds for the disabled, as well. Do you know that we estimate 20% of the enrollment in the Head Start Program (this figure includes Yap Proper) will be children who are handicapped?" The administrator continued, "We do the best we can, but we get along on very little. We recently received funds to renovate the Head Start Centers, but no money for teaching materials. There's one Center each on Falalop, Mogmog, and Fassarai. The minimum enrollment in each Center is 15 children; the maximum number is 20. Five year olds, then four, then three year olds can take part if there are enough spaces left. Children with handicaps are given first priority, then children of low income families, but by U.S.A. federal standards, everybody is low income here in Ulithi. The Head Start program feeds these children their breakfast and lunch, and operates nine months of the year. We provide these children with 2/3 of their meals five days a week for 3/4 of the year. But the food provided by Head Start to us for the children is canned food. Families here prefer that their children are fed local food. High blood pressure and diabetes can result from eating too much canned food. Are you aware of that recent field study in Hawaii that points out the extent to which a local diet enhances well health?"

In terms of the language used to describe people with disabilities in Ulithi, our fieldwork revealed that physical and mental conditions are seen as separate and distinct. For example, *lepapach* means 'can move arms but not legs,' 'paralyzed below the waist,' or 'his/her legs are dead.' On the other hand, *buch* means 'crazy in the head,' 'off balance in the head,' 'cuckoo,' 'crazy,' and typically means mentally deficient. But the term can be used in another way, e.g., 'crazy about women' or 'crazy about men.' If a person is *buchollipich*, a not-uncommon situation for people who are not married, it refers to making frequent and mostly inappropriate sexual advances to others in the community. We were told this situation (sic) "is not a problem" because local people know how to deal with it, especially utilizing ridicule or shame. Even saying the word is not appropriate in public with members of the opposite sex present. Same-sex groups can joke about it within the context of their own groups; it is a way of monitoring the community. We were reminded in the data collection process about the value of gossip, the importance of the extended family, the significant role of reciprocity, and the separateness of men and women in Ulithian society.

In Ulithi, it is said, one describes exactly what is different about a person when one speaks of his or her disability. It is possible to make some local medicines that help ease physical or mental disabilities, and massage can be used. But the human head cannot be directly massaged. This is why disabilities of the mind and body are viewed as being so very different in Ulithi. As a local middle-aged woman observed succinctly, "If you can see it, then you can fix it," that is, a physical abnormality. Mental problems, it would follow, cannot be seen, and therefore cannot be fixed.

We asked what the principle difficulties in Ulithi within daily life are for people with disabilities. A number of Ulithians stated with conviction that it is much worse for women to be disabled than for men. "It is hard for a woman to get up (from where she is seated on the ground) if she is disabled." "It is hard for her to keep her lava lava in place." "It is hard for her to move around." "It is hard for women who are disabled because they have to be so careful when they move about around men; as you know, women have to crouch over when they pass near to where men are. Men with disabilities do not have to deal with those sorts of cultural restrictions." With regard to caring for persons who are disabled, we learned that men with a disability must be bathed by a son or nephew. Women who have a disability must be bathed by other women. A son can bathe his mother who is disabled only if there is no one else who can possibly care for her. From the age of twelve and older in Ulithi, people have the competence to care for a person who has a disability. This is especially applicable for females.

Disability in Ulithi: Reflections

In Ulithi, we learned that people who have disabilities have always been a part of the community. A disability for the most part is seen as a descriptive detail rather than an evaluative measure of a person's worth. A man called Ueg who is identified as the King of Ulithi appears frequently in photos taken during the use of Ulithi Atoll by the US during World War II. He appears to have had a physical disability. He usually appears in the photos seated with his legs crossed in front of him. But there is almost no mention in print regarding King Ueg's disability. One of these was written by Father Victor Walter in 1928: "The island chief, a paralytic, had his family carry him to Catechisms."

The disabled in current times in Ulithi may not be visible on first glance. But then they begin to be noticeable, as they mingle about in the community and are incorporated into community life as much as possible. A cultural or perhaps moral or socio-religious conviction might be discerned. Ulithians state, "It is not right to treat people who are disabled different from others. They will feel badly, because then they will think they are different from everybody else. We don't like to hurt peoples' feelings."

Discussion

To be sure, a comparison/contrast study of disability on Guam and in Ulithi Atoll as undertaken in this chapter is problematic. Guam is a large, modern cosmopolitan community; Ulithi represents a small, more traditional and mostly homogeneous one. Different coping strategies are needed and required for people who are disabled in two such vastly contrasting Pacific Island societies. Yet, some points merit further consideration as set forth. On Guam, it has been noted, special efforts are made to give accommodation to people who are disabled because, "They are entitled to it. They are different." In Ulithi, it appears that special efforts are made not to give accommodation to local residents who are disabled since "They are not different. They are just like everybody else." Legal matters predominate on Guam where the disabled are concerned; whereas, cultural matters predominate in Ulithi with regard to disability. On Guam, the Western model suggests that mental disabilities can be excused, in a manner of speaking, by the non-disabled, whereas physical disabilities tend to make people who are not disabled feel uncomfortable. In Ulithi, physical disabilities are perceived as non-remarkable, merely a descriptive detail about a person such as being short or tall or having long hair. But mental differences bring about considerable comment and may cause people some uncertainty. People in Ulithi said that they are not as able to engage differences that occur among people, if they cannot themselves visualize what those differences are or might be.

Noteworthy changes have occurred since this chapter was initially prepared in 1992. The first B.A. Degree Program in Disability Studies in the USA was offered in 1994 at Syracuse University. Disability studies may be described as (Wikipedia.org, 2017) . . . "an academic discipline that examines the meaning, nature, and consequences of disability as a social construct." Academic programs in disability studies include coursework in disability history, theory, legislation, policy, ethics, and the arts. Interdisciplinary research is encouraged within this relatively new and rapidly growing field of inquiry. Academic journals in print that help to inform the general public include the *Disability Studies Quarterly.*

Acknowledgements

Verna M. Chargualaf, a University of Guam student, assisted in the interpretation of the Chamorro language terms for disabilities used in this chapter, from the point of view of a younger Chamorro language speaker (age 21 and younger). Professor Marjorie Driver of the Micronesian Area Research Center at the University of Guam contributed particular information about Guam's Spanish colonial history for this research endeavor. Any errors in the interpretation of the material at hand are those of the authors.

References

Alkire, W. H. (1992). Perceptions of physical, mental, and sensory disabilities on Woleai and Lamotrek, Caroline Islands. Paper presented at the annual meeting of the Association of Social Anthropology in Oceania, New Orleans, Louisiana.

Arago, J. (1823). *Narrative of a voyage round the world in the Uranie and Physicienne Corvettes commanded by Captain Freycinet, during 1817, 1818, 1819, 1820. 2 Vols.* London: Truettel and Wurtz.

Archibald, J. J. (1992, October 2). Funding cut angers WPAD. *Pacific Daily News,* Guam, p. 3.

Armstrong, J. (1991). Disability in Pacific societies: Contributions from anthropology. Paper presented at the meeting of the Association of Social Anthropology in Oceania, Victoria, British Columbia, Canada.

Austin, L. (1992, September 30). Woman's death casts doubts on mental treatment policies. *Pacific Daily News*, Guam, pp. 1, 4.

Custodio, Z. (1992, February 5). Lytigo-Bodig group offers services. *Pacific Daily News,* Guam, p. 17.

Pacific Daily News. (1992a). Public transit update. *Pacific Daily News*, Guam, October 22, p. 3.

Pacific Daily News. (1992b). Bordallo requests funds for disabled. *Pacific Daily News,* Guam, October 7, p. 6.

Pacific Daily News. (1992c). Guam enforces disability act. *Pacific Daily News,* Guam, July 27, p. 4.

Driver, M. G. (Translator). (1992). *History of the Marianas, Caroline and Palau Islands, by Luis de Ibanez y Garcia, Micronesian Area Research Center Educational Series No. 12.* Mangilao, Guam: University of Guam.

Driver, M. G. (Ed.) and Mallada, V. F. (Translator). (1990). *The Guam diary of naturalist Antonio De Pineda Y Ramirez, February 1792.* Mangilao, Guam: Micronesian Area Research Center, University of Guam.

Fitzgerald, M. H. (1991). Culture and disability in the Pacific: Some questions. Paper presented at the meeting of the Association of Social Anthropology in Oceania, Victoria, British Columbia, Canada.

Jarrow, J. E. & Rengiil, Y. (1991). The language of disability in Micronesia. Paper presented at the meeting of the Association of Social Anthropology in Oceania, Victoria, British Columbia, Canada.

Lessa, W. A. (1950). The ethnography of Ulithi Atoll. Final *Coordinated Investigation of Micronesian Anthropology Report, No. 28.* Washington, DC: Pacific Science Board and National Research Council.

Lessa, W. A. (1964). The social effects of Typhoon Ophelia (1960) on Ulithi. *Micronesica, 1,* 1 – 47.

Lessa, W. A. (1966). *Ulithi: A Micronesian design for living.* New York: Holt, Rinehart and Winston.

Marshall, M. (1991). Congenital and acquired disabilities in a Micronesian atoll population: Case studies from Namoluk Atoll, FSM. Paper presented at the meeting of the Association of Social Anthropology in Oceania, Victoria, British Columbia, Canada.

Peter, J. (1991). Humor and joking relationships: Cultural rehabilitation and disabilities. Paper presented at the meeting of the Association of Social Anthropology in Oceania, Victoria, British Columbia, Canada.

Rensel, J. &Howard, A. (1991). The place of disabled persons in Rotuman society. Paper presented at the meeting of the Association of Social Anthropology in Oceania, Victoria, British Columbia, Canada.

Runquist, P. (October 28, 1992). Visitors Bureau hires beach trash collector, *Pacific Daily News,* Guam, p. 5.

Santos, M. (1992a). Down's syndrome families battle myths, *Pacific Daily News*, Guam, October 15, p. 3.

Santos, M. (1992b). The homebound are not forgotten, *Pacific Daily News,* Guam, September 5, p. 5.

Santos, M. (1992c). American Disabilities Act opens doors, *Pacific Daily News,* Guam, January 29, p. 3.

Santos, M. (1992d). Graduate shows hearing impaired what can be done, *Pacific Daily News,* Guam, January 29, p. 3.

Spiers, J. (1992). Opening doors for the disabled AND finding ways to help keep growing, *Pacific Daily News,* Guam, July 26, p. 28.

Steele, J. C. & Guzman, T. (1987). Observations about Amytrophic Lateral Sclerosis and the Parkinsonism-Dementia Complex of Guam with regard to epidemiology and etiology, *Canadian Journal of Neurological Sciences,14*(3), 358 – 362.

Stephenson, R. A. (1984). *A comparison of freshwater use customs on Ulithi Atoll with those of selected other Micronesian atolls.* Mangilao, Guam: University of Guam, Water and Energy Research Institute of the Western Pacific, Technical Report No. 51 (August).

Stephenson, R. A. & Chargualaf, V. M. (1989). *Lytico-Bodig on Guam: An anthropological inquiry.* Working paper. 30 pages. Privately circulated.

Thompson, L. (1947). *Guam and its people, revised.* Princeton, NJ: Princeton University Press.

Topping, D. K., Ogo, P. K., & Duncga, B. C. (1975). *Chamorro-English dictionary.* Honolulu: University Press of Hawaii.

Wikipedia.org. (11/14/17). Disability Studies. Retrieved 11/14/17, https://en.wikipedia.org/wiki/Disability_studies

Resources in Print Concerning Ulithi Atoll

Deborah Piscusa Bratt with Rebecca A. Stephenson

A set of references were prepared to support the 1992 University of Guam Anthropology Field School in Ulithi, many of which were compiled by University of Guam student Deborah Piscusa Bratt. These should be considered as resources that were available to the authors of the chapters in this volume, but authors did not necessarily quote or cite from all of the references below. As the chapters were revised for publication, some additional Ulithi-related reference resources that were identified after 1992 and that may be of special interest to readers of this publication, have been added by the editors of this volume. In addition, all sources referenced in the Ulithi Field School chapters above have been included here for the convenience of future students and scholars.

Alkire, W. H. (1959). Cultural adaptation in the Caroline Islands. *Journal of the Polynesia Society, 68(*2).

Alkire, W. H. (1965). Lamotrek Atoll and inter-island socioeconomic ties. *Illinois Studies in Anthropology, 5.* Urbana: University of Illinois Press.

Alkire, W. H. (1977). *An introduction to the peoples and cultures of Micronesia* (second edition)*.* Menlo Park, CA: Cummings.

Alkire, W. H. (1978). *Coral islanders, 37,* 47 – 48, 112, 118, 123,131. Illinois: AHM Publishing.

Alkire, W. H. (February, 1992). Perceptions of physical, mental, and sensory disabilities on Woleai and Lamotrek, Caroline Islands. Paper presented at the meeting of the Association for Social Anthropology in Oceania, New Orleans, Louisiana.

Alkire, W. H. (1993). Madrich: Outer islanders on Yap. *Pacific Studies, 16* (2), 31 – 66.

Amemiya, M. (1987). Bone, antler and tusk fishing gear in the Pan-East China Sea Region Busshitsu Bunka (online database). *Journal of Material Culture, 48,* 1 – 26.

Amesbury, S. S., Cushing, F. A., & Sakamoto, R. K. (1986). *Fishing on Guam, Guide to the Coastal Resources of Guam, 3,* Marine Laboratory Contribution #225. Mangilao, Guam: University of Guam Press.

Anell, B. (1955). Contribution to the history of fishing in the South Seas. *Studia Ethnographica Upsaliensia, 9.* Uppsala, Sweden.

Figure 1. Philip Nery and his daughter Shirley of Ulithi Atoll, whose family housed and assisted Dr. Rebecca Stephenson and Dr. Hiro Kurashina during their work with the 1983 water research studies of the University of Guam Water and Environmental Research Institute (WERI). This earlier research and the support provided by the Ulithi community were foundational to the development of the 1992 Ulithi Field School in Cultural Anthropology. (Kurashina, 1983.)

Aoyagi, M. (Ed.). (October 23, 1977). L.A. to Ulithi by bottle. Agana, Guam: *Pacific Daily News*. Los Angeles: *L.A. Times*, p. 5.

Aoyagi, M. (Ed.). (1982). *Islanders and their outside world: A report of the cultural anthropological research in the Caroline Islands of Micronesia in 1980-81* (pp. 77 – 104). Tokyo: St. Paul's (Rikkyo) University.

Arago, J. (1823). *Narrative of a voyage round the world in the Uranie and Physicienne Corvettes commanded by Captain Freycinet, during 1817, 1818, 1819, 1820. 2 Vols.* London: Truettel and Wurtz.

Archibald, J. J. (October 2, 1992). Funding cut angers WPAD. *Pacific Daily News*, p. 3.

Armstrong, J. (March, 1991). Disability in Pacific societies: Contributions from anthropology. Paper presented at the meeting of the Association for Social Anthropology in Oceania, Victoria, British Columbia, Canada.

Ashby, G. (Ed.) & Students of the Community College of Micronesia. (1983; 1989, revised edition). *Some things of value: Micronesian customs as seen by Micronesians* (pp. 56 – 57; 90 – 92). Pohnpei, FSM: Authors.

Austin, L. (September 30, 1992). Woman's death casts doubts on mental treatment policies. *Pacific Daily News*, pp. 1, 4.

Figure 2. Ulithi home compound with WWII bomb artifact. *(Kurashina, 1983.)*

Barratt, G. (1988). Carolinean contacts with the islands of the Marianas: The European record. *Micronesian Archaeological Survey, Saipan, report series (25)*. tDAR (the Digital Archaeological Record). Tempe, Arizona: Center for Digital Antiquity, Arizona State University.

Bell, D., Specht, J., and Ham, D. (1986). Beyond the Reef: Compound Fishhooks in the Solomon Islands. In A. Anderson (Ed.), *Traditional fishing in the Pacific: Ethnographical and archaeological papers, 15th Pacific Science Congress*. Pacific anthropological records #37. Department of Anthropology, Bernice P. Bishop Museum, Honolulu.

Bellwood, P. S. (1978). *Man's conquest of the Pacific: Prehistory of Southeast Asia and Oceania*. Auckland: William Collins Ltd.

Berg, M. (1984). Chronological list of books and articles on German Micronesia in the HRAF translations, *Micronesia Area Research Center working papers, 43,* 7 and 15. Mangilao, Guam: Micronesian Area Research Center, University of Guam.

Boykin, J. C. (1963). The Voyages of the Ulithians, *Micronesian Reporter, 11*(2), 18 – 20.

Carson, M. T. (2013). Austronesian migrations and developments in Micronesia, *Journal of Austronesian Studies, 4*(1), 25 – 50.

Chapman, M. D. (1987). Women's Fishing in Oceania, *Human Ecology, 15*(3).

Christian, F.W. (1899). *The Caroline Islands: Travel in the sea of little lands.* London: Methuen and Company.

Craib, J. L. (1978). *Yap District archaeological survey: Ulithi Atoll, progress report 2.* Agana, Guam: Pacific Studies Institute.

Craib. J. L. (1980). *Archaeological survey of Ulithi Atoll, Western Caroline Island, Monograph 1.* Agana, Guam: Pacific Studies Institute.

Craib, J. L. (1981). Settlement on Ulithi Atoll, Western Caroline Islands, *Asian Perspectives. XXIV*(1), 47 – 56.

Craib, J. L., with Figirliyong, J. & Price, S. T. (1980). *Archaeological Survey of Ulithi Atoll, Western Caroline Islands.* Presented to Historic Preservation Program, Micronesian Archaeological Survey, Trust Territory of the Pacific Islands. Meeting of the Pacific Studies Institute, Agana, Guam.

Craib, J. L. (1983). Micronesian prehistory: An archeological overview, *Science, 219*, 922 – 927.

Crossroads. (November 21, 1969). NAS Hu-16D Visits Ulithi, p 3.

Crossroads. (June 23, 1972). Ulithi, the bustling paradise, p 8.

Custodio, Z. (1992, February 5). Lytigo-Bodig group offers services. *Pacific Daily News*, p. 17.

Dames, V., Hasugulayag, J. G., Natividad, L., & Schwab, G. (2013). Social work for a sustainable Micronesian region.

Figure 3. A Ulithian teenager helps prepare a meal cooking over a fire in the family compound. *(Kurashina, 1983.)*

In S. Furuto (Ed.), *Social welfare in East Asia and the Pacific* (pp. 176 – 203). New York: Columbia University Press.

Damm, H. (1938). Zentralkarolinen: Ifaluk, Aurepik, Faraulip, Sorol, Mogmog. Based on the notes of Paul Hambruch and Ernst Sarfert. In G. Thilenius, (Ed.), *Ergebnisse der Südsee-Expedition, 1908 – 1910. II. Ethnographie, B. Mikronesien, Band 10, Halband 2*, 1 – 379. Hamburg: Friederichsen, De Gruyter and Co.

Descamps, P. (1923). Lerole social de la Pirogue, *L'Anthropologie, 33*, 127 – 145.

Descantes, C. (2004). The martrydom of Father Juan Cantova on Ulithi Atoll: The hegemonic struggle between Spanish colonialism and a Micronesian island polity. *Missionalia, 32*(3), 394 – 418. (available www.micsem.org).

Descantes, C. (2005). Integrating archaeology and prehistory: The development of exchange between Yap and Ulithi, Western Caroline Islands. BAR International Series 1344. Oxford: British Archaeological Reports.

Diaz, H. (July 15, 1973). Learning to live... and to live without. *Pacific Daily News,* p. 32.

Divine, D. (1950). *The King of Fassarai.* New York: Macmillan.

Douglas, N. & Douglas, N. (1989). *Pacific Islands Yearbook: l6th Edition,* p 82. Auckland: Angus and Robertson Publishers.

Driver, M. G. (1989). *The account of Fray Juan Pobre's residence in the Marianas 1606.* Mangilao, Guam: Micronesian Area Research Center, University of Guam.

Driver, M. G. (Translator). (1992). *History of the Marianas, Caroline and Palau Islands, by Luis de Ibanez y Garcia, Micronesian Area Research Center Educational Series No. 12.* Mangilao, Guam: University of Guam.

Driver, M. G. (Ed.) & Mallada, V. F. (Translator). (1990). *The Guam diary of naturalist Antonio De Pineda Y Ramirez, February 1792.* Mangilao, Guam: Micronesian Area Research Center, University of Guam.

Elbert, S. (1947). Ulithi-English, English-Ulithi word lists. Pearl Harbor/Hawaii: US Naval Military Government.

Emory, K. P., Bonk, W. J., and Sinoto, Y. H. (1968). Hawaiian archaeology: Fishhooks. In *Bernice P. Bishop Museum special publication #47*. Honolulu, HI: Bishop Museum Press.

Evans, M. J. (1988). *Political development in Micronesia: A view from the Island of Pohnpei* (Ph.D. dissertation). University of Florida, Gainsville, FL.

Figirliyong, J. (1976). *The contemporary political system of Ulithi Atoll* (M.A. thesis in anthropology). California State University, Fullerton. (See *micsem.org*)

Fitzgerald, M. H. (March, 1991). Culture and disability in the Pacific: Some questions. Paper presented at the meeting of the Association for Social Anthropology in Oceania, Victoria, British Columbia, Canada.

Fitzpatrick, S. M. (2008). Maritime interregional interaction in Micronesia: Deciphering multi-group contacts and exchange systems through time, *Journal of Anthropological Archaeology, 27,* 131 – 147.

Figure 4. A pre-adolescent Ulithian girl prepares a dried pandanus leaf for weaving. (Kurashina, 1983.)

Force, R., & Force, M. (1971). *The Fuller collection of Pacific artifacts* (p. 259). New York: Praeger Publishers.

Furness, W. H. (1910). *The island of stone money: Uap of the Carolines.* Philadelphia: J. B. Lippincott Co. (Republished by Cornell University Library, September 22, 2009, Ithaca, New York)

Good News Press. (1974). *Welcome to Yap District: Island of stone money and lavalavas.* Colonia, Yap.

Gale, R. W. (1978). *The Americanization of Micronesia: A study of the consolidation of U.S. rule in the Pacific.* Washington DC: University Press of America, Inc.

Gailey, H. (1988). *The liberation of Guam, 21 July – 10 August* (pp. 191). California: Presidio Press.

Gardner, D. R. (December 2, 1979). The problem with turtles. *Pacific Daily News: Islander,* p. 3.

Harui-Walsh, E. J. (1985). *Status and roles of island women in the context of cultural change in Ulithi* (Master of Arts Thesis in Behavioral Science). Mangilao, Guam: University of Guam.

Hasugulayag, J. G. (2014). Ulithi, Yap: Navigating the seas of cultural tradition and change. In H. F. Ofahengawe Vakalahi, & M. T. Godinet (Eds.), *Transnational Pacific Islander Americans and social work, dancing to the beat of a different drum* (pp. 91 – 106). Washington, D.C.: National Association of Social Workers Press.

Hauhart, R. C. & Grahe, J. E. (2015). *Designing and teaching undergraduate capstone courses.* San Francisco: Jossey Bass.

Hazell, L. D. (1972). *Folklore and culture change: Andaman, Trobriand, Ulithi and Hopi.* Paper presented at annual meeting of American Folklore Society, California State University, Hayward.

Hezel, F. X., S.J. (1968). Catholic missions in the Carolines and Marshall Islands: A survey of historical materials. *Journal of Pacific History, 5,* 213 – 227.

Hezel, Francis X., S.J. & Del Valle, M. T. (1972). Early European contact with the Western Carolines: 1525 – 1750. *The Journal of Pacific History, 7*(1), 26 – 44.

Hezel, F. X., S.J. (1979). *Foreign ships in Micronesia: A compendium of ship contacts with the Caroline and Marshall Islands, 1521 – 1885.* Saipan, Mariana Islands: Trust Territory Historic Preservation Office and the US Heritage Conservation and Recreation Service.

Hezel, F. X., S.J. (1983). *The first taint of civilization: A history of the Caroline and Marshall Islands in pre-colonial days, 1521 – 1885.* Honolulu: University of Hawaii Press.

Hezel, F. X., S.J. (1991). *The Catholic Church in Micronesia: Historical essays on the Catholic Church in the Caroline-Marshall Islands.* Chicago: Loyola University Press.

Hezel, F. X., S.J. (2001). *The new shape of old island cultures: A half-century of social change in Micronesia.* Honolulu: University of Hawaii Press.

Hezel, F. X., S.J. (2003; 1995). *Strangers in their own land: A century of colonial rule in the Caroline and Marshall Islands.* Honolulu: University of Hawaii Press.

Hezel, F. X., S.J. (2013). *Making sense of Micronesia: The logic of Pacific Island Culture.* Honolulu: University of Hawaii Press.

Howells, W. (1973). *The Pacific Islands.* New York: Charles Scribner's Sons.

Hughes, D. T. & Lingenfelter, S. G. (1974). *Political development in Micronesia.* Columbus, Ohio: Ohio State University Press.

Humphries, J. (July 26, 1964). Loran Station, Ulithi silent among Pacific's many island outposts. *Territorial Sun,* p. 7.

Intoh, M. (1986). Pigs in Micronesia: Introduction or re-introduction by the Europeans? *Man and culture in Oceania, 2,* l0.

Irwin, G. (1992). *The prehistoric exploration and colonisation of the Pacific: Carbon dating, first settlement dates AD 300 – AD 750.* Boston: Cambridge University Press.

Ishikawa, E. (Ed.). (1985). *The 1983 – 1984 cultural anthropology expedition to Micronesia: An interim report.* Tokyo: Committee for Micronesian Research, Tokyo Metropolitan University.

Jarrow, J. E. & Rengiil, Y. (March, 1991). *The language of disability in Micronesia.* Paper presented at the meeting of the Association of Social Anthropology in Oceania, Victoria, British Columbia, Canada.

Johannes, R.E. (1981). *Words of the lagoon: Fishing and marine lore in the Palau District of Micronesia.* Berkeley, CA: University of California Press.

Joseph, A. and Murray, V. F. (1951). *Chamorros and Carolinians of Saipan: Personality studies.* Cambridge: Harvard University Press.

Kirch, P. V. (1997). *The Lapita peoples: Ancestors of the Oceanic world.* Oxford: Blackwell.

Kirch, P.V. (2010). Peopling of the Pacific: A holistic anthropological perspective. *Annual Review of Anthropology, 39,* 131 – 148.

Kluge, P.F. (1991). *The edge of paradise: America in Micronesia.* New York: Random House.

Komatsu, K. (1982). Kinship terminology and respect-avoidance behavior. In M. Aoyagi, (Ed), *Islanders and their outside world: A report of cultural anthropological research in the Caroline Islands of Micronesia in 1980-1981* (pp. 129 – 152). Tokyo: St. Paul's (Rikkyo) University.

Kubary, J. S. (1892). *Ethnographische Beitrage zur Kenntis des Karolinen Archipels.* Leiden: T.W.M. Trap.

Kurashina, H. (1988). *Hotel Nikko Guam archaeological testing in the general vicinity of locality Y at Gognga-Gun Beach, Tumon Bay, Guam.* Mangilao, Guam: Micronesian Area Research Center, University of Guam.

Laimoh, M. (2002). *English-Ulithian Dictionary 1*. Colonia, Yap State, FSM: Yap State Education Enterprising Department.

Lessa, W. A. (1950a). Ulithi and the outer native world. *American Anthropologist, 52*, 27 – 52.

Lessa, W. A. (1950b). The place of Ulithi in the Yap empire. *Human Organization, 9*(1), 16 – 18.

Lessa, W. A. (1950c). The ethnography of Ulithi Atoll. *CIMA Report, no. 28.* Washington, D.C.: Pacific Science Board.

Lessa, W. A. & Lay, T. (1953). The somatology of Ulithi Atoll. *American Journal of Physical Anthropology, 11*, 405 – 412.

Lessa, W. A. & Spielman, M. (1954). Ulithian personality as seen through ethnological materials and thematic test analysis. *University of California publications in culture and society, 2*(5).

Lessa, W. A. (1955). Depopulation on Ulithi. *Human Biology, 27*, 161 – 183.

Lessa, W. A. (1956). Myth and blackmail in the Western Carolines. *Journal of the Polynesian Society, 65*, 66 – 74.

Lessa, W. A. (1959). Divining from knots in the Carolines. *Journal of the Polynesian Society, 68*, 188 – 204.

Lessa, W. A. (1961). Tales from Ulithi Atoll: A comparative study of Oceanic folklore. *Folklore Studies, 13*. Berkeley: University of California Press.

Lessa, W. A. (1962a) The decreasing power of myth on Ulithi. *Journal of American Folklore, 75*, 153 – 159.

Lessa, W. A. (1962b). An evaluation of early descriptions of Caroline culture. *Ethnohistory, 9*, 313 – 403.

Lessa, W. A. (1964). The social effects of Typhoon Ophelia (1960) on Ulithi. *Micronesica, 1*, 1 – 47.

Lessa, W. A. (1966a). *Ulithi: A Micronesian design for living.* New York: Holt, Rinehart and Winston. (Reprinted in 1986. Prospect Heights, Illinois: Waveland Press, Inc.)

Lessa, W. A. (1966b). Discoverer of the sun: Mythology as a reflection of culture. *Journal of American folklore: Special Issue, the Anthropologist Looks at Myth, 79*(311), 3 – 51.

Lessa, W. A. (1968). The social effects of Typhoon Ophelia. In A. P. Vayda (Ed.), *People and cultures of the Pacific* (pp. 330 – 382). New York: Natural History Press.

Lessa, W. A. (1974). Drake in the Marianas? *Micronesica, 10*, 10.

Lessa, W. A. (1975a). The Portuguese discovery of the Isle of Sequeira. *Micronesica, 11*(1), 35 – 70.

Lessa, W. A. (1975b). *Drake's Island of Thieves.* [Betel nut chewing: 1, 7-8, 10, 17, 74, 78, 79, 88, 91, 97, 103, 111, 236, 250, 264; canoes: 85 – 86, 264; clothing: 111; darts: 88, 90, 99; ear lobes lengthened: 92, 93; fingernails, long: 93; population density: 81; population figures: 78-79; sling: 97; thieving tactics: 103-104]. Honolulu: University of Hawaii Press.

Figure 5. Mariano John Laimoh, Editor of the *English-Ulithian Dictionary 1.* Born in Asor and often working in Falalop, Ulithi Atoll, Mariano is a Ulithian linguist. He has also authored children's books for the Yap State Education Enterprising Department that are used in Ulithi, Fais, Sorol, and Ngulu. *(RDK Herman, Pacific Worlds: Retrieved 11/21/17.)*

Lessa, W. A. (1976). The apotheosis of Marespa?. In A. L. Kaepplér and H. Arlo Nimmo (Eds.), *Directions in Pacific traditional literature, essays in honor of Katharine Luomala.* Honolulu: Bishop Museum Press.

Figure 6. Ulithi men and adolescent boys rest and converse in a canoe house on Ulithi Atoll. *(Kurashina, 1983.)*

Lessa, W. A. (1977). Traditional uses of the vascular plants of Ulithi Atoll, with comparative notes. *Micronesica, 13,* 129 – 190.

Lessa, W. A. & Velez, Carols G. (1978a). *Bwang,* a martial art of the Caroline Islands. *Micronesica, 14*(2), 139 – 176.

Lessa, W. A. (1978b). The Mapia Islands and their affinities. In Niel Gunson (Ed.), *Changing Pacific, essays in honour of H.E. Maude.* Melbourne: Oxford University Press.

Lessa, W. A. (1980). More tales from Ulithi Atoll: A content analysis. *Folklore and Mythology Studies, 32.*

Lessa, W. A. (1986). *Ulithi: A Micronesian design for living, revised edition.* Long Grove, Ill: Waveland Press, Inc.

Lessa, W. A. & Meyers, G. C. (1962c). Population dynamics of an Atoll community. *Population Studies, 15,* 244 – 257.

Lessa, W. A. & Vogt, E. Z. (Eds.). (1965). *Reader in comparative religion: An anthropological approach, second edition.* New York: Harper and Row.

Levin, M. J. & Ahlburg, D. A. (1993). Pacific Islanders in the United States Census Data. A world perspective on Pacific Islander migration: Australia, New Zealand, and the USA. In Grant McCall & John Connell (Eds.), *Pacific Studies, Monograph, 6.* Australia: University of New South Wales Printing Section.

Lewis, D. (1972). *We, the navigators.* Honolulu: University of Hawaii Press.

Li, K-C. (1983). *Report of archaeological investigations in the O-Luan-Pi Park at southern tip of Taiwan.* Taipei, Taiwan: National Taiwan University.

Linn, G. (April 9, 197?). Guam pace a change for Ulithi students. *Pacific Daily News,* p. 4.

Lindemann, K. (1988). Operations against Palau by Carrier Task Force, pp. 58, 30, and 31; March 1944 and the shipwreck of World War II, pp V. 121, 152, 157, 171, 283. Belleville, Michigan: Pacific Press Publication Associates.

Lindemann, K. (2005). *Hailstorm over Truk Lagoon: Operations against Truk by Carrier Task Force 58, 17 and 18 February 1944, and the shipwrecks of World War II.* Oregon, USA: Resource Publications.

Low, S. (2014). *Hawaiki rising: Hokule'a, Nainoa Thompson, and the Hawaiian renaissance.* Hawaii: Island Heritage.

Lutz, C. (1988). *Unnatural emotions: Everyday sentiments on a Micronesian atoll and their challenge to western theory.* Chicago: University of Chicago Press.

Lutz, C. & Collins, J. L. (1993). *Reading National Geographic.* Chicago: University of Chicago Press.

Micronesian Reporter. (Second quarter, 1969). Ulithi: Halfway house, pp.10 – 11.

Marshall, M. & Nason, J. D. (Ed.). (1975). *Micronesia 1944 – 1974: A bibliography of anthropological and related source materials.* New Haven: Human Relations Area Files.

Marshall, M. (March, 1991). *Congenital and acquired disabilities in a Micronesian atoll population: Case studies from Namoluk Atoll, FSM.* Paper presented at the meeting of the Association of Social Anthropology in Oceania, Victoria, British Columbia, Canada.

Maskarinec, G. G., Yalmadau, K., Maluchmai, M. R., Tun, P., Yinnifel, C., & Hancock, W. T. (2017). Palliative care and traditional practices of death and dying in Wa'ab (Yap Proper) and in the Outer Islands of Yap. *Hawaii Medical Journal, Nov 11,* Supplement 2, 27 – 30.[1]

Mason, L. (1964). Micronesian Cultures. *Encyclopedia of Word Art, 9,* 915 – 930.

Mason, L. (1968). Suprafamilial authority and economic process in Micronesian atolls. In A. P. Vayda, *Peoples and cultures of the Pacific* (pp. 299 – 329). Garden City, New York: Natural History Press.

Masse, W. B. (1986). A millennium of fishing in the Palau Islands, Micronesia. In A. Anderson (Ed.), *Traditional fishing in the Pacific: Ethnographical and archaeological papers,* 15th Pacific Science Congress. Honolulu, HI: Department of Anthropology, Bernice P. Bishop Museum, Pacific anthropological records #37.

Figure 7. Ulithi boys collect green coconuts and remove the outer husk, in preparation for drinking or grating. *(Kurashina, 1983.)*

Matsumura, A. (1918). Observing the people of Mogmog Island (Ulithi Atoll) at Yokohama (Yokohama ni Mogmog-to Dojin O Miru). *Zinruigaku Zasshi, 33*(4), 111 – 112.

Matthews, L. B. (1982). Turtles and tradition. *Glimpses of Micronesia and the Western Pacific, 22*(2).

Meller, N. (1969). *The Congress of Micronesia: Development of the legislative process in the Trust Territory of the Pacific Islands.* Honolulu: University of Hawaii Press.

Miles, R. (1983). Paul Jacoulet: Portraits of paradise. *Glimpses of Micronesia, 23*(3), 35.

Morrison, S. E. (1963). *The two-ocean war: A short history of the US Navy in the second world war.* Boston: Little, Brown & Company.

Mulford, J. H. (1980). *Lava lavas of the Western Caroline Islands.* (M.A. Thesis in Anthropology), California State University, Northridge.

Mulford, J. H. (1994). Review of exhibition publication: *Traditional Arts of Pacific Island Women.* In J. M. Davidson & D. Minchall (Eds.), *Pacific studies, 17*(3 – 4), 187.

Murdock, J.P. (1948). Anthropology in Micronesia. *Transactions of the New York Academy of Sciences, 11*(1-II), 9 – 16.

---

[1] Co-author Maryann Tangidey Rulmal Maluchmai of Ulithi, is a daughter of John Rulmal Sr. and wife Terry. Maryann is the wife of FSM's First Secretary Maluchmai, Dominic Maluchmai; and mother of son Jalen Seralmal Maluchmai. She has made important contributions to public health research in the Outer Islands of Yap. This article is available for download from: HMJ_Nov11_Suppl2.pdf. Authors discuss the significant activities throughout Yap State when a death occurs. They discuss how death can inspire family unity and trigger rituals and exchanges in the entire community.

Murdock, J. P. (1948). *Social structure.* New York: Free Press.

Nason, J. D. (1975). The effects of social change on marine technology in a Pacific atoll community. In R. W. Caasteel and G. I. Quimby (Eds.), *Maritime adaptations of the Pacific.* The Hague, Paris: Mouton Publishers.

Oliver, D. L. (1989). *The Pacific Islands.* Honolulu: University of Hawaii Press.

Pacific Daily News. (December 3,1960). TT sends aid to Ulithi-Atoll hit by Ophelia, p. 15.

Pacific Daily News. (June 2, 1971). Graduation … island style, p. 17.

Pacific Daily News. (October 21, 1972). Mission Sunday: Devotions, pp. 20 – 21.

Pacific Daily News. (July 27, 1992a). Guam enforces disability act. *Pacific Daily News*, Guam, p. 4.

Pacific Daily News. (October 7, 1992b). Bordallo requests funds for disabled. *Pacific Daily News*, p. 6.

Pacific Daily News. (October 22, 1992c). Public transit update. *Pacific Daily News*, p. 3.

Parkinson, B. (1904). Tatowierung der "Ogemoinknsulanen." (The tattooing of the Mogmog Islanders, in Ulithi Atoll). Translated by *Human Resources Area Files (HRFA, #1187)*, *Globus, 86(15 – 17).*

Peattie, M. (1988). *Nan'yo: The rise and fall of the Japanese in Micronesia, 1885 – 1945.* Honolulu: University of Hawaii Press.

Figure 8. Two Ulithi women engaged in the preparation of threads on the *maliel* spool apparatus (left) for weaving lava lava, on a *thur* (loom, top right) on which a lava lava weaving project is already underway. The woman on the right is likely mentoring the young woman on the left on how to weave *(faesiu). (Kurashina, 1983.)

Peter, J. (March, 1991). Humor and joking relationships: Cultural rehabilitation and disabilities. Paper presented at the meeting of the Association of Social Anthropology in Oceania, Victoria, British Columbia, Canada.

Petersen, G. (2006). Micronesia's breadfruit revolution and the evolution of a culture area. *Archaeology in Oceania, 41*, 82 – 92.

Petersen, G. (2009). *Traditional Micronesian societies: Adaptation, integration, and political organization.* Honolulu: University of Hawaii Press.

Poignant, R. (1967). *Oceanic mythology.* New York: Hamlyn Publishing Group Limited.

Pollock, N. J. (1975). The risks of dietary change: A Pacific atoll example. In R. W. Caasteel and G. I. Quimby (Eds.), *Maritime adaptations of the Pacific.* The Hague, Paris: Mouton Publishers.

Rainbird, P. (1994). Prehistory in the north-west tropical Pacific: The Caroline, Mariana, and Marshall Islands. *Journal of World Prehistory, 8,* 293 – 349.

Rainbird, P. (2004). *The archaeology of Micronesia.* Cambridge: Cambridge University Press.

Rensel, J. & Howard, A. (March, 1991). The place of disabled persons in Rotuman society. Paper presented at the meeting of the Association of Social Anthropology in Oceania, Victoria, British Columbia, Canada.

Figure 9. Teenage girls on Ulithi Atoll prepare leis of orange *hulu* flowers *(Cordia subcordata)* for a celebration. *(Photography, Kurashina, 1983; flower identification, Manner, 2017.)*

Ronck, R. (October 10, 1973a). Ulithi: A story of chance, derring-do. *Pacific Daily News,* pp. 10, 14.

Ronck, R. (October 11, 1973b) Ulithi: Rusty tin midst diamonds. *Pacific Daily News,* p. 14.

Runquist, P. (October 28, 1992). Visitors Bureau hires beach trash collector, *Pacific Daily News,* p. 5.

Sablan, J. (April 7, 2014). Islands mobilize, help storm victims. *Pacific Daily News,* p. 2.

Sablan, J. (April 14, 2015). Storm relief efforts ongoing. *Pacific Daily News,* p. 2.

Sams, (Fr.). (February 29, 1964). Maiden of Ulithi (cover). *Saturday Evening Post.*

Sams, (Fr.). (October 21, 1972). So near, and yet so far … Ulithi (photo essay). *Pacific Daily News,* p. 72.

Santos, M. (January 29, 1992a). American Disabilities Act opens doors. *Pacific Daily News,* p. 3.

Santos, M. (January 29, 1992b). Graduate shows hearing impaired what can be done. *Pacific Daily News,* p. 3.

Santos, M. (September 5, 1992c). The homebound are not forgotten. *Pacific Daily News,* p. 5.

Santos, M. (October 15, 1992d). Down's syndrome families battle myths. *Pacific Daily News,* p. 3.

Senfft, Arno. (1901). Uber einen besuch des Ulithi-Atolls Deutsches Kolonialblatt (translated by *Human Resources Area Files, HRAF). Globus, 88,* pp. 12, 824 – 825.

Severance, Craig J. (1986). Traditional fishing strategies on Losap Atoll: Ethnographic reconstruction and the problems of innovation and adaptation. In A. Anderson (Ed.), *Traditional fishing in the Pacific: Ethnographical and archaeological Papers, 15th Pacific Science Congress, Pacific anthropological records #37.* Honolulu, HI: Department of Anthropology, Bernice P. Bishop Museum.

Sharp, A. (1957). *Ancient voyagers in the Pacific.* Harmondsworth.

Sharp, A. (1960). *The discovery of the Pacific Islands.* Oxford: Clarendon.

Shinberg, D. (Ed.). (1971). *The trading voyages of Andrew Cheyne, 1984 – 1844.* Honolulu: University of Hawaii Press.

Sinoto, Y. (Ed.). (1984). Caroline Islands archaeology: Investigations on Fefan, Faraulep, Woleai and Lamotrek. *Pacific Anthropological Records, 35.* Honolulu: Bernice P. Bishop Museum.

Sinoto, Y. H. (1991). Revised system for the classification and coding of Hawaiian fishhooks. *Bishop Museum Occasional Paper, 31,* 85 – 105.

Sinoto, Y. with Aramata, H. (2016). *Curve of the hook: Yoshiko Sinoto: An archaeologist in Polynesia.* Honolulu, HI: University of Hawai'i Press.

Sledge, E.B. (1979). With the old breed at Peleliu and Okinawa (pp. 178 – 180). New York: Presidio Press.

Sohn, H. & Binder, B. W. (1973). *A Ulithian Grammar.* Canberra: Department of Linguistics, Research School of Pacific Studies, Australian National University.

Solheim, W. G., III. (Ed.). (1984). *Asian perspectives: A journal of archaeology and prehistory of Asia and Pacific.*

Spencer, M. L., Burdge, M., DeLeon, J., Clayton, J., Quitugua, J., Guerrero, A., San Nicolas, H., & Macapinlac, J. (2012). Facilitating program improvement for students with significant cognitive disabilities: Baseline documentation of instructional programs in six Pacific entities. *Micronesian Educator, 16,* 5 – 19.

Figure 10. Young girl playing with her dog in her family compound. *(Kurashina, 1983.)*

Spiers, J. (July 26, 1992). Opening doors for the disabled AND finding ways to help keep growing, Guam *Pacific Daily News*, p. 28.

Spindler, L. & Spindler, G. D. (1978). *Cultures around the world: Fives cases.* Stamford, Connecticut: International Thomson Publishing. (Includes Ulithi.)

Spoehr, A. (1957). Marianas prehistory: Archaeological survey and excavation on Saipan, Tinian, and Rota. *Fieldana: Anthropology, 48.* Chicago.

Spoehr, A. & Sinoto, Y. H. (Eds). (1984). Micronesian prehistory. *Asian Perspectives, 24*(1), 47 – 55. Honolulu, HI: University of Hawaii Press.

Steele, J. C. & Guzman, T. (1987). Observations about Amytrophic Lateral Sclerosis and the Parkinsonism-Dementia Complex of Guam with regard to epidemiology and etiology. *Canadian Journal of Neurological Sciences, 14*(3), 358 – 362.

Stephenson, R. A. (1983). A study of women and water in Micronesia, *Response, 15*(10), 10 – 13, 37. Reprinted: Stephenson, R. (1987). *Land, water, and people: Selected studies in fresh water resources.* Mangilao, Guam: Water and Energy Research Institute and Micronesian Area Research Center, University of Guam.

Stephenson, R. A. (1984). *A comparison of freshwater use customs on Ulithi Atoll with those of selected other Micronesian atolls, Technical Report No.51* (U.S.G.S. Project No. G-837-03). Mangilao, Guam: Water and Energy Research Institute, University of Guam.

Stephenson, R. A. & Chargualaf, V. M. (1989). *Lytico-Bodig on Guam: An anthropological inquiry.* Working paper. 30 pages. Privately circulated.

Sudo, K. (1979). Canoe and kin in Satawalese society, Central Caroline Islands. *Bulletin of the National Museum of Ethnology, 4*(2), 251-284.

Sudo, K. (1984a). Systems of land tenure and resource management on Satawal Island, Micronesia. *Bulletin of the National Museum of Ethnology, 9*(2), 197–348 (in Japanese).

Sudo, K. (1984b). Social organization and types of sea tenure in Micronesia, maritime institutions in the western Pacific. In K. Ruddle and T. Akimichi (Eds.), *Senri ethnological studies, 17,* pp. 203 – 230. Osaka, Japan: National Museum of Ethnology.

Sudo, K. (1984c). Avoidance behavior and kin category in Satawalese society, man and culture in Oceania. *Japanese Society for Oceanic Studies, 1,* 1 – 26.

Sun, W-H. (1969). Changpinian: A newly discovered pre-ceramic culture from the agglomerate caves on the east coast of Taiwan. *Ethnology of China, 9,* 1 – 27. Taipei.

Takayama, J. (1982). A brief report on archaeological investigations of the southern part of Yap Island and nearby Ngulu Atoll. In Aoyagi, M. and Committee for Micronesian Research (Eds.), *Islanders and their outside world: A report of the Cultural Anthropological Research in the Caroline Islands of Micronesia in 1980 – 1981.* Tokyo: St Paul's, Rikkyo University, Japan.

Takayama, J., & Egami, T. (1971). Archaeology on Rota in the Marianas Islands. Preliminary report on the first excavation of the Latte site (M-1). *Report of Pacific Archaeological Survey, 1.* Hiratsuka: Tokai University.

Figure 11. Example of a fresh water catchment on Ulithi, reported by Stephenson, 1984. *(Kurashina, 1983)*

Territorial Sun. (March 29, 1964). TT to return Ulithian canoe: Promotes happy ending for a very unusual story, *8,* p 11.

Tetens, A. (1958). *Among the savages of the South Seas: Memoirs of Micronesia, 1862 – 1868* (Florence Mann Spoehr, translator), (pp. 62, 64 – 66, 71, 80, 92 – 94, 95). Palo Alto: Stanford University Press.

Thompson, L. M. (1945). *The native culture of the Marianas Islands, Bulletin 185.* Honolulu: Bishop Museum.

Thompson, L. (1947). *Guam and its people, revised.* Princeton, NJ: Princeton University Press.

Thone, D. (1983). Tattoo origins, *Glimpses of Micronesia. 23*(3), 38 – 39.

Topping, D. K., Ogo, P. K., & Duncga, B. C. (1975). *Chamorro-English dictionary.* Honolulu: University Press of Hawaii.

Trumbull, R. (1976). *Tin roofs and palm trees: A report on the new South Seas.* Canberra: Australia National University Press.

Tsu, Y-C. (1982). *Yami fishing practices: Migratory fish.* Taipei: Southern Material Center, Inc.

Turbott, I. G. (1950). Fishing for flying fish in the Gilbert and Ellice Islands. *Journal of the Polynesian Society, 59* (4), 349 – 367.

U Matuna Si Yu'us, Archdiocese of Agana, Guam. (October 22, 1972). *The missions near Guam,* pp. 8 – 9.

Useem, J. (1947). Applied Anthropology in Micronesia. *Applied Anthropology, 6*(4).

Ushijima, I. (1982). The control of reefs and lagoons: Some aspects of the political structure of Ulithi Atoll. In Aoyagi, M. (Ed.), *Islanders and their outside world: A report of the Cultural Anthropological Research in the Caroline Islands of Micronesia Committee for Micronesian Research in 1980 – 1981*, pp. 35 – 76. Tokyo: St. Paul's, Rikkyo, University, Japan.

Ushijima, I. (1985). The land holding group on Mogmog Islands, Ulithi Atoll: Matrilineage in a virilocal society. In Eiichi Ishikawa, (Ed.), *The 1983 – 1984 cultural anthropological expedition to Micronesia: An interim report*, pp 5 – 23. Tokyo: Tokyo Metropolitan University.

Ushijima, I. (1987). A reinterpretation of the *Sawai* exchange system of the Caroline Islands. In Eikichi Ishikawa (Ed.), *Cultural adaptation to atolls in Micronesia and west Polynesia: A report of the Cultural Anthropological Research in the Caroline, Marshall, and Ellice Islands Committee for Micronesian Research in 1985*. Tokyo: Metropolitan University.

Van Sinderem, A. (1959). *The other half of the earth (II)*. New York: Privately printed, p. 258.

Vollbrecht, J. (1946). The Ulithian encyclopedia. In Donald Cusenbery Slc, USNR (Ed.), *WVTY, the Armed Forces Radio Station*. Cambridge, MA: Harvard College Library.

Walsh, J. A. (1979, March/April). Language and change in Ulithi. *The New Pacific.*

Walsh, J. A. (1985). *An ethnographic study of the role of the informal environment in the acquisition of Yapese by Ulithians with implications for language teaching*. Unpublished manuscript.

Walsh, J. A. (1987). A comparison of Ulithian and Yapese. *Man and Culture in Oceania, 3*, 73 – 94.

Walsh, J. A. (Ed.) (2013). *Ulithi: A Micronesian anthology*. USA: Bookmasters, Inc.

Walsh, J. A. & Harui-Walsh, E. (1979). Legends of Ulithi. *Pacific Daily News: Islander, December 2,* pp. 6 – 9.

Walsh, J. A. & Harui-Walsh, E. (2013). Loan words in Ulithian. In John A. Walsh (Ed). *Ulithi: A Micronesian anthology*. Guam: Bookmasters, Inc.

Watanabe, M. (1973). *Fishing in the Jomon Period* (in Japanese). Tokyo: Yuzankaku.

Wees, M. P. (1950). *King-doctor of Ulithi: The true story of the wartime experiences of Marshall Paul Wees, M.D., as related to Francis B. Thornton*. New York: Macmillan.

Wenkam, R. (1971). *Micronesia: The breadfruit revolution*. Honolulu: East-West Center Press.

Whaley, F. (May 10, 1993). Living lab: UOG students take classroom to Ulithi. *Pacific Daily News, Vol 24* (No. 98).

Wiens, H. J. (1962). *Atoll environment and ecology*. New Haven: Yale University Press.

Wikipedia. (2016). Ulithi population for 2000. Retrieved May 6. 2016.

Figure 12. John Rulmal, Jr. ("Junior") with his classmates, waiting for his men's group to begin to dance on Graduation Day, 1992. John Jr. has been key to research arrangements and support of researchers in recent years. He worked closely with Dr. Ann Ames and Dr. Todd Ames during their 2013 economic and ecological research, which is reported in later chapters. *(Photograph by R. Stephenson, 1992.)*

PART 2: CULTURE, ECONOMICS, LEARNING, AND LIFE CHALLENGES IN ULITHI

Ulithi, Yap:
Navigating the Seas of Cultural Tradition and Change

Joliene G. Hasugulayag

The foreign captain watched as a small but swift canoe approached the ship. The canoe was filled with men from the island of Wa'ab, who came to inquire about the intent of these foreign visitors. Despite the language barrier, the two parties were able to communicate through body language and gestures. The foreign captain, it seemed, was being invited to the island to talk further with the island chiefs. As the captain boarded the canoe, he asked the islanders what the name of their island was by gesturing toward the shore. The Waabese men noticed that the foreign captain was gesturing toward the bow of the canoe where the *paluy,* or traditional navigator, sat with a canoe paddle in hand. As a result, they believed that the Captain was asking how to say, canoe paddle. They responded by saying *yap.* As a result, the island became known by foreigners as Yap instead of by its true name of Wa'ab (Yap Visitor's Bureau, 2017).

Yap is an island group located in the Pacific region of Micronesia. The many islands that make up Yap span more than 600 miles and are located southwest of Guam (Guahan), east of the Philippines, and northeast of Palau (Belau) (Yap Visitor's Bureau, 2017a). The term Yap Proper is used to distinguish the four main islands of Yap (Yap, Tomil-Gagil, Maap, and Rumung) from the Outer Islands of Yap. Although the Outer Islands of Yap are politically part of Yap, they are culturally and linguistically more similar to the Outer Islands of Chuuk (Hezel, 2001). Yap is regarded as the most traditional island group in Micronesia today (Ridgell, 1995).

According to T. Guiormog (2012), an indigenous Ulithian who was born and raised in Ulithi Atoll, in the Outer Islands of Yap, the Atoll is comprised of approximately 40 small islands. Some of these are close enough to each other to reach on foot when the tide is low. Of these islands, only four are currently inhabited: Falalop, Asor, Fedarai, and Mogmog. Indigenous Ulithian anthropologist, J. Figirliyong (2012), stated that Ulithi is also home to the clan of the Paramount Chief, who serves as the high chief over all of the Outer Islands of Yap.

The culture and lifestyle in Ulithi remain much as they were hundreds of years ago. Some changes have occurred as a result of foreign influences, but many traditional customs and practices are still observed. Although many aspects of Ulithian culture can be generally applied to much of Micronesia, cultural practices vary from island to island. To understand the culture, one must frame it within the context of the environment in which it exists. This chapter focuses on the culture and customs of Ulithi Atoll in the Outer Islands of Yap. In Ulithi, culture equates to rules that, when followed, help increase one's chances of survival in very practical ways. Although the culture includes many different values, this chapter describes three elements that serve as the foundation of Ulithian cultural practices: Relationship to the land, relationships in the family context, and relationships in the community context. In addition, the chapter describes foreign influences on Ulithian culture and provides guidance for social workers and other health professionals working with clients of Ulithian origin.

Relationship to the Land

Role of Land

In Ulithi, the importance of land – which includes the reefs and surrounding waters – and the role it plays in society cannot be emphasized enough (Hezel, 2001). Within Ulithian culture, land is viewed as a living element that, when respected, can provide for all of one's needs, including shelter, clothes, transportation, medicine, and food.

Land is one's direct link to survival; thus, it is not something that is bought or sold (Hezel, 2001). There is no single owner of a piece of land; it is shared communally by lineages. Inheritance of land rights is matrilineal; an individual can never be denied access to the land of his or her mother's clan (Hezel, 2001). People can also be granted rights to their father's land; however, these rights can be revoked if one's father feels it is warranted (J. Figirliyong, 2012). For this reason, children are often encouraged to nurture their relationships with their father's clan as a means of securing access to more land, which ultimately equates to greater access to resources and increased chances of survival.

Because land is kept within family clans, it also serves as a form of identification. By revealing the land on which one was born or raised, one is in essence identifying the clan or clans of which one is a member. The Ulithian word for relative, *chol bugatai,* literally means *person from my land,* which demonstrates the Ulithian belief that land binds the family together (J. Figirliyong, 2012). Land is such a huge part of one's identity, as well as one's survival, that a landless person can be equated to a "nonperson" (Hezel, 2001). Ulithian custom dictates that an individual can never be banished from the land of his or her mother's clan, and in this way, custom serves as a type of safeguard (J. Figirliyong, 2012).

Land can also link a clan with certain responsibilities or roles within the community. For example, certain pieces of land are associated with the chief's clan, and those who live on this land have responsibilities to the community (T. Guiormog, 2012). Another community role linked with land is policing of the island; lineages who reside on this land are tasked with enforcing the traditional laws set forth by the chiefs and elders (T. Guiormog, 2012). Other examples of community roles linked with different parcels of land are overseeing and protecting the outlying reef, distributing food to the island's people during community events, and keeping the chief informed of all that is occurring on the island (J. Figirliyong, 2012).

Subsistence Living and Sustainability

To this day, Ulithians still practice a subsistence lifestyle. They obtain the majority of their food from the land and sea. According to Ridgell (1995), "Yap

State relies more on subsistence than any other [FSM] state." Although foreign food items such as rice, canned goods, and flour are periodically delivered by ship, the people are not dependent on these items for survival.

Subsistence living is the main form of economy in Ulithi; therefore, the concept of sustainability is significant. Ulithians take care not to overuse a particular parcel of land or overfish in a particular part of the sea. They observe seasons during which certain crops are harvested and certain sea animals are caught. This tradition gives the plants and animals time to grow, mature, and reproduce, which is necessary to preserve these resources for future generations. The people's understanding and awareness that their survival depends directly on the land's survival have allowed the traditional subsistence lifestyle to continue to flourish in Ulithi. Although these traditional sustainability practices are still observed, they are sustained primarily by members of the older generations; awareness of the importance of seasonal harvesting and fishing practices is lessening in younger Ulithian generations (J. Figirliyong, 2012).

Education

From a young age, Ulithians are taught the knowledge that is necessary to survive in a subsistence economy. Girls learn how to maintain taro patches and other land crops, and boys learn the necessary skills to fish and navigate the ocean. In this sense, the land also serves as a classroom in which children learn the skills they need to survive. Although Western education now exists in Ulithi in the form of schools, traditional education is still relevant because the subsistence lifestyle dominates.

Figure 1. Joliene Hasugulayag, MSW, LSW, author of Navigating the Seas of Cultural Tradition and Change.

***Palul Wolfulu,* or Land Navigator**

Because land is such an integral part of the Ulithian culture and survival, clans keep "records" of who has rights to which land parcels. Like many Micronesian cultures, Ulithian culture is based on oral tradition. It is through this oral tradition that the *Palul Wolfulu,* or land navigator, is taught the various lineages and the land that these lineages are from (J. Figirliyong, 2012). Whenever confusion or disputes arise regarding land, the *Palul Wolfulu* is tasked with determining who is in the right. Because survival depends on access to land, this knowledge is very valuable and important in the Ulithian culture.

Relationships in the Family Context

Family Structure

Traditional Ulithian society is extremely collective in nature. Ulithians are taught from a young age to put the needs of the clan before their individual needs. The foundation of social structures is the family unit, which encompasses not just the nuclear family but also the entire extended family. Often the extended family lives on a single parcel of land, using separate small dwellings for sleeping and a shared central cookhouse (Hezel, 2001). As in many other traditional Pacific Island cultures that practice a subsistence lifestyle, food plays an important role. Whatever food is gathered or caught is shared equally among extended family members and is often prepared in the central cookhouse. This living and eating arrangement is an outward demonstration of the interconnectedness within families. By living on and surviving off the same land, Ulithians are identifying themselves as a family unit. Cooking their food in a central cookhouse and sharing it equally is both an acknowledgment that as family they are responsible for each other's survival and a demonstration of solidarity (Hezel, 2001).

One of the most important roles the extended family plays is as a safety net when challenges or problems arise. In Ulithi, child rearing is a shared responsibility among family members. Children develop close relationships with various relatives who serve as a buffer and intervene should conflict or difficulties develop. Because the family unit includes the entire extended family, a large amount of support is available to assist family members when needed. This safety net can be viewed as the traditional version of Western public assistance programs; it helps fulfill individuals' needs when they are unable to fulfill them on their own.

Figure 2. Author with family members: *Left:* Joliene Hasugulayag with husband Derwin Rolmar, daughter Nayana Harosulwol, and brother, Kyle Yolrag, 2016. *Right:* Brother Alex Carleton Lugwa, father and mother – Josede and Dana Figirliyong, with Joliene Hasugulayag, 2010.

Authority

Relationships within the family are based on respect for authority figures, cooperation, and trust. Unlike the culture of Yap Proper, Ulithian culture is primarily matrilineal; nevertheless, men are viewed as the head of the family and

Figure 3. Joliene's childhood in Ulithi Atoll, with her father Josede and mother Dana, and shown at home as a preschool child.

make most of the important decisions. In addition to gender, age and relationship also determine one's rank or level of authority within a family. Showing respect for an authority figure is important and often manifests as "classic respect avoidance" (Hezel, 2001), which includes refraining from or limiting one's speech when in the presence of an authority figure and intentionally avoiding direct eye contact. Although in more Western societies this type of body language is often misinterpreted as disrespect, in Ulithi it is a show of respect; in essence, it is an acknowledgment, through one's body language, that one is not on the same level as the authority figure (J. Figirliyong, 2012).

Brothers, Sisters, and First Cousins of the Opposite Sex

Because chances of survival are increased in a subsistence lifestyle when greater numbers of people share the work, large families are very common (J. Figirliyong, 2012). Even more important than having children, however, is having healthy children free from defects, which, from a biological viewpoint, helps ensure the survival of the human species. For this reason, romantic relationships between relatives, regardless of how distant, are highly discouraged. Because the islands in Ulithi are very small, some less than a mile long, options for mates who are not related are sometimes limited. To prevent inappropriate relationships between close relatives, a strict code of behavior between brothers and sisters and first cousins of the opposite sex (who are perceived as siblings) is still enforced today (J. Figirliyong, 2012).

Once children reach puberty (Hezel, 2001), the sexes begin to segregate. Boys usually begin sleeping in the "men's house," a communal home for young, unmarried men, and girls continue to sleep at home under the protection of the clan. Brothers and sisters are not allowed to share dishes, eat from the same plate of food, or drink from the same cup (Hezel, 2001). When a young woman menstruates, she keeps her distance from her brothers and anything they may come into contact with, such as food or personal belongings. She moves from the family

Figure 4. Joliene and Derwin's wedding day on Ulithi.

compound to the "women's house," a communal home where men are prohibited, and remains until menstruation ends. (J. Figirliyong, 2012).

Although brothers and sisters are segregated, their protective instincts toward each other do not diminish. Brothers are highly protective of their sisters and may even get into fights in their defense. Likewise, sisters are very protective of their brothers. When in each other's presence or in mixed company, they use polite language and strictly avoid any references to bodily functions or topics that are sexual, romantic, or suggestive. If a man were to use such language in the presence of an unrelated woman, even if the comments are not directed at her, the woman's brothers would likely confront, and possibly fight, the offender.

A custom that is often misinterpreted by outsiders is a woman's physical lowering of herself to pass a brother or male first cousin who is sitting down. This custom is commonly perceived from a Western perspective as degrading and sexist. It is important to avoid an ethnocentric approach, however, and to understand this practice within the context of the culture of origin. There are several reasons a woman lowers herself, and crawls if necessary, when passing a brother or cousin who is seated. The first reason is to discourage inappropriate relationships between brothers and sisters; if the brother or cousin is seated, he might have an easy view of her upper leg because she is standing above him (J. Figirliyong, 2012). A woman's leg above her knee is considered a private part that should be viewed only by her spouse, so it is taboo to expose her upper leg to brothers or cousins. By eliminating this possibility by lowering herself when passing, the woman prevents inappropriate exposure and relationships. In addition, this custom serves as a way for brothers and sisters to show mutual respect. By lowering herself and crawling by her brother, the woman is showing him respect. Whenever possible, however, brothers stand up and move to prevent their sisters from having to crawl, thus reciprocating the respect. This respect strengthens the bonds between relatives and contributes to the atmosphere needed to survive in subsistence living.

Adoption

Adoption in Ulithi is perceived very differently than in Western cultures. Like so many other Ulithian customs, this one is directly linked to survival in a subsistence lifestyle. Adoption is the rule and not the exception in Ulithi. Because the subsistence lifestyle of Ulithi motivates many families to have numerous children, it is common for parents to allow one or more of their children to be adopted to relatives (J. Figirliyong, 2012). Unlike Western cultures, in which biological parents give up their legal rights to the child, in Ulithi adoption does not have any formal paperwork and is viewed as a way for the child to gain an extra set of parents, as opposed to losing a set of parents (Hezel, 2001). Just as biological first cousins are viewed as siblings, adoptive parents are perceived just as biological parents would be (J. Figirliyong, 2012). Similarly, biological children of the adopted parents are connected to the adopted child in the same way their biological brothers, sisters, and first cousins would be (J. Figirliyong, 2012).

Adoption is an important part of the family structure because of the various functions it serves. First, it gives a child a larger safety net and support system. The child often lives with the adoptive parents but is not usually prohibited from visiting the biological parents when he or she feels so inclined (J. Figirliyong, 2012). Because large families are necessary to help ensure survival in a subsistence lifestyle, children are highly valued. For couples who are unable to have children, adoption provides a means to become parents and to have someone to whom they can pass on land rights. It also provides someone who can care for the adoptive parents in their old age.

Lastly, adoption is a way to strengthen the bond between relatives and increase access to resources. Like marriage, which unites two families, adoption can help create a closer bond or relationship between families. Because the adopted child will have access to land and resources through the adopted parents, he or she can provide additional resources to the biological parents if needed. Because survival in a subsistence lifestyle depends completely on access to land and other resources, adoption is a type of alliance that can help ensure the survival of both families.

Relationships in the Community Context

Social Structure

A subsistence lifestyle is the primary way of life in Ulithi; therefore, high value is placed on cooperation, trust, and reciprocity. Everyone understands that they must be interdependent to maximize their chances of survival. The more people work together to grow and harvest crops, fish, and build shelters, the more efficiently the work is completed. Thus, large families are very common in Ulithi, because labor is a valuable resource for survival.

As with brothers and sisters in a family unit, the sexes are usually segregated in the community. Women socialize with women and men with men. Public displays of affection or intimacy between couples who are dating or even married are strictly taboo.

Gender Roles

Gender roles in Ulithi are very different. Men's duties include fishing, sailing, building and repairing houses, protecting the women and children, and hard labor, and women's responsibilities include caring for the children and elders, cooking, cleaning around the house and island, growing crops such as taro, and weaving the traditional clothes still worn in Ulithi. The distinction between the genders and their roles serves to reinforce their interdependence and is seen as necessary for survival. The men recognize that they will not survive if the women do not do their jobs, and the women recognize that they, too, will not survive if the men do not do their jobs. Awareness of this interdependence helps reinforce the respect, cooperation, and reciprocity that are needed to survive. Men are considered the heads of their families and the leaders of the community (J. Figirliyong, 2012). The position of chief is held by a man, and it is customary for the island's men to gather at the men's house in the morning hours to plan and discuss the community's activities for the day (J. Figirliyong, 2012). After making plans, the men usually share them with the women.

This is not to say, however, that women do not possess power; they do. As described by Hezel (2001), men's power is more public, whereas women's power is more private. When necessary, women exercise their power when they feel it will benefit the community. For example, it is a common daily task for men to harvest *faluba* or *tuba,* a liquid obtained from the coconut tree that, when fermented, becomes an alcoholic beverage. If a man becomes intoxicated and disturbs the peace in the community, especially in a violent fight that causes serious bodily injury, the women often prohibit the cutting and consumption of *faluba* until they feel it is safe to lift the ban (J. Figirliyong, 2012). When this happens, the men must follow the women's mandate until instructed otherwise.

Reciprocity

Throughout the year, seasons are designated for harvesting different types of plants and fish and other sea life. These events provide yet another arena for the sexes to acknowledge and demonstrate their interdependence and reciprocity. When certain fish are in season, the men designate a day to fish as a collective whole for the women of the island. The fish are distributed equally among the women and families on island, in a custom called *heler fefel,* or "food for the women." Likewise, when crops such as taro are ripe, the women designate a day to harvest the crops together. They then distribute the taro equally among the island's men and families, in a custom called *heler mal,* or "food for the men" (J. Figirli-yong, 2012). This exchange of food between men and women is symbolic of the interdependence and mutual respect between the sexes (Hezel, 2001).

Foreign Influences on Ulithi Culture

Although to an outsider Ulithians' way of life appears relatively untouched, the evidence of foreign influence is visible to those familiar with Ulithi and its culture. As early as the 1500s, European explorers arrived in Micronesia (Ridgell, 1995). With the Spanish occupation of the Mariana Islands, Guam in particular, it did not take long for Catholic priests to arrive and attempt to convert the indigenous people to Catholicism. Eventually, these efforts expanded to Ulithi with the arrival of Father Juan Cantova in the early 1700s (Yap Visitor's Bureau, 2017b).

The Spanish maintained their presence in the region throughout much of the 1800s until after the Spanish-American War, when they sold the Caroline Islands (which included Ulithi) to the Germans (Ridgell, 1995). German control was eventually replaced by Japanese occupation in 1929 as a result of the League of Nations mandate (Ridgell, 1995).

World War II and the Trust Territory of the Pacific Islands

US planes strafed and bombed the Ulithi island group six times, killing a half-dozen islanders as they did so, including the daughter of the atoll chief. US forces seized the island group in late September and promptly bulldozed meeting houses and dwellings to make way for US military installations (Hezel, 1995, p. 239).

According to T. Guiormog (2012), when the islands of Ulithi were occupied by the US Navy in 1944, many Ulithians from Falalop, Asor, and Mogmog were relocated to Fedarai, freeing up those islands for military use. Because Falalop had the only airstrip in Ulithi, it was used for equipment and planes. Asor was used for administrative functions. Mogmog, the island that is traditionally home to the Paramount Chief, was used by American military personnel for recreation.

Ulithi changed hands once again in 1947 when the United Nations granted control of various islands to the United States after World War II (Hanlon, 1998). These islands, which included the Northern Marianas, Palau, Marshall Islands, Yap, Chuuk, Kosrae, and Pohnpei, were referred to as the Trust Territory of the Pacific Islands (TTPI) (Hezel, 2001).

Western Education

The US naval administration introduced a Western education system to Yap State, and schools were built at various locations. In 1963, construction of the first Western high school in the Outer Islands of Yap began in Ulithi on the island of

Asor (J. Figirliyong, 2012). The school, called Outer Island High School, was built by locals, many of whom were high school students at the time. (J. Figirliyong, 2012). The students attended classes in the morning and worked on building the high school during the afternoon (J. Figirliyong, 2012). The high school continues to function in Falalop, and many Ulithians and people from other Outer Islands of Yap have graduated and gone on to pursue higher education beyond the borders of Yap.

For many Ulithians, the presence of Western education is an opportunity that provides an alternative to remaining in Ulithi and living a traditional lifestyle. Unfortunately, some have the notion that without a Western education, one is "not educated," and that traditional knowledge and skills passed down through oral customs are not a type of education. The basic purpose of education, however, is to provide the necessary skills to survive in a particular environment. Americans go to school because the knowledge and resulting diploma or degree they obtain helps increase their chances of obtaining a cash-paying job, and in an environment in which a cash economy dominates, cash is necessary for survival. Cultural knowledge and skills related to subsistence living that are passed down from one generation to another also constitute a form of education, because these skills are necessary to survive in a subsistence economy (J. Figirliyong, 2012).

Cable Television

Another aspect of Western culture introduced in Yap in 1979 was cable television. In O'Rourke's documentary, *Yap: How Did You Know We'd Like TV?* (1981), he explored and questioned the circumstances surrounding this major event. Despite the objections of local leaders, cable television made its way to Yap in the form of prerecorded videotapes donated by the US-based Pacific Taping Company. Because the shows and commercials were filmed for American audiences, much of the content was culturally inappropriate for Yap. For example, commercials for products like Nair hair removal cream depicted women's upper thighs, often being caressed by a man. Because the upper leg is considered a private part within Ulithian and Yapese cultures, these commercials were highly inappropriate. O'Rourke also noted that when cable TV was introduced, the majority of Yapese households did not have electricity, let alone a television set. Cable TV was introduced during a time when the trusteeship was coming to an end and discussions about a new form of relationship with the United States were being held. According to O'Rourke, Yapese participants in the documentary questioned whether cable television was being used as a tool to Americanize Yap and give the United States a stronger foothold in this island group once the trusteeship ended.

The trusteeship ended on May 10, 1979 when Yap, along with Chuuk, Kosrae, and Pohnpei officially formed the Federated States of Micronesia (FSM) (Ridgell, 1995). Their relationship with the United States changed from a trusteeship to a free association, a relationship that would be further defined by an important document known as the Compact of Free Association (COFA).

COFA

The COFA is an agreement between the FSM, the Republic of Palau, and the Republic of the Marshall Islands, collectively referred to as the Freely Associated States (FAS), and the US (Ridgell, 1995). COFA went into effect on November 13, 1986, and in 2004, an amended version was implemented (Hezel, 1996). The agreement allows for citizens of the FAS to migrate freely throughout the US and its territories to obtain education, employment, and medical care (Federated States of Micronesia Delegation, 2011). In addition, the US federal government also gives financial assistance to the FAS to develop their own education, health care, and infrastructure. In exchange, the FAS granted the US exclusive defense rights in times of war, meaning that no other country but the US will be allowed to set up military defenses in the FAS should the US federal government feel it is necessary to protect US interests.

Migration Experiences

Because COFA allows the free migration of FAS citizens throughout the US and its territories, many Ulithians have moved to US states and territories such as Guam, Hawai'i, California, and even Texas (Hezel, 1996, 2006). For many Ulithians, relocation is an opportunity to pursue a different lifestyle through Western education and cash-paying jobs (Hezel, 1996, 2006). For others, it is a way to gain access to much-needed health care. Regardless of the reasons, the transition that comes with migration is difficult.

One of the biggest challenges Ulithians face is the difference in culture. Ulithian culture and American culture are based on different value systems, and Ulithians often experience a clash between the two sets of values when trying to exist in a new environment. In a subsistence lifestyle, a person's chances of survival are increased when people work together and share resources, hence the significance of the extended family and community in Ulithi. In a cash economy, however, a person's chances of survival increase when there are fewer people to support. Thus, *family* in America is usually perceived as the nuclear family, and when children reach adulthood, they are commonly expected to move out and support themselves. In the context of survival and practicality in specific environments, both cultures have strengths and purpose. Unfortunately, because the differences in culture are so vast, assimilation does not always come easily for Ulithians and other FAS citizens, and members of the host community often misunderstand and discriminate against them (Diaz, 1995).

Migrating to the US frequently brings change to Ulithian family structure. Whereas in Ulithi people are dependent on their family for day-to-day survival, the cash economy in America provides a way for people to support themselves without the family. Ulithians who attempt to maintain the traditional Ulithian concept of family quickly find that it is harder to survive when the cash they earn must support extended family members. The trend toward limiting household size has weakened the safety net that the extended family once provided. Unfortunately, family problems and hardships still exist, and Ulithians are sometimes forced to seek support from community service programs (Celes, 1995).

In Ulithi, English is taught in schools, but Ulithians migrating to the US often encounter difficulty in communicating. Although many younger Ulithians understand English, they may not be comfortable speaking it. With time, however, they are able to pick up enough to communicate verbally. Writing in English presents additional barriers. The structure of the Ulithian language differs from that of English, so writing in English is difficult. In addition, in the Ulithian culture knowledge is passed on orally, whereas in the US the only form of official documentation is written.

Despite the challenges Ulithians face when they migrate to the US, many have been able to create a balance between their home and host cultures (Hezel, 2006). Ulithians have pursued higher education and work in fields such as tourism, law, medicine, education, entomology, landscaping, construction, music, business, nursing, writing, academia, and social work. Not only do they contribute to the society in which they live, but they often send money and other goods to their relatives in Ulithi (Hezel, 2006).

Although the family structure often changes with migration, familial bonds continue to exist. Ulithians in the US often come together as a community to support each other in times of need (Figirliyong, 2012). When there is a death in the Ulithian community, regardless of where the death takes place, each household gives what it can toward a pool of money given to the family of the deceased to help with expenses (Figirliyong, 2012). In the case of medical emergencies, fundraisers are often held, with everyone donating a good or service to help raise money for expenses. Although manifested in new ways, these expressions of cooperation and reciprocity are integral aspects of Ulithian culture.

Social Work Practice: Some Considerations

One of the most important aspects of social work practice is cultural competence. Many social work models of intervention are based on Western concepts and cultures and may not always be appropriate to use with Ulithian clients. In addition, Micronesia is not homogeneous. Although there are many cultural similarities within the Micronesian islands, there are also many different languages, dialects, cultures, and lifestyles. Social workers must be careful not to assume that all Micronesians have the same beliefs and practices. Recognizing the need to explore the specifics of clients' culture is the first step in establishing awareness and maintaining cultural competence in practice.

Significance of Family Strength

Because American culture is more individualistic than Ulithian culture, social workers and other health professionals may perceive the extended family as a barrier that prevents an individual from functioning independently. However, the extended family and the role it plays can be a strength if used as a source of informal support. Practitioners who disregard the significant cultural role of the family risk creating a barrier between themselves and clients. Because Ulithians are taught from a young age that the needs of the family must come before individual needs, family has a major influence on the individual. Ewalt and Mokuau (1995) highlighted the distinction between perceptions of maturity within Western and Pacific cultures. In America, people are viewed as having reached maturity once they are able to live independently and support themselves. In many Pacific islands, including those in Ulithi, people are considered mature when they are able to put the needs of the family and community before their own (Ewalt & Mokuau, 1995).

For a family that has moved away from Ulithi, the transition from a collective culture to an individualistic one can be difficult. Often Ulithian families continue to observe their customs in their homes while trying to assimilate to the host culture when away from home. For example, in Ulithi, older children, particularly girls, help care for younger siblings and the household as part of their role within the family, and they are often expected to maintain this role even after moving away from Ulithi. A teenage girl may have the time to perform her role in Ulithi, but in the US she must also meet the demands of going to school and doing homework. So she faces difficult decisions about whether to follow her culture by putting her family first and performing her role even at the expense of her schoolwork, or putting her schoolwork first to do well at the expense of her family's well-being.

Elders in the family also experience change in their family roles when they leave Ulithi. In Ulithi, elders are afforded great respect. They are viewed as the keepers of vital cultural knowledge and skills necessary to survive in Ulithi. Even when they are too old to participate in the physical aspects of an activity, they supervise and instruct younger Ulithians on the correct way of doing things. This role changes drastically for Ulithian elders who migrate to the US. Instead of the active contributors they once were, they may be perceived as noncontributing members of the family and community who must be cared for. Ulithian elders may experience a sense of loss and even depression and feelings of disempowerment.

Social workers and other health professionals must be aware of the conflicts that clients may experience in fulfilling their cultural roles as members of Ulithian families and residents of the Western world. In addition, the issue of whether all family members migrated from Ulithi or some family members were born and raised in the US after the other family members migrated can influence family dynamics and the assigned or perceived roles of individual family members. When faced with conflicting expectations of the culture of origin and the host culture, many people choose their culture of origin, especially in the family context. The practitioner's task is to help family members find methods to balance both cultures in a way that allows them to assimilate while maintaining their cultural identity. A dual-culture approach can help practitioners ease the family's transition and maintain cultural competence.

In Ulithi, because individual identity is framed within the context of the family and community, Ulithians tend to be more comfortable in group settings. If singled out or put in the spotlight, they may become embarrassed and hesitant to respond. This information can be helpful when working in micro- and mezzo-level practice.

Importance of Gender Roles

The importance of recognizing the different gender roles in Ulithian culture cannot be emphasized enough. Although these roles may change when both women and men obtain cash-paying jobs to support the family, when Ulithians are at home with the family, they often revert to the duties traditionally assigned to their gender (Hezel, 2006). Because of the strict etiquette expected of certain relatives, such as brothers and sisters, it is important for practitioners to be aware of the relationships of clients to others in the family unit. If the client is in the presence of an adult relative who is of the opposite sex, the client may be hesitant to talk or discuss certain subjects openly. For example, a Ulithian woman who was hospitalized was being visited by relatives, one of whom was a man. The nurse on duty came in and began asking the patient important health questions dealing with bowel movements and other bodily functions. Everyone in the room remained silent and avoided talking with the nurse, causing her to become frustrated. It was not until the male relative left the room that the woman felt comfortable enough to answer the nurse's questions openly.

Importance of Respect for Authority

Within Ulithian culture, respect for authority is extremely important (Hezel, 2001), and the value of respect does not diminish in the least for Ulithians who migrate. People gain authority on the basis of factors such as age, gender, familial relationship, and social position (Hezel, 2001). The great respect afforded to family and community elders is a strength that provides practitioners with a tool for culturally competent interventions; because of the respect they are given and the position of authority they hold, elders and other traditional authorities can sometimes get through to a client when others cannot.

This respect may hinder clients struggling for self-determination, however, if an authority promotes a route that client does not feel is in his or her best interest. For clients who feel pressured to comply with an authority's wishes because of cultural expectations, practitioners can help them review all possibilities and decide on the course of action that is best for them. If this means taking a route contrary to the wishes of the authority, practitioner and client can review the potential consequences and, if necessary, find alternative means of support for the client. This could come from other family members or authority figures in the Ulithian community.

Acknowledging Positive Contributions

Ulithians who have migrated to the US have contributed in many positive ways to their host communities. First, a provision of COFA grants exclusive defense rights to the US should war break out, providing a strategic advantage to the US in the Pacific during times of war. The general American public often overlooks this contribution because they are not aware of COFA or its provisions. Despite the belief of some that Ulithians and other immigrants migrate to the US to take advantage of public assistance programs (Celes, 1995), many Ulithians are tax-paying citizens in their host community and thus contribute to the overall welfare of that community (Hezel, 2006).

A major contribution to Hawai'i that was made by the Outer Island of Yap community is the knowledge of traditional ocean navigation (Mita & Anthony, 2010). This skill had been lost to the Hawaiians until traditional master navigator Mau Piailug, from Satawal in the Outer Islands of Yap, agreed to share his knowledge. Although sharing this knowledge with people beyond his clan broke with culture and tradition, Piailug understood the importance of keeping this valuable traditional knowledge alive and forever connected the Outer Island of Yap with Hawai'i (Mita & Anthony, 2010).

Conclusion

Ulithians and other FAS citizens have demonstrated their resilience as a people through all the challenges and hardships they have faced when migrating. They have found ways to maintain their cultural identity while adapting to new ways of life. They have taken the strengths of their culture and discovered ways to apply them to life in their new homes. Maintaining a sensitive balance between two opposing cultural forces is not an easy task, and yet this is what FAS citizens who migrate to the US do every day.

Ultimately, although Ulithian culture is very different when compared to most other cultures of the US, they all serve the same purpose – to increase people's chances of survival in a particular environment. To avoid an ethnocentric approach when trying to make sense of an unfamiliar culture, practitioners must challenge themselves to view new cultures within the context of those cultures' environments. Because Ulithians continue to live a traditional lifestyle based on a subsistence economy, their standard of living is very different than that found in America. This is not a bad thing; it is just different. US Navy Rear Admiral Carleton H. Wright summed up the difference as follows:

> If civilization were measured by flush toilets, ice cubes, machine guns, and sewing machines, then Micronesians were indeed savages. If, however, civilization meant an economic system in which there was no relative poverty, but rather adequate food, shelter, physical security, and a social system in which all participate equally and actively in the material and aesthetic standards of community life, then the people

of Micronesia were indeed civilized and had much to teach the rest of the world (quoted in Hanlon, 1998).

Wright's observations and ensuing comments encourage one to consider what it truly means to be "civilized." Is it something that can only be measured in terms of material goods and the degree of industrialization as it often is? Or is it more accurately measured by the degree of social harmony, social equity, and relative quality of life? The key to answering these questions lies in social work practice that is firmly rooted in cultural competence.

References

Celes, R. (1995). No more free rides. *Latte Magazine, the Essence of Guam,* December, 39 – 57.

Diaz, T. A. (1995). From the mouths of babes: What are we teaching our children? *Latte Magazine, the Essence of Guam,* December, 52 – 53.

Ewalt, P. L., & Mokuau, N. (1995). Self-determination from a Pacific perspective. *Social Work, 40,* 168 – 173.

Federated States of Micronesia Delegation. (2011). *Information provided in the Federated States of Micronesia President's meeting with FSM citizens.* Dededo, Guam: Author.

Figirliyong, J. Personal communication, May 8, 2012.

Guiormog, T. Personal communication, June 10, 2012.

Hanlon, D. (1998). *Remaking Micronesia: Discourses over development in a Pacific territory 1944-1982.* Honolulu: University of Hawai'i Press. (pp. 46; 47.)

Hezel, F. X. (1995). *Strangers in their own land: A century of colonial rule in the Caroline and Marshall Islands.* Honolulu, HI: University of Hawaii Press. (p. 239.)

Hezel, F. X. (1996). *New trends in Micronesia migration.* Retrieved from http://micsem. org/pubs/articles/migration/frames/trendsfr.htm

Hezel, F. X. (2001). *The new shape of old island cultures.* Honolulu: University of Hawai'i Press. (pp. 3 – 5; 7; 28 – 32; 35; 38; 40;46 – 65; 58; 68; 115;122 – 126.)

Hezel, F. X. (2006). *Micronesians abroad* [motion picture]. Federated States of Micronesia: Micronesian Seminar.

Mita, M., & Anthony, N. (2010). *The wayfinder* [motion picture]. United States: Paliku Documentry Films.

O'Rourke, D. (1981). *Yap: How did you know we'd like TV?* [Motion picture]. United States: Direct Cinema, Ronin Films.

Ridgell, R. (1995). *Pacific nations and territories: The islands of Micronesia, Melanesia, and Polynesia.* Honolulu: Bess Press. (p. 86).

Yap Visitor's Bureau, old site. (2017, February 18). *Myths, legends, and factual tidbits: How Wa'ab became Yap.* Retrieved 2/18/17 from http://www.visityap.com/oldsite/funfacts.html

Yap Visitor's Bureau. (2017a). Getting to Yap and things to know once you're here. Tourist information. Retrieved 2/18/17 from www.visityap.com/getting here/

Yap Visitor's Bureau. (2017b). History of Yap, a timeline of Yap's history and cultural development. Retrieved 2/18/17 from www.visityap.com/history/

My Parents Named Me Joshua

Joshua Depmar Walsh

My English professor father would have loved the "call me Ishmael" ring to this first line.

My last name is Walsh – a good Irish name that my father carried with him from New York to Ulithi. He fell in love with my mother, and she fell in love with him.

My mother, a native of Fassarai, Ulithi, gave me the middle name *Depmar.* In her language – a language that my cousins have reminded me I speak like a rookie Peace Corps volunteer – *Dep* means "love." *Mar* calls to mind the *marmar* traditional head floral crown. My name, therefore, is most directly translated as something like, "love for the traditional crown." My mother explained to me that a better translation would be "loyal." She would remind me that I am, by name, destined to be loyal to Ulithi. When I was younger, I really didn't like the name Depmar. My friends had normal middle names like Michael or Paul. Some had cool ones like Phoenix. I eventually came to realize what a gift a name like Depmar is, and I have remained grateful for being given it.

Mom died a few a years ago.

My dad – who would smile at the Camus reference of the prior line – passed away three years after her. During those years he, my brother, and I would often reflect on Mom and Ulithi. Mom and Dad did much joint academic work together about Ulithi, and I like to believe that he found joy in continuing with his boys the "Ulithi conversation" he and Mom engaged in so often. I know Mom would have loved that. Dad was afflicted with Parkinson's, but that did not stop him from compiling his reflections on Ulithi into a short anthology that amounted to an old professor's last published work. This is my reflection.

This reflection was started as I began my most recent journey across the Pacific. I am, of course, not the first person of Western Caroline island heritage to trek across the deep ocean. I certainly will not be last. This particular trek, however, was taking place 37,000 feet above the ocean in Seat 3A aboard a United 777 headed to Houston. I was on my way to litigate an international arbitration matter for a client. A company was paying my firm handsomely to actively attack defendants who had committed a wrong against them. My path (a flight to Houston), my chosen *wa* – canoe – (a lie flat seat on a wide body airliner skimming the sky), and the reason for my journey (beating an opponent who had committed an offense) seem as foreign to Ulithian identity as one can get. There was fish on the journey, albeit it poached Salmon served with capers, followed by a Port wine and cheese cart. There were celestial bodies involved, but only the technological man-made orbiting wonders that guided the aircraft's computerized navigation and communication systems. There was community and fellowship through food, but only because it makes the most sense for the airline to feed 300 passengers at the same time.

There I was jetting across the pacific with my fancy hat on to wreak litigation destruction, as opposed to finding a way through humble and quiet interaction to find reconciliation. Would Fernando Harui, my mother's stoic father whose back had been weathered into leather by a lifetime of fishing the Ulithi Lagoon, recognize me as his Kin? What does it mean to be his Kin, and what does my "Ulithian-ness" mean to me? Would he think of me as still "loyal?"

Ulithi in the Mirror

I can see my mother in my face. My receding hairline and the shape of my head that is being slowly revealed confirm that I have inherited my grandfather's features as well. I cannot, however, navigate a canoe or turn the leaves of a bush into medicine that can heal a wound. I cannot climb a coconut tree, and I'd be a bit jittery husking a coconut without taking my time. My fishing these days involves casting a Shimano Rod with my boys, or drinking a Corona and trolling on a boat that is dragging a line that someone else has set for me. Being Ulithian seems distant. But it is not.

I can see Ulithi in ways that move beyond my physical countenance. While my Ulithian spoken language skills may be lacking, I cannot help but find Ulithi in the way I communicate.

If you know Ulithians, you know that they have a drive for humor and a comedic timing that would make the ghost of Johnny Carson take note. I can hear my mother's wicked sense of humor every time a sophomoric smile cracks across what should otherwise be a stoic face. The command "don't laugh" might as well be laughing gas. The laughing continues into the world of the crass, and that is very much Ulithian.

Lessa, as only a dry mid-20th century anthropologist can, wrote that "Ulithian curses and profanity are overwhelmingly lewd." Lessa focused on the anger that was behind the profanity, but Lessa missed how often those lewd remarks – even when

Figure 1. Joshua Walsh with his two boys, Elijah Depmethou Walsh and Jeremiah Harui Walsh.

uttered in anger – carried with them a level of humor that served as an almost instant balm because of the absurdity of the curse. Indeed, some of the expressions are ridiculous in their content, and their literal English translations are indeed bawdy. "The inside of your mother's rectum is very, very, very, very, very, red." Lewd yes, but Lessa forgot that lewd gets reactions, and lewd absurdity can get the best laughs – just ask George Carlin. I can

Figure 2. Joshua and brother John with their families: L-R: Jeremiah, Cara, and Elijah; John, Conan, Lily, and Tiffany; Joshua.

assure you, as can my wife, that this vein of *schtick* is intact. My brother, a medical professional tempered by years of Emergency Department practice, has a gallows humor that will make you both cringe and smile. As an attorney, I have an appreciation for the first amendment that does not scare me away from finding humor in even those topics that might make you exclaim "too soon."

Humor is language, and language is incredibly important to Ulithians. Pacing, rhythm, situational syntax, and voice tone all are used as instruments to convey multiple subtle layers of communication. Ulithian chant and dance are obviously great examples of this. Ulithian language is all those things, but it is also resilient, changing, and quite alive. Mom and Dad spent time writing about how the language shifted – and continues to shift – with the times. My favorite example of this is the account Mom and Dad wrote about in the journal *Anthropological Linguistics* about the native language adoption by the Ulithians of some of the foreign machines they were confronted with as the twentieth century rolled through World War II: The Ulithian word, *wa,* means *canoe* in English. (It has been extended to mean *motorboat.*) A car, jeep, or truck are called a *wal wol fului*, canoe of the land. An airplane is a *wa yal,* a flying canoe, and a helicopter is a *wa tagulul,* a canoe turning around. A bulldozer is designated as *wal borbor,* a canoe that digs (as a pig does with its snout). Sil wa yal, mother of the flying canoes is, aptly enough, an aircraft carrier.

I find the adaptability of the Ulithian language much like the resiliency and adaptability of the Ulithian people themselves. In his essay, Language and Change in Ulithi (1979, p.20; 2013, 82-87), Dad wrote:

When strong winds and seas work on a coral island its configuration changes. Part of the beach that you saw a month ago may be gone now and the other end of the same island may have an addition to it. This resembles what is happening to Ulithi culture and to its language. What was part of life before, seen and talked about daily, may now be awash, not mentioned, invisible. But most likely there is something new and different around somewhere. (Walsh, 1979; 2013)

Perhaps Dad was writing about more than language. Perhaps my Ulithian-ness, like the evolving Ulithian language, is simply "something new and different," yet still Ulithian. The configuration of the beach has changed, but the coral island is still there.

I also see Ulithi in my reactionary instinct to initially not confront new situations without first sitting back and, as the Yapese say, – *Bay ea lawan' u way* – finding the wisdom that is still in my basket. The wisdom to be found in my *basket* is betel-nut, and, as Stefan Krause (2014) has summarized, the expression is meant to convey the advice that whenever a problem seems difficult to solve, one should take a minute to chew a betel nut and think about it. "The calming effect of the betel nut will help in providing the focus needed to make a wise decision." Francis Hezel, speaking to Krause about the expression, explains: "A betel-nut break [also provides] a check against impulsive speech. Nothing is so detrimental to the peace and climate of respect as an ill-considered remark."

My mother would often tell the analogous well known account of how a typical Ulithian boatman, upon approaching his destination island, would lower his sail and approach slowly. When he arrived on the shore, he would immediately go to the men's house and tell the occupants, even if the only occupants at the time were the ghosts and spiders, *tor kaptat wai.* His "boat had no news," even if the next words out his mouth were indeed important, extraordinary, and newsworthy. This opening phrase assuring the audience in the men's house that there was "no news" served as a verbal pause – a verbal betel-nut break and moment of thought before speaking. My default mode is to indeed "fix the betel nut" before taking impulsive action. I often will speak to others in the manner of *tor kaptat wai,* and seek the verbal pause to keep things calm before moving on to more newsworthy matters. I speak and work in this manner, and I know I do so because of the preference for truly measured, as opposed to speedy action, that permeates the islands of Yap.[1]

And yes, I even find Ulithi in the litigator I see in the mirror, even if that mirror is aboard a jetliner headed to an international arbitration with no quarter being given to the opponent. Lessa found "exquisite restraint" in the way Ulithians, even when faced with conflict, are a society that "values conformity and deprecates controversy…" Because of this, he wrote that in Ulithi "litigation is weak" and that this is due to the fact that "the relationships that people have to one another have been worked out over many years and are predominantly personal and kinship in character." Because of the extreme insular nature of Ulithi lagoon, there is a "sheer need for cooperation." Despite what you may think about lawyers, our profession is supposed to be a healing art. Much like the exchange of *lava lava* or woven rope, the lawyer's words, letters, and papers are meant to replace the sticks, stones, and spears that have been the traditional method of dispute resolution for much of

---

[1] See chapters in Lessa (1966); e.g., Chapter 2, Basic Social Relations; Chapter 3, Political Organization.

human history. I litigate with *Lessa-inian* "exquisite restraint" because I work as a conflict resolver. I fix my betel nut before I respond. I calm my clients with what isn't news, to make sure that when we discuss the real news, we are collected and can make proper decisions. My clients are best served by the resolution of conflict, and I bring a very Carolinian sense to that work.

I have reflected on this Caroline island mentality in the recent work I have been doing with convicted prisoners from the FSM – all men – who are the subject of removal proceedings from the United States and deportation to their home islands. Without disclosing particulars, you should under-

Figure 3. Joshua Walsh in the FSM Supreme Court room in Palikir.

stand that the convicted felons that are the subject of removal proceedings like these across the United States face an invariably forgone conclusion. Department of Homeland Security statistics show that 91% of the foreigners removed from the United States are removed for having been convicted of a felony, and that almost none of those that challenge their removal are ever successful in being allowed to stay. Counseling these inmates requires directness, but it is also best accomplished with a Carolinian sensibility.

It is difficult to admit, but when I meet with these men, I cannot help but be grateful that I am, put bluntly, not them. I have a family of my own, and the means and education to lead a comfortable life. I am surrounded by an incredible community of others who have made my Micronesian experience on Guam truly blessed. It could easily have not been so.

When hoodie wearing black teenager Travon Martin was shot, President Obama remarked that if he had a son, he could look like him. But for the blessed connection of events that made me the son of John Walsh and Eulalia Dolomog Harui, my Micronesia experience on Guam could have ended up like one of these men facing deportation. I look like them.

My work with marginalized and societally despised Micronesian men keeps me reflective on the broad range of what it means to be a Ulithian – a Micronesian man – on Guam. That reflection sometimes turns to the reflections of others, and Ulithi has been a place that invites such reflection. This wonderful collection is certainly proof of that. Much has been written about Ulithi. I believe that is so because Ulithi is much more than a merely interesting place on the map. Ulithi and its people, and their continuing and evolving story and challenges that are faced, transcends Ulithi from geographic point to Pacific Island ethos.

Ulithi as Ethos

In 1945, Armed Forces Radio Station WVTY published *The 'Ulithi' Encyclopedia*, a 41 page guidebook about Ulithi written and edited by US Navy officers about a place "which was a terrific change for a lot of us." The volume offers this pessimistic thought at the close of its chapter on Ulithi's people:

> It is not a pleasant final thought, but unless there is a noticeable addition of young people in the next few years, the Ulithians will be extinct within three generations. When the Japanese took all the young men and women with them, they seriously endangered the continuation of Ulithi as a society. In peace once more, those young people may be returned; the problem may be solved by integration with people from nearby islands, whereby some of the family and cultural characteristics may be preserved. But it is likely that we have seen Ulithi in its last days as a separate social unit.

My sons are 7 and 4, and three generations removed from Fernando Harui's Ulithi. Fortunately, the Ulithians are not "extinct" as our Navy friends once feared they would be. However, it is undeniable that times have changed significantly. Ulithians are neither "extinct" nor in their "last days," but they certainly have been changed in the many decades since those words foretelling their demise were written. Fran Hezel (1995), writing about the Micronesia that had been remade in the post war period, explained succinctly that:

> Times had changed in Micronesia. The people of remote Ulithi, who for years had scorned western clothes, were wearing sunglasses and shirts and zories after the typhoon that devastated their atoll in 1960.

But, change does not necessarily mean the death of tradition. When the boatman approaching the men's house left his sails behind in the last century and changed to fiberglass hulls and Yamaha outboards, the tradition of *tor kaptat wai* did not end. The engine was slowed on approach to an island, as opposed to the sail being lowered. The boatman still goes to the men's house. The loss of the canoe did not end the drive for measured speech, or the desire to keep your audience calm.

The real change that threatens Ulithi is well beyond the decision of individual islanders to keep traditions or halt the influx of modern technology onto the atoll. Depending on what UN or NGO report you read, it is more likely that Ulithi itself may be extinct before the last Ulithians disappear. Whereas Bikini was lost to the literal fallout of war, Ulithi may be underwater because of the larger world's love affair with the combustion engine. Ulithi may, within our lifetime, move from a place that is the subject of academic anthologies such as this, to a place of remembrance and reverence for the past. To borrow a line from Camelot, Ulithi may become little more that a place of the past where we whisper to each other, "Don't let it be forgot, that once there was a spot, for one brief shining moment, that was known as Ulithi."

But even this threat may help to strengthen Ulithi, as those who love Ulithi band together in community to confront this new challenge.

John Rulmal, Jr. has picked up the role of Ulithian leadership his father once carried and has done great work in researching Ulithi's ecosystem, and assisting in overlaying a cultural lens across that study. If you know Ulithi, you understand that Ulithians have since time immemorial adhered to certain taboos and cultural strictures regarding the methodology and rules of harvesting turtle. As it turns out, those cultural rules have direct connections to maintaining sustainable and respectful harvesting of turtles and health for the lagoon. The Ulithians, unsurprisingly, had been conservationists well before Teddy Roosevelt set up his first National Park. These connections are what Jr. and the researchers he works with are trying to understand. One of the people he works with, Nicole Crane, a Professor in the Department of Biology at Cabrillo College in Aptos, California, has even given a TED talk on the intersection of Ulithi traditions and conservationism (Crane, 2017). For those of you not in the TED know, TED is the cool kids global educational forum, where learned men and women gather to share, "ideas worth spreading," in elaborate lecture halls with advanced multimedia presentations. Those ideas worth spreading have exceeded a billion internet video views, and cover such diverse and catchy topics as "10 things you didn't know about orgasm" and "The economic injustice of plastic." Dr. Crane's Ted Talk on "Sustainable Ocean Management – Back to the Future in Micronesia" is a reflection on Ulithi that links the traditions of Ulithians with modern sensibilities of sustainable living. Simply put, Dr. Crane and her cohort are examining a Ulithian way of doing conservation. Ulithi has moved beyond a geographical location, and has become an ethos; a model of action.

Part of the ethos of Ulithi, I also suggest, is a model for academic research; a place rooted in oral tradition where researchers – researchers who have become part of the community they study – continue to draw us in to gather and tell stories. More, they gather and tell those stories arm in arm with the native people themselves.

My father was an American missionary and teacher and my mother a student and academic from Ulithi. Together, they collaborated on much reflection about Ulithi. The academic skills my mother gained that helped her in that effort were gathered at the University of Guam, where she connected with many great friends who were interested in learning all they could about Ulithi. I cannot help but think of the smile mom must have about my essay appearing in a work edited by Mary Spencer and Rebecca Stephenson – two women who taught, collaborated with, and shared so much about Ulithi with her. Mom would especially like the presence of strong women at the core of a volume of a matrilineal society like

Ulithi. Beyond that, my mother would also love that my appearance in this volume comes alongside my cousin Joliene Hasugulayag. We shared the experience of being children of Ulithian parents who married beyond the lagoon, and today Joliene and I are united in sharing our reflections about the place – Ulithi – that has kept us linked all these years.

There is something incredibly special about Ulithi and the fellowship of those who have spent time trying to understand Ulithi. That special connection can be seen in the relationship between Mom and Dr. Stephenson. Aunt Becky transcended the role of university professor and anthropological researcher, and was simply my aunt while I was growing up and moving into adulthood. She was there as I finished school, got married, baptized my sons, and buried my parents. She has watched my boys run with their blond hair amongst their Ulithian cousins. I cannot help but have a great feeling of fellowship as I contribute just a bit to the work she and Dr. Spencer have put together, and beyond that, I am making that contribution in a collected volume where my mom also "speaks." Her words are contained in two other essays in this collected work, and they stand as a wondrous bridge that, without this volume, might not otherwise exist. My mother and I are speaking in the same space, and that is blessed indeed.

When my parents were married in 1979, the reception was held at the newly built UOG student center. The wedding party included Joliene's father, Josede; Jr. Rulmal's father, John; and Aunt Becky. It is indeed a beautifully Ulithian happening that this academic work brings together not just teachers and students, researchers and subjects, or even similarly minded collaborators. Research about Ulithi has brought together family.

Figure 4. Eulalia Harui and Jack Walsh's wedding party, 1979

Moving Forward

To be sure, Ulithi is now one of the cool kids. Ulithi and the Caroline Island identity that it anchors embodies the spirit of these Micronesian islands. One only needed to spend a few hours at the recent Festival of Pacific Arts hosted on Guam in 2016 to see just how true that was, as the Carolinian canoe became the dominant cultural image of the festival. My Chamorro brothers and sisters are slowly stirring toward cultural resurgence, and it appears that they will be navigating their path forward with Ulithi and the rest of the Caroline Islands as their guiding star. I have also heard from surfers from around the world and watermen of all variety about how Ulithi is on their dream list of exploration. They speak the name "Ulithi" with a reverence that lies somewhere between the sacred and the stoked.

I have come to realize that Ulithi means so much more than the geographic contours of the lagoon.

"Ulithi" is a place, to be sure, but it is also a way. It has become understood by many who know it to be a way of existence, and a model for how we should be interconnected with each other. Lessa called it a "Micronesian design for living." I'd suggest that Ulithi is now more an *ideal* for living; the embodiment of harmonious interaction with our fellow people and our environment that so many of us are currently searching for. "Ulithi" has become for many observers some form of magical Pacific shangri la – a Rogers and Hammerstein "Bali Ha'i" come to life. Too much? Perhaps. But, as the rest of the world continues to march further into the realm of the digital and the fleeting, I cannot help but think that Ulithi stands as a beautiful reminder of authenticity and rooted tradition.

Of course, Ulithi has its problems – educational difficulties, the continuing clash of a Micronesian biology and western prepackaged food, lack of economic opportunities, etc. Ulithi is not simply a stylized image from a Jacoulet painting. Ulithi, as part of the sphere of Yap, is still a place where the content of your character may indeed mean less at times that the identity of your village, family, or mother. But, the idea of Ulithi as an ideal is certainly real. Dr. Marshall Wees, telling Francis Thornton about his time in Ulithi as a doctor in World War II (1950), said of the Ulithians that, "They were without exaggeration the most amazing people I have ever met. In the purity of their personal lives and the strength of their social solidarity they offered me lessons and insights which completely altered my basic patterns of thought."

This is what I feel, and because of this I know that Fernando Harui would recognize me, and also those many people who have crossed paths with the atoll. We are Ulithi, and that makes me proud.

References

Armed Forces Radio Station WVTY. (1945). *The 'Ulithi' Encyclopedia,* 1 – 41.

Crane, N. *One people, one reef; hofagie laamle!* Retrieved 3/20/17: http://ulithimarinecon-servation.ucsc.edu/

Hezel, F. X. (1995). *Strangers in their own land: A century of colonial rule in the Caroline and Marshall Islands,* (p 298). Honolulu, HI: Center for Pacific Island Studies, University of Hawai'i.

Krause, S. M. (2014). *Micronesia: The art of communication in Yap, FSM: Traditional forms of respectful interactions.* (Retrieved March 21, 2017. Search for: Stefan M. Krause The art of communication in Yap, FSM)

Lessa, W. A. (1966). *Ulithi: A Micronesian design for living.* NY: Holt, Rinehart and Winston.

Walsh, J. A. (1979). Introduction to language and change in Ulithi. *The New Pacific,* 20 – 21.

Walsh, J. A. (Ed.). (2013). Introduction to language and change in Ulithi. In J. A. Walsh (Ed.), *Ulithi: A Micronesian anthology* (pp. 82 – 87). Ohio: Bookmasters, Inc.

Wees, P. & Thornton, F. B. (1950). *King-doctor of Ulithi* (*vii*). NY: The Macmillan Co.

LAVA LAVA:
HALLMARK OF ULITHIAN CULTURE[1]

Eulalia J. Harui-Walsh with Rebecca A. Stephenson

The distinctive hand woven *lava lava* of Ulithi have a significance far beyond being used as an article of clothing. In addition to being classic Ulithian woman's daily attire, the lava lava or *ghow* is an extremely important cultural artifact. Lava lava can likewise be viewed as a Ulithian cultural icon. Lava lava serve to bond Ulithians together, to allow them to obtain forgiveness for wrongdoings, to help them maintain ties with the people of Yap, and to afford them a way of showing honor and respect (Walsh & Harui-Walsh, 1989, p. 13; Welborn & Bothmer, 1977).

In early academic works concerning Carolinians in Micronesia, there are only a few references made to women's garments. Some examples of these include: "The women wear only a piece of material around the waist, which falls to the middle of the thigh" (Arago, 1822, as cited in Barratt, 1988, p. 55), and "Women could be distinguished…by their brightly coloured aprons, falling to below the knees" (von Lutke, n.d., as cited in Barratt, 1988, p. 61). Mertens (1828, as cited in Barratt, 1988, p. 66) observed that women "…go naked, like the men, but for a broad girdle of striped material, which they wrap around their lower ribs." Graviere (n.d., as cited in Barratt, 1988, p. 73) indicated, "…the waist alone of the young woman was covered by a yellowish cloth which stopped above the knee."

Field research in the 1990s for this study of Ulithian lava lava revealed that noticeable sociocultural changes were continuing to occur within the Caroline Islands. Development and modernization were bringing about variations within classic Ulithian customs and lifeways. The lives of Ulithian women seem to have changed considerably within that time period. For example, marked differences were noted between and among Ulithian women, especially with regard to age-sets and formal educational experiences (Harui-Walsh, 1984, reprinted in Walsh, 2013; Stephenson, 1984; Walsh & Harui-Walsh, 1989, reprinted in Walsh, 2013). Significant Ulithian language changes have been noted for some time (Walsh 1979). However, the importance and value of lava lava for women within the context of Ulithian culture and society did not seem to have been impacted.[2]

During the course of anthropological field research conducted in Ulithi Atoll, William Lessa (1977, pp. 129-190) completed an extensive study entitled, *Traditional Uses of the Vascular Plants of Ulithi Atoll, with Comparative Notes.* In the document, Lessa identified twelve species of plants found in Ulithi as being directly utilized within the context of the making of lava lava.[3] Lessa's well known

---

[1] This is an augmented version of the earlier paper prepared for the Museum of New Zealand *Te Papa Tongarewa* in Wellington, NZ. First released August 1992.

[2] See former Peace Corps Volunteer Carolyn Vernimen's blog on her contemporary and fashion forward views on weaving and wearing lava lava on Ulithi: https://caroistaa.wordpress.com/tag/lava-lava/

[3] Friends identified by Lessa who assisted him in the field research in Ulithi Atoll for the 1977 *Vascular Plants* study included Melchetthal, Pedro Yamalmai, King Wegelemar, Iourmar, Sorekh, Ithuweiang, and Eulalia Harui.

ethnography of Ulithi Atoll, entitled *Ulithi: A Micronesian Design for Living*, was first published in 1966. Earlier works by Lessa concerning Ulithi that are of particular interest to this paper highlight aspects of Ulithian perception and cognition (Lessa, 1961, 1962, and 1963).

Welborn and Bothmer (1977, p. 23) have noted that, "…in the water-born micro worlds of the Caroline Islands, where manual skills and practical crafts abound, the weaving of the lava lava is the most refined of the island skills." In the 1990s, as in the past, young women learned to weave lava lava from older women. A girl's mother, or perhaps an aunt or an older sister would teach her the intricate skills of using the loom.

Weaving the Lava Lava

For Ulithians, weaving a lava lava is a two-step process. Before putting a lava lava on a loom, a weaver must first set up the lava lava on four pegs that stand upright on a footed board. The board is called *maliel*. The four pegs are called *lol maliel*, "the children of the *maliel*."

The weaver first sets the pegs for the width of the lava lava to be made. Next the weaver loops each strand of thread around each peg until the desired lava lava width is obtained. Then this arrangement of looped thread (called *chow*, meaning loop) is transferred from the board *maliel* to the loom, which is called *thur*.

Mulford in 1980 described the classic Ulithian backstrap loom including detailed textual notations and vivid diagrams. Mulford resided on Fassarai in Ulithi for two months in August-September 1978, to gather field research data for her M.A. Thesis in Anthropology at California State University, Northridge. She expressed great concern that the weaving of lava lava by women in Ulithi was a cultural endeavor that would soon disappear. Earlier, in 1977 (p. 24), Welborn and Bothmer offered in print the following synthesis of the weaving process for women in Ulithi, based on their own field research:

> The warp portion of the weaving is done on a backstrap loom which is tied to a tree or some sturdy support. The backstraps themselves are intricately hand woven using sennit twine made from coconut husks. The backstrap is attached to the loom and looped around the woman's lower back. The woman is then able to control the tension of the warp threads by movements of her arms and torso.

Clearly, the weaving of lava lava in Ulithi requires considerable skill and know-how for women. In the 1990s, the weaving of lava lava, nonetheless, was an expected and rather everyday undertaking for most Ulithian women. But not every Ulithian woman who knows how to weave lava lava is acknowledged to be a master weaver. Ulithian women pride themselves on their weaving. It has been said that they "talk about it from generation to generation."

The weaving of lava lava for Ulithian women involves a carefully defined dynamic process in and of itself, as well as a noteworthy finished product. In her

Figure 1. Linda Ylmareg and her *maliel,* where she prepares the threads *(chow)* for the loom *(thur). (Photo by Rebecca Stephenson.)*

graduate research paper in Pacific Islands Studies at the University of Hawaii, Manoa, Lynn Martin (1981) explained that she learned how to weave Ulithian style lava lava from Eulalia Harui at the University of Guam in 1976. At that time, Lolly was funded by the University of Guam's financial aid program as a work-study student to teach weaving hands-on for the Department of Art on campus. Mulford recalled an occasion when she was reprimanded by Lolly for talking casually with a friend while weaving lava lava. Lolly explained that a weaver must fully respect the weaving process. One must offer the weaving process one's full attention, as well as the final product. Martin (1981, p. 60) stated: "Lolly's teaching method developed in me a philosophy that there is a certain intuitive process involved that draws inspiration from the natural rhythms of nature, the environment, and human activity…Thus only an approach which encompasses all facets of this lifestyle can lead to true mastery."

Ceremonial Uses of Lava Lava in Ulithi

Within Ulithian marriages and funerals up to the present time, lava lava serve as an important symbol of cooperation and unity. For a traditional Ulithian marriage, the relatives of the bride and groom hold a ceremony in which they exchange lava lava. The bride comes forward to the relatives of the groom wearing about six lava lava wrapped around her regular lava lava. She gives these extra lava lava to the female relatives of the groom, who are waiting to receive her. These women then anoint her with tumeric and oil and give her several lava lava which they wrap around her.

Lava lava are likewise presented at Ulithian funerals. In the same way that flowers serve as a sign of sympathy within a Western-style funeral, lava lava serve as an expression of shared grief among Ulithians. When a Ulithian dies, the relatives of his or her spouse will present gifts of lava lava. The lava lava presented on these occasions serve a threefold purpose: a wrapping for burial *(hadugdug)*, a farewell *(hartel haebuel loy)*, and an expression of love *(wortag)*. The children, nieces and nephews of the deceased, also bring lava lava to show their love and respect.

Family members and in-laws give lava lava to the deceased person's close blood relatives, who then decide which of the lava lava will be used in the burial. Lava lava that do not accompany the deceased into the ground are redistributed among the relatives and in-laws, serving both as a remembrance of the departed one and as a sign of unity.

When a high-ranking Ulithian is buried, as many as fifty lava lava may be offered, and half of these may go into the ground with the deceased. Considering the many hours of work involved in weaving lava lava, this is a loving farewell, indeed, as well as a mark of prestige. When Jesuit priest Father Walter died of cancer in 1977, he was buried on Mogmog, Ulithi in a grave with hundreds of lava lavas (Mulford, 1980, p 31).

Walsh and Harui-Walsh (1989, 2013) have discussed other means by which lava lava are highlighted within Ulithian culture. These include the giving of lava lava to relatives and friends traveling away from Ulithi, and the gift of lava lava among families in Ulithi when seeking forgiveness for an offense. Lava lava continued to be important in the 1990s in maintaining traditional cultural ties between Ulithians and the people of Yap who reside in Gagil Village. From past times up to the present, Ulithians are very generous in giving lava lava to important visitors to Ulithi as a sign of honor and respect.

The Ulithian Lava Lava Collection in the Museum of New Zealand, *Te Papa Tongarewa*

Early in 1992, Dr. Janet M. Davidson, then the Senior Curator-Pacific at the Museum of New Zealand *Te Papa Tongarewa* in Wellington, sent out a call for women's fiber arts items to be prepared within the Western Pacific region. These items could then be donated to the museum for its upcoming special exhibit entitled, "Traditional Arts of Pacific Island Women." Dr. Hiro Kurashina, then Director of the Richard Flores Taitano Micronesian Area Research Center at the University of Guam, brought this invitation to the attention of the UOG Ulithi Field School team leaders. The UOG Field School in Anthropology was expected to commence in Ulithi Atoll beginning in May 1992 (see Part 1 in this book). Perhaps it would be possible to commission the weaving of lava lava for the upcoming exhibit in New Zealand to occur during the UOG team's time in residence in Ulithi? The Ulithian lava lava could then be donated to the Museum of New Zealand *Te Papa Ton-*

garewa in Wellington. Dr. Davidson offered to provide women weavers in Ulithi with special recognition if they would be willing to contribute newly woven lava lava for inclusion in the exhibit. Ulithian women responded enthusiastically to this invitation.

The outcome of this unique situation is that, since 1992, there are ten Ulithian lava lava housed in the permanent Pacific women's fiber arts collection in the Museum of New Zealand *Te Papa Tongarewa* in Wellington. The Ulithian lava lava were first displayed for public viewing within the special exhibit entitled *Traditional Arts of Pacific Island Women,* which opened at the museum January 1, 1993. The *Te Papa Tongarewa* Ulithian lava lava may be seen online: http://collections.tepapa.govt.nz/search?searchTerm=lava+lava+of+Ulithi&scope=all

Dr. Hiro Kurashina, Director Emeritus of the Richard Flores Taitano Micronesian Area Research Center at the University of Guam, and Dr. Rebecca A. Stephenson, Professor Emerita of Anthropology at UOG, had the opportunity to view these Ulithian lava lava in July 2014 during a visit to *Te Papa Tongarewa* in Wellington. The ten lava lava, woven in Ulithi in May through June in 1992, are in excellent condition. They are very well curated, and are viewed as unique and noteworthy items within the museum. Two distinct types of Ulithian lava lava are included in the collection: traditional fiber lava lava and thread lava lava. There are five traditional fiber lava lava and five thread lava lava in the collection.

Ulithian lava lava in general can be divided into two varieties that are called *golitet* and *golfang.* These two varieties of lava lava encompass both fiber and thread lava lava. *Golitet* lava lava are high class lava lava and of high quality. They are given to people whom one cares about and feels close to. *Golitet* lava lava are not normally given to a person whom one does not know. *Golfang* lava lava, on the other hand, can be given more casually. They may be given as a token exchange, for example, in return to a person who has given some taro. *Golfang* can be given to anyone. *Golitet* lava lava are recognizable because the weaving in them is fine; i.e., close together. How can one tell whether a lava lava is *golitet*? Ulithi women offered the following suggestion: "Pour some water on the lava lava. If the lava lava is *golitet,* the water will not seep through."

Traditional Ulithian lava lava made from natural fibers may take a skilled weaver about 30 hours to complete, from the gathering of the raw materials to the drying of them as well as the time spent weaving. Lava lava that are woven using commercial cotton thread, on the other hand, can be completed within about ten hours of working at the loom. This is one of the reasons why Ulithian women from the 1990s up to the present time who reside in Ulithi prefer to wear thread lava lava for daily use. Lava lava woven from thread are more comfortable for women to wear, and thread lava lava are easier to launder. Another consideration is that if and when a major typhoon occurs in Ulithi, such as Typhoon Ophelia in 1960 and Typhoon Maysak in 2015, natural materials that are needed by the women for weaving lava lava might not be readily available for quite some time.

Traditional Fiber Lava Lava

There are four types of traditional Ulithian fiber lava lava included among the five natural fiber lava lava of Ulithi in the *Te Papa Tongarewa's* collection. The descriptions of them that appear below were prepared in 1992. These descriptions accompanied the Ulithian Lava Lava Collection donated to the Museum of New Zealand *Te Papa Tongarewa* for the *Traditional Arts of Pacific Island Women Exhibit,* which opened there on January 1, 1993.

The four types of traditional Ulithian fiber lava lava located in *Te Papa* in New Zealand are identified as follows:

peg (wide stripe on each side)
ilotol gulfoy (all hibiscus)
marub (plain)
dorol satawal (weaving of Satawal Islands)

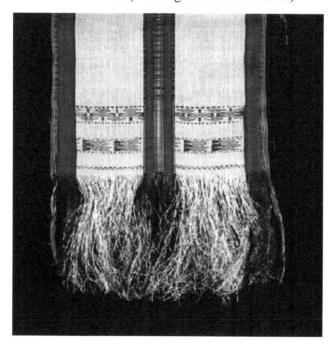

Figure 2. Ulithi Lava lava No. 1, a peg lava lava by Carmen Haduemog. *(Photo by Museum of New Zealand Te Papa Tongarewa.)* (Note: The New Zealand *Te Papa Tongarewa* Museum attributes this lava lava to Alberta Ului Dipwek.)

Ulithi Lava Lava No. 1 (Figure 2) is a *peg* lava lava of banana fibers. It has wide white sections, a traditional design down the middle, and bordering on each side.

The weaver was Carmen Haduemog, age 56, recently widowed. From the island of Asor in Ulithi, she now lives on the island of Falalop. Carmen is a master weaver, the number one specialist for traditional medicine in Ulithi, and she likes to farm bananas, potatoes, taro, and "anything that can grow." Carmen uses her late husband's name by choice; Ulithian women usually do not take their husband's name at marriage.

Ulithi Lava Lava No. 2 (Figure 3) is an *ilotol gulfoy* lava lava. It has seven dark stripes of about two inches in width which are interspersed with six brown-

Figure 3. Ulithi lava lava No. 2, *ilotal gulfoy,* by Lourdes Ydwechog. *(Photo by Museum of New Zealand Te Papa Tongarewa.)*

ish-white stripes of about one inch in width. This lava lava was made from hibiscus fibers. The weaver was Lourdes Ydwechog, age 49, from Mogmog (the island of the Paramount Chief), now living on Falalop. She is a master weaver and a homemaker.

Ulithi Lava Lava No. 3 (Figure 4) is a *marub* lava lava. It is a plain brownish-white color and was made from banana fibers. This lava lava was woven by Carmen Haduemog. Carmen's mother was from Woleai, an island that lies some distance from Ulithi Atoll in the Caroline Islands. This is probably the reason why Carmen weaves *marub* lava lava. Unlike all of the other nine lava lava represented in this collection, a *marub* lava lava of this type can be worn by a man or a woman. It is a high class lava lava, a chief's garment.

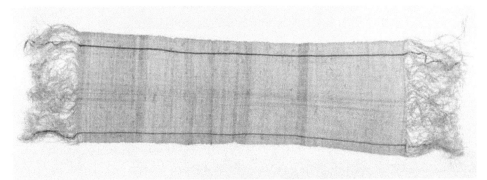

Figure 4. Ulithi lava lava No. 3, *marub,* by Carmen Haduemog. *(Photo by Museum of New Zealand Te Papa Tongarewa.)*

Ulithi Lava Lava No. 4 and No. 5 (Figures 5 and 6) are *dorol satawal* lava lava. Such lava lava are characterized by having many stripes. Both of the lava lava are made of a combination of hibiscus and banana fibers. These lava lava are called *dorol satawal* because this particular design which calls for many stripes with no set pattern was transmitted to Ulithi from Satawal Island during the Japanese colonial period in Micronesia (1914-1945). The weaver of Lava Lava No. 4 was Maria Pemadaw, age 22. From Mogmog, she recently married and is now living on Fassarai. Maria is one of the few young master weavers in Ulithi. Maria likes to work with natural fibers in weaving, and she is experimenting with the use of traditional dyes. Maria acknowledges that these traditional practices are very time-consuming. The weaver of lava lava No. 5 was Carmen Haduemog.

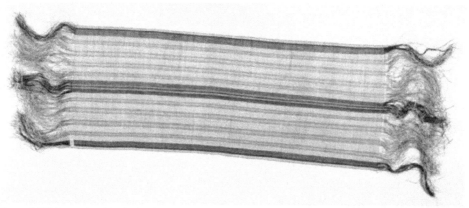

Figure 5. Ulithi lava lava No. 4, *dorol satawal,* by Maria Pemadaw. *(Photo by Museum of New Zealand Te Papa Tongarewa.)*

Figure 6. Ulithi lava lava No. 5, *dorol satawal,* by Carmen Haduemog. *(Photo by Museum of New Zealand Te Papa Tongarewa.)*

Thread Lava Lava

The five thread lava lava of Ulithi Atoll represented in the New Zealand collection are of two types: *peg rang* (wide yellow stripe on each side); and *pad chig* (small stripes within stripes).

Ulithi Lava Lava No. 6 (Figure 7) is a *peg rang* lava lava. *Peg* means wide stripes on each side. *Rang* means yellow. This particular lava lava was woven by Maria Rosogmar of Mogmog, who now divides her time between Fassarai, Asor, and Mogmog. A longtime master weaver, she is now 75 years old. She is also

Figure 7. Ulithi lava lava No. 6, *peg rang,* by Maria Rosogmar. *(Photo by Museum of New Zealand Te Papa Tongarewa.)*

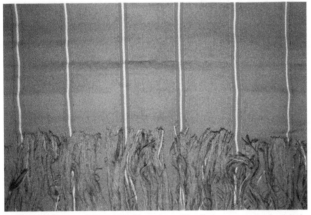

Figure 8. Ulithi *pad chig* thread lava lava, No. 7, green, woven by Maria Rosogmar. *(Photo by Hiro Kurashina.)*

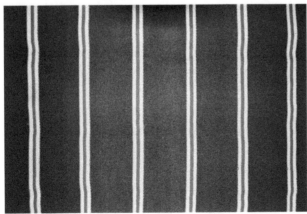

Figure 9. Ulithi *pad chig* thread lava lava, No. 8, purple, woven by Linda Ylmareg. *(Photo by Hiro Kurashina.)*

a master tattoo specialist, but does not do tattoo anymore because of the coming of Christianity to Ulithi. She is likewise a massage specialist and a medicine woman.

Ulithi Lava Lava No. 7, No. 8, No. 9, and No. 10 (Figures 8, 9, 10, and 11, respectively) are thread lava lava known as *pad chig. Pad chig* lava lava are made of seven stripes about two inches wide interspersed with smaller stripes of about one inch in width. The wide stripes will be of a dark color like blue, black, purple or green. These stripes cannot be red, white, or yellow. The one-inch stripes are composed of three sub-stripes forming a pattern of a central color with a second color on each side of it. Any two colors may be used for these sub-stripes, but the pattern must be consistent across the lava lava. This is the most popular type of lava lava woven in contemporary Ulithi.

Lava Lava No. 7 (Figure 8), No. 8 (Figure 9), No. 9 (Figure 10), and No. 10 (Figure 11) may be further identified according to their predominant color. The use of English language color terms in three of the four cases is noticeable. No. 7 may be called "green;" No. 8 may be called "purple;" No. 9 may be described by the Ulithian word *dololtad,* "color of the ocean;" and No. 10 may be called "pink." The weaver of Lava Lava No. 7 was also Maria Rosogmar. Linda Ylmareg, age 44, wove Lava Lava No. 8. Of Asor, now living on Falalop, Linda is a woman of two worlds. She is both a Ulithian-trained master weaver and Western-trained dental technician. Linda uses the term "yo yo" to describe herself, acknowledging the necessary movement back and forth between two very different cultures that characterize her daily life.

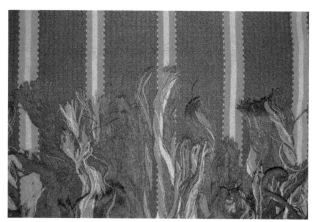

Figure 10. Ulithi *pad chig* thread lava lava, No. 9, *dololtad,* "color of the ocean," woven by Alberta Ului Dipwek. *(Photo by Hiro Kurashina.)*

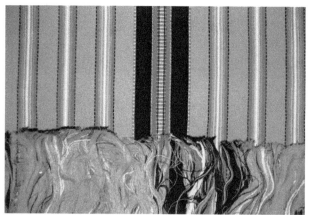

Figure 11. Ulithi *pad chig* thread lava lava, No. 10, pink, woven by Alberta Ului Dipwek. *(Photo by Hiro Kurashina.)*

Lava lava No. 9 (Figure 10), and lava lava No. 10 (Figure 11) were woven by Alberta Ului Dipwek, age 42. Alberta is a master weaver from Mogmog and a current resident of Falalop.

Up to the present time, the color patterns and stripe width in Ulithian lava lava identify a lava lava as having been woven by members of a certain family. Individual weavers develop their own border patterns. Thus, Ulithians can often tell by the pattern which woman wove a particular lava lava. The width of the lava lava is to some extent a matter of style and personal preference. Traditional-minded women insist that lava lava when worn should reach to a few inches below a woman's knees. Many younger women, however, wear their lava lava at knee length or even slightly shorter.

These days, it is more likely that traditional-minded women in Ulithi will not be wearing a blouse or shirt to accompany their lava lava. Customarily, the lava lava was worn by itself with no upper garment. Younger women in recent times more typically choose to wear some kind of top. Fashion choices for them include a tee-shirt in a solid color that favorably matches one of the colored stripes in the lava lava. At Ulithi in June of 1992, the matter of "going topless" was discussed with local women. Ulithian women of various ages offered the astute observation that, if one goes about uncovered, the tropical sun is very hard on one's skin and one ages visibly very fast. This may partially explain why considerably fewer bare breasted women can be seen in Ulithi Atoll in contemporary times.

Discussion

All of the ten lava lava woven in Ulithi Atoll that are now in the permanent collection of the Museum of New Zealand *Te Papa Tongarewa* are high quality lava lava with no mistakes made in the weaving of them. Ulithian women who are weavers, those who wove the lava lava for the collection, offered comments about the lava lava that were given to *Te Papa,* including the following:

> "When you wear one of these lava lava, you can keep your chin up. You don't have to keep looking down at your lava lava because you are concerned about its defects…"

> "When you give a lava lava like these away as a gift, you can look the person who received it in the eye, and you don't have to look down at the ground…"

The above quotes refer to the pride in weaving skills that Ulithian weavers have with regard to their work. The comments of the weavers also refer to the fact that even little mistakes in the weaving of a lava lava can be detected, and may be commented upon by everyone. High quality lava lava like the Ulithian lava lava in *Te Papa* may be used as gifts for chiefs and also for weddings, as gifts to the bride. Lava lava may be given to relatives of the deceased at a funeral or used to adorn the deceased.

In summary, the ten lava lava of Ulithi Atoll that are housed in the permanent collection at the *Te Papa Tongarewa* in Wellington, New Zealand, are garments. To be specific, they are women's clothing. The lava lava are also, and perhaps more importantly, the fabrics into which contemporary Ulithian women, old and young, weave their culture. The continued demand, use, and need for lava lava up to the present day appears to link with keeping the traditional weaving skills of women alive. This in turn helps in a very significant way to keep Ulithian culture alive. Perhaps no other item of material culture in Ulithi is as important as the lava lava for maintaining the traditional Ulithian ways of expressing togetherness, forgiveness, and respect; and therefore, Ulithian sociocultural integration.

As mentioned above, the University of Guam's Field School in Anthropology was scheduled to be held in Ulithi in early Summer 1992. Ulithian women weavers were consulted about their interest in and willingness to weave lava lava for the upcoming New Zealand special exhibit. Could these lava lava possibly be woven during the period when the UOG Field School team members would be in residence in Ulithi? The Ulithian women enthusiastically agreed. However, at the close of the UOG Field School in Anthropology in Ulithi in Summer 1992, the women needed additional time to finish preparing their lava lava collection for the exhibit. An arrangement was made for the ten completed lava lava to be sent by postal mail from Ulithi to the University of Guam. The Ulithian lava lava then would be sent from UOG to the Museum of New Zealand *Te Papa Tongarewa.*

When the parcel sent from Ulithi containing the ten lava lava arrived on campus, the UOG project team leaders opened the box with great anticipation to view the contents. The lava lava woven in Ulithi for the NZ exhibit emerged as being visually stunning in appearance (see the above photos of the lava lava). An extensive variety of colors, designs, and materials had been utilized in their making. Each lava lava in and of itself was a treasured cultural artifact from the central Caroline Islands. Truly, the women in Ulithi had woven lava lavas of remarkable quality, quantity, and variety to be exhibited in New Zealand.

Nonetheless, a question emerged. Some of the type of contemporary lava lava that Ulithian women wear on an everyday basis, woven at home on their looms with big spools of colored thread, and which we had commissioned, were not in the package. This particular variety of lava lava was also to be included within the collection prepared in Ulithi to be sent to Te Papa in New Zealand. Fortunately, a few were included.

The Ulithian women were warmly acknowledged for their outstanding lava lava, which were then posted onward from UOG to *Te Papa* in Wellington. The Ulithian lava lava collection arrived safely at *Te Papa* with great appreciation and enthusiasm. The special exhibit at *Te Papa* on *Traditional Arts of Pacific Island Women* became a landmark event. Later, for us, an opportunity presented itself to make a polite inquiry about the matter mentioned above. Why, we asked the Ulithian women, were some of the contemporary thread lava lava that women regularly wear in Ulithi not prepared for the *Te Papa* exhibit? The response from the Ulithian women weavers was earnest and heartfelt. They explained: "The thread lava lava that we weave on our looms for everyday wear in Ulithi are ordinary items for us. They are not special. They do not belong in a museum!"

References

Barratt, G. (1988). *Carolinian contacts with the islands of the Marianas: The European record. Micronesian Archaeological Survey Report No. 25.* Saipan, MP: Division of Historic Preservation, Department of Community and Cultural Affairs.

Cusenbery, J. D. (Ed.). (n.d.). *The "Ulithi encyclopedia.* Ulithi, Yap, FSM: WVTY, Armed Forces Radio Station.

Davidson, J. M. & Minchall, D. (Eds.) (1993). *Traditional arts of Pacific Island women* (exhibition publication). Wellington, NZ: Museum of New Zealand *Te Papa Tongarewa.*

Harui-Walsh, E. (1979). Ulithi: Dancing and diplomas. *Glimpses of Micronesia and the Western Pacific, 19*(4 winter), 52 – 57.

Harui-Walsh. E. (June, 1984). Changes in the lifestyle of women in Ulithi, Micronesia. *Cultural Survival,* 81 – 88. (Reprinted in Walsh, 2013, 88 – 103.)

Harui-Walsh, E. (1986). *Status and roles of island women in the context of cultural change in Ulithi.* MA. Thesis in Behavioral Science, University of Guam.

Harui-Walsh, E. (1992). Lava lava of Ulithi. Collection archived in the Museum of New Zealand, Te Papa Tongarewa, Wellington, New Zealand. http://collections.tepapa. govt.nz/search?searchTerm=lava+lava+of+Ulithi&scope=all Retrieved July 3, 2017.

Lessa, W. A. (1950). *The ethnography of Ulithi Atoll. Final CIMA Report, No. 28.* Washington, DC: Pacific Science Board and National Research Council.

Lessa, W. A. (1961). Tales from Ulithi Atoll. *University of California, Folklore Studies, 13,* 1 – 493.

Lessa, W. A. (1962). An evaluation of early descriptions of Carolinian culture. *Ethnohistory, 9*(4), 313 – 403.

Lessa, W. A. (1963). The decreasing power of myth on Ulithi. *Journal of American folklore, 75,* 153 – 159.

Lessa, W. A. (1964). The social effects of typhoon Ophelia (1960) on Ulithi. *Micronesica, 1*(1), 1 – 47.

Lessa, W. A. (1977). Traditional uses of the vascular plants of Ulithi Atoll, with comparative notes. Micronesica, 13(2), 129-190.

Lessa, W. A. (1986). Ulithi: A Micronesian design for living. Prospect Heights, Il: Waveland Press. (also, 1966, NY: Holt, Rinehart, & Winston, Inc.)Martin, L. (1981). An approach to Central Carolinian aesthetics (1 – 104). Submitted to Professor Deborah Waite, Art 677, University of Hawaii, Manoa, Plan B Paper. Pacific Islands Studies.

Mulford, J. H. (1980). *Lava lavas of the Western Caroline Islands* (1 – 140). M.A. Thesis in Anthropology, California State University, Northridge.

Mulford, J. H. (1994). Review of exhibition publication: *Traditional Arts of Pacific Island Women,* J. M. Davidson & D. Minchall (Eds.), *Pacific Studies, 17*(3 – 4), 187.

Pacific Daily News. (2015). *Typhoon Maysak.* Guam: Pacific Daily News.

Spindler, G. & Spindler, L. (Eds.) (1977). *Cultures around the world: Five cases* (includes Ulithi, pp. 107 – 230). NY: Holt, Rinehart, and Winston.

Stephenson, R. A. (1984). A comparison of freshwater use customs on Ulithi Atoll with those of selected other Micronesian atolls. *Technical Report of Water and Energy Research Institute of the Western Pacific, University of Guam, 51,* 1 – 27.

Walsh, J. A. (April, 1979). Language and Change in Ulithi. *New Pacific,* 20 – 21.

Walsh, J. A. (Ed.). (2013). *Ulithi: A Micronesian anthology.* Yona, Guam: Bookmasters, Inc.

Walsh, J. A. & Harui-Walsh, E. (1989). Ulithian Lava Lava: Fabric of a Culture. *Guam and Micronesia Glimpses, 4th Quarter,* 12 – 15. (Reprinted in Walsh, 2013, 39 – 46.)

Welborn, S. & Bothmer, J. (1977). Lava lava: More than a simple wraparound, this woven skirt holds ceremonial significance. *Guam and Micronesia Glimpses, 3rd Quarter,* 23 – 25.

Acknowledgements by Eulalia Harui-Walsh (1993)

I wish to gratefully acknowledge Dr. Janet Davidson of the Museum of New Zealand *Te Papa Tongarewa* in Wellington for making it possible for the Ulithian Lava Lava Collection to be included within the special *Traditional Arts of Pacific Island Women Exhibit,* which opened on January 1, 1993. Dr. Rebecca A. Stephenson, Professor of Anthropology at the University of Guam, is thanked for her general assistance to this lava lava research endeavor during our UOG Field Team's research stay in Ulithi Atoll. Dr. Hiro Kurashina, Director of the Micronesian Area Research Center at the University of Guam, is warmly acknowledged for his guidance in the administration of the paperwork for the permanent donation of the Ulithian Lava Lava Collection to *Te Papa Tongarewa* in New Zealand.

ECONOMIC WELL-BEING IN A SUBSISTENCE ECONOMY:
PRODUCTION, MARKETING, AND MICRO-FINANCE
ON YAP PROPER AND FALALOP ISLET, ULITHI, YAP STATE

Ann Ames

This research is part of an on-going project focusing on innovative marketing strategies and micro-finance in Yap State. In 2007, 2008, 2010, 2013, and 2016, I went to Yap Proper with two other researchers (Dr. Todd Ames and Dr. Harley Manner) to conduct research on stakeholders' identified problems in production and marketing, as well as stakeholders' identified solutions. In 2008, 2010, and 2013, I went to Ulithi Atoll to continue my work on economic well-being, marketing initiatives, and micro-finance. Of special interest during this stage of data collection was change in small-scale atoll economies and the use of micro-finance as a market initiative. This paper focuses on some of the more fundamental issues surrounding production and marketing, particularly raw resources, management training and support, access to capital, export issues, local market issues, climate change,

and cultural economies. One objective of the paper is to identify problems and solutions associated with production and marketing by conducting a index between Yap Proper and Falalop Islet in the Ulithi Atoll. Another objective of this paper is to conduct a needs assessment for small-scale business development, in particular micro-finance on Falalop Islet, Ulithi Atoll. What are the similarities and differences in production and marketing? And, is there a need or potential for micro-market development on Falalop Islet?

Figure 1. Maria Luhudul (above) and Emanual Hadhomar (left) both provided outstanding assistance and insights to the research on Ulithi Atoll that was conducted by Dr. Ann Ames for this chapter, and also to other related research by Dr. Todd Ames, which is reported in other chapters in this volume. *(Ann Ames, 2008, 2010.)*

Central to this research is the development of micro-markets at the community level. Micro-markets are designed to improve upon the productivity of Yap State's informal food systems of exchange by generating employment and increasing family incomes. Micro-markets combine traditional forms of economic exchange already in place in Yap State with the continued development of monetary markets. Primary income generation is through crop production, linking subsistence with cash-crop cultivation. The continued development of small-scale business activities through production and marketing research benefit small and medium family farms by promoting subsistence and cash-crop production *plus* providing an outlet to distribute goods. Innovated marketing models, such as micro-finance, target low and no-income farming populations and is linked to economic mobility for members. But will this type of innovative marketing work on Falalop Islet, Ulithi Atoll?

Method

Setting

It is important to understand the general layout of the Islet to get a better understanding of the market's true nature. Based on observations during my various research trips, the following is an accurate account of the Islet's infrastructure in the 21st century.

Most homes are made of tin, with a few exceptions in which homes are made of concrete. Concrete structures also include the church, the men's house, the airport terminal, and the Ulithi Adventure Resort. The walls and roofs of such buildings are made of corrugated tin. For windows, owners cut three-sided openings in the tin, lifting up the resulting flaps and holding them outward with two-by-fours. With the exception of the airport-post office building, the medical dispensary, Head Start school, and the Ulithi resort, I have not yet seen windows with glass panes. There are some homes with split glass but very few. Most windows are cut in the tin siding and lack screens.

Most homes have doors. Looking inside reveals that floors are made of plywood. One informant reported having a tile floor. The Resort has concrete floors. I was told that many of the floors are concrete. Some of the homes were built on cinder blocks, lifting them slightly up off the ground. It appeared that a number of people sleep either on mattresses laid directly on the floor or box springs. There is very little furniture inside these homes, and only one person reported a refrigerator, and this is at the Resort. A number of computers were reported (used to play DVDs), and a number of fans are visible. Inside homes, individual bathrooms are apparent, including toilets and showers. This is quite different from Fais, another outer island of Yap State, where people rely on rain catchment to shower, and where there is no indoor plumbing.

Most of the people I interviewed reported that they cook outside with wood. Small outdoor cooking areas are evident throughout the Islet. Generally, cooking is done on the ground in a thatched area with a single black pot. Firewood serves as fuel. I did not observe propane tanks, stoves, or coal. The Resort, however, has an electric stove and microwave. I observed women collecting coconuts for cooking oil.

A number of the homes have pigs; fewer have chickens, and some cats. Even fewer homes have domestic dogs. Interviews took place in thatched areas outside the homes, generally the cooking area. There were large wooden benches to sit on, made of plywood and two-by-fours. Some of the thatched areas have looms for weaving and hammocks made of fishnets.

I was told there are four general stores on Falalop. Stores sell cans of ice tea, pineapple, orange, and strawberry sodas. Tinned meats (ham and tuna), cookies from Indonesia, and sea biscuits are available. These goods come in on the field trip ship. I did not see local produce being sold at the stores. It was reported that husked and cold coconuts are sold at the airport for 25 cents a piece. The Ulithi Women's Association also sells goods in their store at the airport, including hand-icrafts and thread. There was also a store in Asor village, but it has since closed down because the people running it moved off the islet. There is a coin-operated laundromat on Falalop ($1.00 to wash and $1.00 to dry) with three washers and dryers. The laundromat is most often being used to dry things. It is constructed of tin, with sliding glass windows, and a concrete floor.

The infrastructure on Falalop is far less developed than the infrastructure on Yap Proper. For example, Colonia, the capital of Yap State, has paved roads, con-crete homes, electricity, indoor plumbing, a hospital, the College of Micronesia, commercial and cooperative markets, small-scale family stores and micro-markets, and a micro-finance project known as Micro-Traders. Micro-Traders started in 2000 in association with Yap's Small Business Development Center (SBDC). The SBDC is partnered with the Yap State Department of Resource and Devel-opment, in partnership with the US Small Business Administration – sponsor of the University of Guam's Pacific Island's Small Business Development Center Network (PISBDCN). Evidence from related studies elsewhere supplied useful comparisons. Micro-Traders,[1] along with the PISBDCN's micro-finance project in Chuuk, and other micro-finance projects such as the P4K[2] in Indonesia and CARE[3] in Malaysia, provided guidance and comparative data that informed this needs assessment on market and micro-finance development on Falalop Islet.

Data Collection Methods

Methods of data collection included interviews, surveys, case studies, obser-vations, and stakeholder meetings. Interviews took place at respondents' homes and gardens. Surveys took place during Stakeholder meetings at the Small Busi-ness Development Center on Yap Proper and the Community Center on Falalop Islet. Stakeholders included subsistence producers, cash-crop producers, sellers, buyers, livestock producers, handicraft producers, women's associations, gov-

---

[1] For a detailed analysis of micro-finance in Yap, see Ames, A. (2012).

[2] For a detailed analysis of micro-finance in Indonesia, see Ames, T.T. & Ames, A. L. (2007).

[3] For a detailed analysis of micro-finance in Malaysia, see Ames, A. & Ames, T. (2010).

ernment officials, agricultural experts, and small business practitioners. Research assistants and translators also participated as stakeholders (Table 1).

Table 1. Methods of data collection and analysis.

Methods	Stakeholders/Data	Analyses	Indicators
Interviews	farmers	comparative	cultivation
	entrepreneurs	longitudinal	crop types
	business practitioners	statistical	crop quantity
Surveys	micro-finance members	profiles	crop values
	farmer co-opts		crop usages
	women's groups		amounts grown
Stakeholder	agricultural experts		amounts sold
Meetings	government officials		unit price
	extension specialists		incomes
	COM faculty		new crops
	COM students		inputs
			outputs
Case Studies	daily sale records	statistical	losses
	monthly sale records	descriptive	value-added
	yearly sale records		consumers
	inputs/outputs records		problems
			solutions
Observation	small farms	typologies	training
	medium farms		sustainability
	mixed/kitchen gardens		consumption
	backyard gardens		e-commerce
	crop cultivation		resource mgt.
	business activities		businesses
	community markets		markets
	entrepreneur networks		consumers
			needs
			produce quality
			added-value
			cultivation
			ecosystems

Results

Previous analyses of Yap Proper's Micro-Traders data, along with the PISBDCN's micro-finance project in Chuuk, and other micro-finance projects such as the P4K in Indonesia and CARE in Malaysia, are used as baseline comparisons for conducting the needs assessment for micro-finance development in Falalop.

A Comparative Analysis

Stakeholders' identified problems and solutions in production and marketing in relation to their contemporary island economies. Although membership in a farmers' association or other cooperative is very evident in the Yap Proper data, only 2 of the 30 stakeholders surveyed on Falalop indicated membership in a structured organization designed to promote crop and market production. Crops grown for family consumption were for the most part identical between the Yap Proper and Falalop data sets with the exception of spinach, corn, and sugar cane which were reported as a subsistence crop on Falalop. There is also much more of a variety of subsistence crops reported in Falalop than in Yap Proper. Several varieties of potatoes were reported on Falalop, including *Kimote Hadogmar* and *Kimeti Woleai*. Although Falalop stakeholders grew more subsistence crops than Yap stakeholders, there is without a doubt more market development in Yap Proper.

During my last trip in 2016, I observed several micro-markets in Colonia. One of these was the Micro-Traders market known as The People's Market. One of Micro-Traders' key indicators of success (2007 – 2013) has been The People's Market. The People's Market was, at one time, the only market in Colonia that sold local produce. Part of the marketing problems members said they are facing today is the number of other small vending stores that have opened up over the past several years. What you see now in Colonia, are several small stores that equate simply into more competition in crop sales. Interestingly enough, members and staff saw this as less of a marketing problem as demonstrated through their innovative solutions. For example, some of the original members of Micro-Traders said they are now taking their produce to the smaller shops to sell, taking on more of a middleman role then a seller role. Plus respondents said it eliminated the need to sit at the market all day. One staff member said she thought the opening of new local markets were helping members sell more because it gives members the opportunity to sell produce all month long (The People's Market is open twice a month). Nevertheless, members still rely on the micro-finance project, demonstrating innovative market skills as they continue to redefine themselves as markets shift.

Falalop stakeholders reported selling directly to the customers, the Resort, government employees, or to tourists; exporting items such as handicrafts, lava lavas, and marmars to Yap Proper, Guam, Pohnpei, and Hawai'i. One stakeholder reported selling copra to the Yap Cooperative Association (YCA), but said he no longer sells to YCA because they stopped coming to Falalop. Other markets in Falalop include the Ulithi Women's Association and small family owned shops. Pigs, copra, and coconut products such as tuba, vinegar, syrup, and oil were the top three items sold on Falalop. Pandanus woven purses and mats were also reported. As findings indicate, subsistence activities take precedence over cash-crop production in Falalop although the contemporary islet economy is definitely a mixed economy. Stakeholders' surveys indicate that economic opportunity, such as jobs off-island, has an impact on subsistence cultivation; followed by other impacts such as cash-crop production and wage labor. Limited land access and family obligations were also listed as problems in subsistence cultivation. Lack of arable land is also evident as a constraint in Yap Proper.

Yap Proper data were collapsed into three separate categories: Raw resources, training and support management, and access to capital. Below is a summary of the problems in production.

Raw resources. Needs or concerns were identified for:
1. More quality seeds suitable for island conditions;
2. More nursery facilities;
3. Lack of arable land;
4. Some people, like Outer Islanders, have no land for farming.

Training and support management. Needs were identified for:
1. Better support for disease management;
2. Training and materials to deal with crop pests;
3. More training for growing crops for market;
4. More training on how to do farming;
5. Training and benchmarks for produce quality.

Capital. Obstacles and needs were identified as including:
1. Limited capital to buy new tools and supplies, with the resulting need for low interest loans;
2. Many producers only grow enough to feed their families; so in order to have enough to market, they must increase production. To enhance production, capital is needed.

Member access to capital is a key indicator of success for any micro-finance project. Members of Yap and Chuuk's micro-finance projects, as well as members of Indonesia's P4K and Malaysia's CARE micro-finance projects all reported access to capital through the projects. Money was used to buy new tools and supplies through low interest loans, resulting in increases in production and family incomes.

Access to capital is evident in stakeholder data from Falalop, as are raw resources. Falalop categories that are not evident in the Yap Proper data include climate change and other economic and community activities. Below is a summary of the problems in production on Falalop.

Climate Change
1. Rising sea levels and salt water;
2. Drought, not enough water, flood;
3. Heat;
4. Dry weather;
5. Global warming.

Other Economic or Community Activities

1. No time after fulfilling community obligations;
2. Preparing children for school, baby-sitting;
3. Not enough time;
4. Taking care of the sick and old;
5. Government or DOE jobs.

Raw Resources

1. Poor soil;
2. Not enough space or land area for gardening (also evident in Yap Proper);
3. Lack of arable land (also evident in Yap Proper).

Capital

1. Limited capital to buy new tools and supplies (also evident in Yap Proper);
2. Need funds for fertilizer.

Most micro-finance models include access to capital to buy tools and supplies, like fertilizer, to assist with crop production. Micro-finance is not, however, designed to deal with climate change or other economic and cultural activities evident in Falalop. The more successful micro-finance projects are the ones that work within existing economic structures. In other words, if community obligations and subsistence farming are more important to community members than cash-crop production, then the amount of loans and loan group activities will be limited. With the exception of a few of the P4K projects in Indonesia, I have not seen micro-finance production as the one and only economic activity for members.

As noted, cash-crop production in conjunction with market development is part of a successful micro-finance project. The problems in marketing identified by stakeholders in Yap and Falalop are listed below. Yap categories include export issues and local market issues.

Export Issues

1. Shipping costs off-islet are too expensive;
2. Shipping and flight schedules are unfriendly to local producers wanting to ship;
3. Training is needed on how to ship crops and produce, and how to package them for shipping;
4. Better understanding is needed of outside markets in the region, like Guam and Saipan;
5. Better understanding is needed to overcome regional quarantine restrictions.

Local Market Issues

1. Some method for uniform pricing of crops and produce is needed;
2. Transporting crops and produce to market is difficult for many people;
3. An increase in local and regional market demand for crops is needed.

Stakeholders in Falalop Islet also identified export and local market issues as problems in marketing. Of interest to the discussion is the third category - economic and cultural issues.

Export issues

1. The costs of shipping off-islet are too expensive (also evident in Yap Proper).
2. A better understanding is needed of markets outside the region (also evident in Yap Proper).
3. Better access to transportation for moving products to Yap Proper is needed.

Local Market Issues

1. Transporting crops and produce to market is difficult for many people (also evident in Yap proper).
2. Increased local and regional market demand is needed for crop products (also evident in Yap proper).
3. The crops and goods available to market are limited.
4. There are no markets on the islet in which crops can be sold.
5. Rising sea-level.

Economic and Cultural Issues

1. Crops are needed for subsistence. Food for the family is more important than cash-crops.
2. There are not enough jobs to support buying over and beyond subsistence.
3. Cultural economies.

Taking into account the ways in which culture affects local economies is central to the analysis. Understanding and incorporating cultural economies into micro-finance designs is key to defining solutions to the problems in marketing. This is a greater consideration in Chuuk's micro-finance project (Ames, A., 2014 unpublished field notes) and it is echoed in the data from Falalop. As noted by one Falalop stakeholder, "Families do not sell, we share." And another Falalop stakeholder said, "In this kind of society, where everyone's related or knows each other, it does not seem right that I sell to my neighbor or relative. Everyone or most people ask for and expect to get from their friend or relative what they're asking for." As evident in Chuuk's cultural economy, getting what someone asked for became a big problem in terms of selling goods through the micro-finance project. The solution here was to have the goods in the store be owned by the micro-finance project, not the micro-finance member; hence, the goods are not theirs to give away. Because of this cultural practice, Chuuk's project as well as the CARE project in Malaysia is not as successful as Micro-Traders in Yap or the P4K in Indonesia. Cultural issues are evident in both the production and marketing problems identified by Falalop respondents, a red flag with regards to Falalop's micro-finance trajectory.

Before assessing the possible need or potential for micro-finance development on Falalop Islet, I want to briefly discuss the solutions identified by stakeholders in Yap Proper. These solutions are transferable in addressing some of the problems identified on Falalop.

Stakeholder Identified Solutions for Production: Raw Resource Solutions

1. Use of greenhouses with plastic roofs for new crops and palm fronds for traditional crops.
2. Arranging with individuals to donate or loan land.

Training Solutions: Internal

1. Producers can provide training to each other (through such organizations as the Farmers Association).
2. Government can help in training (through the Department of Agriculture and Agriculture Extension Office).
3. Better distribution of information, such as pesticide use (through the Department of Agriculture and Agriculture Extension Office).
4. Value-added training (Micro-traders and Small Business Development Center).

Stakeholder Identified Solutions for Market Issues and Export Solutions: Representation and Training

1. An agent is needed for the farmer's market who will arrange shipping and sales, and appoint a middleman.
2. Band together to form a cooperative, so as to be better heard by the government.
3. Set up workshops to build understanding of shipping and import restrictions and requirements.

Local Market Solutions: Community Supported Agriculture

1. Better financing is needed, or small loans such as micro-finance.
2. Existing educational materials need to be translated into the local language.
3. People need to be encouraged to buy local products in order to boost local demand.
4. Small-scale local markets are needed to sell agricultural and other goods.

POSITIVE FACTORS TO PRODUCTION AND MARKETING

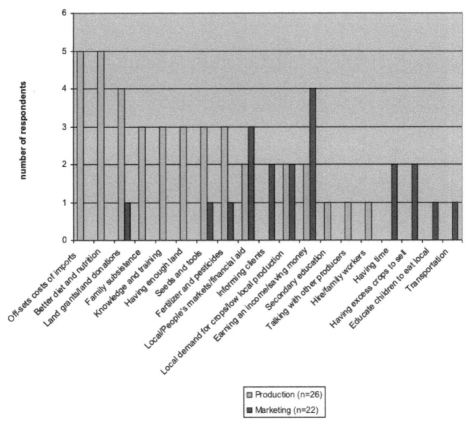

Figure 2. Positive factors to production and marketing.

Value-added training, better financing through small loans such as micro-finance, and the development of small-scale local markets to sell agricultural and other goods are parts of the micro-finance design. They would serve as a solution to some, but not all of Falalop stakeholders' concerns with regards to production and marketing. As noted in Figure 2, positive factors to production include: Off-setting costs of imports; better diet and nutrition; and contributions to the family subsistence economy. Positive factors to marketing include earning money and The People's Market, a part of a micro-finance design.

Solutions and positive factors for expanding production and developing markets are the underlying rationales of micro-finance, successful or otherwise. With this in mind, the discussion will now address micro-finance development in Falalop.

Discussion

Falalop Trajectory

The analysis above supports the idea of micro-finance as a solution to some of the problems identified by Falalop stakeholders. Access to capital is certainly first and foremost. Key also are the projects' contributions to family economies, earning money, and market development. There is very little micro marketing on the Islet, in terms of crop cultivation or marketing development. However, respondents did report selling to the high school, Head Start, Ulithi Adventure Lodge, individuals for local festivals, and selling small amounts of produce and handicrafts to Yap Proper. Goods are imported, generally from Yap Proper, and include gasoline. Respondents reported a need for market development to distribute canned goods, drinks, fuel, paper products, and the other products in general demand. There are three family owned stores on Falalop. The one pictured below is normally the only store opened.

Figure 3. General store on Ulithi that is most often open.

Rice, soy sauce, coffee, sugar, salt, batteries, tobacco, canned meats, and mosquito coils fill the store (Ames, Ames, & Manner, 2010). Respondents reported spending an average of $100.00 a month for such goods. As previously noted, there was limited cash-crop development reported for Ulithi. However, several other outlets served community needs for food products. Coconuts and bananas were collected and sold at the airport. The Ulithi Women's Association (UWA) has a store in the airport terminal and reported average earnings of $200.00 a month.

Micro-finance Development

Research respondents in this study said they would be interested in setting up a micro-finance project. Respondents wanted to borrow money to either: a) buy boat gas for fishing, and/or b) buy a baby piglet to then sell to the school. Respondents indicated that they would participate in a micro-finance project. As one respondent from Asor told me:

> Yes, we would really want micro-finance. Our small business would be small pigs. After we paid the money back, then we would use the money we earned from the piggery to buy a big water tank to catch water.

It is questionable whether there is a need for a micro-market to sell local produce, largely due to the abundance of subsistence crops and the lack of consumers.
Based on evidence presented in Table 2, crops are grown to fill community-based
needs such as subsistence, medicine, decoration/ornamental, rituals, and construction (Manner, 2008). What would be more likely to succeed would be the selling
of imported goods. Hence, a micro-finance model in Falalop would need to shift
its focus away from cash-crop production.

Respondents reported that the most marketable items were the following:
Cigarettes, candies, cooked food, rice, canned goods, drinking coconuts (husked
and cold), handicrafts such as bags and marmars, but not lava lavas. For handicrafts, a store would need to be set up in Yap Proper, and this would require having
an agent. Agents are evident in Chuuk's micro-finance model. Agents in Guam are
on the receiving and selling end, where fish and skirts are sent from Chuuk and
sold in Guam. Agents would need to be incorporated into Falalop's micro-finance
design, especially with regard to handicrafts. As noted by one respondent, "We all
weave lava lavas; we all have lava lavas."

In terms of market development, respondents said they would buy *Yot* taro,
sweet potatoes, vegetables, and pigs but only for special occasions. Respondents
said they would not buy breadfruit, chickens, coconuts, bananas, yams, papaya, or
cucumbers. Out of the three farmers interviewed on Falalop, subsistence farming
was reported - not cash-crop cultivation. Respondents said micro-finance would
be good for younger people who were stronger and who could pay back loans. In
terms of business development, access to capital is a very evident need and is a key
component of a micro-finance design:

> There is no money to start a business. That is why we do not start a
> business; no money for us.

In summary, respondents wanted access to capital and market expansion but
business development would revolve around selling imported goods. The selling
of imported goods does quite well in Chuuk's project (Ames, A.L., 2014) and
would need to be incorporated into a project on Falalop. Ulithi's family and community economies would need to take precedence over market economies. The
project would only help families meet subsistence needs and products sold would
need to be in demand by the community. Bananas and coconuts are not in demand,
whereas the market for rice, cigarettes, and coffee is established. This was evident
in Fais, where a tablespoon of instant coffee sold for 50 cents and one cigarette
sold for 75 cents. The most marketable crop in Fais is tobacco (Ames, A.L., 2009).

For micro-finance to be successful in Falalop, the design would need
to incorporate informal economies, such as family producers and sellers. These
are family economies where husbands and wives, and parents and children work
together in collective fashion, not as individual producers. The markets need to
be developed around informal community economies, not a formal market economy. With these factors in mind, the project could be very successful. The key to

Table 2. A listing of the species found in the gardens and agroforests of three Ulithi households.

Family	Scientific Name	Local name	Planters 1	2	3	Uses F	M	D	R	C	O	Comments and Notes
Apocynaceae	Plumeria rubra	Sour, Sowur	*		*		*	*				More often found in village sites.
Araceae	Alocasia macrorrhiza	Fôle		*		*	*	*	*		*	Giant taro, common.
	Colocasia esculenta	Ióth	*	*	*	*		*	*			True taro, found mainly in taro pits.
	Cyrtosperma chamissonis	Bwolokh, Buloh	*	*	*	*		*	*			Dominant aroid of the taro pits.
	Xanthosoma sagittifolium	Ióth minado		*	*	*						Presumed introduction after 1977 as it is not listed in Lessa (1977).
Arecaceae	Areca catecu	Bu, Buu	*		*		*	*	*		*	Stimulant, Occasional distribution.
	Cocos nucifera	Lu, Liu	*	*	*	*	*	*	*	*	*	Abundant food tree.
Asteraceae	Chromolaena odorata			*								Presumed introduction after 1977 as it is not listed in Lessa (1977).
	Wollastonia biflora	Eatheuth			*		*					Commonly found shrub. Listed in Lessa (1977) as Wedelia biflora.
Calophyllaceae	Calophyllum inophyllum	Fôtôi	*				*		*	*	*	Common, One of the largest trees on the atoll.
Capparidaceae	Crateva speciosa	Iabwuch		*	*	*	*			*		Occasional tree with edible fruit.
Caricaceae	Carica papaya	Bwebwae, Beabaay	*	*	*	*	*	*	*			Common, sub-canopy fruit tree.
Convolvulaceae	Ipomoea batatas	Kômôti, Komooeti		*				*				Abundant food plant with 9 locally named varieties.
Cucurbitaceae	Curcubita maxima	Kôlôbwäs			*	*	*					Squash, common in agroforests.
Cyperaceae	Mariscus javanicus				*							Presumed introduction after 1977 as it is not listed in Lessa (1977).
Dioscoreaceae	Dioscorea spp.	Palai, Iär	*		*		*					Two species reported for the atoll.
Euphorbiaceae	Acalypha sp.		*									Shrub with heights to 8 feet.
	Euphorbia atoto	Habwubwuleng			*		*					Spontaneous herb.
	Euphorbia hirta	Tekherokhar			*		*					Spontaneous herb.
	Manihot esculenta	Tiyohum		*		*					*	Presumed introduction after 1977 as it is not listed in Lessa (1977).
Fabaceae	Casssia occidentalis	Haeleng		*	*							Spontaneous herb.
Fabaceae	Vigna marina	Holu	*	*	*		*					Common vine of the strand.
Lamiaceae	Premna obtusifolia	Iar	*		*		*		*	*		Abundant mid-sized tree.
Malvaceae	Hibiscus tiliaceus	Hulifôi	*		*				*	*	*	Abundant midsized tree.
	Sida acuta				*							Presumed introduction after 1977 as it is not listed in Lessa (1977).
	Sida rhombifolia			*								Presumed introduction after 1977 as it is not listed in Lessa (1977).
Moraceae	Artocarpus altilis	Mäi; Maaey	*		*	*		*	*	*	*	Seedless breadfruit, abundant.
	Artocarpus mariannensis	Maifeul		*	*			*	*		*	Seeded breadfruit, common.

Table 2. A listing of the species found in the gardens and agroforests of three Ulithi households, *continued.*

Family	Scientific Name	Local Name	Planters			Uses						Comments and Notes
			1	2	3	F	M	D	R	C	O	
Musaceae	Musa spp.	Uch; Yuuch	*	*	*	*					*	8 local varieties of cooking and eating bananas.
Myrtaceae	Eugenia malaccensis	Harafath		*	*	*	*		*	*	*	Occasional fruit tree in village.
Onagraceae	Ludwigia octovalvis	Hól	*				*					Common in taro swamps.
Pandanaceae	Pandanus tectorius	Fach; Faach	*	*		*	*		*	*	*	Abundant tree of coastal sites.
Poaceae	Elusine indica				*							Common; grass of trail and waste sites.
	Pennisetum polystachon				*							Grass; presumed introduction after 1977 as it is not listed in Lessa (1977).
	Paspalum conjugatum			*	*							Grass: presumed introduction after 1977 as it is not listed in Lessa (1977)
	Unidentified grass	Siadome		*								
Polypodiaceae	Polypodium scolopendria	Chichi	*				*					Abundant fern of agroforests and open sites, often epiphytic.
Pteridaceae	Tectaria fernandensis		*	*								Large fern of salinized and abandoned swamps
Rubiaceae	Guettarda speciosa	Iuth	*				*	*	*	*		Mid-sized tree with multiple uses; common throughout the atoll.
	Morinda citrifolia	Lól	*	*	*		*	*	*	*	*	Small tree; fruit used as a starvation food and medicine.
Sapindaceae	Allophylus timorensis	Ngoi		*			*		*		*	Small tree of secondary woodlands.
Solanaceae	Physalis minima	Pengpeng		*	*		*		*			Spontaneous herb with edible fruit.
Urticaceae	Pipturus argenteus	Iourama	*	*	*		*		*	*	*	Common regrowth tree
Verbenaceae	Stachytarpheta spp.				*							Presumed introduction after 1977 as it is not listed in Lessa (1977).
	Unidentified shrub		*									
	Unidentified fern	Matalosi	*				*					On Fais, matalosi is either the introduced food, non-fern species, Rungia klossii and Cnidoscolus acontifolius.

Key: F= Food; M= Medicine; D=Decoration or Ornamental; R= Ritual; C= Construction; O= Other
1= Margarite (taro patch and surrounding agroforest (80m²);   2=Maria and Emmanual (taro patch and surrounding agroforest (150m²);
3= Marianne and Bian (garden, taro patch and surrounding agroforest (199m²)

Additional notes: Ulithian orthography after: Elbert, S.H. 1947. Ulithi-English and English-Ulithi word lists with notes on linguistic position, pronunciation, and grammar. United States Naval Military Government, photocopy; Lessa, W.A. 1977. Traditional uses of the vascular plants of Ulithi Atoll, with comparative notes. *Micronesica*, 13(2): 129-190; Mellen, N., and J. Uwel. 2005. Ulithian-English Dictionary, 38 pp.

Plant usage after Lessa (1977).
Data from Manner, H.I. 2008. Fieldwork notes.

that success is stakeholder input, stakeholder participation in the development process, and stakeholder assessment and solution contributions. Lastly, it needs to be remembered that micro-finance is designed to generate subsistence incomes only; the accumulation of wealth is not evident in Chuuk, Yap, Indonesia, or Malaysia. What is evident within these successful projects is a community-based economy, the final factor needed in any plan for a micro-finance design in Falalop.

References

Ames, A. L. (2012). Micro-traders: A case study of micro-finance on Yap Proper, Federated States of Micronesia. *Pacific Asia Inquiry, 3*(1), 102 – 115.

Ames, A. L. (2014). Unpublished Chuuk field notes on development and micro-finance.

Ames, A. L, Ames, T. T., & Manner, H. I. (2010). "Traditional Agricultural Systems and Emerging Markets in Yap, Federated States of Micronesia", in *Proceedings of the* 11th *Pacific Science Inter-Congress*, Haut Commisariat de la republique en Polynesie Francaise et Polynesie Francaise.

Ames, A. L. (2009). Unpublished Fais field notes on community-based economies.

Ames, A. L. & Ames, T. T. (2010). The effects of microcredit on the Orang Asli of Malaysia. In A. Goenka & D. Henley (Eds.), *Southeast Asia's credit revolution: From money-lenders to microfinance.* New York, NY: Routledge, Taylor & Taylor Group.

Ames, T. T., & Ames, A. L. (2007). The role of micro-finance and community development in Indonesia. *Micronesian Educator, 12,* 25 – 36.

Manner, H. I. (2008). Unpublished Ulithi field notes on species of Ulithi.

Field Notes from Ulithi

Todd Ames

Ulithi Atoll lies like an emerald necklace in the Western Pacific, with its verdant green islands and islets floating on a turquoise sea. Ulithi is part of the Outer Island portion of Yap State, Federated States of Micronesia. I first saw Ulithi in 2008 from a height of about 5,000 feet. We were flying in a Beechcraft Queen Air. This particular aircraft was one of two twin-engine Beechcraft passenger planes operated by Pacific Missionary Air Service, or PMA. Their two planes were made in 1968 and 1969, respectively, and have been beautifully maintained by PMA. PMA is the only regular air-service operating between the four Yap Proper islands and Falalop, Ulithi Atoll and Fais Island (another Yap Outer Island located about 40 miles east of Ulithi). PMA flies out to Falalop and Fais twice a week, or more often if there is a medical emergency or a charter flight. They also occasionally fly on to Woleai, further east. But often the flooded runway there precludes landing. PMA is a mission-based air-service, which operates in Yap, Palau, and the Philippines, to help provide better access to food, medical care, and educational services.

The Yapese operation of PMA provides the one regular locally available air-service to Ulithi and Fais. The cost for a ticket is a modest fee, about $120 each way. Most flights are operated to provide normal air service to the people of those islands, and for free medical emergency flights for local people. I was to find out later how important the flights could be for someone suffering a medical emergency. The only other way to reach the outer islands in Yap is on the field trip ship, which leaves Yap Proper once every 6 to 8 weeks. However, this schedule is not always followed, and could be changed due to bad weather, ship breakdowns, or (at one point) lack of fuel with no credit or money to buy fuel in Yap Proper. Islanders use the field trip ship to transport everything heavy, from building materials, boat motors, appliances, or large amounts of food supplies; as well as using it for passenger service. A trip with a deck passage to Ulithi takes about 24 hours but only costs $6. Cargo on the fieldtrip ship is considerably cheaper than sending it by air.

The trip by air starts in Yap Proper at one end of the commercial airport. PMA has its own building, hanger, and terminal. One needs to arrive early in the morning, about 8:00, for weighing in and loading of baggage. All passengers and baggage are weighed so the pilot can calculate maximum gross take-off weight. At times, some cargo is left behind if the entire load is too heavy for the plane. There is usually a festive atmosphere at the terminal when a flight is scheduled, with passengers arriving, friends and relatives coming to see them off, or to greet them on the return flights. Other people are coming and going to drop off cargo being sent out to the outer islands. This includes everything from tires, to building materials, to small appliances, to gasoline for boats and generators, to bags of rice. Occasionally bodies are sent back and forth on PMA, as most people wish to be buried on their home island. Once the plane is wheeled out onto the tarmac, it is fueled, then the luggage loaded, then the passengers. The plane only carries about eight passengers in two single-seat rows, with an aisle between them. On our flight Amos Collins (Figure 2) was the ticket taker, baggage loader, and pilot. I was lucky in that I was able to ride in the copilot's seat on this trip, which provided me with a fantastic view.

Once we were all stuffed into the plane, Amos ran us down to the end of the runway, ran the engines up, and did all of his pre-flight checks. Sitting in a small plane on a runway in Yap with no air conditioning is stifling. Once we started our take off run, we got a nice breeze through the cockpit vents. After takeoff, I got my first view from the air of Yap Proper, flying over Chamorro Lagoon before turning west. On the commercial flight in and out of Yap one arrives and leaves in the middle of the night, so I had never before seen Yap Proper from the air. Flying at 5,000 to 6,000 feet, it took about 40 minutes to get to Ulithi Atoll, 115 miles away. The Island of Falalop, with the only airstrip in Ulithi, is on the east end of the atoll, so you can see the entire atoll as you cross over it on the way to Falalop. We over-flew the airstrip and then flew in a wide circle around Falalop. While it provided a great view of Falalop (Figure 1), I was later to learn that Amos regularly did this both to warn people to get off of the runway, as well as to let them know the plane had arrived. As we completed our circle, we lined up for final approach and settled down onto the tarmac strip. By the time Amos had the propellers in reverse pitch, and the brakes on, we had reached the far end of the runway. The entire runway is only half a mile in length, so bigger planes are precluded from landing there.

Figure 1. Falalop from the air. (Photo by T. Ames, 2008.)

If the airport in Yap had a festive atmosphere, it was doubly so at the airport on Falalop. A number of people came down to pick up relatives; others to retrieve cargo, still others just to watch the plane's arrival and the passengers disembark. All around the terminal, small children ran and played. While there is a concrete, tin-roofed building that houses the terminal operations and the post-office, most people sat in the shade of an open-air thatch-roofed shelter next door which was far cooler and had a better view. On this trip there were three of us: Dr. Harley Manner, a geographer specializing in Pacific Island ecosystems and agriculture; Dr. Ann Ames, a sociologist and micro-credit specialist; and myself, Todd Ames, a sociologist (Figure 2.). Waiting for us was John Rulmal, Senior, who owned and ran Ulithi Adventure Lodge. John had one of only several cars or trucks on Falalop. We all piled into the back of his truck with our luggage, except for Ann who got to sit in the front. We drove across the runway and down a dirt road, winding between a number of houses, small buildings, and gardens. Most houses on Falalop are wood frame with corrugated metal roofs. There are a few buildings that are concrete, such as the church and the power station. Some are partially concrete, such as the public schools. The Ulithi Adventure Lodge is a delightful two story building with ten rooms set back about 100 feet from the beach. It has a second story with a wrap-around veranda, as well as electricity and running water throughout. It is one of the more comfortable places to stay in the outer islands of Yap. The downstairs contains the reception desk, a nice sitting area, a dining room, and a kitchen.

We were taken to meet Chief Yach of Falalop, an elderly man wearing a baseball cap. Our research assistant, Derwin Rolmar, explained to us that it was considered polite behavior to bring a gift, so we had brought several cans of Spam and corned beef. The chief politely listened to the explanation of our work, and gave his approval.[1] The next day we started visiting gardens, many of which were flooded taro

pits where Ulithians were growing giant swamp taro (Figure 3). In other places people were growing sweet potatoes and a variety of tree crops: banana, cassava, and breadfruit all mixed together (Figure 4). Taro pits were dug

Figure 2. Research team. *(Photo by M. Spencer, 2010.)*

into the ground between 18 to 24 inches below ground level. This allows them to fill naturally from the fresh water lens that collects below the soil surface. This lens is fed by rainwater, but if sea levels rise, or a storm surge goes over the island, it can contaminate the fresh water.

---

[1] See a 2010 photo of the Chief in Figure 7.

In the taro pit the water is usually 3 to 4 inches above the rotting organic material in the bottom of the pit. Where giant swamp taro is being grown, the taro plants usually reach 2 to 3 feet above ground level. Conducting transect measurements of the flooded taro pits became quite a chore, as it entailed wading around the perimeter, often in several feet of thick mud, covered by several inches of water.

Figure 3. Healthy taro pit with Harley Manner. *(Photo by T. Ames, 2008.)*

One of the taro gardens we visited was owned by an 80-year-old man, Immanuel, who told us that when the Japanese came to Falalop during World War II (WWII), everyone tried to cover up the taro pits with palm fronds and leaf debris to hide them from the Japanese. After the war they were able to uncover the taro pits and still recover much of the taro. He also told us how he and other men from Falalop were forcibly taken to Fais before the war to dig out phosphate for the Japanese. They were paid less then 10 Japanese dollars a month to do this. He also mentioned that his son was currently serving in Iraq, and that he was raising a pig to serve at a celebration for when his son returned home to Falalop. He told of another son living in Hawaii who sent him $50 a month. He and his wife used it to buy rice, sugar, soy sauce, coffee, and canned goods at one of the local stores on Falalop (Figure 5). For the other food that they consume, they take about five sweet potatoes a day from his garden. These are for him and his wife, one son and one daughter, and their families. He and

Figure 4. Falalop garden with H. Manner, A. Ames, and D. Rolmar. *(Photo by T. Ames, 2008.)*

his daughter also buy a 25-pound bag of rice every three weeks. They also eat banana and breadfruit. For him, his wife, and his son's and daughter's families, they pick and eat about three breadfruit every day, five to six big bananas each day, and three pieces of giant taro each week. He told us that he does not fish anymore, but that his son-in-law gives him some of the fish he catches. Immanuel went on to tell us that he collects five coconuts a day for drinking.

After several hours of measuring garden activities and crop densities, we would be dripping wet from sweat and the high humidity; so it was always a plea-

Figure 5. Store goods. *(Photo by A. Ames, 2008.)*

sure to return to the Lodge about midday for a swim and a cold drink. During our first stay at the Lodge, there were a number of other guests. There was a tour group that had come out from Los Angeles, who were staying on Falalop for several days and then visiting other islands in the FSM. There were also several men from the Navy's ordinance disposal unit. They told us that night that they were there to recover a missile that had been test fired and lost at sea off the coast of California. They had received reports from locals that it had washed up on one of the islands in the Ulithi Atoll. It always seemed much more likely to me that it had been lost from the landing area in Kwajalein, which is the US military site in the Marshall Islands from which missiles are test fired, as the lagoon there allows for their recovery.

Later on that night I heard several local men talking about the Navy personnel. One Ulithian man was mentioning how he had found the missile and removed its stainless steel nose cone, which had made a great chicken coop once he had cut a door in it for the chickens. His friend was warning him that he better take it back first thing in the morning, before the Navy men went out to the island where the missile had been found. Another was saying how it was too bad that the Navy had come for its missile, as he had been removing stainless steel screws and bolts, which worked great on his boat.

We continued our work the next day, measuring garden plots and categorizing crop varieties, and interviewing local farmers. One older woman, Maryann, whose gardens we visited that next day, told us that she and her daughter eat one to two coconuts a day, three to four small sweet potatoes, two to three small taro roots, one can of Spam if they have money, and usually buy a 50-pound bag of rice each month. She went on to add that her children who have moved away send her money each month, usually about $100. Of that, $20 is for the power bill, and the rest is to buy food from the store.

When visiting another garden site, one very industrious woman in her early 50s, Marguerite, told us that she collects one pick-up load of coconuts each week. She uses them for milk, grating, and for pig food. Her two pigs eat about eight coconuts each day. The little pig eats three and the bigger one eats five. Marguerite said that she was going to sell one pig, and keep the other to eat. She said that a large pig (150 pounds) would sell for about $200, whereas a piglet would sell for about $20. She also uses another three to four coconuts for drinking. Marguerite also told us that she grows taro, sweet potatoes, bananas, and breadfruit, and that she fishes twice a week. She sells some of her produce to the Ulithi Adventure Lodge when they have guests, and also to the local Headstart Program. She earns $10 for each banana stalk, $16 for a basket of sweet potatoes, and 25 cents per coconut. She also told us that she raises chickens and cats, (cats, she explained because they eat rats, which attack her sweet potatoes). Marguerite went on to tell us that she raised chickens, not for food, but for their eggs. However, other people have in the past come and stolen some of her chickens in order to eat them. She eats some of the eggs and keeps the rest to hatch and raise more chickens. Her husband works for the power company on Falalop, so they live off of his salary and what she makes selling her crops.

Most chickens on Ulithi are loose free-range chickens. Pigs are not penned, but tied by one leg and a length of line to a large tree. I was speaking to one farmer about penning up the chickens. He told us that there had been a demonstration project several years before with a visiting agricultural officer who showed them how to build inexpensive chicken pens. But when they tried it locally, having the chickens penned up in one area smelled so bad that no one wanted to do it.

I always went in for a swim in front of the lodge when we were done for the day. There were beautiful reef flats in front of the lodge, with extensive fish life. About 100 feet out there was a steep drop off where I encountered blacktip and whitetip sharks. I talked with the Navy guys later that night. They had apparently stayed up late the night before drinking palm wine (tuba) with some local men. So, they must not have gotten out very early to retrieve their missile.

The next day, I started to feel somewhat sick to my stomach. I assumed I had eaten something to upset myself. By that night I was quite sick, and developed a fever. By the next morning it was obvious that I had an infection in my lower leg. I had scratched it in the taro pit, and flies had bitten the scratch several times. I spent the next several days with a high fever and hallucinations. Ann would bring me meals and water. Ann and Harley continued the fieldwork, while I slept and hallucinated. The Navy guys kindly gave me some antibiotics they had and some antiseptic scrub, and the local public health nurse came by and gave me a bottle of penicillin. At this point my lower leg had swollen up considerably and much of the skin on my shin and calf were raw and oozing pus and blood. Our research team had originally planned on going on to the island of Fais to continue our work. I was game to go, but my two colleagues wisely vetoed that idea, and insisted I return to Yap on the next flight for medical care.

Harley did go on to Fais, for an eventful week. Once the flight had taken Harley on to Fais, the plane returned to pick up Ann and me for the return trip to Yap Proper. Ann took me to the hospital on Yap, where a visiting doctor from Papua New Guinea put me on intravenous antibiotics, with a heavy dose of oral antibiotics as well. I returned to Guam where I continued the antibiotics. The doctors on Guam ultimately decided that I had a combined strep and staph infection. Overall, it would be about six weeks before I was fully recovered.

The Work on Yap

Our research team returned to Yap in 2010 (Figure 2). This time we had been generously funded by the United States Department of Agriculture to address issues affecting production and marketing of crops in Yap State. Once again we flew out with Amos of PMA, on one of their Beechcrafts. It was a gorgeous flight between large cumulus clouds. Visibility was probably about 10 miles. This time we were picked up at the Ulithi airstrip by John Rulmal Sr.'s son, John Jr. John Sr. had passed away since our last visit. Becky Stephenson had mentioned this to us, and asked if we would visit John Sr.'s grave on Falalop and leave a shell necklace from her and her husband Hiro Kurashina as a memento and symbol of their remembrance of him. The graveyard on Falalop is made up of concrete slabs covering the graves, and also small concrete crypts. Near John's grave was another recent grave of a young

Ulithian who had joined the US Army and been killed in Iraq. As Francis Hezel has noted (2005, p. 3), "While the average death rate in Iraq for individual states in the US is 5 per million, the figure for Micronesia is

Figure 6. Stakeholders meeting. *(Photo by T. Ames, 2010.)*

25 per million, or 5 times the US rate." Across Micronesia and in Guam, many young people join the US Military because they see it as an opportunity for economic advancement, education, travel, and US citizenship. For many it offers the one sure way to leave their small island communities. Sadly, this young Ulithian's courageous decision had earned him a permanent place in the soil of Falalop.

Figure 7. Chief Yach of Falalop with Derwin Rolmar. (Photo by A. Ames, 2010.)

On this trip we were conducting a far more extensive survey of Falalop's gardens and we held several stakeholder meetings and problem solving workshops with Ulithian farmers (Figure 6). We again visited Chief Yach of Falalop, with Derwin Rolmar to gain permission for our research (Figure 7). Chief Yach listened intently to the expanded project we were conducting and gave his approval. To our delight he also attended the stakeholder meetings.

When we were measuring some of the taro pits on our first trip, we noticed that a few taro plants had been dying in the pits closest to the ocean. On this trip, many more taro plants were being affected and some of the pits in the center of the island were experiencing die offs as well. While talking to one of the farmers, and asking if salt water was seeping into the pits, he replied that, "No, the rising ocean is raising the water lens on the island and the taro is drowning in fresh water that is too deep. There are some taro pits closest to the ocean that are getting brackish from ocean water, but the ones in the center of the island are suffering from too much fresh water." I asked innocently if more organic material could not simply be added to raise up the level in the pits. I was told that it had taken almost ten years for the debris initially put into the pits to achieve decay. It would simply take too long for a new batch of leaves and fronds to decay and raise the bottom of the pits to save the current crops. (Reported earlier: Ames, 2013, pp. 9 – 10.)

One of the alternatives that the Ulithians were experimenting with was growing taro in tanks. We had noticed this on our first trip. Several landing craft had been left over from WWII. These had been filled in with organic debris and then successfully planted with taro. We were told that several years before our arrival a United Nations grant had been given to provide concrete to build some more above-ground tanks. These were being used while we were there. One drawback that was mentioned to us was that they did not naturally fill with water as do the below ground taro pits. If there is plenty of rain they fill on their own. But if it is dry for an extended period, the tanks have to be filled by hand. Then of course there is the expense of the concrete, and the difficulty of transporting it to Ulithi.

Building a *Wa*

One interesting activity that we stumbled onto on this second trip was a traditional *wa* (outrigger canoe) being built at the high school. We were told that it was part of an Australian aid project to provide basic health care education to local students. The students who took part in the training were allowed (as their reward) to work on building the *wa*. Once complete, it was going to be sailed to Yap Proper where it would take place in the Yap Day *wa* races. There were several master *wa* builders who were directing the construction activities next to the high school (Figure 8). While we were on Falalop, they had completed the main part of the hull and were attaching the planks to build up the sides and the carved bow and stern carvings of the tern's tail that is traditional for a *wa*. (A *wa* has no permanent bow and stern. They sail back and forth depending on which direction they are tacking.) The students and men had been using adzes to chop out the main hull from a log, and then to shape the side planks,

Figure 8. Wa builders. (Photo by T. Ames, 2010.)

bow, and stern fixtures. As in traditional construction, these additional pieces were held in place by drilling adjacent holes in the pieces and then lashing them together with sennet fiber made from coconut husks.

I had read that the various pieces had traditionally been sealed with heated sap from the breadfruit tree (LeBar, 1964, p.133). On closer inspection, I could see that the builders had been using heavy monofilament fishing line to lash the pieces together. I could also see a white sticky substance oozing out between two pieces of the *wa* (Figure 9). I asked one of the men working there if they were using breadfruit sap as a sealant? He chuckled and reached down next to the half finished *wa* and held out a long tube to me, "No, we are using this." Then he went back to work. I was looking down at a tube of white 3M Marine Sealant, something I was intimately familiar with myself. I use 3-M Sealant on my own boat all the time. It is a great sealant. I grinned to myself, thinking that this was a fine example of the Ulithians adapting modern products to their traditional practices. (Reported earlier: Ames, 2013.)

Figure 9. Ulithian *wa* detail. *(Photo by T. Ames, 2010.)*

A Wedding

In the Spring of 2013, Ann and I were contacted by Ann's friend Joliene Hasugulayag and her fiancée Derwin Rolmar (our research assistant on previous trips to Ulithi). Joliene and Derwin were getting married and they were inviting us to their wedding on Asor in Ulithi. We were told this would be conducted as a traditional wedding. We were thrilled to be invited and readily accepted. We had already planned on making a research trip to Yap that summer, so including a trip to Ulithi was easily manageable. We learned later that two of our friends, Becky Stephenson and Hiro Kurashina, would also be attending due to their long friendship with Joliene and her family. My mother Jan, who would be visiting from Denver, CO at the time, was included in the invitation when we told Joliene that she would be with us.

Once again arriving back on Falalop on the stalwart PMA Beechcraft, we were transported to the Ulithi Adventure Lodge to leave our belongings. This time there were several guests at the Lodge. Other than myself, Ann, my mother, Becky, and Hiro were staying there, as were several of Joliene's visiting uncles from Hawaii. As soon as we were checked in we had to leave for Asor, as the

wedding was that afternoon. We were taken down to the shore near the airstrip, where two 18 foot outboards and several other guests waited for us. There was a fair bit of surf and chop that day, so we gingerly waded out a few feet to one of the boats. Crossing the channel between Falalop and Asor was quite rough, with waves and spray breaking over the bow, soaking all of us who were sitting in front of the steering console. Hiro bravely took out his camera to take pictures on the way, risking it to a salt water soaking.

Figure 10. Hiro Kurashina, Todd Ames, Becky Stephenson, and Jan Ames at the wedding on Asor. *(Photo by A. Ames, 2013.)*

Once we reached Asor, we again waded ashore, with my mother and Becky being partially carried. We were very impressed with how my mother was treated. The Ulithians were so considerate to her and very impressed that an older woman (she was 85 at the time), would travel all the way to Ulithi from Denver and then take a small boat over to Asor. We walked on a path along the shore to the site of the wedding. The wedding was being held in front of a local school on Asor. A canopy on a frame

Figure 11. Wedding on Asor. (Photo by T. Ames, 2013.)

had been erected near the shore, with chairs underneath (Figure 11). In front of the canopy on the edge of the beach, a framework of peeled poles, holding up garlands of flowers and aromatic strands of local leaves arrayed the framework, which was also liberally decorated with cut palm fronds. A small cloth-covered table, strewn with flowers, was used as a pulpit by the priest. The ceremony was going to be conducted by a Catholic priest, assisted by a local catechist.

All members of the wedding party were attired in traditional dress: For the men this entailed a thu, or loincloth and a marmar (a flowered garland worn on the head); and the women wore *lava lavas* (the traditional wrap around skirt), *marmars,* and leis. In Ulithian society men and women are traditionally topless. Joliene wore a beautiful long-fringed lei, which kept her very modestly covered. She warned the guests several times however that, "I don't want to see pictures of me posted on your Facebook pages!" Once the ceremony was ready to begin, the guests were seated, with my mother being taken up to the VIP seating area, along with Joliene's mother, Becky, Hiro, and Derwin's aunt and uncle. Derwin's mother, father and other family members were also present. The ceremony was beautiful, with the priest and the catechist conducting simultaneous ceremonies, and the guests sitting next to us singing hymns in Ulithian. There was a steady breeze blowing through the palms, and the sound of waves could be heard breaking on the beach.

With the ceremony progressing, so many guests and relatives came up to take photos with digital cameras and video recorders that at times it was hard to see the ceremony, but it was all tolerated very good naturedly by the wedding party. I was rather surprised at the extensive array of electronic photographic devices. Considering that we were on an island with no regular electricity, the variety and amount of photographic equipment would have put any medium size department store to shame. Once the ceremony was completed and many more photos were taken of the wedding party and the relatives (Figure 12), a meal was served consisting of a mix of local and store bought foods, such as fish, taro, sweet potatoes, turtle, rice, sausage, canned meats, and local fruits.

Finally, after a colorful and exhausting day we made our way back to where the boats were moored for our return trip to Falalop. I was talking to one of the younger men riding back to Falalop with us and I asked him how the fishing was going. He replied, "In most places it is pretty good, but there are still places in the lagoon where ships were sunk during the war, and many of those places if you eat the fish caught there, they will make you sick. We think there are still chemicals leaking in some places." Being in such a beautiful and idyllic location makes it easy to forget that Ulithi, like many places in Micronesia, has a long history of occupation and raging battles involving Germany, Britain, Japan, and the United States.[1] During WWII, the Japanese routinely used Ulithi as an anchorage, until 1944 when Japanese

---

[1] Ulithi was first occupied by Japan in 1914, as Japanese naval forces swept through both the eastern and western islands of Micronesia, taking possession away from Germany. Japanese occupation eventually evolved into diplomatic annexation through a long period of political debate in which the Versailles Treaty awarded Micronesia to Japan; i.e., the Japanese Mandate. See Hezel (1995), pp. 146-156.

Figure 12. Wedding party on Asor. (Photo by T. Ames, 2013.)

forces were driven out and the US established an airbase on Falalop. There are a number of accounts of fierce air battles over Ulithi. While visiting Falalop, I have found small pieces of battered aluminum structures, which are clearly pieces of wrecked aircraft. Ulithi lagoon was also used as an anchorage for U.S. Naval forces from 1944 on. The U.S.N. *Missasinegwa*, a Navy oiler, was sunk in Ulithi lagoon and was one of the few casualties of the Japanese *kaitans,* or suicide submarines during the war (Mair, 2008).

Subsistence and Sea Turtles

After the wedding we stayed on for a few extra days to conduct some follow-up work on our earlier field research. During our discussions with local people, I asked one man on Falalop if they caught and ate sea turtles. He explained to me that one of the islands in the lagoon was an important turtle nesting site. If a person wanted to catch a sea turtle, he had to get special permission from the chief. In general, the turtles were considered off limits when they were coming ashore to lay their eggs. However, special permission could be obtained – such as for a wedding or a special feast. If someone caught a turtle without permission of the chief, then the turtle would be taken away and the person would be fined. It is worth noting that the Ulithians, like many indigenous peoples, are allowed under local law to take sea turtles for personal use. Certainly the tight controls imposed by the chiefs on sea turtle harvest, and the limited amounts that are taken, do not impose any great threat to the local sea turtle population.

These same practices of controlled and limited sea turtle harvesting are practiced throughout the outer islands of Micronesia. When Ann, Harley, and I were staying on Fais for research in 2009, early one morning our host Terry Palifer brought out a plate of what looked like cooked cubes of beef for breakfast. Without telling me what it was, she urged me to try a piece. I did and to my amazement it tasted like mild beef. I asked her where she had gotten fresh beef, as there is no refrigeration on Fais. She told me that a neighbor had caught a turtle the night before and given her some of the meat. She had also been given one prized egg, which she presented to me. It looked like a white golf ball, with leathery skin. I suggested that since it was such a treat we should save it for Ann who was not yet up (described earlier in: Ames, 2013, p.13).

Commerce on the Islands

A day or two after the wedding, we visited one of the two stores on Falalop, and spent several hours there with one of the owners. She explained that they made about $700 in sales per month. Their biggest selling items were rice, sugar, ramen noodles, coffee, and soy sauce. They currently bring in 80 bags of rice every 4 months. A 25 pound bag sells for $20. They also bring in eight 14 kilo boxes of sugar. A 2 kilo bag sells for $4.00. They also bring in 30 cases of ramen noodles with 24 packs of noodles in each case. The ramen noodles sell for $1.00 each. What the owners of this store do is to arrange with the other store to carry different items so they do not both stock the same items. We were also told that there had been a store on Asor, but it closed when the owners moved away. John Jr., one of the other owners, told us that they have had a long issue with people wanting credit. Family members, especially, wanted extended credit from their store. John explained to us that after the war, the people on Ulithi received large war reparation payments; in some cases as much as $40,000, $60,000, and $90,000. With these payments, many people stopped performing their subsistence activities. Now, John said, people expect the government to give them money and goods. John also noted that he will not bring in Spam and corned beef any more, but that is what people keep asking for. I asked John what wage paying opportunities there are on Falalop. He told us that income is very limited. There was a solar installation project, a coral reef research project, and a turtle research project; but those were all for short periods of time. There were also jobs teaching in the local schools, working in the community health clinic, and working for the power company. In all, there were only about 30 permanent jobs on an island of about 450 permanent residents.

Figure 13. Effects of salt water intrusion. (Photo by T. Ames, 2013.)

Climate Change and the Islander's Plight

One of the days after the wedding, we returned to some of the taro gardens we had visited on our first trip and were dismayed to see that whole taro gardens had since died. The local farmer we were interviewing confirmed to us that many taro pits now had saltwater intrusion (Figure 13 and 14). Just as worrying, one local

Figure 14. Farmer shows dying taro pit. *(Photo by T. Ames, 2013.)*

woman took us to see her prized breadfruit tree. She told us that in the last year it had become infected with some sort of white fly she had never seen before. These caused the leaves to die and breadfruit to fall off and rot before it became ripe. She said that the blight also seemed to be spreading to her coconut trees (Figure 15).

On one of our last days on Falalop, I took a walk around the southern and eastern shores, which are uninhabited. A lane runs around the edge of the island which people use to access the coconut groves there. Throughout Micronesia, people used to harvest coconut to produce copra. However, about 20 years ago, with competition from Indonesia and the Philippines, copra prices fell to half of their previous value. It just was not worth the effort to produce it in Micronesia any more. Now, as noted earlier in this chapter, people still grow and harvest coconut, but it is mainly for personal use. Many people rely on them for drinking. I was told by several people that in the dry months all they drink is coconut water. Several times when we were out in the field surveying gardens, our local companions would pick several coconuts for us to drink. I was told by one young Ulithian man that if you were really thirsty, it was alright to pick a coconut from someone else's tree, but it was not

Figure 15. Blighted breadfruit. *(Photo by T. Ames, 2013.)*

alright to take more than a couple. Coconuts are also widely used as a food source. Coconuts are grated and added to dishes, squeezed for coconut milk, and used to make oil. Coconuts are also used extensively for pig and chicken feed.

On the southeastern shore of Falalop, I came to a spot where the shoreline had been undercut and swept away by the ocean. Hundreds of coconut trees, now dead, lay in the surf. The road had been completely washed away for several hundred feet (Figure 16).

When I went back to the lodge I spoke to John Jr. and he explained that the erosion along the windward side of the island where I had been, had just happened the previous winter as the result of an extreme storm surge. He said that for his whole life the road had been there, and there had never been any shore loss like this. John Jr. said that he knew that some of the trees that were washed away were over 40 years old. The highest point on Falalop is only six feet above the high tide line, so Falalop and the other islands of Ulithi are particularly susceptible to being inundated by rising sea levels and storm based erosion. Before I left I talked to several other people on Falalop about the issue of rising sea levels. They were all aware of it and all knew about the case in Chuuk in 2008 when one inhabited outer island was completely swept over by a series of high storm waves. As one local Ulithian commented to me, "What are we supposed to do? There is no where else higher in Ulithi to go."

Figure 16. Shoreline erosion. (Photo by T. Ames, 2013.)

On our last night on Falalop, a woman came to the Lodge to tell the wedding guests that we were all invited to a traditional dance that they were putting on later that night. At the appointed time we all walked down the road to where the dance was to be held. Most of the Lodge guests and Ulithians sat on the front steps of several houses facing the road, others sat across the road in the grass and on lawn chairs. About a dozen women, and several children came out dressed in lava lavas with overskirts of palm frond fringe, marmars, and leis. They proceeded to dance for the next hour while singing a lovely melodic song in Ulithian (Figure 17).

The man I was sitting next to at the dance inquired what I did and I told him about working at the University of Guam. We got into a long discussion about how important he felt it was for his daughter to attend the University of Guam and he asked my advice about how she should apply for admission to the University. He went on to explain how he felt it was necessary for her to leave Ulithi, and get a good education so that she would have a bright future. I was impressed at this man's determination that his daughter would attend a university, despite it meaning she would leave Ulithi. As the dancing ended, and the singing faded into the night, we made our way back to the Lodge under a star-studded sky, with the palm fronds rustling in the wind.

Figure 17. Women dancing on Falalop. (Photo by T. Ames, 2013.)

Ulithi is the type of place that people dream about: Emerald isles on a turquoise sea, beautiful beaches, abundant fish-life, prolific vibrant reefs, coconut palms swaying in the wind, large cumulus clouds passing overhead, a very slow-paced idyllic lifestyle, and friendly, charming people. I think about Ulithi and I wonder when will I return?

References

Ames, T. (2013). Maritime culture in the Western Pacific: A touch of tradition. *Pacific Asia inquiry, 4*(1), 94-108.

LeBar, F. (1964). *The material culture of Truk.* New Haven: Yale University Publications in Anthropology.

Hezel, F. X. (1995). *Strangers in their own land: A century of colonial rule in the Caroline and Marshall Islands.* Honolulu, HI: University of Hawai'i Press.

Hezel, F. X. (2005, October). The call to arms: Micronesians in the military. *Micronesian counselor, 58.*

Mair, M. (2008). *Oil, fire and fate: The sinking of the USS Mississinewa AO-59 in WWII by Japan's secret weapon.* Platteville, Wisconsin: SMJ Publishing.

GLIMPSES OF ULITHIAN AND OTHER YAP OUTER ISLAND LEARNING TRADITIONS FOR CHILDREN

Mary L. Spencer[1]

Seated on a rock-studded coral beach platform, as the tide gradually crept closer to her, an American psychology professor prepared lecture notes and activities for tomorrow's educational psychology class. Most of her students, teachers and principals from a variety of Yap State's Outer Islands, were in the deep blue waters of Falalop Island, Ulithi Atoll, fishing for the beautiful silver skipjack that would feed them and others tonight. Tomorrow they and the two women teachers would join the professor at the Outer Islands High School (OIHS) where summer courses for educators were conducted by the University of Guam.

Observing the natural beauty, she picked up her field book and wrote:

> The tidal seashore on the windward side of Ulithi, with fluctuating wave heights swinging from low to high, reveals the luxurious depths of green splashing water. Rushing forward like clockwork in broad proud waves, it alternately covers and exposes rusty spam cans. The black, pocked, and pitted moonscape of a beach stretches out and looks with watery eyes toward the lapping shallows. The long continuous rim beyond is ever slammed, ever drummed by white froth.

Throughout the latter part of the 1970s and throughout the 1980s, the Yap Department of Education and the University of Guam (UOG) collaborated in implementing degree-oriented summer teacher training. For its part, UOG's College of Education (COE) maintained careful records of Yap's participating teachers, continuously updating information on which courses they had successfully completed, planning future schedules with statistics on the courses that were either a requirement for their education majors or an option for fulfilling UOG's General Education requirements. Based on this information, the courses with the largest number of potential enrollees were scheduled for the summer session – if faculty with matching teaching qualifications could be identified to spend much of the summer in Yap. Federal funds from both the waning Trust Territory of the Pacific Islands (TTPI) and the US Department of Education's Office of Bilingual Education and Minority Language Affairs (OBEMLA) supported the program. In 1985, at the time I sat on the beach preparing for class, UOG's College of Education was operating a very large OBEMLA contract, Bilingual Education Assistance in Micronesia (Project BEAM), which took its multi-lingual/multi-ethnic team of trainers and faculty to all entities in Micronesia to respond to the requests of the school systems for various types of training and technical assistance.

Because I am a psychologist specializing in cross cultural child development, testing and assessment, and bilingual education, Robert Underwood, Director of

---

[1] Mary L. Spencer is Dean Emerita of the College of Liberal Arts and Social Sciences, and Professor of Psychology and Micronesian Studies (Retired), University of Guam, Mangilao, Guam. class_uog@yahoo.com

BEAM, determined that the Educational Psychology and Evaluation courses would be appropriate courses for me to teach. However, he and the COE Dean, Michael Caldwell, were somewhat worried about whether I would collapse under the burden of culture shock and four to six weeks on location. They turned to our colleague, Tony Tawerilmang, an indigenous Woleaian scholar of Micronesian language, culture, and Pacific Island education, for his assessment of my potential. Tony had already been my culture teacher and "minder" on multiple training trips to islands

Figure 1. Falalop Island, Ulithi Atoll, December 7, 2004, 10° 01' 01.96" N, 139° 47' 24.40" E, elev 6m

in both Eastern and Western Micronesia. I was proud to know that he thought I could be trusted to go to Ulithi, a more traditional and remote outer island, not offend the people, and actually serve as a relevant and effective instructor. Nevertheless, Tony and Robert determined it would be wise to have Tony drop into Ulithi about half way through the summer session to see how things were going.

Objectives and Goals

Beyond the priority of the course preparation and instruction, I hoped to carry out several research objectives as well. My method would be to conduct and document naturalistic observation. Foremost among my topics for observation were the following: Socialization to literacy; children-parent teaching/gendered behavior and issues; and interrelationships of language, culture, and education. I aspired to develop notes and a formative first-hand understanding of some or all of these topics that could serve as a foundation for later more full-bodied research activities. I also engaged my students in the exploration of the learning traditions in their own com-

munities. Although I could not have forecast it at the time, my field notes, photographs, and memories of the children, families, and educators on Ulithi in the summer of 1985 would congeal into one of several perspectives from the field that guided my research,

Figure 2. One of my 1985 Ulithi UOG classes with Yap Outer Island educators.

teaching, and administration in Micronesia for the next 30 years.

Children and their Activity Groups

My opportunities to observe children often occurred when I could approach a naturally formed grouping of children. Because I seemed to be such a novelty in the community, some of my observations seem very "me-oriented" as children registered reactions to me. This is also true because I was trying to find my way, trying to find strategies for achieving non-disruptive observation.

Figure 3. Another of my 1985 Ulithi UOG classes with Yap Outer Island educators.

6/28/85 Field Notes

On arrival at the Ulithi airport following the Pacific Missionary Airlines (PMA) flight from Yap, many children stared at me as I sat waiting for two of the male teachers who made arrangements for my luggage. Later, at the house where I was assigned to stay, the four children seemed to simply ignore me – continuing their group play, the little eight-year old girl, Julita, paying more attention, hanging around the table where I was talking with Rita and Juanita, women who were making me comfortable and welcome. Later, at the OIHS office, three year old

Cass hung around watching me as I talked with two of the male educators who administered the summer courses. She had a package of gum and slowly made her way to an interaction with one of the men in which she offered him a piece of gum and handed it to him under the table where we were sitting. He suggested she give a piece to me. She told him (in her language) that she was afraid of me. She seemed to make a few approaches to me as we continued to talk, but always withdrew.

Later in the afternoon, I walked over to the "musical group" where I sat and quietly observed. At first they noticed, accepted, and seemed pretty unaffected by my presence. But later, as they selected songs, especially for my reaction, I could see that they were to a substantial extent directing their behavior in ways meant to impact and please me. Much more of this happened today. The little girl in this group wants to be near me, touch me, interact with me. She initiated a hair combing session that ended with a small ponytail on the top of my head. Others – all boys – want to display their skills and interests to me – and to entertain or teach me. Of course, I am far from the only thing they have on their minds, but when they react to me, it is in that way, at least today.

The music group. The sounds of a small band could be heard from the little thatched hut 30 feet from the house. About 8–10 children had been gathering there. The hut is about 8' x 5' and about 8' high from ground to top exterior beam. It is open and seems a perfect size for children, although it is often used by adults as well. The children have a collection of empty tin cans used for drums. Most have a plastic top. The cans have been modified for sound – some gouged; some with the bottom gone; one with an additional lid tied with a cloth string, a cymbal like apparatus. Clarence, a very small boy, used a large sardine can with a ribbed bottom – running a stick over it to get a washboard sound effect. The group seems to have a repertoire of 10 to perhaps 20 pieces. Not all of them know all of the pieces, but that seems to be part of the fun – teaching one another. Some songs are paired with specific dances. Some have specific percussion patterns. Most of the songs are in Ulithian, a few in English with the English mixed with Ulithian passages. There seemed to be some aspects of the activity, such as drumming, that were reserved for the boys. Julita was welcome in the predominantly male group and she was often a song leader. She may know the dances better than anyone. The group was very cohesive most of the time – sitting close, speaking one to a subgroup or one to the whole group, with varying speech initiators. The main tasks at hand were: 1) to select a piece to perform via discussion or a false start for demonstration; 2) to try out the piece, teaching some who do not know the words, trying to get the tune and instrumentation straight; or 3) ceasing if someone or more persons decided it is a failure or are not interested in it. In watching them learn together, I saw the main drummer make a trial pass at the percussion part of the score – some kids showed or told about changes or additions they were suggesting. The main drummer then incorporated some of these. For words, I saw one child make serious eye contact with another, saying the words more slowly than usual, trying to synchronize

Preschool boys explore picture books while visiting author at Principal's home

Three young girls following their swimming session in the ocean

Figure 4a. Sampling of Ulithi children's activities at varying ages, by girls and boys, and in varying contexts, including some visiting children from other Yap Outer Islands. *(Photos by Mary Spencer.)*

with the other child's prediction effort. When the learner stumbled or erred, one child-teacher ignored. Another corrected and required another try. The children's attention spans were quite long. They were engaged in this activity intermittently all afternoon. I sat with them about 3:00 pm and they did not disperse for 40 minutes. There were some comings and goings among the group members, but the group had at least five constant members. One mover did not make music, but instead climbed the supporting poles and the rafters. A young boy,

Young girl and boys enjoy playing in a sand pile near their home

Boys and girls, ranging in age, stroll a path on Falalop Island, as part of their common "hanging out" activities

Figure 4b, Continued sampling of Ulithi children's activities at varying ages, by girls and boys, and in varying contexts, including some visiting children from other Yap Outer Islands. *(Photos by Mary Spencer.)*

Clarence, played quite independently around the group, trying only occasionally to make music with it (as with the sardine can). The children entertained me and then played a good trick on me. As I sat there listening to their songs and watching their dances, they suddenly began singing in unison: "We don't smoke marijuana in Muskogie, and we don't take no trips on LSD." They broke up laughing at my shocked reaction. Next they sang, "She'll be comin' round the mountain." I believe that most of the children in this musical group are from Mogmog, Ulithi, just staying on Falalop temporarily with relatives. My new friends include Julita (8 years old, 3rd grade), Julian, Walter, Norman, Quincy, Vana, Clarence, and Roland.

6/30/85 Field Notes

More music. On this occasion, I observed a direct teaching lesson between eight-year old Julita and a younger child, Alton, that took place by the steps of the Principal's house where I stayed. They sat cross-legged, facing each other, each with a two-foot stick in their hands. Julita was trying to teach Alton one of the sitting stick dances. She made intense eye contact with him and they began their rhythmic chant slowly – trying to hit the ground and then hit one another's stick at the right time. The hardest part seemed to be alternately striking the stick by either your right or left knee, according to the pattern of the song. Julita was a split beat ahead so Alton could imitate her. When it looked like he was getting it, she increased the pace ever so slightly. Once he struck several stick strokes correctly, she appeared to relax a bit. Then he erred, striking the stick in the wrong direction. She took her hand and moved his stick to the right place without expression. Then they proceeded for a few more strokes. He erred again. Now her face and head movement show exasperation. She again moved his stick to the correct position and manually moved it through more sequences as she talked the words of the song. After a few more attempts, each ending with Alton erring, they agreed to go do something else.

Figure 5. Ulithi families and children maneuver their boats to ferry out to a ship that has anchored briefly off shore to supply the island. *(Photo by Mary Spencer.)*

7/1/85 Field Notes

Singing and drawing. I found a group, including some of the same children observed in earlier music activities, sitting on a piece of plywood on the concrete patio behind the house, facing the ocean. There was a bit of singing and drumming going on. I sat down at the corner of the plywood and listened. I had paper, pen, and pencil with me. The children started singing a local version of the 12 days of Christmas in Ulithian. I started taking notes on each day of Christmas as they sang it. They took a great deal of time with me, helping me get the words for each day understood phonetically, then transcribed, then vocalized. As with Julita's earlier instruction with Alton, eye contact was involved, along with slow motion speaking and repetition of the words. I write; I say. If I am not close enough, they repeat the words, separating each syllable, and emphasizing the ones giving me trouble. They wanted me to pronounce correctly. They seemed pleased when I could sing along with them. Then I started asking the meaning of each of the Christmas gifts mentioned. They said the "haluf" was a crocodile. It turns out that it was probably a monitor lizard. I drew a picture of a coconut tree and a lizard. They took the pencil away and drew a better picture. Then one boy, Norman, drew an excellent picture of a swordfish on the plywood. I gave him paper and he drew another one, with a diploma in its mouth. As he drew, the other children entertained themselves by forming a group wheel, heads in the center, bodies forming spokes. Some of them rose and abruptly left. Shortly afterward, they returned with Rolan's excellent drawings. He offered three pages of drawings to me and told me to choose one to keep. Then he drew a picture for me of Jesus on a new page.

The Kung-Fu group. One afternoon after classes, I spotted a group of children hanging out at the "graduation area." This is a clearing near the school where graduation ceremonies are held. I walked over and found Julita and Sylvia sitting the activities out as each boy tucked his *thuw* (loin cloth) up high and undraped, practicing throwing one another to the ground in the sand pit area. At first I wanted to watch closely to see if this could really be part of something traditional. But soon it was clear that this was an effort to practice some type of Asian martial art. Several times someone got the wind knocked out of him and lay there feeling badly. Each time, one of the children came and comforted the child until all was well. Then there was an extended tree chase in which one boy was high in the tree, holding a long stick. Clarence tried to climb after him, always getting outsmarted. The tree suffered a number of broken branches, and Clarence got no satisfaction, but everyone else was an onlooker. Then the children regrouped on the raised concrete stage with one child dividing the boys up, half on one end and half on the other end. Then one boy from each end stood on his hands, walked to the center, and kicked the other as hard as he could until one toppled. Then a new pair of boys walked on their hands toward each other.

The girls obviously could not join this activity because their lava lavas would be upside down, exposing everything. Later on the back terrace, where I was going to sit and read, I encountered an upended child doing the handstand. It was Sylvia with her lava lava tucked up – almost *thuw* style. She acted a bit scared as though she had been caught red handed. I winked and smiled at her. Later, I showed her a photograph of my daughter Laura doing gymnastics.

by Norman

by Rolan
Figure 6. Ulithi children's drawings.

This observation of the Kung Fu group took on more importance later when there was a parent-community involvement workshop held on island in which the imported videotapes became a major topic of discussion. The participants were first briefed on how to count acts of violence, and to look for the role of women and the purpose of violence. Then the tapes were shown. The result was very revealing to the participants, judging from later discussions in my Educational Psychology class. One educator said, "TV is the best reinforcement," meaning that it is the most liked activity. But the prevailing view was that TV had to be controlled somehow. (There is some irony in this view because Falalop, Ulithi is a fairly remote Atoll island with limited electricity and access to imported television equipment and videotapes, but it reflects the feeling of some families that they have little control over what is brought to the island.) In a later discussion about this with a culture teacher from Mogmog, he said the Kung Fu video presented still another problem: "In our culture, we don't like to tell children they can't do something. So, if they want to watch, it's hard to stop them."

Mid-July Field Notes

The young group. By mid-July the older children of the previous groups had either returned to Mogmog or were spending more of their time in the village on the side of the flight tarmac opposite the area around the OIHS. The dominant group of remaining children near the school included Arvin, the three-year old son of a young Woleaian administrator from Yap DOE who had come to make preparations for the parent-community involvement workshop. Bright-eyed, curly haired Arvin had long eyelashes, a ready smile, and a gently mischievous turn to his behavior. He was popular with the teachers as well as other children. In the absence of the older children, Arvin, Clarence, and a few other small ones were left to take over the territory. Whereas they had previously sat on the sidelines, now they created their own group activities. Although their performances were not as polished as those of the older children, now they practiced and exerted their own personalities without the constraints of the older children's privileges. Two small girls were usually included in the group. Once I observed them practicing dance in the graduation area for 30 minutes or more. Most often they played in a sand pile under a tree. (Sand and gravel had been hauled to an area near the house where I stayed where more teachers' housing was being built.) At times they would bury one another's legs. At times they concentrated for 20-40 minutes on digging holes with broken coconut shells.

Later July Field Notes

A home visit. One day Arvin, Clarence, Romeo, and Marvin, a slightly older boy, all walked into the living room of the house where I was staying. As was typical of children of this young age, only Marvin wore clothing. Since this is the home of the Principal, who is currently off-island, I assumed that the children had been here on other occasions. They spent some time just sitting and "reading" the predictable text picture books that I had brought with me for demonstration in my classes. Arvin found my navy blue NIKE tennis shoes with Velcro fasteners and wore them about the room as his only clothing. Clarence liked the books upside down. The Sesame Street book was particularly popular, perhaps because videotapes of Sesame Street programs have been shown on Ulithi. After a while, the boys opened a cupboard that I had not even noticed before and discovered that it was full of toys. They pulled everything out and played both cooperatively and independently with the toys for at least 20 minutes. Two of the children's mothers came to fetch them, but the children were not inclined to leave. One boy kept looking at the toys and seemed to be refusing to make eye contact with his mother. She reached toward him as if to pick him up from the chair. He quickly pulled away and she just as quickly withdrew her hands. My perception was that she felt constrained from commanding him to go with her, or from carrying him out physically, although he was physically small enough for her to lift and carry him. Her next step was to call the older child back in and ask him to disengage his little friend and help her get him home. This brief moment of mother-child tension surrounding the mother's request for his compliance presented an interesting topic for analysis of culturally affected learning/teaching style and familial negotiations. One possible explanation could be that in some families children are given a great deal of credit for being able to direct their own behaviors judiciously and without interference from parents. It occurred to me to wonder if the same narrative would have occurred if the child had been female.

Language and Literacy

The Spoken Word and Rules of Silence

Providing instruction in the assessment of children's language proficiency was one of my instructional duties. Gauging a child's speaking proficiency in any language requires that the child must be induced to talk. If she does not talk when prompted by the examiner, it is virtually impossible to draw an accurate conclusion about whether this is because she can speak fluently in the target language but simply chooses not to speak; or conversely, does not have the language competence to speak. At the time I was teaching language assessment in Ulithi, the remedy I recommended for the lack of vocalization of the child was to begin the assessment session with rapport building activities, making him or her feel comfortable, allowing the child to play with appealing toys, and gradually building some conversational give and take. Another approach was to explore whether assigning a gender-matching or culture-matching examiner increases the child's speaking performance. I presented these strategies to my students and I still believe they are appropriate. But I was beginning to understand that another dynamic was at work. Children's silence is not always just a manifestation of shyness, fear of the examiner, or discomfort with an adult with different language and ethnic-racial characteristics. It could also be part of a larger pattern of language behavior suited to cultural rules for context determined orality; something like the familiar old fashioned rule in Anglo-American homes, "Speak when spoken to;" i.e., speech needing familial and contextual cues.

I began to notice that something larger was at work in regional contexts when Nelia Vela and I were conducting research assessments of Chamorro language proficiency in Inarajan Village in southern Guam in 1984 (Spencer, Palomo, Vela, 1987). When we saw children in more contexts and with a variety of other role players, we suspected that a child who was completely silent in a school assessment situation might have a larger speaking vs silence repertoire in varied family and community contexts. If this is true, it is possible that the language proficiency of children can be seriously underestimated by traditional language testing. Another regional example of this is the statement of respected researcher Ann Fischer on Romonum, Chuuk Lagoon in her research shortly after World War II (1950). She suggested that Romonum children may be language deficient because her field records showed low levels of orality. This hypothesis was unfounded because of her lack of systematic observation of the children. It was certainly not supported by my recent recorded language observation samples of children on Romonum (Spencer, 2015). Unaisi Nabobo Baba has researched silence patterns in the social life of her native Fiji. She has provided a taxonomy of silence that would be a useful starting point for validating and developing a clearer picture of child silence patterns in the various Micronesian cultures (2006). I detected hints of these patterns during my observations of the everyday life activities of Ulithi children: Silence while in the presence of adults, particularly those of high status, until explicitly called upon; fully active and spontaneous speaking and verbal interchange during the activities of the children's groups.

The Written Word

In the study of language in a society, it is usually appropriate to first examine the structure and content of the language in its oral form - speaking and listening – because the codification of a language into reading and writing occurs much later, if ever. Many of us take the spelling of our languages for granted. However, for people with a language that is in the process of having a literate form of their oral language created, nothing can be taken for granted. This has been very true for the languages of Micronesia. Approaches to spelling – known as the creation of an orthography – is usually directed by a linguist or perhaps by missionaries. The linguist and missionaries are most often outsiders. The successful adoption of the orthography will depend significantly on the ability of the person leading the orthographic project to involve and be guided by the opinions of the indigenous language community. The University of Hawaii PALI dictionary projects in Micronesia were admirable in the steps taken to engage a team of indigenous Micronesian linguists in formal academic linguistic training, and to then employ their talents in the development of dictionaries and reference grammars. The Yapese and Woleaian materials were early successful examples of this process (Jensen, 1977; Jensen, Iou, Defeg, Pugram, 1977; Sohn, 1975; Sohn and Tawerilmang, 1976). Work on the Ulithian materials had not come to fruition at the time of my 1985 teaching visit. However, in 2002 the Yap State Education Enterprising Department (SEED) published the *English-Ulithian Dictionary 1,* edited by Mariano Laimoh. Following is a discussion of the emergence of literacy in the Outer Islands of Yap.

Socialization to Literacy

The topic of socialization to literacy came to my attention when I was working with language minority children in California schools. My colleague, Eduardo Hernandez Chavez, had written about how academic success for the children of Hispanic and Native American families in American schools required much more than simple instruction in reading and writing. He saw literacy in those settings as a broader and more complex cultural development. Access to textbooks and instruction from well-trained reading and writing teachers were not sufficient to engender deep family and community commitments to literacy learning. For students living where the livelihood and well being of the family depend upon the development and application of manual skills, and/or coordinated group work – as is often true of family farm situations – the type and content of literacy and the practical uses of this literacy will suit local economic and cultural needs. What is generally considered by American educators to be literacy may be quite limited where families do not feel it creates concrete advantages.

The term "socialization to literacy" connotes the welling up of reasons, circumstances, and means that influence the growth of what we traditionally consider to be literacy in a society at both a macro and micro level. In the remote insular contexts of the Outer Islands of Yap, the spoken word has reigned. Long before European missionaries brought their forms of literacy, the indigenous peoples of these islands developed sophisticated oral methods of communication, logical elaboration, and historical recording.

Another facet of the concept of literacy that I have discussed elsewhere (Spencer, 1996) is the possibility that the graphic symbolism involved in modern literary material is part of pictorial traditions; e.g., pictograms in Chinese lettering; drawings used to communicate and document as in ancient Chamorro and Polynesian petroglyphs; or abstract representations establishing rank or telling a story in woven fabrics or tattoos such as those found in Indonesia or the Outer Islands of Yap.

In my 1985 stay on Ulithi, I hoped to have opportunities to notice the different types of literacy apparent throughout the various sectors of the community and how literacy development was currently being nurtured. My observations on this topic were limited because of my short stay and busy schedule. However, observations from that trip, when combined with those of subsequent trips and exploration of historical and new materials create a useful foundation.

The Written Ulithian Language

Ulithian was a mostly unwritten oral language at the time of my teaching assignment on Ulithi. Where I found it, written Ulithian seemed to be prepared in almost individualistic versions. Very little public material seemed to be written in Ulithian. However, my students told me that they all wrote letters and kept notes on various things by using their personalized form of the Ulithian language. During my stay, one of my students left island for a meeting where she would help translate the FSM constitution into a written form of Ulithian.

There is a post-contact history of Ulithian dictionary development, going back to the document developed by the famous Pacific linguist, Samuel H. Elbert, when he was Lieutenant Commander, US Navy Reserve, US Naval Military Government, January 1947. It included Ulithi-English and English-Ulithi word lists of more than 900 words, as well as notes on linguistic position, pronunciation, and grammar. His instructions to native speakers of the Ulithian language indicate that he intended them to be the primary audience for the book. In the introduction, he shares some interesting language information for the time:

Introduction:

This is the fifth study made by Naval Military Government of languages of the Micronesian area formerly mandated in Japan. The field work was done during one week spent at the village of Fassarai in November 1945.

Ulithian is spoken by 418 people on Ulithi and 236 on Fais. The natives of the Woleaian-Satawal area, 1,134 by one count, speak related dialects. On Ulithi itself there are two dialects, one spoken at Falalop and Asor, the other at Fassarai and Mogmog. The differences are slight, usually in the quality of the vowel.

In the 1970s and 80s, a major collaboration was underway by indigenous and academic linguists to create a series of dictionaries and reference grammars in Micronesian languages. Known as the PALI series, it was funded and managed by the TTPI and the University of Hawaii. These volumes were fundamental to the development of bilingual education materials, curriculum and instruction plans, and teacher training throughout the islands to which they corresponded. However, the work was often controversial among some portion of the receiving communities. Commonly, complaints were made when the PALI spelling system for an indigenous language was different from the spelling system used in earlier religious materials in the indigenous language. Other complaints arose when linguistic devices such as double vowel lettering were used to signal subtle vowel usage on the grounds that it made the words too long. Although work on a Ulithian PALI dictionary was underway at the time of my Ulithi assignment, it was not completed in that particular format (see Laimoh, 2002).

Field notes on local dictionary development. One of the teachers in my class, Isaac Langal, was working on the Ulithian dictionary. He explained that an earlier, linguistically technical version exists, but that a version more understandable to teachers and the average person is needed. Somewhere the process had stalled. In my efforts to find a Ulithian dictionary, I failed to find one at the Falalop or Mogmog elementary schools, nor at the high school. I was also told that a science series had been developed in Ulithian, but it was not visible either. Several teachers told me that they themselves do not know the new spelling system well enough to use it in Ulithian language arts instruction yet. I was told by the PMA pilot that he planned to go to Ulithi that August to work with the Catholic Church to make a dictionary and to translate the Bible. Isaac Langal was widely considered to be an indigenous language authority.

Vernacular writing. Within the Falalop and Mogmog communities, evidence of the use of vernacular writing during that summer included: 1) a parting phrase on a sign as one passes through to the airport; 2) several vernacular graffiti phrases written on the walls of the Falalop elementary school; and 3) a series of short handmade children's picture books in Ulithian. The signs of a literate environment in English were abundant. In the principal's house where I stayed there were magazines, books of short stories, American literature curriculum materials, and Pacific Daily News issues from Guam. At the high school there were textbooks in the bookshelves of the classrooms, and in the office. There was a library, and there was a very popular ditto machine that we were able to use for class handouts, projects, and bulletins. Each day the bulletin board outside the office had new notices from the office, from the administrator, and teachers. There were also notices in the cafeteria, one for signing up for team sports, one long complaint about things being stolen from the office and how people were forgetting their proud culture if they would steal from the OIHS students. I saw FSM newspapers being passed around. One of the teachers in my class received a *Time* magazine regularly from the mail coming in on the plane. The signs on the front of the church, the apostle center, the dispensary, and the "Danger – No Smoking" sign on the gasoline tank near the beach were all in English. American comic books were sometimes seen in these public places. I noted that I had not seen many reading materials in the few family homes I had visited.

After my summer on Ulithi, much more work was done on the Ulithian dictionary. The socialization of Ulithi students in their indigenous language was further extended by the Yap State Vernacular Language Program of Yap's State Education Enterprising Department (SEED). They published a series of beautiful full color children's picture storybooks in Ulithian in 1998: *Kawawa; Wool Moa Geech; Serea Sufi Soomw Somwoy; Kofel Tamag Moa Ddoelel Semat Moa Semat.* SEED provided the following explanation on each text: "This book is a part of the first project developed to address a community need to enhance language and culture instruction. All materials developed for this project were translated into the four languages of Yap – Satawalese, Woleaian, Ulithian, Yapese; and English. The contents were defined by local communities. Illustrations were done by local artists, manuscripts were written in the vernacular by local teachers and community members, with texts translated by local language specialists." Mariano Laimoh of Asor and Patrick Chotaifil of Falalop authored the first two of these books, respectively. Laimoh translated the other two books into Ulithian.

The *English-Ulithian Dictionary 1* was printed for students by Yap SEED in 2002 under Director Henry Falan, and funded in part by the US Department of Education. It was edited by Mariano Laimoh, and developed by the Ulithian Dictionary Group, which included: Jesse John Salalu, Mariano John Laimoh, Pedrus Paul Ramaliol, Juanito Juanito Faurang, Albert Mathias Haped, Ygnasia Victoria Lahasudep, and Priscilla Killa Lamaleg. Cesar A. Hidalgo served as a consultant to the work. He explained that the book was curriculum based, and that its main

Figure 7. Ulithian language picture books. *(Photo by Mary Spencer.)*

goal was to support instruction of the English language. He said it was based on the model for his earlier publication of a Filipino-English dictionary. Somewhat later, Walsh and Walsh (1979) reported using the Ulithian-English dictionaries by Mellen and Uwel (2005) and Mellen and Hancock (2010).

Students' Explanations of Learning Style

In the latter part of the 1960s, and continuing today, social science scholars have vigorously engaged in research, analysis, and collaborative discussion of cross cultural comparisons of speech use and the learning dynamics of children within family and social contexts. Some of the important discussions centered on the developmental experiences of Native American children in home and school. The research of anthropologist Susan C. Phillips on the Warm Springs Indian Reservation in Oregon was one of the most stimulating and widely discussed of these studies (1970). She attributed studies with other Native American tribes as the impetus for her research (e.g., Wax, Wax, and Dumont, 1989 with Pine Ridge Sioux; Wollcott, 2003 with Kwakiutl school children; Cazden and John, 1971; Cazden, John, and Hymes, 1972; and Hymes and Bittle, 1967). The focal points of these studies were observations of resistance of the Indian children to the way classroom activities were typically organized; observations of persistent silence from the Indian students; contrasts in home versus school approaches to enculturating *styles of learning;* and sociolinguistic interference when non-Indian teachers

Figure 8. Course students explore the cognitive development and learning styles of local children of different ages through the use of Piagetian conservation tasks. *(Photos by Mary Spencer.)*

did not understand or know how to accommodate this contrast. Contemporary research along similar lines has been conducted in a variety of Hispanic settings by psychologist Barbara Rogoff and her colleagues (e.g., Rogoff, 2003; Rogoff, B., Moore, L., Najafi, B., Dexter, A., Correa-Chávez, M., and Solis, J., 2007). They have used a broader construct that they call *learning traditions,* rather than the more individualized construct of *learning style.* They also see the blending of some features of these three traditions for some children in various contexts and on some occasions*: Intent Community Participation; Guided Repetition;* and *Assem-*

bly Line Instruction. The third form is most similar to American school formats and the first two are more similar to forms I have found in the traditional Pacific Island settings I have studied (e.g., Spencer, 2014).

During the course on Educational Psychology that I taught on Ulithi in 1985, I gave the educators who were students in my class the assignment of reading Susan Phillips' research and reflecting on how children's lives and learning in their own cultures might compare and contrast with her analysis. Although situated on Ulithi, the OIHS serves students from all of the Outer Islands of Yap. That was also true of the summer college courses there. Therefore, some of the students' explanations reflect their lives on islands such as Lamotrek,[2] Woleai, and Farraulap, as well as those of the students from Ulithi. All but one of these students were male. Their narratives on the subject of learning style, related to Phillips study, are presented below. The island and gender of each reporting student are cited. I have abbreviated and smoothed the language of some of their narratives.

Male 1 from Woleai

To begin with, learning aspects or knowledge in our culture is private, not shared with members of the community or public. In private homes, the father, uncle, or mother share their knowledge with sons, daughters, nephews, or nieces. In some cases, when time comes for the possessor to pass his or her knowledge, then s/he becomes very selective. The heir should be someone who cares for people, be secretive, care for the father, mother, and uncle, respect traditional culture, and be able to learn. That particular heir should be able to meet all of these requirements. This new possessor of the knowledge should not be known to the public until need arises for his particular skills. That is the time that he will show his skills to the public. After that, people will look up to him as one individual with skills. I think learning in traditional culture is not separated from life. You actually learn the importance of the learning throughout life. The child learns more at home, and is taught at an early age to respect people and tradition as a whole. So there is no separation between learning and life. They all started together.

Male 2 from Woleai

The important aspects of the *learning* styles in my culture are different from American learning styles. I will list some of the important styles in my culture:
1. Be well respected by your own community and by other people from different islands;
2. Always respect others;
3. Many youngsters will always be willing to come and learn the skills from you;
4. Do most of the work or know most skills in your community;
5. Always bow down when coming to places where lots of people are sitting;

---

[2] Readers will find Alkire's book on Lamotrek Atoll (1965) invaluable in developing a deeper understanding of the culture of the Lamotrek students mentioned in this chapter.

6. Always respect the chief and uncle;
7. Never speak in a meeting if there are older people;
8   Know all your relatives within the clan;
9. Know all your lands that belong to your father and mother;
10. Know all the people who share your father's and mother's lands.

The important aspects of home *teaching* styles in my culture are almost the same as the Warm Spring Indian students, families, and teachers. Some of the important aspects are:

1. One to one teaching styles;
2. Father teaches only his sons and daughters;
3. Mother teaches only her sons and daughters;
4. Uncle teaches only his nephews and nieces;
5. Skills are passed only to family members;
6. No outsider is allowed to learn the skills;
7. The skills are never told to anyone who does not belong in the family;
8. Skills are taught only when sons or daughters ask the father or mother to teach them;
9. Skills cannot be taught just at any time the father or mother want to; if no one in the family asks to be taught the skill, then it will never be taught, and they will never know it;
10. Skills are very secret to teach.

Male 3 from Woleai.

Around the world learning styles and home teaching styles are different for each culture. Even Yap Proper has styles that are different from the cultures in the neighboring islands. The neighboring islands themselves have most of the same aspects of learning styles and home teaching styles. There might be a little difference, but as I see and understand it myself, they are similar.

Let me begin by using myself as an example. I was born in Falalop, Woleai and I grew up with all the environmental surroundings there. But (formal skill) learning in my culture is optional. If I want to learn, then I'll ask. In home teaching styles, the mother has her own responsibilities over her children to teach the girls to cook in different ways. Not only cooking, but also weaving lava lavas and mats, respect for the household members and the community, how to become better people in the future, how to become a good mother, how to take care of the family if father or mother died, about land owned and the relationships with other related people.

As for the father, he has his own responsibilities. He has to look over the family and to teach his sons about making ropes, respect the elders and the community, ways of fishing, navigation, land owned by the family, making canoes and fish traps, making fishing net, how to cut tuba for the family and teach them how to become good leaders of the family when the mother and father die.

Figure 9. In a private home, a child (left) begins the creation of an intricately woven traditional *mwarmwar*, closely observing and practicing her mother's expert work (right). Earlier, the mother dispatched several children with instructions for picking the correct flowers and greenery. *(Photos by Mary Spencer.)*

These learnings only depend on how much you care to learn. The mother and father will teach the most, but if one of them lacks one thing (for example, the father), we can seek other people besides him, like an uncle, an aunt, cousins, or the most known person in a certain skill. Some people with such skills are hard to obtain. Maybe it is because of their selfishness that they do not want to pass their skills to anyone. Only if, like the old saying, "You give me <u>that</u> and I will give you <u>this</u>." Or, "You care for me and I will care for you."

In one of our learning styles, children got some of the skills through observation. That is, when the men are in the canoe house doing something, like making ropes, fish traps, making net, and other things. This is done for boys only.

As for girls, most of their learning experiences are at home. The father can pass his skills to the girls, one who he trusts, if he does not want to give his sons the skills because of their bad reputations.

If we want to be a navigator, we seek a good skilled navigator. If we want to learn about medicine, we seek people who have that skill. But if we want to acquire all the skills, we seek all of them. With the advisors we have, we must follow their advice. They are our mothers and fathers.

Male 4 from Woleai.

Learning style through culture is very much like the case study of the Warm Springs Indian children as they grew up and were capable of deciding where and what to do. Parents are very concerned about them and therefore advise them to learn different kinds of skills that exist on the island and about their life.

Back home as I see, children especially look where there are elders and adults meeting and gathering. They sit around silently watching and listening to what the adults are doing or discussing. Taking me as an example, I will be interested. All the people on the island will participate. At this time the adults will do the work and at the same time, tell the children to help. The children will become involved in the work by imitating. Back to me, if there is a job like this, I will come to the working area to watch the adults. Whatever they ask me to do, I will try to do, but with their help and instruction all the time.

Another example: The drinking circle is required back home. All the men from each village will come down to their canoe house especially in the evening. Stories and important topics will be discussed at this moment. Also, the younger people will ask many things about different skills. At this point, if the question is concerning navigation, the person known to be a navigation master will do the talking while everyone else will remain silent unless they ask him a question. He will talk about some important things, but only not in detail and not with demonstration. He will only talk briefly, summarizing everything. If the question on navigation is asked, he will only name the stars used for navigation. Traditionally, few verbal directions are given, no demonstrations of the skills, and no actual testing of students in the application of knowledge. This is for boys but girls stay at home and the same procedure for men is also used for them.

On my island, the home teaching style is not the same as the learning styles (culture). Things such as skills are taught both verbally and through demonstration in very detailed ways until the child masters the particular skill.

The family will gather together especially in the evening time. All of their children are asked to sit with them. The adults will tell the children what they think the child is poor in. Children are deliberately taught many skills, but one at a time. For example, as the child grows up, the first thing s/he will do is learn the relationship of people on the islands, like the clans, individuals, etc. After this, they will learn their lands, where did it actually come from, how, and why. Many skills will be taught like this.

During the time when they are capable of working, many teaching experiences will be required. They will learn with more verbal instruction, including practicum. They will apply what they learn in practice, in sort of tests to make sure they learn or master the particular skill. Afterwards, a relative who is teaching the skill to the children will test them.

For example, if that person is ready for navigation, the tester will take him (the learner) on a canoe traveling around the far islands. He will not supervise the student or take charge of the canoe. He will watch every single mistake he commits or does for correction. Actually, the final test for those skills does not involve verbal performance. However, the learner will learn a lot at this time. Whatever the student fails will be re-taught or reviewed until he gets the mistake or problem solved. This kind of teaching is applied to every skill taught in that family. We can also learn from observation. Girls are also taught in the same way. Finally, home learning is verbal and applied until it reaches the mastery level.

Male 5 from Woleai.

We have different learning styles that the children grow up with. But it is quite similar in a way to the ones for the Indian children. The children's learning styles depend on what children (boys for instance) will do when they get together in the men's house and listen and learn from the elders - the skilled men. The men, especially the ones with more skills, will do some lecturing on certain skills and every participant will have to listen. A few ideas will be contributed by the other men. After the lecture is done, each of the children will learn by doing it by hand and this is most important (learning to do it by hand). The older men will check on the individual or group to see that they are doing the right thing. However, in the men's house not every skill is taught. They only generalize everything out for the boys, but when they go home the closely related men (for instance, the father) will then give some additional or correcting information of what has been taught at the men's house. This is also the same for the girls. But there are other skills that are not to be taught in public, only in homes. For instance, skills for medic will remain secret and only the household and other favorable relatives can learn these from either the uncle or father. The children are told not to mention any of the skills taught to them to any other children or elder people. In addition, each individual has his/her responsibility to ask questions any time and the father is always glad to answer.

Father sits privately with his children close and looking on while he does paperwork.

Nearby children (not shown) look on as a group of men weave food baskets and prepare for a barbeque.

Figure 10. Men take an active role in teaching children in both private and community settings. *(Photos by Mary Spencer.)*

Male from Ulithi.

I would say that the learning style of children here is somewhat similar in some cases to that of the Warm Spring Indian children. Older children are also given a good deal of responsibility for the care and training of their younger brothers or sisters. They are taught many skills around the home and outdoors at an early age by the parents and other relatives. Each family is responsible for teaching its own children the family's own skills and values in life. Special skills are usually learned from other relatives and friends. Traditionally, silent listening and watching is the first step in learning skills. Often a parent or relative who is teaching a skill to a child divides it up into several parts, giving the simple parts to the child first and gradually giving the other parts only when he/she feels that the child has already mastered the first parts. For example, in teaching the skill for preparing medicine from herbs, the elder will be inclined to move on to a more complex type of medicine only when the child can go out and collect, bring back, and prepare the medicine successfully under the elder's watchful observance. Unlike the Indian children though, these children are put to test almost always and always under an elder's watchful eyes to make sure the child is ready for the next step, although he is of no help to the child during each testing period. Often, when a child fails to do something, the parents or relatives are put to blame for not teaching their children properly. So, home learning becomes the most important in a child's life.

In the old days and even nowadays, children learn by observation and listening to elders. It is usually a relative who passes on knowledge to children but not always. In the cases of families who are poor of certain knowledge or skills, local valuables are used in exchange for someone to teach their children. But this is very rare, only when a child proves worthy of the knowledge or skill.

Female from Ulithi.

The most important aspects of learning styles of children from my culture are listening, observing, and practicing. I think this is true in that children learn everything from listening to and observing their parents, family members, and people within their community. This is mostly customs, stories, legends, etc. As for skills, they listen and observe whoever is teaching them the skill and then they practice the skills. This practicing, they can do it individually or in groups, with always someone available for supervision or help should there be any problems or questions.

There is something I think is important in groupings in my culture. There is always the division of men and women in almost anything: learning skills, working, playing, etc. Men or boys usually learn things they need to learn from their fathers or other older men and the same goes for girls. They learn from their mothers or other older women.

Children from my culture usually find it somewhat hard or uncomfortable to learn in the American schools where they would be learning or working with children from the opposite sex, and they would be learning the same skills and things. I think this is true, especially for the girls. They are used to learning things from women and working or practicing skills (women's) in the presence of women.

Male 1 from Lamotrek.

The aspects of the child's learning styles from his own culture was that a child has his own father and mother. As the child grew older he learned from his father and mother. He imitated what he saw the parents doing. When he grew older he learned what his parents were doing. He helped his parents doing things. His father took the child with him to do men's job so the child learned from his father about the men's job. After that he can go by himself and do the job. This idea applies to women also. A girl went with the mother for her job. After the children learned from the parents, and the parents knew that their children are perfect of the skills, then the parents can free the children to go out in the community to do the skills. They move out in the community and practice the skills and learn from the community those skills they never face from the parents. But the skills that children learn from the community are only a few because they learned almost everything earlier from the parents.

Figure 11. A Ulithian women's village cooking circle, in which children of varying ages observe, pitch in, and occasionally receive requests or suggestions. *(Photo by Mary Spencer.)*

After all these things are done and the parents know their children are perfect of the skills, the children will work independently. If they are old enough to get married and have children then the same thing will be done to their children also. Parents will teach their different skills to their different children growing up in the same family.

The parents cannot teach their children the skills they knew among different people or in the meetings or while gathering. The parents usually teach their children in the evening at home, usually when there are no people around. The parents can teach the children any place where they cannot be seen or heard by different people who are not related to them. The reason for this is because the parents don't allow their skills or their knowledge to be known by different people. The skills or knowledge pass from generation to generation only in the same family group of people living together. So, the parents teach their children all the skills they know and also some skills they adapted from different families of people.

After the teaching, the children will go out and stay in the community and the community will teach them about minor things or skills. This teaching occurs during the gathering of people or in meetings, and also when legends or stories of their own culture are told.

Male 2 from Lamotrek

The learning and teaching styles are traditionally taught through family in my culture. For example, the father will teach his skills to his sons only if they ask. If they don't ask, then the father won't give his skills to them. Let's say the father has four sons and two of them listen and obey him. They are the ones their father will teach every skill to them. He will, however, teach the other two sons but not all the skills he knows.

We could learn the other skills from other people, although we don't have any relationship to them. All we have to do is to give that skilled man some valuable things such as lava lavas, cloth, and so on. And in return he will teach us some of his important skills. If that person is a canoe builder, you ask for the necessary skills in making a canoe. He might know other skills but not sufficient. You only offer things to whom you are not related to, but not true for father, brother, and uncle.

The girls learn the women's skills from their mother, aunt, or sisters; but not secretly as boys do. The mother can teach her daughter any time of the day, but it doesn't really matter if one unrelated woman is with them. I have no idea regarding this, but this is how it happens in my culture. Girls can also learn some skills from their fathers as well as from the other relatives.

Boys and girls can also learn through observation. This is how some learn. Boys gather in the men's house and observe men when they are working. They will take turn helping the men. This is also true for girls. They will observe the women and then help them out. Women can even learn navigation from their fathers. One in Satawal knows native medicine, history, origins, but probably not how to build a canoe. So in my culture we learn from our relatives and through observation. Teaching is secretly done.

Regarding the situation with adopted children or when relatives other than parents teach important skills: There is no difference. If I have four sons and three listen to me and takes care about what I tell them what to do, and only one doesn't, I'm not going to teach all my skills – some – but not all. If I have adopted son and he listens to me, I will teach him – secretly. I don't want to pass our skills to every-one unless they give us some things.

Secret skills are navigation, native medicines, building houses, carving and making canoes, and the origin of our clan. Almost all skills are secret. On Satawal, navigation is taught more publically because the navigators are afraid that if it is kept secret the skill will vanish. With girls it is the same. For example, making lava lavas is not as secret as navigation, medicine, origin of the clan, but there are some secrets. Cooking might be public.

Regarding how a child asks parents to teach him/her a valuable and secret skill: The child must verbally make a request. If you don't it means you don't respect him. If you respect him, you do ask him for his skills. Fathers say to sons (and other relatives, daughters), if you pay attention to me, care for me, respect me, I'm going to teach you my skills. My father asked me, "Don't you want to learn about navigation? He was a navigator. I said, "No, I really don't want to sail between islands. I'm afraid. You know, they don't even have radios." I talked to him about these things. I left for school, and I came back and then I left again. When I came back he was sick, and then he died. But I have an uncle who is a navigator. He came to me and asked me. I didn't want to learn about navigation. I was about 18. I told him the same thing I told my father before. "I am afraid. I love my life. I don't want to sail between islands." He really got mad. He picked up this 2 x 4. Later he really got mad with my mother. He told her that maybe I don't know he's my relative. When I didn't learn navigation skills, some people thought it meant that I had not respected my father, and so my father had decided not to teach me.

A group of men carry out a summer canoe carving project at the OIHS in 2010. Interested children wander around the work area, observe, and pitch in.

A Ulithian woman engages in her loom weaving of a traditional lava lava in the outside kitchen of her home while children of varying ages move about, occasionally fetch something she needs, and watch.

Figure 12. Traditional skills observed in 1985 continued in 2010. *(Photos by Mary Spencer.)*

My father in law makes canoes. I went to him to ask how. Even though he is my father in law, I still take tuba and I work with him and he shows me. When I make the first canoe he worked with me, and when he looked at it he found things I did wrong and he told me – showed them to me. "You really didn't do this right. Next time, don't do it this way. Make it like this." Then on the second canoe, he watched me and asked me questions about everything. I could answer some, but when I couldn't answer, he would say, "Hey, come on. How are you going to build this good canoe if you don't know this?" So maybe some time I am going to make a third canoe. He said he is not going to help me that time, just watch. So maybe I can answer all the questions that time.

Regarding the men's house, people go there both day and night. Some things, such as work, happen there. At night there is a drinking circle there. Women cannot go. The oldest men tell what they will all do the next day. Sometimes the others protest. There is no place for women to have meetings, but women sometimes meet outside church. If the chief calls a meeting for everyone, women would be at the men's house. That is the only time.

Regarding the work of culture teachers at the schools in light of the secrecy surrounding skill teaching, culture teachers just teach in a very general way, but not in detail. For example, they could teach how to count in our language, a little bit on navigation, or making a canoe. You couldn't really do these things from this amount of information.

Regarding rules or expectations of silence, if a person has high clan status, he will have to voice up at a meeting. If low clan, he will ask chief to grant him permission to speak. Being high clan does not mean all of you have to talk. The Chief does most of the talking. If he is not present, the next person in line talks. If you feel something, you can ask permission. But it probably must be pretty important. Like in the recent cafeteria discussion where all teachers at the summer school were called by the highest ranking educational leader a few days ago, most teachers knew the answers to the questions but if they gave answers, others would think, "Hey, what are you doing?"

Regarding traditions of oratory in his island, in my island, there are three main people: the chief who is from the high clan; the second man who is also from the high clan and could be the chief in the future; and the third man who is from the low clan. The third man cannot be the chief, but often he is the orator.

Male from Farraulap

In a family, children learn secretly through their father, mother, and their uncle. These are the children's important sources of learnings. They can also learn from their close relatives and their brothers and sisters after their parents and their uncles die.

In a family, male children have tried their best to accomplish all the culture skills their father and their uncle have mastered. The female children have tried the same way on the opposite side. Mother and the uncle do the instructions. Children are carefully taught by their parents everything they wish to learn but they also have to be aware of one important thing to follow in their life time with their parents. Their parents love them very much so they keep watching and observing, mainly to find out who and which one of their children love and care for them a lot. If they find out that one of their kids doesn't care about them, then they will not teach him/her as well as the others.

Our children can learn the culture skills generally from the drinking circle, especially in the evenings. They always come to the drinking circle and carefully listen to the men's stories. They also can learn the skills by participating in helping the men at work in the men's house. At night time, they come home and ask their father about what they have seen and their father is very happy to help them out.

Children are preferred to try themselves out in all kinds of skills secretly either with their father or with their uncle. They hate to show themselves to the public that they have failed to do the work. They have always tried hard to accomplish all the culture skills their father and their uncle have given them in order for their names to be popular among the people in the community. If they have failed the work the first time, they could have tried again, and again until they have done it properly. In the community it is awful and shameful for the children without understanding the knowledge of their parents or their uncles, especially when they die and nobody will ever know their fortune.

Parents are blamed if the child doesn't learn well or fails to do something. During the learning process the parents test the child at each step. The task is divided into steps, and the simple one is demonstrated first. The teaching depends on the teacher. The teacher tries to just find ways student would learn most quickly. The student takes a bottle of tuba to the man and goes and sits by him every evening.

Themes of the Educators' Descriptions of Learning Traditions

There was substantial agreement across the 10 educator-students' descriptions of the learning traditions in children's lives on their respective neighboring islands. The majority explicitly explained that certain important forms of knowledge and skill transfer are very secret and restricted to specific members of a family. This knowledge is typically shared with only worthy sons, daughters, nephews, or nieces by mothers, fathers, and uncles. The Woleai men described this worthiness in more detail, mentioning that the recipients of teaching must be able to keep the secrets; have already demonstrated that they care for the mother, father, and uncle; that they respect their culture and tradition, that they are able to learn and can demonstrate success in acquiring the skill or knowledge. Woleai and Lamotrek respondents said that the child must explicitly ask the prospective teacher of the valuable skills to teach him/her; and that if the child fails to take responsibility for making this request, the family experts will withhold the secret and very valuable training. The children selected to receive the secret knowledge must not only show respect to their mentors, but already be respected by the community and have evidenced work for the community and respect for its traditions.

Although all 10 educator-students spoke of the gender division of types of learning (e.g., weaving, native medicine, navigation, canoe building, certain kinds of cooking and food preparation), two explained that if a girl is worthy and explicitly asks a master, she may receive some or most kinds of typically male skills or knowledge. The example was given of one girl who had learned navigation and of another on Satawal who had learned native medicine, history, and origins – "but probably not how to build a canoe." The critical topics of teaching/learning for each family include the identity of all relatives in the clan, the mother's and fathers' lands, people who share the mother's and father's lands, and the relationship details of related people. All children will receive some types of traditional teaching, but the depth and range of teaching will be calibrated to the teachers' estimation of each individual child's worthiness. Customs, stories, and legends seem to be widely shared. Parents will be held responsible if a child lacks important skills or knowledge. According to two respondents, if a family lacks important skills they would like to see their child develop, they may be able to arrange for an expert to accept certain local valuables (e.g., lava lavas) in exchange for teaching these to their child.

For many of the educator-students, the men's house on their island was the prime location for the sharing of traditional knowledge by older men to male children. Other venues included private sessions in the master's home or in a natural site. They indicated that the home was the typical teaching location for girls. (On Ulithi at that time, a large thatch women's house existed. Among other things, women did some of their weaving there.) Several descriptions of observation and imitation learning were given. Several others described masters analyzing the skills or body of knowledge into components differentiated by difficulty or stage into a series of learning objectives. These were then presented sequentially to the child, who practiced them, and were then tested on them by the master. The master then gave feedback and additional training. Only after the child demonstrated mastery would the expert proceed to the next steps in the learning sequence.

The relevance of the ten educators' narratives to academic theories of learning style and learning traditions is readily seen. As important, or more so, are other social dynamics specific to the indigenous Yap Outer Island cultures. Knowing these helps us paint a more complete portrait of how the children access, process, and are nurtured in the information and skills important to their cultures and communities. That this has been shared with us deserves our respect and gratitude.

Discussion

Life in Ulithi has both changed and stayed the same since my 1985 work there. Many of the young men and women who were students in my classes have had accomplished careers in the intervening years. The Ulithi OIHS continues to be a year-round magnet for some of Yap Outer Islands' most promising students and educators. Indigenous traditions and explorations of technical communication and computer innovation thrive side-by side. The educator-students and local families of 1985 Ulithi, particularly those on Falalop Island, generously shared their approaches to life and child rearing with me that summer. I have presented my observations and their words as objectively as I am able so readers can judge for themselves. In addition, I will suggest a few of my own interpretations.

Child observations were easily arranged. Both parents and children were tolerant of me inconspicuously sitting near groups of children, taking notes, and occasionally photographing them during observations that were relatively non-participatory on my part. The children themselves were endlessly creative in their abilities to devise play-worthy activities in the absence of commercially developed play materials and toys. Notable were their frequent "hanging out" sessions around the women and men of their families, as they quietly observed, pitched in, or created child-centered activities nearby. Both women and men seemed to welcome the presence of both girls and boys. Either away from the adults or nearby, the children constructed group singing activities in both Ulithian and English. They combed one another's hair and played music on homemade musical instruments. They drew and told stories. Gender separation was evident at early ages in some activities such as climbing trees and Kung Fu; but mixed gender and mixed age play groups were also frequent. Leaders emerged in these play groups, but collaboration was evident from young ages.

An analysis of the degree of child agency on Ulithi would take notice of the relative independence of these children's groups and their activities; i.e., a high degree of child agency. Moreover, a consideration of the extent of child agency raises the topic of the nature, context, and extent of adult disciplinary behavior toward children. Two instances in the observations seemed to reinforce the idea that child agency was viewed as something to be respected and nurtured. First, we saw a mother, late in the afternoon, who wished to bring her pre-school child home from a neighbor's house. Rather than directly picking him up or ordering him to come with her, she gently suggested he come. When he did not obey her, instead of insisting herself, she quietly requested another child to persuade her little boy to come home. Second, in one of the OIHS educator's discussions of learning styles, he made the comment about shielding children from Kung Fu movies: "In our culture, we don't like to tell children they can't do something. So, if they want to watch, it's hard to stop them." In contrast to these instances of free rein being given to child agency, the educators' narratives on traditional teaching illustrated adults, especially those holding high status and highly respected skills, in firm control of interactions with children, teens, and young adults. As interesting as these clues are, the topic of child agency and family views on discipline would need much more observation and discussion before a clear understanding could be reached.

The importance and prominence of child-to-child teaching among Ulithian and other Outer Island children should not be underestimated. It was very frequent in my observations and had an underlying organization (e.g., the sitting stick dance lesson). The child teachers were observed to employ an almost fierce eye contact method of keeping the learner's attention, combined with imitation teaching-learning routines, teaching with participation, intentionally pacing the flow of the activity, and using repetition strategies. We are left with the questions of how the teaching child received her or his teacher training, and what are the cultural expectations of child-to-child teaching relative to various forms of adult-to-child teaching.

A final word about socialization to literacy: I found only meager evidence of written Ulithian in 1985. However, there was a history of early field dictionaries and some additional but incomplete dictionary development that grew in the following decades into the production of a children's dictionary and a small series of quality storybooks. The Ulithian and other Outer Island languages continue the vibrant oral forms of communication in Ulithi and between indigenous Outer Island Yap islanders of all ages and circumstances. Graphic symbolism underlies some forms of Ulithian weaving – a robust and paramount indigenous art form of the atoll that continues even now. The question of contemporary Ulithian literacy would require new study, but it is noteworthy that a team of curriculum specialists at the Yap State Department of Education met with me in 2010 and described their continued material development in the indigenous languages of the Outer Islands of Yap.

The educators in my classes provided significant details about the intergenerational learning traditions in their Outer Island communities, including Ulithi. They believed that important commonalities existed among the learning traditions of Ulithi, Woleai, Lamotrek, and Farraulap. For all, secrecy surrounded the content, the receiver, the provider, and the method of transfer of knowledge. Gender divisions were strictly applied, although a few exceptions were cited. Neither gender nor family position was sufficient to guarantee that a child would be given the gift of valued knowledge. He or she must achieve community respect and demonstrate deep and long-lasting respect and obedience to the master teacher. In addition, the child must explicitly ask to be taught a valued skill and incrementally master each of a hierarchy of increasingly difficult skill elements. Even then, the master teacher would withhold the ultimate levels of the curriculum if he felt the child lacked the ability or loyalty to receive them.

In retrospect, headway was made on most of my objectives for the 1985 University of Guam summer session on Ulithi. But as it turns out, I was the student and the children, community, and educator enrollees were the teachers.

Acknowledgements

I would like to acknowledge the excellent academic efforts made in my classes by the teachers and administrators enrolled in them. They include the following students from the Educational Psychology class and those in the Evaluation class whose names I have from their assigned papers. (Unfortunately, I no longer have the class list for the evaluation course.) I extend my deep thanks to all of these students for their insights, hard work, and cooperation with me in my efforts to achieve the course objectives.

Patrick Chotaifil
George Fagolfeg
Isaac F. Langal
Robert L. Petalmai
Peter S. Mangiemar
Augustine Igeral
Willy Radolfetheg
Francis Haleylabeg

Johannes L. Sapwetil
Lorenzo L. Sartilug
Vincent A. Souwemal
John Mailus
Juanita Yatchdar
Luke J. Yauritik
Lazarus M. Ulith
Nicholas Figer

Sesariyo Harong
Phillip Raigumai
Thomas Hapitmai
Vincent Yangremal
Clare Yothog

Titus J. Rapsilug   Jerome I. Rakilur

Paul P. Rassug   Thomas T. Sefairal

Martin S. Remiltalug   John F. Taweryan

Ramon T. Retwalut   Stanley Retogral

I would also like to extend my sincere gratitude to the Falalop Ulithi community who cared for me during the summer course work. Several women visited me to make sure I was not lonesome, brought me food, and gave me cultural guidance. Juanita Yatchdar and Clare Yothog, the two women students, helped me significantly both at home and in class. In addition, thanks are due to all of those on Mogmog who extended their hospitality to me on several trips I made there. Jean Thoulag, is an American woman who served Ulithi as a Peace Corp Volunteer and later married Bernard Thoulag. She introduced me to Bernard's family on Mogmog who offered their help and kindness to me. Jean also shared her knowledge and work on Ulithi legends, contemporary story writing, and the OIHS Library where she had made important contributions to the creation of a well-organized and comfortable literate environment.[3] I also express my appreciation to Rosa Huffer Tacheliol and her husband Hilary Tacheliol. Rosa and I were colleagues during the Project BEAM years at the University of Guam. As an indigenous Chamorro woman, who was married to a prominent Ulithi leader,[4] she counseled me on cultural and educational matters for many years. The warmth of her friendship has nourished my continuing interest in the indigenous people of Yap State and Guam.

References

Alkire, W. H. (1965). *Lamotrek Atoll, inter-island socioeconomic ties.* Prospect Heights, ILL: Waveland Press, Inc.

Cazden, C. B., & John, V. P. (1971). Learning in American Indian children. In M. L. Wax, S. Diamond, & F. O. Gearing (Eds.), *Anthropological perspectives in education.* New York: Basic Books.

Cazden, C. B., John, V. P., & Hymes, D. (Eds.). (1972). *Functions of language in the classroom.* New York: Teachers College Press.

Chotaifil, P. (1998). *Wool moa geech.* Colonia, Yap State, FSM: Yap State Education Enterprising Department.

Dumont, R. Jr., & Wax, M. (1969). Cherokee school society and intercultural classroom, *Human Organization, 28*(3), 217 – 226.

Elbert, S. H. (1947). *Ulithi-English and English-Ulithi word lists with notes on linguistic position, pronunciation, and grammar.* U.S. Naval Military Government.

Fischer, A. M. (1950). *The role of the Trukese mother and its effect on child training: A report to the Pacific Science Board of the National Research Council on research*

---

[3] In later years, Jean and Bernard moved to Pohnpei, Capitol of the Federated States of Micronesia. They made important contributions there, Bernard as an officer of the FSM national government and Jean as an administrator of the Catholic school and then at the national campus of the College of Micronesia. Jean is now a faculty member at the Hamilton Library of the University of Hawaii, Manoa campus.

[4] Hilary Tacheliol was Lieutenant Governor of the State of Yap from 1980 to 1987 and continues to provide leadership in Yap and FSM. Rosa Tacheliol has played an important role as an academic leader in secondary and post-secondary education on Yap Island for decades. Among her many contributions, she was Director of the Yap State Department of Education and faculty at the Yap Campus of the College of Micronesia.

done under the program entitled Scientific Investigation of Micronesia (Contract N7-onr-291. Task Order IV). Washington, DC: The Office of Naval Research & The National Academy of Sciences.

Hymes, D. H., & Bittle, W. E. (Eds.). (1967). *Studies in southwestern ethnolinguistics meaning and history in the languages of the American Southwest.* New York: Mouton and Company.

Jensen, J. T. (1977). *Yapese reference grammar.* Honolulu, HI: University Press of Hawaii.

Jensen, J. T., Defeg, R., Iou, J. B., & Pugram, L. D. (1977). *Yapese-English dictionary.* Honolulu, HI: University Press of Hawaii.

Laimoh, M. (1998). *Kawawa.* Colonia, Yap State, FSM: Yap State Education Enterprising Department.

Laimoh, M. (Ed.). (2002). *English-Ulithian dictionary 1.* Colonia, Yap State, FSM: Yap State Education Enterprising Department.

Maag, E. F. (1998). *Kofel Tamag moa ddoelel semat moa semat.* Colonia, Yap State, FSM: Yap State Education Enterprising Department.

Mellen, N., & Uwel, J. (2005). *Ulithian-English dictionary.* www.habele.org/downloads/ULITHIAN_DICTIONARY.pdf

Mellen, N., & Hancock, J. (2010). *Ulithian-English dictionary, first edition.* Columbia, SC: Lulu Press, Inc.

Nabobo-Baba, U. W. (2006). *Knowing and learning: An indigenous Fijian approach.* Suva, Fiji: Institute of Pacific Studies Publications, University of the South Pacific.

Philips, S. U. (1972). Participant structure and communicative competence: Warm Springs children in community and classroom. In C. B. Cazden, V.P. John, & D. Hymes (Eds.), *Functions of language in the classroom* (pp. 370 – 394). New York: Teachers College Press.

Rogoff, B. (2003). *The cultural nature of human development.* New York, NY: Oxford University Press.

Rogoff, B., Moore, L., Najafi, B., Dexter, A., Correa-Chavez, M., & Solis, J. (2007). Children's development of cultural repertoires through participation in everyday routines and practices. In J. E. Grusec, & P. D. Hastings (Eds.), *Handbook of socialization, theory, and research* (pp. 490 – 515). New York, NY: The Guilford Press.

Sohn, H. (1975). *Woleaian reference grammar.* Honolulu, HI: University Press of Hawaii.

Sohn, H., & Tawerilmang, A. F. (1976). *Woleaian-English dictionary.* Honolulu, HI: University Press of Hawaii.

Spencer, M. L., Palomo, R., with Vela, N. (1987). Studies in Chamorro and English oral language proficiency with Chamorro children in Guam. In M. L. Spencer (Ed.). *Chamorro language issues and research on Guam.* Mangilao, Guam: University of Guam. Retrieved from http://www.uog.edu/dynamicdata/mlipublications.aspx?siteid=1&p=499

Spencer, M. L. (2015). *Children of Chuuk Lagoon: A 21st Century analysis of life and learning on Romonum Island.* Mangilao, Guam: University of Guam Press.

Walsh, J. A., & Walsh, E. (1979). Loan words in Ulithian. *Anthropological Linguistics, 21*(3). (Also see Wikipedia: http://en.wikipedia.org/ wiki/Ulithianlanguage)

Wax, M. L., Wax, R. H., & Dumont, R. V. (1989). *Formal education in an American Indian community: Peer society and the failure of minority education.* Long Grove, ILL: Waveland Press Inc.

Wolcott, H. F. (2003). *A Kwakiutl village and school (updated version).* Lanham, MD: Altamira Press.

Yap State Education Enterprising Department. (1998). *Serea, sufi, soomw, somway.* Colonia, Yap State, FSM: Yap State Education Enterprising Department.

ULITHI:
PHYSICAL ENVIRONMENT BIBLIOGRAPHY

Harley I. Manner

The reader may be wondering why there are two long sections of bibliographic listings in this book. In Part I, which was dedicated to the research reports of the 1992 Ulithi field trip students and faculty scholars, the reference section was developed by Deborah Piscusa Bratt and Rebecca Stephenson shortly following their field work. It was then augmented by team members over time as further analyses and editorial work occurred. The focus of the first reference section is closely calibrated to the activities and interests underlying that particular field trip. In contrast, the Ulithi bibliography which follows has a focus that is more international, has a longer historical range, yet is more interdisciplinary. It includes an important strain of research works dedicated to the cultural context of topics on environmental sustainability, subsistence economic issues, agriculture, and environment. Since this bibliography was substantially inspired by my work in Ulithi, as well as work in other parts of Micronesia, Hawaii, and the South Pacific, I will preface the bibliography with some contextual reflections.

I first visited Ulithi in January 1990 while working on the "LISA" (Low Impact Sustainable Agriculture) grant funded by the United States Department of Agriculture (USDA). Former University of Guam President, Dr. Fred Leon Guerrero, was instrumental in bringing me into that project because it included Micronesian states that typically practice a viable low input sustainable form of agriculture in contrast to the high input (e.g., fertilizers, insecticides, machine-based techniques) agricultural approaches that are frequently the subject of USDA funding. The grant was conducted as a cooperative project involving the American Samoa Community College, University of Hawaii, University of Guam, College of Micronesia, and USDA, focusing primarily on taro as a sustainable type of agriculture.

Figure 1. Harley Manner discusses survey with Ulithi men at research gathering in 2010. *(Photo by Mary Spencer.)*

During three trips between 2008 and 2010, I joined Todd Ames and Ann Ames on their research grant with Yap State. The study encompassed the outer islands of Ulithi and Fais as well as Yap Proper and examined market development, micro-market development, and agriculture. We collected data on these islands to document features of the agricultural processes there and to make comparisons of marketable items from Ulithi and Fais for Yap Proper. For example, we examined applications of indigenous agriculture that had potential to lead to a more commercialized agricultural economy on Yap Proper. One question of interest was whether this could lead to increased income for farmers in Ulithi and Fais. Research questions included: What were the people growing? What species were selected? What were the methods, agricultural systems, and problems? And, what was the potential viability of these systems?

There were several young people and students working on the Ulithi and Yap research projects (e.g., Derwin Rolmar in Ulithi and Alex Langowa in Fais). We interacted with their families and many other community members in both locations. It was my impression that numerous young people of Ulithi hoped to leave, with favored destinations being Yap Proper or Guam – sometimes so other family members would have better access to the health care options they needed. I knew at least two such young men who were students at UOG. Although I saw few high school aged youth, younger children were a common sight. (See page 190 of the *Specialty Crops for Pacific Islands* book for photos of some friends from these trips.)

Some of the main findings of the research observations on Ulithi may be of interest to readers. The Ulithi people had a very viable system of agriculture. They still used traditional techniques and they were not relying on commercial fertilizer or pesticides. Nevertheless, they appeared to be quick to adopt and adapt agricultural techniques that suited their needs. For example, they grew taro in concrete tanks and other military equipment such as landing barges that had been left over from the WWII US military presence on Ulithi. Although I cannot document it here, it is likely that they have also adopted some of the agricultural approaches that they learned about during the Japanese Mandate years of occupation.

Figure 2. Derwin Rolmar and Ulithi men discuss environmental research survey in a 2010 study visit. *(Photo by Mary Spencer.)*

During my first trip to Ulithi in 1990 for the purpose of providing technical assistance, I shared information about the nature of global warming and sea level rise, and on some of the methods they could use to mitigate effects of these phenomena (see the South Pacific Regional Environment Programme pamphlet, *A Climate of Crisis* by P. Hulme, 1989). I pointed out the benefits of their use of the concrete tanks for growing taro and encouraged them to use this approach more extensively. Later, following the construction of a hotel on Ulithi, there was more salt-water intrusion into the Ulithi taro patches. One possible contributing factor was a greater draw-down of fresh water due to increased hotel consumption of water. This, added to tidal changes, may have impacted the fresh water in the ground water supply. (See the illustration on page 167, *Specialty Crops for Pacific Islands*.)

I have conducted research in many parts of the Pacific. These experiences have taught me that people who live on atolls have the best expertise and skill for living in a relatively inhospitable environment. They must select their crops carefully, considering all the factors that help them decide which species grow best. Although taro is not particularly well suited to the atoll environment, people take great pains to cultivate it because of its great cultural significance. Lessa (1977, p. 44) wrote that Ulithi had three species of taro: *Alocasia macrorrhiza* (*file* in Ulithian) with five varieties; *Cyrtosperma chamissonis* (*bwolok* in Ulithian) with four varieties, and *Colocasia esculenta* (*ioth* in Ulithian) with two varieties. While in Ulithi in 1990, I found at least one variety of a fourth species, *Xanthosoma nigrum* (*yothol minedo* in Ulithian). To contrast these results to another Yap State outer island, Alkire (1974) listed 19 varieties of *Colocasia esculenta* on Woleai Atoll.

Figure 3. Ulithi gardener examines newly planted and mulched taro plants in one of the concrete tanks, 1990. *(Photo by Harley I. Manner.)*

An interesting question is "Why does Ulithi have so few varieties of *Colocasia* taro?" On Ulithi, as on many other atolls, we would expect there to be considerably more varieties (cultivars) than species. It seems that once the people have determined that a particular species, such as taro, is important to them and can tolerate the limited growing conditions of their atoll, they find diversity in the different varieties of that species. In larger geographic locations that possess a greater variety of growing conditions, people have the opportunity to grow a greater number of species as well as varieties because they have more favorable environmental conditions.[1] These interesting issues are further complicated on atolls where the range of possible food plants and hospitable space for planting them is smaller than on larger landmasses. Often atoll inhabitants try to expand the number of varieties of the species that are already growing successfully on their atoll. For an interesting comparison, consider that on Ulithi, *Colocasia* taro has two varieties, but in Hawaii there were over 300 named varieties of *Colocasia* at one time. Another

---

[1] See discussions in Boserup, 1963, or Agricultural Involution by Clifford Geertz. Bill Clarke and Harold Brookfield discussed these issues for Papua New Guinea. Timothy Bayless-Smith has also written about the issue of land use theory and the consequences of population changes for land and agriculture.

interesting kind of comparison could be to compare the species and varieties of taro among the different outer islands in Micronesia, and to consider the relative importance of each to the cultures specific to each island. Other extraneous factors may also account for Ulithi's relatively small number of taro species and varieties. Likely among these factors is the impact of Japanese occupation during the Mandate years and US occupation during World War II.

Ulithians and other atoll peoples continue to try to find the resources that combat salt-water intrusions, typhoons, storm surges, and other threats. Examples of potentially useful approaches include the taro pits, the *maas* (taro islands), mulching techniques, guides for determining amounts of water to use for different purposes, and guides for determining the size of populations they can support. A parallel can be found in the Marshall Islands where islanders are identifying crops that are resistant to drought and that can tolerate salt water, as well as learning about techniques to protect their crops and conserve fresh water. (The Secretariat for the Pacific Community and the USGS Climate Science Center are among the organizations sponsoring some of this work.) Historically, the use of sophisticated sea-going technology provided the option of leaving an island if environmental distress becomes so severe that the island can no longer support its population. When they do move away from the atoll, atoll people seem to do very well and are very industrious. The drawback is that the migration process seems to result in the loss of young adults, leaving an imbalance of young children and the elderly. Atoll people did not create the problem of sea level rise, but they are the ones who are bearing the costs.

We believe it is important to organize and disseminate the research resources on Ulithi and other Pacific islands that could prove helpful to current and future generations who strive to learn and use the science and discovery to protect and enhance the environmental quality of their islands. For Ulithi, this knowledge is the result of work performed by earlier Ulithians, and in more recent times by collaborations of Ulithians and some outside researchers. Ulithians should have access to these resources as well as to others that relate to their islands and to the issues of importance to them. There is a rich literature if you look carefully for it. It is often said that much important historical and scientific information about Micronesia exists only in the "grey literature." That means that it may be in government reports or other forms of documentation that may not be easily found on a library shelf. Therefore, we have attempted to include both the easily found and the more difficult to find reference resources in the bibliography below. The reader will notice that some entries are European or Asian, as well as American. I feel it is important to take an international approach to examining the research resources relevant to Ulithi. We should keep in mind that we can request the assistance of librarians in our colleges and universities to help us locate them.

This bibliography will be useful to Ulithians and other Pacific Islanders who have migrated, or who are studying at universities, or just asking questions about their heritages to find out who they are and what the lessons are of their ancestors. Using the literature about their islands can support efforts that Ulithians and others can initiate in order to perpetuate their sustainable agricultural techniques for use at home and perhaps also make available to other parts of the world. Already techniques similar to those of the Ulithians are being used by other people. They just use new terms to characterize them; e.g., perma-culture; sustainable agriculture. (See Clarke, 1974, *The Structure of Permanence,* in the context of Papua New Guinea and other sustainable cultural systems.)

I believe that one natural consequence of Ulithians becoming familiar with their history of environmental and social research is that they will become interested in taking the next step: Defining their research agenda for the future. What might they see as important? We can only guess. As the population gets older, would more assistance be needed in the collection of crops for their individual use (e.g., harvesting coconuts and breadfruit from trees will be difficult for the elderly). Will this stimulate the growing of different kinds of crops? If out-migration increases, what will be the structure of agriculture on Ulithi? Is there an agricultural future for Ulithi? What will it be? Are there desalinization projects that could potentially be cost effective for Ulithi? What are the pros and cons of such development for the Ulithi population? What are the potential solar electricity and communication prospects for Ulithi? What are the advantages and disadvantages of such development? What are the conveniences or protections that people on Ulithi would like to have in order to live there? Does knowing the research of the past help Ulithians examine and understand their past and plan for their future?

A big part of the trend of globalization has been for people to move from the small to the big. But for a variety of reasons, many people prefer small-scale environments. For people who want to live in smaller places, or for those who want to maintain their heritage lands, what do they need to live safely, hygienically, nutritiously, and have their health and happiness well supported? When applying these questions to Ulithi, it is paramount that the younger generations also be called upon to describe their needs and their wants, for they shall inherit their atoll and the seas and skies that surround it.

Bibliography

To use the bibliography that follows, the reader may want to simply skim through it in its entirety in order to find topics of interest. It reflects the philosophy that students should read widely, looking across disciplines and across time. One will find valuable information about culture in a book on botany, or about strategies for coping with global warming by learning how elders historically coped with drought or rainy seasons. The reader will notice that some references are accompanied by an annotation that describes the general content or approach of the reference. Most of these are repeated from Sachet and Fosberg's two extensive annotated bibliographies for tropical Pacific islands, first in their 1955 publication, and further in their 1971 publication. The annotated references from Sachet and Fosberg's publications that are relevant to Ulithi have been individually integrated into the current bibliography. To aid readers who wish to look more closely at original sources, the annotations of these references are identified by the initials SF55 or SF71, referring to the year of the relevant Sachet and Fosberg publication.

Alkire, W. H. (1965). *Lamotrek Atoll, inter-island socioeconomic ties.* Prospect Heights, ILL: Waveland Press, Inc.

Alkire provides a classic and in-depth anthropological analysis of Lamotrek Atoll, a sister Atoll in the Yap Outer Island constellation of which Ulithi figures so importantly. It features an abundance of photographs of the people of Lamotrek engaging in their everyday life activities. Alkire's descriptions and analysis address the Atoll and island setting, kinship and political organizations, economic activities, religion, inter-island communication concepts and technology, inter-island socioeconomic ties and a 1989 epilogue. It should be recommended reading for anyone interested in Ulithi or other Yap Outer Islands.

Figure 4. William H. Alkire, Department of Anthropology, University of Victoria, British Columbia, Canada. Dr. Alkire wrote one of the most widely read books on the people and cultures of Micronesia, and also conducted research on specific principles of societal organization in the Outer Islands of Yap.

Alkire, W. H. (1972; 1977). *An introduction to the peoples and cultures of Micronesia.* Menlo Park, CA: Cummings Publishing Company.

Alkire, W. H. (1978). Cultural adaptation in the Caroline Islands. *Journal of the Polynesian Society, 69* (2), 123 – 150.

Alkire, W. H. (1993): Madrich: Outer islanders on Yap. *Pacific Studies, 16(2),* 31 – 66.

Alkire, W. H. & Fujimura, K. (1990). Principles of organization in the outer islands of Yap State and their implications for archaeology. *Micronesica Supplement, 2,* 85 – 88, 1990.

American Anthropological Association. (2015). *AAA guidelines for the evaluation of ethnographic and visual media.* http://www.americananthro.org/ConnectWithAAA/Content.aspx?ItemNumber=1941 Retrieved 3/30/17.

American Association of Geographers. (2009). *Statement on professional ethics.* http://www.aag.org/cs/about_aag/governance/statement_of_professional_ethics Retrieved 4/3/17.

American Psychological Association. (2010). *Ethical principals of psychologists and code of conduct.* Washington, DC. Author

American Sociological Association. (1999). Code of ethics and policies and procedures of the ASA Committee on Professional Ethics. http://www.asanet.org/membership/code-ethics Retrieved 4/3/17.

Ames, A. (2012). Micro-Traders: A case study of micro-finance on Yap Proper, Federated States of Micronesia. *Pacific Asia Inquiry, 3,* 101 – 115.

Ames, A., Ames, T., & Manner, H. (2010). Traditional agricultural systems and emerging markets in Yap, Federated States of Micronesia. In *Proceedings of the 11ᵗʰ Pacific Science Inter-Congress, Haut Commisariat de le Republique en Polynesie Francaise et Polynesie Francaise, Tahiti, French Polynesia.* Honolulu, HI: Pacific Science Association.

Ames, T. (2012). The greening of Yap: The transformative reemergence of subsistence agriculture and its impact on rural community development in Yap, FSM. *Pacific Asia Inquiry, 3,* 76 – 86.

Ames, T. (2013). Maritime culture in the western Pacific: A touch of tradition. *Pacific Asia Inquiry, 4,* 94 – 108.

Ames, T., Ames, A., & Manner, H. (2009). The application of innovative marketing to traditional subsistence agriculture. Paper in *Project director meeting handbook for the agribusiness markets and trade and agricultural prosperity for small and medium sized farms programs.* Washington, DC: Cooperative State, Research, Education and Extension Services (CSREES), USDA.

Figure 5. Ann Ames discusses environmental survey with Ulithi woman at community meeting, 2010. *(Photo by Mary Spencer.)*

Ames, T. T. & Ames, A. L. (2007). The role of micro-finance and community development in Indonesia. *Micronesian Educator, 12,* 25 – 36.

Andersen, K. (1908). Twenty new forms of Pteropus. *Annual Magazine of Natural History, VIII*(2), 361 – 370.

Includes Pteropus (bats) yapensis from Yap and Mackenzie Islands (Ulithi), p. 365. (SF55)

Anon, L. N. P. (1945). *Tropical and Exotic Diseases of Naval Importance,* 1 – 107. Bethesda, Md. (LC: RC 986, U62, 1945)

Anon. L. N. P. (1960). Settlement at Falalop. *Micronesia Reporter, 8*(3), 16 – 17.

Account of settlement of claims for land taken by U.S. Government on Ulithi.

Anon. L. N. P. (1961). Ophelia the Second. *Micronesia Reporter, 9*(2), 4 – 7.

Account of typhoon that devastated Ulithi on Nov. 30, 1960. See photo. (SF71)

Figure 6. Todd Ames, Derwin Rolmar, and Ulithi man discuss environmental and food production matters after 2010 workshop. *(Photo by Mary Spencer.)*

Aoyama, T. (Ed.). (2003). The Progress Report of the 2000 and 2001 Survey of the Research Project, "Social homeostasis of small islands in an island-zone, Yap Proper and Ulithi Atoll, Micronesia." *Occasional Papers, 39.* Kagoshima, Japan: Kagoshima University Research Center for the Pacific Islands. Retrieved from http://cpi.kagoshima-u.ac.jp/

Aoyama, T. (2003). Politics of dancing: Cultural and social negotiation among the islands of Ulithi Atoll and Yap Proper. In T. Aoyama (Ed.), The Progress Report of the 2000 and 2001 Survey of the Research Project, "Social homeostasis of small islands in an island-zone, Yap Proper and Ulithi Atoll, Micronesia." *Occasional Papers, 39* (section 1, report 2), 11 – 15. Kagoshima, Japan: Kagoshima University Research Center for the Pacific Islands. Retrieved from http://cpi.kagoshima-u.ac.jp/

Baker, R. H. (March 11 – 13, 1946). Some Effects of the war on the wildlife of Micronesia. *Transactions of the 11th North American Wildlife and Natural Resources Conference,* 205 – 213.

Includes a few remarks on the effects of war on the vegetation and animal life of Ulithi. (SF55)

Baker, R. H. (1948). Report on collections of birds made by United States Naval Medical Research Unit No. 2 in the Pacific war area. *Smithsonian Miscellaneous Collection, 107*(15), ii, 1 – 74, and 6 plates.

Aerial photo of Falalop Islet showing area cleared for military operations; photo of "jungle" vegetation on Ulithi; list of various birds from Ulithi; map of atoll; some excellent photos showing vegetation of several Micronesian islands, including Ulithi. (SF55)

Barratt, G. (1988). *Carolinean contacts with the islands of the Marianas: The European record. The Micronesian Archaeological Survey Report No. 25.* Saipan, MP: Divi-

sion of Historic Preservation, Department of Community and Cultural Affairs, info@
cnmihpo.net

For readers interested in Ulithi, the other outer islands of Yap, and Yap itself, Barratt's deeply
researched report will provide rare and valuable information about the people of these islands
and their earliest interactions with Europeans and Chamorros. There were a few reports from
the 1500s and 1600s, but greater focus was given to later contacts. Of particular interest is
the review of Spanish Padre Juan Antonio Cantova's knowledge of the Ulithi language and
culture, life in the Carolines, and particularly life on Ulithi in the 1700s. Barratt also discusses
information about Cantova's "martyrdom" on Ulithi in the 1730s. Cantova issued a letter in
1722 that described the physical geography of the Carolinian islands. Based on his interviews
with Carolinians, Cantova created a map of the Carolinian islands and outlined their political,
language, and economic relationships. Palau constituted the western boundary and Truk formed
the eastern edge. Cantova's map echoed island naming information given earlier by Padres
Clain and Somera, but was considered to be more correct geographically. In Barratt's opinion,
Cantova's map was still the best available in 1816 when Russian Captain Otto Kotzebue sailed
the area. Readers will also be interested in the documentation of voyages by Ulithians and other
Yap outer island mariners to Guam, and their lives on Guam following these voyages. It reveals
that descriptions of the isolation of Ulithi and other outer islands before the Europeans landed
on their shores were not altogether true. The navigators of these islands were actively exploring
the world, bringing home important economic materials such as iron, obtaining an international
education, and establishing diplomatic relationships throughout the Pacific.

Borja, J. I. (October 10, 2017). Kicking the nut, betel nut study investigates ways to help chewers quit the addiction. *Pacific Daily News, 49*(271), 1, 3.

Boykin, J. C. (1963). The voyage of the Ulithians. *Micronesia Reporter, 11*(2), 18 – 20.
Canoe with 6 men sailed from Ulithi to the Philippines in 3 weeks. (SF71)

Bryan, E. H. Jr. (1971). *Guide to place names in the Trust Territory of the Pacific Islands.*
Honolulu: Pacific Science Information Center, Bernice P. Bishop Museum.

Buden, D. W. (2011). The Odonata of Fais Island and Ulithi and Woleai Atolls, Yap State, Western Caroline Islands, Federated States of Micronesia. *Micronesica, 41(2)*, 215 – 222.

Buden, D. W., & Tennent, W. J. (2011). New records of butterflies from Yap Outer Islands, Micronesia: Fais Island and Ngulu, Ulithi, and Woleai Atolls. *Pacific Science, 65(1)*, 117 – 122.

Chamisso, D. A. Von (1821). Remarks and opinions of the naturalist of the expedition. In O. von Kotzebue (Ed.), *A voyage of discovery into the South Seas and Bering's Straits for the purpose of exploring a north-east passage* (Vol. 3, pp. 1 – 318; 436 – 442). London: Longman, Hurst, Rees, Orme, and Brown.
Includes valuable information on various atolls visited by the ship, the Rurick: Marshalls, pp. 140-180, Carolines (especially "Ulea" and "Mogemug," information apparently compiled), p 181 – 216; Penrhyn, pp. 217 – 219; Tuamotus, pp. 220 – 223; The Johnstone I. mentioned in the chapter on Hawaii is really Gaspar Rico (Pokak). The information includes notes on plants, vegetation (especially for the Marshalls), fauna, water supply, material culture, etc. (SF55)

Chiang, L-H. N., Lidstone, J., & Stephenson, R. A. (2003). *Global processes, local impacts: The effects of globalization in the Pacific-Asia region. Session proceedings, 10th Pacific Science Inter-Congress: "Globalizaiton in the Pacific and Asian Regions-*

Figure 7. Chandra Legdesog of Ulithi is a Master of Arts graduate student in the Micronesian Studies Program at the University of Guam. She is active in research on climate change and also participates in federally funded health research on betel nut use and treatment (see Borja, 2017). Her environmental research explores the perceptions of Ulithians about climate change phenomenon, and their adaptations to climate change impacts.

New Perspectives in the 21ˢᵗ Century. Honolulu: Micronesian Area Research Center, University of Guam and Pacific Science Association.

Clark, E. (1951). Field trip to the South Seas. *Natural History, 60,* 8 – 15; 46.
Popular account of collecting trip in Western Carolines. Some notes and photos on Ulithi and Ngulu. (SF55)

Clark, E. (1953). *Lady with a spear,* 1 – 243. New York: Harper and Brothers.
Popular account of author's fish collecting trips; includes some notes on native life on Kayangel, Ulithi and the southwestern Caroline atolls, LC:QL31, C56 A3. (SF55)

Close Up Foundation. (2000). *Micronesia: A guide through the centuries.* Alexandria, VA: Close Up Foundation.

Cogswell, H. S. (1946). Bird study aboard a transport to the western Pacific. *Elepaio, 6,* 46 – 48; 53 – 54; 62 – 63.
Lists birds seen, passing near Johnston Island and Bikar Atoll; records some birds on Ulithi. (SF55)

Corner, E. J. H. (1960). Taxanomic notes on Ficus Linn, Asia and Australasia, I-IV. *Gardner's Bulletin, Singapore, 17,* 368 – 385.
Includes F. prolixa var. subcordata, N. var., from Ulithi and Fanning Islands. (SF71)

Craib, J. L. (1979). Archaeological survey of Ulithi Atoll, Western Caroline Islands, *Monograph Series, 1.* Guam: Pacific Studies Institute.

Craib, J. L. (1983). Micronesian prehistory; an archaeological overview, *Science, 219,* 922 – 927.

Craib, J. L. (Nov. 14, 2014). Review: *Prehistoric architecture in Micronesia,* by William N. Morgan, *Archaeology in Oceania, 26*(1).

Crane, N. (2017). One people, one reef; *hofagie laamle!* Retrieved 3/20/17. http://ulithimarineconservation.uese. edu/

Damm, H. (1938). Zentralkarolinen: Ifaluk, Aurepik, Faraulip, Sorol, Mogmog. Based on the notes of Paul Hambruch and Ernst Sarfert. In G. Thilenius, (Ed.), *Ergebnisse der Südsee-Expedition, 1908 – 1910, part II. Ethnographie, Band 10, 2. Mikronesien, Halband.* Hamburg: Friederichsen, De Gruyter and Co.
Monographic, treating geography, flora, fauna, but emphasizing anthropology, with information on geology, climate, typhoons, water supply, vegetation, economic plans and animals, agriculture, etc.; bibliography, photographs. (SF55)

Divine, A. D. (1950). *The King of Fassarai,* 1-296. NY: The Macmillan Company.
Historical novel set in Ulithi, based on the story of M. P. Wees. LC: PZ3, D6387 Ki. (SF55)

Doutt, R. L. (1951). The parasite complex of Furcaspis oceanica Lindinger. *Annals of the Entomological Society of America, 43*(4), 501 – 507.
Describes anabrolepis oceanica, parasite of Furcaspis from Ulithi, and mentions Marietta carnesi as a probable parasite of Anabrolepis, also from Ulithi. (SF55)

Doutt, R. L. (1955). Hymenoptera: Trichogrammatidae and Mymaridae. *Insects of Micronesia, 19*(1), 1 – 17.
Includes Oligosita hilaris (Perkins) recorded from Ulithi, and Aphelinoidea oceanica Timberlake, from Wake. (SF71)

Figure 8. Isadore Dyen, was a Professor of Linguistics at Yale University, and was one of the original members of the small research team that the US Navy placed on Romonum Island in Chuuk State immediately after WWII hostilities ceased. His task was to study the linguisitics of the Chuukese and other Proto-Austronesian languages. He focused on the classification of the Austronesian language (often referred to as Malayo-Polynesian languages). He conducted field work in 1947 and 1949 on Micronesian languages in Chuuk and Yap. He later applied his methods to other language groups (e.g., Indo-European). After he retired from Yale, he joined the University of Hawaii faculty, where linguist Margaret Sharpe worked with him to catalog and digitize his Proto-Austronesian files. (Photo courtesy of Yale University.)

Elbert, S. H. (1947). *Ulithi-English and English-Ulithi word lists with notes on linguistic position, pronunciation, and grammar.* U.S. Naval Military Government.
Extensive vocabulary, including words for economic plants, animals, and foods. (SF55)

Falgout, S., Poyer, L., & Carucci, L. M. (2008). *Memories of war: Micronesians in the Pacific War.* Honolulu, HI: University of Hawai'i Press.

Farner, D. S. (1945). A new species of *Aedes* from the Caroline Islands. (Diptera, Culicidae). *Proceedings of the Biological Society of Washington, 58,* 59 – 62.
Aedes (Stegomyia) hensilli described from Ulithi. (SF55)

Figirliyong, J. (1976). *The contemporary political system of Ulithi Atoll.* (Unpublished master's thesis). California State University, Fullerton.

Fosberg, F. R. (1946). Botanical aspects of the U.S.C.C. economic survey of Micronesia. Paper presented before the general, microbiological, paleobotanical, physiological, and systematic sections and joint sessions of the Botanical Society of America, Boston, Massachusetts December 26 to 31, 1946. Abstract. *American journal of botany, 33(10),* 25a. Retrieved from http://www.jstor.org/stable/2437280

Fosberg, F. R. (1946). E. Y. Hosaka's photographs. *Economic survey of Micronesia, 13.* Honolulu: U.S. Commercial Company.

Fosberg, F. R. (February, 1947). Botanical report on Micronesia. *Economic Survey of Micronesia, 13(1),* (I and II), 1 – 349. Honolulu: U.S. Commercial Company.
Contains a description of atoll vegetation and information on economic plants, a bibliography, and figures 1 – 447.

Fosberg, F. R. (1948). *Economic survey of Micronesia, v.11, Botany.* Honolulu: U.S. Commercial Company. Microfilm. Washington, DC: Library of Congress Photoduplication Service. On reel 4 of 5 35mm low reduction microfilm reels. Retrieved from https://uhhilo.lib.hawaii.edu/vwebv/searchBasic?sk=hilo

Fosberg, F. R. (1958a). Notes on Micronesian pteridophyta, II. *American Fern Journal, 48,* 35 – 39.
Includes an atoll record of Ceratopteris thalictroides from Ulithi. (SF71)

Fosberg, F. R. (1960)[2]. The vegetation of Micronesia: General descriptions, the vegetation of the Marianas Islands, and a detailed consideration of the vegetation of Guam. NY: *Bulletin of the American Museum of Natural History, V119*(Article 1).

Fosberg, F. R., Sachet, M. -H., and Oliver, R. (1979). A geographical checklist of the Micronesian Dicotyledonae. *Micronesica, 15*(1 – 2), 41 – 295.

Figure 9. Samuel H. Elbert is the linguist who developed the Ulithi-English word lists for the US Navy immediately after World War II. These formed the basis for many other Ulithi language activities such as work with Peace Corps volunteers. He may be known even more widely for co-authoring the Hawaiian-English Dictionary with Mary Kawena Pukui. He also published articles and books on Hawaiian folklore.

Figure 10. Renowned island botanist F. Raymond Fosberg who worked at the Smithsonian Institution, documenting and creating an archive of plant materials from the Micronesian region. He is credited with playing a significant role in the development of coral reef and island studies. (1908-1993). (Photo by H. Gray Multer, appearing in Atoll Research Bulletin, February 1994.)

---

[2] Although Ulithi is not specifically mentioned in this book, the discussions on coral atoll vegetation have relevance to Ulithi.

Fosberg, F. R., Sachet, M. -H., and Oliver, R. (1982). A geographical checklist of the Micronesian Pteridophyta and Gymnospermae. *Micronesica, 18*(1), 23 – 82.

Fosberg, F. R., Sachet, M. -H., and Oliver, R. (1987). Geographical checklist of the Micronesian Monocotyledonae. *Micronesica, 20*(1 – 2),19 – 129.

Goldberg, A. (1967). The genus Melochia L. (Sterculiaceae). *Contributions from the United States National Herbarium, 34*(5), 191 – 363.
Reports *M. compacta* from Ulithi Atoll. (SF71)

Goodenough, W. H. (1978). Property, kin, and community on Truk (2nd ed.). Hamden, CT: Archon Books, p172.
In this classic book, Ward Goodenough provides detailed genealogical, cultural, and historical information on how lineages in Chuuk are represented in land ownership, land use, and land transfer. On page 172, he provides a detailed map depicting plot ownership by lineage throughout the island of Romonum. The land distributions he discusses are critically important to the way life has been lived on this island (and perhaps more widely in the Trukic domains of Micronesia) in the past. They may also represent key forces in the present. Any student of land use and land inheritance in Micronesia would want to be familiar with Goodenough's research on these topics.

Gräffe, E. (1873). Die Carolinen-Insel Yap oder Guap nebst den Matelotas-, Makenzie-, Fais und Wolea-Inseln, nach A. Tetens and J. Kubary. *Journal Museum de Godeffroy, 1*(84 – 130).
Includes brief descriptions and notes on foods for Ngulu, Ulithi and a vocabulary for Ulithi. pp. 127 – 130. (SF55)

Hanlon, D. (1998). *Remaking Micronesia: Discourses over development in a Pacific territory 1944-1982.* Honolulu, HI: University of Hawai'i Press (pp. 46, 47).

Harry, H. W. (1966). Land snails of Ulithi Atoll, Caroline Islands: A study of snails accidentally distributed by man. *Pacific Science, 20*(2), 212 – 223.
Includes an ecological discussion as well as an annotated systematic list. Illustrations. (SF71)

Hartlaub, G. (1867). On a collection of birds from some lessknown localities in the western Pacific. *Proceedings of the Scientific Meetings of the Zoological Society of London for the Year 1867, Part 1,* (828 – 832). London: Messrs. Longman, Green, Reader, and Dyer.
Records Tachypetes minor, from the "Mackenzie group" (possibly Ulithi): several records from l'Echiquier (Ninigo), two of them new species. (SF55)

Hartlaub, G. & Finsch, O. (1872). On a fourth collection of birds from the Pelew and Mackenzie Islands. *Proceedings of the Scientific Meetings of the Zoological Society of London for the Year 1872,* (87 – 114). London: Messrs. Longman, Green, Reader, and Dyer.

Hatta, A. (2001). School education of the Federated States of Micronesia and small islands of South Japan. In T. Aoyama (Ed.), The progress report of the 1999 survey of the research project "Social homeostasis of small islands in an island-zone." *Occasional papers, 34,* (section 1, report 4), 33 – 40. Kagoshima, Japan: Kagoshima University Research Center for the Pacific Islands. Retrieved from http://cpi.kagoshima-u.ac.jp/

Figure 11. Ward H. Goodenough, at 90 years of age, one of the original Yale University members of the anthropology team sent to Micronesia immediately after World War II by the US Navy's Coordinated Investigations of Micronesia. In meticulously detailed in situ linguistic and cultural research, Goodenough worked with the people of Romonum Island in Chuuk Lagoon to document the Chuukese language, lineage structure, and cultural traditions. In doing so, he provided a conceptual structure for further research throughout other parts of Micronesia that would be considered part of the "Chuukic continuum." In his long career his work has served as a model for all of Micronesia, and he provided collegial assistance to countless numbers of students and officials from Micronesia. Goodenough's vast scholarly influence on knowledge and thinking about Micronesia have also been built on his linguistic work (Trukese-English and English-Trukese dictionaries) and his research on pre-Christian Trukese religious traditions. (Courtesy of Ward Goodenough and family.)

Higuchi, W. (2013). The Japanese administration of Guam, 1941 – 1944: A study of occupation and integration policies, with Japanese oral histories. North Carolina: McFarland & Company, Inc.

Hezel, F. X. (1970). Catholic missions in the Caroline and Marshall Islands. *Journal of Pacific History, 5*, 213 – 227.
Reports on archival manuscripts material uncovered by the author, including an 18th century description of Ulithi. (SF71)

Hezel, F. X. (1995). *Strangers in their own land: A century of colonial rule in the Caroline and Marshall Islands.* Honolulu, HI: Center for Pacific Island Studies, University of Hawai'i Press.

Hezel, F. X. (1996). *New trends in Micronesia migration.* Retrieved from http.//micsem.org/pubs/ articles/migration/frames/trendsfr.html

Figure 12. Father Francis X. Hezel, author of multiple books on the history of Micronesia. Father Hezel has also conducted original research on important issues such as the high rate of suicide among Micronesian teens and young adults, and census studies. *(Photo courtesy of Vid Raatior.)*

Hezel, F. X. (2001). *The new shape of old island cultures.* Honolulu: University of Hawai'i Press.

Hezel, F. X. (2005, October). The call to arms: Micronesians in the military. *Micronesian counselor, 58.*

Hezel, F. X. (2006). *Micronesians abroad* [motion picture]. Federated States of Micronesia. Micronesian Seminar.

Hosaka, E. Y. 1946. Botanical report on Micronesia. *Economic survey of Micronesia, 13*(2), 1 – 68. Honolulu: U.S. Commercial Company.
Includes sections on vegetation and agriculture of Ulithi, Kapingamarangi, Nukuoro, and Eniwetok, and a list of useful plants with native names, some of which are from these atolls; two photographs of Kapingamarangi. (SF55)

Hosaka, E. Y. (1948). *Economic survey of Micronesia, 11,* Botany. Honolulu: U.S. Commercial Company. Microfilm. Washington, DC: Library of Congress Photoduplication Service. On reel 4 of 5 35mm low reduction microfilm reels. Retrieved from https:// uhhilo.lib.hawaii.edu/vwebv/searchBasic?sk=hilo

Hulm, P. (1989). A climate of crisis: global warming and the island South Pacific. Papua New Guinea: The Association of South Pacific Environmental Institutions. Retrieved from: http://www.sprep.org/virtual-library

Hunt, E. E., Jr., Lessa, W. A., & Hicking, A. (1965). The sex ratio of live births in three Pacific island populations (Yap, Samoa, and New Guinea). *Human Biology, 37,* 148 – 155.
Includes incidental data on the human population of Ulithi Atoll. (SF71)

Ichitani, K., Hikida, M., Kamada, N., Nagayama, H., Onjo, M., Tsuda, K., & Tominaga, S. (2003). Genetic diversity of coconut (*Cocos Nucifera* L.) in Yap State. In T. Aoyama (Ed.), The progress report of the 2000 and 2001 survey of the research project "Social homeostasis of small island in an island-zone, Yap Proper and Ulithi Atoll, Micronesia." *Occasional papers, 39,* (section 2, report 2), 45-49. Kagoshima, Japan: Kagoshima University Research Center for the Pacific Islands. Retrieved from http:// cpi.kagoshima-u.ac.jp/

Ishiguro, E., Kashiwagi, S., Kikukawa, H., Higashi, M., Yoshinaga, K., Fukuda, R., & Moriyama, M. (2003). Probability of monitoring and analyzing seashore environments in Yap using satellite data. In T. Aoyama (Ed.), The Progress Report of the 2000 and 2001 Survey of the Research Project "Social Homeostasis of Small Island in an Island-Zone" Yap Proper and Ulithi Atoll, Micronesia. *Occasional Papers, 39,* (section 2, report 6), 65 – 71. Kagoshima, Japan: Kagoshima University Research Center for the Pacific Islands. Retrieved from http://cpi.kagoshima-u.ac.jp/

Ishihara, G. N., Terada, R., Higashi, A., & Noro, T. (2003). A study of the coastal sea water in Yap Island and Ulithi Atoll, Federated States of Micronesia, 2001. In T. Aoyama (Ed.), The Progress Report of the 2000 and 2001 Survey of the Research Project "Social Homeostasis of Small Islands in an Island-Zone," Yap Proper and Ulithi Atoll, Micronesia. *Occasional Papers, 39,* section 2, report 1, 35 – 43. Kagoshima, Japan: Kagoshima University Research Center for the Pacific Islands. Retrieved from http:// cpi.kagoshima-u.ac.jp/

Kawai, K. (2003). Influences of wave action on shell shape of marine snail *Nerita plicata* and oil spill on marine coastal environments. In T. Aoyama (Ed.), The Progress Report of the 2000 and 2001 Survey of the Research Project "Social Homeostasis of Small Island in an Island-Zone" Yap Proper and Ulithi Atoll, Micronesia. *Occasional Papers, 39,* 59 – 64, section 2, report 5. Kagoshima, Japan: Kagoshima University Research Center for the Pacific Islands. Retrieved from http://cpi.kagoshima-u.ac.jp/

Kawai, K., Kuwahara, S., Terada, R., Tominaga, S., Noda, S., & Nagashima, S. (2011). Influence of environmental changes on the Micronesian region: Case study of islands in Yap State, Federated States of Micronesia. South Pacific Studies, 31(2), 23 – 43.

Klingman, L. & Green, G. (1950). *His majesty O'Keefe, the incredible true story of a south seas adventurer.* NY: Scribner.
Fascinating, well written historical novel based on life of David O'Keefe; mainly about Yap, but with information on Nauru, Palau, Ulithi, Sonsorol, Mapia and other islands; including casual mentions of plants, vegetation, etc., but important in its historical information; seemingly written with scrupulous attention to accuracy. (SF55)

Krämer, A. (1908). Studienreise nach den Zentral – und Westkarolinen. *Mitteilungen aus den Deutschen Schutzgebieten, Berlin, Band 21*, Heft III, 169 – 186.
Includes a word on Ontong Java, and minor references to typhoon damage on Tobi, Pulo Anna, Merir, Mokemok (Ulithi) and in Mortlock Islands. Mentions Ngeiangl (Kayangel) in Palau Islands. Most of the article concerns the high Carolines. (SF55)

Kurtz, Born, Martens and Fritz. (Marz, 1907). Der Taifun in den West-Karolinen vom 26, bis 31. *Annalen der Hydrographie und Maritimen Meteorogie, 35*, 501 – 505. Berlin: E. S. Mittler and Sohn.
Partly reproduced from Born et al., 1907, with added information by various other observers. Concerns effects of typhoon on Lossop, Ifaluk, Oleai, Sorol and Ulithi. (SF55)

Kuwahara, S. (2001). Tourism, traditional culture and autonomy in a small island: Yap faces a new millennium. In T. Aoyama (Ed.) The Progress Report of the 1999 Survey of the Research Project, *Occasional Papers, 34* (part 1, section 1, report 2), 15 – 24. Kagoshima, Japan: Kagoshima University Research Center for the Pacific Islands. Retrieved from http://cpi.kagoshima-u.ac.jp/

Kuwahara, S. (2003). Traditional culture, tourism, and social change in Mogmog Island, Ulithi Atoll. In Aoyama, T. (Ed.), The Progress Report of the 2000 and 2001 Survey of the Research Project "Social Homeostasis of Small Island in an Island-Zone" Yap Proper and Ulithi Atoll, Micronesia. *Occasional Papers, 39,* Section 1, Report 1, 1 – 9. Kagoshima, Japan: Kagoshima University Research Center for the Pacific Islands. Retrieved from http://cpi.kagoshima-u.ac.jp/

Laimoh, M. (Ed.). (2002). *English-Ulithian dictionary 1.* Colonia, Yap, FSM: Yap State Education Department.

Lancy, D. F. (2016). Teaching: Natural or cultural? In Geary, D. C. & Berch, D. B. (Eds.), *Evolutionary perspectives on child development and education* (pp. 33 – 64). Switzerland: Springer Palgrave.
This chapter takes an interdisciplinary social science stance at examining evidence for alternative explanations of how children from many different cultures learn, including some that place emphasis on child self-agency versus direct teaching. It includes Barbara Rogoff's model, whose research was done in a number of Hispanic contexts. Lancy's discussion is useful when considering child development and education in settings such as Ulithi and other Micronesian islands.

Langal, I. (1990). Ulithian Orthography and Dictionary. In M. Spencer, V. Aguilar, G. Woo (Eds.), *Vernacular language symposium on new and developing orthographies in Micronesia* (p. 40). Mangilao, Guam: University of Guam Press.

Lange, W. H. (1950). The biology of the Mariana coconut beetle, Brontispa mariana Spaeth, on Saipan, and the introduction of parasites from Malaya and Java for its control. *Proceedings of the Hawaiian Entomology Society, 14*(1), 143 – 162.

Includes, p. 144, notes on distribution of species, including Woleai, Nukuoro, Ulithi, Nomwin; B. chalybeipennis reported from the Marshalls (Esaki). (SF55)

Lessa, W. A. (1950a). *The ethnography of Ulithi Atoll. Final CIMA Report, No. 28.* Washington, DC: Pacific Science Board and National Research Council.

Ethnological, with sections on geography, habitat, animals, agriculture, and, as appendices, lists of wild economic plants with their uses, and cultivated plants; bibliography. (SF55)

Lessa, W. A. (1950b). The place of Ulithi in the Yap empire. *Society for Applied Anthropology,* 16 – 18.

Lessa, W. A. (1950c). Ulithi and the outer native world. *American Anthropologist, 52,* 27 – 52.

Principally cultural and social anthropology, but contains some information on materials and products imported into and exported from the atoll, including some plant products. Map of part of Pacific. (SF55)

Figure 13. William Lessa, a UCLA anthropologist who conducted extensive field work on Ulithi, working with Ulithians to describe their way of life, as well as contemporary challenges presented to them in events such as typhoons. (Photo retrieved 8/3/16: http://wanderling. tripod.com/lessa.html)

Lessa, W. A. & Spiegelman, M. (1954). Ulithian personality as seen through ethnological materials and thematic test analysis. *University of California Publications in Culture and Society, 2*(5), 243 – 301.

Lessa, W. A. (1955). Depopulation on Ulithi: A record of research. *Human Biology, 27*(3), 161 – 183.

Includes historical notes and estimates, and author's analytical census of 1949. Depopulation theories discussed, including mortality from disease and typhoons. (SF71)

Lessa, W. A. (1961a). Sorcery on Ifaluk. *American Anthropologist, 63*(4), 817 – 820.

In the *Brief Comments* section, Lessa commented on Burrows' and Spiro's earlier claim that sorcery was absent on Ifaluk. Lessa explained the relevance of his findings on Ulithi to Ifaluk culture, and his conclusion that aggressive spirits play a role in many Micronesian cultures. He noted that they are sometimes applied to the gardens of a victim.

Lessa, W. A. (1961b). Tales from Ulithi Atoll. *University of California, Folklore Studies, 13,* 1 – 493.

Extensively annotated volume of folk tales, with interpretations and much incidental information. (SF71)

Lessa, W. A. (1962). An evaluation of early descriptions of Carolinian culture. *Ethnohistory, 9*(4), 313 – 403.

Discusses early Spanish and other documents and discoveries, and their bearing on certain problems, including aspects of human biology and demography. Includes atolls. Bibliography. (SF71)

Lessa, W. A. (1964). The social effects of typhoon Ophelia (1960) on Ulithi. *Micronesica, 1*(1), 1 – 47.

Introduction includes geographical setting, account of typhoon and its immediate results. Map, photos. (SF71)

Lessa, W. A. (1966). *Ulithi: A Micronesian design for living.* 1-118. NY: Holt, Rinehart, & Winston, Inc.

Contains descriptions of general environment and traditional life, including land tenure and external contacts. (SF71)

Lessa, W. A. (1977)[3]. Traditional uses of the vascular plants of Ulithi Atoll, with comparative notes. Micronesica, 13/2, 129 – 190.

Lessa, W. A. & Lay, T. (1953). The somatology of Ulithi Atoll. American Journal of Physical Anthropology, 11, 405 – 412.

Lessa, W. A. & Meyers, G. C. (1962). Population dynamics of an atoll community. Population Studies, 15, 244 – 257.
    Analyzes comparable censuses of 1949 and 1960. Stresses effect of gonorrhea upon fertility. Graphs, data, tables. Ulithi. (SF71)

Levine, R. A. & New, R. S. (Eds.). (2008). *Anthropology and child development, a cross-cultural reader.* MA: Blackwell Publishing.

Lingenfelter, J. E. (1981). *Schooling in Yap: Indigenization vs. cultural diversification* (Doctoral dissertation). University of Pittsburgh, Pittsburgh, PA.
    This dissertation focuses primarily on schooling in Yap Proper for people indigenous to that area. However, Lingenfelter provides some information and insights about the schooling received there by students from outer islands (e.g., see the section, Social Relations in Yap High School: Equality and Inequality, 66-71).

Mangefel, J. A. (1958). Medical party on a field trip (Yap). *Micronesia Reporter, 6*(5), 1, 19.
    Notes on the medical dispensary on Ulithi and neighboring atolls. (SF71)

Manner, H. I. (1991). Ulithi. In A. Vargo & L. Ferentinos (Compilers), *A rapid rural appraisal of taro production systems in Micronesia, Hawai'i and American Samoa: Surveys conducted in conjunction with the project, "a comparative study of low-input and high-input taro production systems in the American Pacific, with special reference to pest control"* (pp. 145 – 153). Honolulu, HI: Pacific Agriculture Development Office, University of Hawai'i.

Manner, H. I. (1993). Taro (*Colocasia esculenta* (L.) Schott) in the atolls and low islands of Micronesia. In L. Ferentinos (Ed.), *Proceedings of the Sustainable Taro Culture for the Pacific Conference*, September 2425, 1992. In *HITAHR Research Extension Series, 140* (pp. 88100). Honolulu, HI: EastWest Center.

Manner, H. I. (1993)[4]. To Micronesia via Suva: A tale of two universities and their regions. In E. Waddell & P. D. Nunn (Eds.), *The margin fades: Geographical itineraries in a world of islands,* (pp. 121 – 136). Suva, Fiji: Institute of Pacific Studies, The University of the South Pacific.

Manner, H. I. (1993). Ulithi. In L. Ferentinos & A. Vargo (Eds.), Taro Production Systems in Micronesia, Hawaii and American Samoa, *HITAHR Research Extension Series, 139* (pp. 7984). Honolulu, HI.

Manner, H. I. (1995). Humans and island biogeography: examples from Micronesian atolls. *South Pacific Journal of Natural Sciences, 14*, 133 – 166.

Manner, H. I. (2011)[5]. Giant swamp taro (Cyrtosperma chamissonis). In C.R. Elevitch (Ed.), *Specialty crops for Pacific Islands* (pp. 159 – 176). Holualoa, HI: Permanent Agriculture Resources.

Manner, H. I. (2015)[6]. Sustainable traditional agricultural systems of the Pacific Islands. In C. R. Elevitch (Ed.), *Agroforestry landscapes for Pacific Islands: Creating abun-*

---

[3] The reader will want to note the multiple photographs showing how plants have been used on Ulithi; e.g., coconut leaflets used in dancing for aesthetic and magical value; the ritualistic distribution of nutritious breadfruit; the use of Hibiscus tileuceus bast for the weaving of the post-pubertal wraparound skirt for girls; the preferred use of Calophyllum inophyllum for making canoe hulls, the highest expression of Ulithian craftsmanship; the chel tree, Messerschmidia argentea, which is used for medicine, canoe parts, and earth ovens.

[4] See Plate 8.2, page130 for a photograph of a World War II landing barge used for the hydroponic cultivation of taro on Ulithi Atoll. This method has recently been adopted for use in many places in the world as a mitigation against sea water incursion into gardens caused by global warming.

[5] Of note is the photograph of Marianna Chim, 81 year old successful subsistence cultivator of the giant swamp taro on Falalop Islet, Ulithi Atoll, p. 172-173.

[6] Photographs illustrate the presence of giant swamp taro in 2008 on Falalop Islet, Ulithi Atoll (p. 29), and a developmental succession in response to sea level rise and salt water intrusion of the taro swamp (p. 29).

dant and resilient food systems (pp. 2 – 58). Holualoa, HI: Permanent Agriculture Resources.

Matsumura, A. (1918). The physical characteristics of the natives of Mokmok Island. *Journal of Anthropological Society, Nippon, 33*(4), 112 – 113.
    Anthropometric observations made on occupants of a canoe which drifted to Japan. In Japanese. (SF71)

McNight, R. E. (1964). Handicrafts of the Trust Territory of the Pacific Islands. *South Pacific Bulletin, 14*(2), 37 – 40.
    Includes weaving on Kili; Tobi and Ulithi "monkey men;" navigational charts. Photos. (SF71)

Mellen, N. & Hancock, J. (2010). Ulithian-English Dictionary. Columbia, South Carolina: Habele Outer Island Education Fund.
    This 38-page free download dictionary provides English definitions for Ulithian words. One author (Neil Mellen) is a former American Peace Corps Volunteer and another (Juan Uweil) is Ulithian. The document was published in 2005 and a revised 127-page hard copy print version was published by Mellen and John Hancock in 2010. This version is available for purchase from Lulu Marketplace (www.lulu.com). Preparations have been made to publish a further expanded and corrected version when time and funding permit. Habele Outer Island Education Fund, a US 501c3 nonprofit organization, located in Columbia, South Carolina, is the publisher of these dictionaries. Habele also works to aid outer island students who wish to attend private primary and secondary schools in the FSM capitols, and to establish host families. Interested donors may contact the fund via www.habele.org to learn more about the directors, scholarships, and goals of the Fund.

Merlin, M., Kufas, A., Keene, T., & Juvik, J. (1996). *Gidii nge gakiyy nu Wa'ab. Plants, people and ecology in Yap.* Honolulu: East-West Center.

Mertens, K. H. (1830). Mémoire sur l'archipel des Carolines, particulièrement sur les iles basses. *Recueil des Actes de la Séances Publiques de l'Académie des St Petersbourg,* tenue le 29 decembre 1829, 93 – 186.
    Includes information on geography and native life on the atolls,

Figure 14. Marianna Chim, a Falalop Ulithi woman, reviews a report of environmental research conducted on Ulithi and in her garden by the Ames, Ames, Manner, and Rolmar team, 2010. *(Photo by Mary Spencer.)*

especially Lukunor, Woleai, Ulithi, and the Hall Islands. Some mention of vegetation, much information on economic plants, with botanical and native names. Brief notes on birds. (SF55)

Mueller-Dombois, D. & Fosberg, R. R. (1998)[7]. *Vegetation of the tropical Pacific Islands.* NY: Springer-Verlag.

Nakano, K., & Onjo, M. (2003). An overview of aroid cultivation on atolls in the Pacific Ocean. In T. Aoyama (Ed.), The Progress Report of the 2000 and 2001 Survey of the Research Project "Social Homeostasis of Small Island in an Island-Zone" Yap Proper and Ulithi Atoll, Micronesia. *Occasional Papers, 39*(section 3, report 1), 87 – 91. Kagoshima, Japan: Kagoshima University Research Center for the Pacific Islands. Retrieved from http://cpi.kagoshima-u.ac.jp/

National Museum of Natural History (2010 – 2013)[8]. *Search the Department of Botany Collections.* Department of Botany. Washington, D.C.: Smithsonian Institution. Retrieved from http://collections.nmnh.si.edu/search/botany/
    Database of herbaceous plant specimens collected from Ulithi and other Pacific islands.

---

[7] Although Ulithi is not specifically mentioned in this book, the discussions on coral atoll vegetation have relevance to Ulithi.

[8] Many specimens gathered in Ulithi and other islands of Micronesia by scientists, over a long period of time, are housed in this collection.

Nelson, P. (2014). Building capacity for community management of marine resources. Ulithi Atoll, Yap, Federated States of Micronesia. In *Case studies of social-ecological resilience in island systems: Resilience sourcebook*. New York, NY: Center for Biodiversity and Conservation, American Museum of Natural History. Retrieved from http://www.amnh.org/our-research/center-for-biodiversity-conservation/events-exhibitions/conferences-and-symposia/2013-island-systems/case-studies

Nishihara, G. N., Terada, R., Higashi, A., & Noro, T. (2003). A study of the coastal seawater in Yap Island and Ulithi Atoll, Federated States of Micronesia, 2001. In T. Aoyama (Ed.), The Progress Report of the 2000 and 2001 Survey of the Research Project "Social Homeostasis of Small Islands in an Island-Zone" Yap Proper and Ulithi Atoll, Micronesia. *Occasional Papers, 39*(section 2, report 1), *35 – 43*. Kagoshima, Japan: Kagoshima University Research Center for the Pacific Islands. Retrieved from http://cpi.kagoshima-u.ac.jp/

Noda, S. (2014). Review, mosquito fauna in the Federated States of Micronesia: A discussion of the vector species of the dengue virus. *South Pacific Studies, 34(2)*, 117 – 127.

Noda, S., & Gilmatam, J. (2003). A survey of the mosquito fauna in Ulithi Athol (sic), Yap State, Federated States of Micronesia. In T. Aoyama (Ed.), The Progress Report of the 2000 and 2001 Survey of the Research Project "Social Homeostasis of Small Islands in an Island-Zone" Yap Proper and Ulithi Atoll, Micronesia. *Occasional Papers, 39*(section 3, report 5), 111 – 114. Kagoshima, Japan: Kagoshima University Research Center for the Pacific Islands. Retrieved from http://cpi.kagoshima-u.ac.jp/

Noda, S., Gilmatam, J., Ogino, K., Toma, T., & Miyagi, I. (2005). Mosquitoes collected on Yap Islands and Ulithi Atoll, Yap State, Federated States of Micronesia (Diptera: Culicidae). Medical Entomology and Zoology, 56, 349 – 353.

Noro, T., Nishihara, G.N., Terada, R., & Yoropiy, A. (2003). Ciguatera fish poisoning in Ulithi Atoll, Yap State, Micronesia. In T. Aoyama (Ed.), The Progress Report of the 2000 and 2001 Survey of the Research Project "Social Homeostasis of Small Islands in an Island-Zone" Yap Proper and Ulithi Atoll, Micronesia. *Occasional Papers, 39*(section 2, report 9), 83-86. Kagoshima, Japan: Kagoshima University Research Center for the Pacific Islands. Retrieved from http://cpi.kagoshima-u.ac.jp/

Onjo, M., Hayashi, M., & Matsuo, T. (2003). Comparision of tuber proteins of yam introduced from Pohnpei Island and Yap Proper, The Federated States of Micronesia. In T. Aoyama (Ed.), The Progress Report of the 2000 and 2001 Survey of the Research Project "Social Homeostasis of Small Islands in an Island-Zone" Yap Proper and Ulithi Atoll, Micronesia. *Occasional Papers, 39*(section 2, report 4), 55 – 58. Kagoshima, Japan: Kagoshima University Research Center for the Pacific Islands. Retrieved from http://cpi.kagoshima-u.ac.jp/

Onjo, M., Nakano, K., Tominaga, S., Tsuda, K., Ichitani, K., & Park, B. J. (2003). Agriculture and food supply on Ulithi Atoll. In T. Aoyama (Ed.), The Progress Report of the 2000 and 2001 Survey of the Research Project "Social Homeostasis of Small Islands in an Island-Zone" Yap Proper and Ulithi Atoll, Micronesia. *Occasional Papers, 39*(section 1, report 3), 51 – 54. Kagoshima, Japan: Kagoshima University Research Center for the Pacific Islands. Retrieved from http://cpi.kagoshima-u.ac.jp/

Pacific Daily News. (2015). *Typhoon Maysak*. Guam: Pacific Daily News.

Pacific Worlds & Associates. (2003). Pacific Worlds Yap-Ulithi Website: Chronology for Yap and Ulithi. Baltimore, MD: Pacific Worlds. Retrieved on 2/18/17 from http://www.pacificworlds.com/yap/memories/chronol.cfm

Pacific Worlds & Associates. (2003). Pacific Worlds Yap-Ulithi Website: Sources and Links. Baltimore, MD: Pacific Worlds. Retrieved on 2/18/17 from http://www.pacificworlds.com/yap/arrival/sources1.cfm

Pacific Worlds & Associates is a non-profit "indigenous-geography education project for Hawai'i Pacific schools." It produces webpages for government and education organizations in the Pacific. Examples of these are multiple Yap State web pages that provide historical, cultural, educational, and economic information. Funding for this work is provided by organizations such as Pacific Educational Research Laboratory (PREL), the Hawaii Council for the Humanities, the Center for Pacific Island Studies at the University of Hawaii, and a variety of private foundations.

Pemberton, C. E. (1953a). Economic entomology in Guam and Micronesia. *Proceedings of the 7th Pacific Science Congress, 4,* 94 – 96.

Includes information on insect pests, and the parasites introduced to control them, with examples from Majuro and Ulithi. (SF71)

Poyer, L., Falgout, S., & Carucci, L. M. (2001). The typhoon of war: Micronesian experiences of the Pacific war. Honolulu, HI: University of Hawai'i Press.

The main thrust of this book is to share the perspectives of Micronesia's Islanders who lived through the World War II events. It begins by overviewing the Japanese Mandate years in Micronesia, and moves on to the harrowing experiences of warfare, invasion, and occupation as America prevailed. Ulithi is part of the coverage of war memories in Yap, including mistaken US attacks on Ulithi civilians (p. 168).

Purcell, D. C., Jr. (1976). The economics of exploitation: The Japanese in the Mariana, Caroline, and Marshall Islands, 1915 – 1940. *Journal of Pacific History, 11*(3), 189 – 211.

Ridgell, R. (1995). *Pacific nations and territories: The islands of Micronesia, Melanesia, and Polynesia.* Honolulu: Bess Press.

Riesenberg, S. H. (1975). The ghost islands of the Carolines. *Micronesica, 11*(1), 7 – 33.

Rubinstein, D. H. (1992). *Power and enchantment, ritual textiles from the islands.* Mangilao, Guam: ISLA Center for the Arts, University of Guam.

Rubinstein, D. H. (1993). The social fabric: Micronesian textile patterns and social order. In R. L. Anderson & K. L. Field (Eds.), *Art in small-scale societies, contemporary readings* (pp. 70 – 83). New Jersey: Prentice Hall.

Rubinstein, D. H. (2003). A tale of two islands: Tourism, culture, and conflict in Yap State. In T. Aoyama (Ed.), The Progress Report of the 2000 and 2001 Survey of the Research Project "Social Homeostasis of Small Islands in an Island-Zone" Yap Proper and Ulithi Atoll, Micronesia. *Occasional Papers, 39*(section 1, report 4), 25 – 34. Kagoshima, Japan: Kagoshima University Research Center for the Pacific Islands. Retrieved from http://cpi.kagoshima-u.ac.jp/

Rubinstein, D. (2007). Seeking safety from the storm: The impact of climate change on inter-island relations and human migration in Micronesia. In Climate changes and globalization – environment and people's life in the Pacific Islands. *Occasional Papers, 48,* 59 – 64. Kagoshima, Japan: Kagoshima University Research Center for the Pacific Islands. Retrieved from http://cpi.kagoshima-u.ac.jp/

Abstract in Japanese.

Sachet, M. –H. & Fosberg, F. R. (1955). *Island bibliographies: Micronesian botany, land, environment, and ecology of coral atolls: Vegetation of tropical Pacific Islands, Publication 335.* Compiled under the auspices of the Pacific Science Board, National Academy of Sciences, National Research Council (Mimeograph).

Figure 15. Marie-Helene Sachet, pre-eminent botanist with the Smithsonian Institution, and curator in the Department of Botany, National Museum of Natural History. She was particularly dedicated to collecting, organizing, and disseminating research and information on the botany of islands. (1922–1986) (Photo courtesy of the Smithsonian Institution, siarchives. si.edu.)

Sachet, M. –H. and Fosberg, F. R. (1971). *Island bibliographies, supplement: Micronesian botany, land environment, and ecology of coral atolls; vegetation of tropical Pacific Islands.* Washington, DC: National Academy of Sciences, National Research Council.
Bibliography of the land environment and ecology of coral atolls – Ulithi, beginning p. 86. (SF71)

Schlanger, S. O. & Brookhart, J. W. (1955). Geology and water resources of Falalop Island, Ulithi Atoll. *American Journal of Science, 253*(1), 553 – 573.
General geological study with considerable emphasis on terrestrial features; geological and topographic map, a few photos showing geological features and vegetation; bibliography. (SF71)

Senfft, A. (1901). Ueber einen Besuch des Uluti-Atolls (Westkarolinen). *Deutsches Kolonial Blatt, 12,* 824 – 825.
Brief note, with a word on foods, and mention of sick coconut trees. (SF55)

Sinoto, Y. H., Aramata, H., Stewart, F., & Nagado, M. (2016). *Curve of the Hook: An Archaeologist in Polynesia.* Honolulu, HI: University of Hawai'i Press.
Yoshihiko Sinoto, Senior Anthropologist, at the Bernice Pauahi Bishop Museum in Honolulu, conducted research that has shaped and reshaped the world's understanding of the history of indigenous life in the Pacific. His colleagues point to such important topics as early Polynesian migration, ancient ocean voyaging and navigation, sacred places, and the everyday life of the Pacific's indigenous people. In nearly six decades of field research on almost every island group of the Pacific, his research has built a view of Oceania as one vast community that is also linked with Asian and North American communities. In introducing his most recent book, *Curve of the Hook,* University of Hawaii Press lists some of his accomplishments: His "1972 discovery of an ancient canoe-building workshop, buried for a millennium, on Huahine Island. At the same site in 1977, he unearthed the remains of a large Tahitian voyaging canoe; previously, such magnificent Polynesian canoes, capable of sailing vast distances, were known only through legends and chants. The material evidence of Polynesia's impressive cultural achievements before Western contact—along with Sinoto's restorations of sacred sites – helped encourage a cultural reawakening on many Eastern Polynesian islands, as well as renewed interest in Hawaiian navigation and voyaging. His study and restoration of *marae* (religious structures) in Tahiti during the last forty years have focused on cultural and environmental preservation, particularly on Huahine."

Smithsonian National Museum of the American Indian. (2009). *Nine guidelines for research with indigenous peoples.* Washington, DC: Author.

Solomon, A. M. (1963). National Security Action Memorandum No. 243, Survey Mission to the Trust Territory of the Pacific Islands. Washington, DC: The White House.
Anthony M. Solomon conducted a major study and report for President John F. Kennedy regarding the status, development, and needs of the Trust Territory of the Pacific Islands. It addressed: A. the political development of Micronesia; e.g., problems of the Trusteeship status; territory-wide factors affecting a plebiscite, district political patterns, problems, people, attitudes toward affiliation, many factors surrounding arrangements for a plebiscite, and government at the district and municipal levels; B. The

Figure 16. Anthony Solomon (right), Undersecretary of the Treasury, 1977, author of the famous and potentially consequential Solomon Report for President Kennedy on the development of Micronesia. (Photo by Frank Johnson. © The Washington Post.)

economic and social development of Micronesia; e.g., private and public sector economic surveys and recommendations; C. Administration of the Trust Territory; e.g., authority of the Trust Territory government; administrative relationship with Washington; administrative organization under the High Commissioner; execution of the Master Plan; budgeting; supply; personnel;

judiciary. This became a controversial report, called by some "a ruthless blueprint," and seen by many leaders in Micronesia as an extension of US colonialism. It was sent to President Kennedy only a month before his assassination. Therefore, its consideration and implementation was in the hands of his successor, President Lyndon B. Johnson. Many of the Solomon Report recommendations were over-ridden by the forces of self-determination among the local leaders of the various delegations of Micronesia. Many other provisions of the report influenced the directions and decisions made by these and US leaders for the development of the new nations.

Spencer, M. L. (2015). *Children of Chuuk Lagoon: A 21ˢᵗ century analysis of life and learning on Romonum Island.* Mangilao, GU: Micronesian Area Research Center, University of Guam.

This book is based on direct observations of children of Romonum, Chuuk in the Federated States of Micronesia. It provides a useful comparison to the observations and analysis made by Spencer in Ulithi that are reported in this book.

Spindler, G. & Spindler, L. (Eds.). (1977). *Cultures around the world: Five cases* (includes Ulithi), pp 107 – 230. NY: Holt, Rinehart, and Winston.

Stephenson, R. A. (1984). A comparison of freshwater use customs on Ulithi Atoll with those of selected other Micronesian atolls. *Technical Report of Water and Energy Research Institute of the Western Pacific, University of Guam, 51,* 1 – 27.

Sternfeld, R. (1918). Zur tiergeographie Papuasiens und der pazifischen inselwelt. *Abhandlungen Herausgegeben von der Senckenbergischen Naturforschenden Geselldchaft, 36,* 375 – 436.

Includes enumeration of reptiles and amphibians collected by the "Natuna," some species from various atolls: Ulithi, Tuamotus. (SF55)

Strand, E. (1915). Indoaustralische, papuanische und polynesische spinnen des Senckenbergischen Museums, gesammelt von E. Wolf, J. Elbert u.a. In Wissenschaftliche Ergebnisse der Hanseatischen Südsee-Expedition 1909. *Abhandlungen herausgegeben von der Senckenbergischen Naturforschenden Geselldchaft, 36*(2), 179 – 274.

Mostly based on collections made by the Natuna expedition: includes some species collected on atolls, especially Tuamotus and Ulithi. (SF55)

Strohecker, H. F. (1958). Coleoptera: Endomychidae. *Insects of Micronesia, 16*(2), 105 – 108. http://hbs.bishopmuseum.org/pubs-online/pdf/iom16-2endo.pdf

Includes Trochoideus desjardinsi recorded from Fassarai, Ulithi atoll. (SF71)

Takayama, J. (1982). A brief report on archaeological investigations of the southern part of Yap Island and nearby Ngulu Atoll. In M. Aoyogo (Ed.), *Islanders and their outside world.* (pp. 77 – 104). Tokyo: Committee for Micronesian Research, St. Paul's (Rikkyo) University.

Tajima, Y. (2001). Dabach, new settlement, constructed for outer islanders of Yap in Micronesia. *South Pacific Study, 22 (1),* 13 – 30.

Tajima, Y. (2001). Outers moving in: The residence of outer islanders in Yap Proper. In T. Aoyama (Ed.), The Progress Report of the 1999 Survey of the Research Project "Social Homeostasis of Small Islands in an Island-zone." *Occasional Papers, 34*(section 1, report 3), 25 – 32. Kagoshima, Japan: Kagoshima University Research Center for the Pacific Islands. Retrieved from http://cpi.kagoshima-u.ac.jp/

Tajima, Y., & Harong, S. (2003). Migration of Mogmog Islanders in Ulithi Atoll, Yap State, FSM. In T. Aoyama (Ed.), The Progress Report of the 2000 and 2001 Survey of the Research Project "Social Homeostasis of Small Islands in an Island-Zone," Yap Proper and Ulithi Atoll, Micronesia. *Occasional Papers, 39*(section 1, report 3), 17 – 23. Kagoshima, Japan: Kagoshima University Research Center for the Pacific Islands. Retrieved from http://cpi.kagoshima-u.ac.jp/

Takatsukasa, S., & Kuroda, N. (1915). A table of birds known at present from the various islands and island groups of western Pacific, formerly belonging to Germany but now occupied by Japan, *Tori, 1*(2), 60 – 64.

An article in Japanese. A table of birds known at the time of writing to be from the various islands and island-groups of the western Pacific that earlier belonged to Germany and occupied at the time of writing by Japan. A table may be legible to non-Japanese readers because it is in Roman type. It includes Mackenzie and Ngoli, as localities for various species. (SF55)

Taura, S., Park, B. J., Ichitani, K., Onjo, M., & Kawabe, K. (2003). Random amplified polymorphic DNA (RAPD) analysis of yams collected in the Yap islands and the Ulithi islands. In Aoyama, T. (Ed.), The Progress Report of the 2000 and 2001 Survey of the Research Project "Social Homeostasis of Small Islands in an Island-Zone" Yap Proper and Ulithi Atoll, Micronesia. *Occasional Papers*, *39*(section 2, report 8), 77 – 81. Kagoshima, Japan: Kagoshima University Research Center for the Pacific Islands. Retrieved from http://cpi.kagoshima-u.ac.jp/

Tominaga, S., Ichitani, K., Onjo, M., Tsuda, K., Park, B. J. Nagayama, H., Kamada, N., & Kohno, R. (2003). Preliminary report on soil conditions in Yap Island and Ulithi Atoll of the FSM. In T. Aoyama (Ed.), The Progress Report of the 2000 and 2001 Survey of the Research Project "Social Homeostasis of Small Islands in an Island-Zone" Yap Proper and Ulithi Atoll, Micronesia. *Occasional Papers*, *39*(section 3, report 3), 99 – 105. Kagoshima, Japan: Kagoshima University Research Center for the Pacific Islands. Retrieved from http://cpi.kagoshima-u.ac.jp/

Tominaga, S., Yamamoto, M., Kohno, R., Park, B. J., Tsuda, K., Onjo, M., & Ichitani, K. (2003). Classification of citrus species on Yap Island and Ulithi Atoll of the FSM. In T. Aoyama, (Ed.), The Progress Report of the 2000 and 2001 Survey of the Research Project "Social Homeostasis of Small Islands in an Island-Zone" Yap Proper and Ulithi Atoll, Micronesia. *Occasional Papers*, *39*(section 3, report 2), 93 – 98. Kagoshima, Japan: Kagoshima University Research Center for the Pacific Islands. Retrieved from http://cpi.kagoshima-u.ac.jp/

Tsuda, K., Watanabe, M., Tominaga, S., Onjo, M., & Ichitani, K. (2003). The biogeography of the insect fauna of the Ulithi Islands, Micronesia. In Aoyama, T. (Ed.), The Progress Report of the 2000 and 2001 Survey of the Research Project "Social Homeostasis of Small Islands in an Island-Zone" Yap Proper and Ulithi Atoll, Micronesia. *Occasional Papers*, *39*(section 2, report 7), 73 – 75. Kagoshima, Japan: Kagoshima University Research Center for the Pacific Islands. Retrieved from http://cpi.kagoshima-u.ac.jp/

United States Weather Bureau. (1965). *Climatography of the United States, no. 86 – 44*: *Dicennial census of the United States climate, climatic summary of the United States; supplement for 1951 through 1960, Hawaii and Pacific*. Washington, DC: US Government Printing Office.
Includes data from Ulithi, Marcus, Wake, Kwajalein, Majuro, Eniwetok, Midway, French Frigate Shoals, Johnston, and Canton; maps. (SF71)

Uowolo, A. L. (2017). Melai Mai Breadfruit Project in Yap, FSM. Islandpacifica. Aug 17, 2017. www.youtube.com

US Navy. (1945). Base facilities summary, advance bases, Central Pacific Area, 1 – 242. Pearl Harbor, HI.
Contains some general geographical information on the "Line Islands" (Christmas, Johnston, Palmyra, Canton, Midway), Marshalls, Gilberts, and Ulithi; information on water supply; maps. (SF55)

Ushijima, I. (1982). The control of reefs and lagoons: Some aspects of the political structure of Ulithi Atoll. In M. Aoyagi (Ed.), *Islanders and their outside world* (pp. 35 – 75). Tokyo: St. Paul's (Rikkyo) University.

Van Zwaluwenburg, R. H. (1948). New species and new records of elaterid beetles from the Pacific III. *Proceedings of the Hawaiian Entomological Society, 13*, 265 – 276.
Systematic enumeration, includes simodactylus lineatus, n. sp., from Nukuoro, p. 269, and records of other species from Wake, Eniwetok, Ulithi. (SF55)

Vargo A. (1991). Summary and conclusion. In A. Vargo & L. Ferentinos (Compilers), *A rapid rural appraisal of taro production systems in Micronesia, Hawai'i and American Samoa: Surveys conducted in conjunction with the project, A comparative study of low-input and high-input taro production systems in the American Pacific, with special reference to pest control* (pp. 161 – 166). Honolulu, Hawai'i: Pacific Agriculture Development Office, University of Hawai'i.

Figure 17. Navy physician Marshall Wees being taken on a turtle hunt by Ulithian youth during his WWII assignment to Fassarai. *(U.S. Navy photo, reprinted from Wees, 1950)*

Wagner, W. L., Herbst, D. R., Tornabene, M. W., Weitzman, A., & Lorence, D. H. (2012). Flora of Micronesia website. Retrieved from http://botany.si.edu/pacificislandbiodiversity/micronesia/index.htm

Wees, M. P. (1950). *King-doctor of Ulithi.* 1 – 128. NY: The Macmillan Company.
Popular account of experiences of an American naval doctor, with some incidental and sometimes inaccurate information on natural history and general environmental conditions on the atoll; good information on diseases current among the natives; photographs. (SF55)

Wenkam, R. (1971). *Micronesia: The breadfruit revolution.* Honolulu, HI: East-West Center Press.

Wharton, G. W., & Hardcastle, A. B. (1946). The genus Neoschongastia (Acarinida: Trombiculidae) in the Western Pacific area. *The Journal of Parasitology, 32*, 286 – 322.

Figure 18. King Ueg of Ulithi. *(U.S. Navy photo, reprinted from Wees, 1950).*

Includes five new species of Acarina from Ulithi, all parasites on birds. (SF55)

Wiles, G. J. (2004). A Record of *Perochirus* cf. *scutellatus* (Squamata: Gekkonidae) from Ulithi Atoll, Caroline Islands. *Micronesica, 37(1)*, 163 – 166. Retrieved on August 4, 2016 from: University.uog.edu.172-31-22-36.previewmywsisite.com/up/micronesica/abstracts_37/pdfs_37/163-166 wiles 37(1).pdf

Wood, J. B. (1921). Yap and other Pacific Islands under the Japanese mandate. *National Geographic Magazine, 40,* 591 – 628.

Wynn, A. H., Reynolds, R. P., Buden, D. W., Falanruw, M., Lynch, B. (2012). The unexpected discovery of blind snakes (Serpentes: Typhlopidae) in Micronesia: two new species of *Ramphotyphlops* from the Caroline Islands. *Zootaxa , 3172*, 39 – 54.

Yamamoto, S. (2014). Food Security in Small Islands: Case Studies in the Federated States of Micronesia. In S. Yamamoto & S. Raharjo (Eds.), New horizon of island studies in the Asia-Pacific Region, *Occasional Papers, 54, 27 – 33.* Kagoshima, Japan: Kagoshima University Research Center for the Pacific Islands. Retrieved from http://cpi.kagoshima-u.ac.jp/

Yamashina, Y. (1932). On new bats found in Polynesian region (Japanese Mandate). *Transactions of the Natural History Society of Formosa, 22,* 240 – 241. Description of new subspecies, including Pteropus marianus ulthiensis from Ulithi; in Japanese, title in English in table of contents. (SF55)

Yangerluo, R. B. (2012). *Land acquisition and disputes: Contemporary political and socioeconomic issues of Outer Islanders in Yap State, FSM.* (Unpublished master's thesis). University of Guam, Mangilao, Guam.

Yap Office of the Governor. (c.1995). *Yap State.* Colonia, Yap: Yap State Government.

Yap Visitor's Bureau. (2000). *Yap.* Colonia, Yap: Yap State Government.

Figure 19. Robert Yangerluo of Woleai, receiving the Presidential Thesis Award for Outstanding Thesis at the University of Guam. His research explored political and socioeconomic land issues for outer islanders of Yap. Yangerluo received the Master of Arts degree in Micronesian Studies in 2012 and is now a faculty member at the College of Micronesia, Yap State. Robert Yangerluo also worked as a Research Associate with University of Guam faculty, Todd Ames, Ann Ames, and Harley Manner. His work in Yap Proper served as the foundation for the later work presented in their respective chapters in Part 2 of this book.

Figure 20. In 1983, while conducting a Fresh Water Resources field project in Ulithi for Dr. Steven J. Winter at WERI, University of Guam, Dr. Rebecca Stephenson was able to view this large traditional structure on Fassarai that featured a high gabled roof. Note also the elevated airplane pontoon on the left that was used as a rainwater catchment device. *(Photo by Hiro Kurashina.)*

AFTERWORD

This book was written with the people of Ulithi at the forefront of the authors' minds. We thought of them as the primary readers of the book. Beyond them, we imagined that the book could be useful to teachers and students in Yap, other parts of Micronesia and Oceania, and perhaps in some college and university courses in the US and other parts of the world. Each one of us has been able to spend time in Ulithi and conduct our educational activities there only because of the generosity and participation of citizens of Ulithi – ranging from the very young to the very old. They have collaborated with us, fed us, cared for us when we were tired or ill, and they have enriched our lives. We hope this book provides good stories of our shared work in Ulithi and satisfactorily reflects the entertwining experiences we have had with our Ulithi sponsors and friends.

More specifically, the purposes of this book are to share the research and learning that the various authors have acquired from their teaching and field-work on Ulithi, or with Ulithians in other locations, at specific points in time. The authors accept the long-tested reality that research and writing are constantly subject to analysis and evaluation; open to review and critique; and invite revision and updating. We invite Ulithian as well as all other readers to give serious consideration to what has been written and illustrated in each chapter, and to share their questions, reactions, advice, or concerns. We are happy to receive and use these to revise future forms of the book.

Photographs and Our Purposes for Printing Them

There are many photographs in this book. We would like to comment on three main purposes for them:

1) To help readers visualize and understand the words and themes of each chapter. We expect that readers will differ in their ages, place of residence in the Atoll and/or other places in the world, and in their heritage. English may not be the first language of many people interested in the book. So, we provided pictures that will make it easier for all readers to grasp the main messages.

2) To help educators and students from other places and cultures who want to use the book to learn about Ulithi, Yap State, or Micronesia. We hope our chapters and photographs will allow them to see a little piece of life on Ulithi Atoll and the culture and lives of the people of Ulithi.

3) To fulfill some of the purposes of the social sciences in which we have been trained – anthropology, social work, psychology, sociology, legal studies, and geography – which would be to document aspects of life and culture at particular moments in time; to try to learn the meaning and lessons of what we have been shown; and then to use these lessons to plan for and cope with the future. We hope both students and educators will learn from the photographs and descriptions about procedures used

by the researchers, the generosity of the Ulithi people to the authors, and how this combination led to the research results discussed in this book. Examples are given in every chapter of Ulithian involvement or leadership in research and analysis on their atoll. Undoubtedly, Ulithian research leadership will increase in years to come.

Examples of the Use of Photographs

There are examples of the usefulness of photographs in almost every chapter. In the reporting of Rebecca Stephenson and her students, the reader who is preparing to teach either a high school or possibly a college level *capstone course,* will find much to aid in preparing and implementing such a course. The photographs in the papers of Dr. Stephenson and her students make this more understandable and useful to those planning similar activities in the future. Some of the photographs in these chapters also introduce Ulithians who helped arrange and support the Field School. Dr. Sinoto's chapter on the intricacies of catching flying fish becomes much more understandable because of the drawings and photographs he included. The Ulithian men who collaborated with him contributed to preserving that knowledge. Melvin Cruz illustrated certain economic conditions through his photographs of commercial enterprises on Ulithi.

In her chapter on lava lavas, Eulalia Harui-Walsh shares rare details on the materials, weaving process, varieties, and purposes of this culturally and historically important article. The photographs of each type clarify the qualities and distinctions among them.

In his chapter, Joshua Walsh, not only discusses the dual-culture/dual-location of his life's development, he also shares a beautiful photograph of the marriage of his mother and father and members of the wedding party. We think that upon seeing this assembly of close and loving family and friends, the reader will gain an emotional sense of the positive and supporting foundation that helped Joshua's parents launch their family's future. This is an instance in which a photographic image can tell a story that otherwise might have required a thousand words and been less effective. Likewise, seeing the photographs of Joshua and his brother John with their families, helps us see the longer path of their heritage. Joshua's photo in the FSM Supreme Court room in Palikir enlarges our understanding of the cultural blends in his life even further.

Dr. Ann Ames illustrates additional economic principles in graphic and photographic forms in her chapter. She is seen engaged in some of her research discussions with Ulithi women in Dr. Manner's chapter.

Dr. Todd Ames' chapter brings the reader into his recent fieldwork on Ulithi by supplying photographic examples. In so doing, he provides an educational case study to students who are learning how to participate in – or teach about – the procedures of field work—whether it be in Ulithi, other places in Micronesia, or the world at large. His sharing allows readers to learn about a concrete example of what one might expect to see during research on environment and ecology on an atoll, and while learning about island economies. Whether student or teacher, the reader could see an example of how researchers sought permission from the Chief of Ulithi for their activities and how they worked closely with community members for mutual sharing of environmental and economic information and opinions. Part of this exploration included documenting a few educational and social activities on Ulithi, images that help the reader appreciate portions of the important cultural context of the island.

In Mary Spencer's chapter, she used photography as an educational tool in her teacher education courses for Yap State Outer Island teachers in summer 1985. It aided her observation and illustration process for addressing the learning objectives and activities in these two University of Guam courses. For example the college students in each of her courses voluntarily posed for their respective class photos. The two courses each explored child development, focusing especially on the way cognitive skills such as thinking, problem solving, and learning the various forms of language (speaking, listening, reading, writing) develop within cultural context. She photographed examples of Ulithi and other outer island children as they developed these skills while their parents participated in the University summer school. Associated with understanding these forms of development is the opportunity to learn about the social and cultural ways of life that surround children as they grow and learn. The outer island teachers who were students in Dr. Spencer's class thought deeply about these culturally connected ways of teaching and parenting children. Their own descriptions of these processes appear in Dr. Spencer's chapter. As this dialogue took place, Dr. Spencer captured examples of culturally-guided practices in both her notes and her photography. She then used these examples in her Ulithi courses, and used both notes and photographs in teacher training and technical assistance activities with Yap teachers on later occasions. By sampling the activities of the Ulithi and other outer island children on the island that summer, and bringing them into course discussion of child development, educational psychology, assessment of language and academic growth, and cultural factors known to interact with learning, both the instructor and the college students were able to make the courses relevant to the purposes established by the Yap State Department of Education and the University. The children and their families were routinely asked for permission to be photographed, and these parents were often present when pictures of their children were taken. College students and other adults were also asked, and only those who consented were photographed. In this chapter there are a few more recent photographs of adults (e.g., several culture teachers at the Outer Island High School, and a neighbor in a nearby home, who gave permission for Dr. Spencer to photograph her working at her loom and her children as they pitched in to help her from time to time). The purpose of all of these community photographs is to illustrate naturally occurring teaching and learning interactions and arrangements of children and adults, within cultural context. In her chapter, Dr. Spencer discusses how these examples relate to evolving theories of child cognitive development within a variety of cultural contexts.

In the final chapter of the book, Harley Manner uses an annotated bibliography about the environments and ecological issues of Ulithi to directly encourage and guide Ulithians toward past, present, and promising future resources of their atoll. For all readers, he discusses global warming and sea level rise and methods to mitigate the negative effects of these phenomena. He speaks about effects on Pacific plants and possible effective approaches for coping with impacts. He stresses the importance of their development of knowledge about their environment and taking the next steps, which might include defining their own research agendas for the future. As part of this message, Dr. Manner includes photographic examples of Ulithians participating in a workshop and survey on environment and food supply issues in 2010, an example of a Ulithi man using one possibly effective technique to protect taro plants, and a woman reviewing a report based on an earlier study on Ulithi in which she had been involved. Also interspersed are photographs of some of the American and Canadian scholars who have conducted research on Ulithi and written extensively about the Atoll and its people. The purpose for all of these photos is to give readers the more personal sense that an image of relevant research in progress can convey, and of some of the visiting scientists who have spoken extensively about Ulithian life and culture. For the same reason, photographs of all of the lead authors of the book appear in various other parts of the book. A photograph of King Ueg of Ulithi, taken during the WWII occupation years by author and Navy doctor M.P. Wees in his book *King-doctor of Ulithi* (1950), is shown. This photo is of historic importance and is included to show that Wees's book, though not recent, may be of interest to readers. Finally, a photo is provided of Woleaian researcher and scholar, Robert Yangerluo, during the University's award of merit for his study of land issues on Yap (Yangerluo, 2012). The intent of this image is to draw attention to the importance and implications of Yangerluo's research for Ulithi and other outer islands.

In all of the photographs presented in this book, authors strived to insure the dignity and well being of those photographed. Photographs included in the book accord with the ethical standards of the professional associations of the researchers (American Anthropological Association, 2015; American Association of Geographers, 2009; American Psychological Association, 2010; and American Sociological Association, 1999), and are consistent with other legal and ethical discussions of the matter (e.g., Goldstein, 2008; Smithsonian National Museum of the American Indian, 2009).

References

American Anthropological Association. (2015). *AAA guidelines for the evaluation of ethnographic and visual media.* http://www.americananthro.org/ConnectWithAAA/ Content.aspx?ItemNumber=1941 Retrieved 3/30/17.

American Association of Geographers. (2009). *Statement on Professional Ethics.* http://www.aag.org/cs/about_aag/governance/statement_of_professional_ethics   Retrieved 4/3/17.

American Psychological Association. (2010). *Ethical principals of psychologists and code of conduct.* Washington, DC: Author.

American Sociological Association. (1999). *Code of ethics and policies and procedures of the ASA Committee on Professional Ethics.* http://www.asanet.org/membership/code-ethics Retrieved 4/3/17.

Goldstein, A. (2008). *Cardozo Arts & Entertainment Law Journal.* Privacy from photography: Is there a right not to be photographed under New York State law? (1-27).

Smithsonian National Museum of the American Indian. (2009). *Nine guidelines for research with indigenous peoples.* Washington, DC: Author.

Wees, M. P. (1950). *King-doctor of Ulithi.* 1-128. NY: The Macmillan Company.

Yangerluo, R. B. (2012). *Land acquisition and disputes: Contemporary political and socioeconomic issues of Outer Islanders in Yap State, FSM.* (Unpublished master's thesis). University of Guam, Mangilao, Guam.

INDEX

A

Adoption, 119
Agricultural training, 152
Alkire, William, 34, 91 – 92, 199, 217, 220
American Anthropological Association, 241
American Association of Geographers, 241
American Psychological Association, 241
American Sociological Association, 241
American with Disabilities Act, 85, 89 – 90
Ames, Ann, 38, 109, 152, 154, 159, 162 – 63, 169 – 71, 174, 177, 215, 221, 230, 237, 239
Ames, Jan, 177
Ames, Todd, 38, 81, 109, 152, 162, 167 – 70, 173, 175 – 77, 179 – 83, 215, 230, 237, 239
Ames, Todd and Derwin Rolmar, 221, 230
Amesbury, S., 59
Anell, B., 59 – 60, 64, 67
Angkel, Fr. Julio, 35
Anthropology, 47 – 50, 52, 64, 97, 140, 142 – 43, 149, 151, 220, 225, 238; cultural anthropology, 36, 47, 54 – 55, 62, 90, 97
Arago, J., 87, 139
Armed Forces Radio Station WVTY, 134
Armstrong, J., disability in Pacific, 84
Asor, 3, 9, 10, 12 – 13, 15 – 16, 18 – 21, 23, 27, 38, 51, 73 – 74, 90 – 91, 102, 113, 121 – 22, 144, 146, 148, 154, 162, 176 – 77, 179 – 80, 196 – 97
Authority, 116

B

Barratt, G., 4, 139
Bechiyal Cultural Center, Yap, 50
Bernardo de Equi Zabalaga, Don, 4
Bernice P. Bishop Museum, 36, 48, 50, 64
Breadfruit, 30, 57, 74, 76, 78 – 79, 163, 169, 171 – 72, 176, 181, 219
Brothers, Sisters, and First Cousins, 117
Bunshitsu (weather station), 19

C

Cable television, 122
Caldwell, Michael, 185
Canoe carving, 207
Canoe house, 103, 201 – 2
Capital, 152, 157 – 58
Capstone course, 47, 239
Cash economy, 75, 122 – 23
Catholic Church, 77, 79
Celes, R., 124, 127
Ceremonial use of lava lava, 141
Chamorro (CHamoru) language and Culture, 88, 95
Chamorro Lagoon, Yap, 168

Chief Yach of Falalop, 169, 174
Child activity groups, 186 – 87, 190 – 91
Child agency, 211
Child development, 38 – 39, 184, 240
Child-to-child teaching, 211
Children, 4 – 5, 10, 12, 16, 21, 37 – 38, 56, 77, 79, 84, 87 – 88, 92, 102, 114 – 15, 117, 119 – 20, 123, 125, 136, 140, 142, 158, 163, 169, 172, 182, 185 – 94, 196 – 212, 216, 218, 240 – 41
Chim, Marianna, 230
Chuuk, 14, 32 – 33, 35, 113, 121 – 22, 154 – 55, 157, 159 – 60, 163, 166, 182, 193, 223, 225
Climate change, taro die off, 152, 157, 180
Coconut husking, 104
Coconuts, 181
commerce, 180
community activities, 157
Compact of Free Association (COFA), 37, 92, 122 – 23, 127
comparative analysis, 152
comparisons of disability on Guam and Ulithi, 84, 94
Congress of Micronesia, 29, 31 – 32
Congress of Micronesia Status Commission, 32
Coordinated Investigations of Micronesian Anthropology (CIMA), 28, 34
Council of Chiefs, 29
Council of Micronesia, 29
Council of Pilung, 4, 33
Council of Tamol, 4, 33
Craib, J. L., 59, 61
Crane, Nicole, 135
Cruz, M. D., 36, 48 – 49, 73, 239
cultural tradition and change, 113, 115, 139

D

Damm, H., 6
dance, traditional, 53, 182
Davis, S. H., 36
Department of Homeland Security, 133
Deutsche Jaluit-Gesellschaft, 8
Diaz, T. A., 123
Die West-Karolinen-Gesellschaft, 8
difficulties of disability in Ulithi, 94
Dipwek, Alberta Ului, 144, 148
disabilities in Ulithi; on Guam, 84 – 96
disability and culture, 87, 91
drawing, 190
Driver, M., 66, 68, 87, 92, 95
Dyen, Isadore, 223

E

economics, 36, 48, 73, 81
economic solutions: stakeholders, training, 160
education, 21, 35, 37 – 38, 115, 121 – 24, 133, 174 – 75, 183 – 85, 196, 240
Elbert, Samuel H., 195, 224
Ellis, S. J., 4
English-Ulithian Dictionary, 102, 194, 197
environment, 13, 38, 74, 113, 122 – 23, 127, 137, 141, 196, 213, 215, 217, 240 – 41
European Contact and Control, 4
Executive Orders No. 8683; No. 10265; No. 10408; No. 10470; No. 11045, 26, 28
export issues, 152, 158

F

Fais, 3 – 4, 13, 17, 22 – 24, 102, 153, 163, 167, 170, 173, 179 – 80, 196, 215 – 16
Falalop, 3, 9 – 10, 12, 15, 16, 19, 23, 34, 38, 49, 51, 52, 53, 56, 68, 71, 73 – 74, 76 – 81, 90 – 92, 102, 113, 121 – 22, 144 – 45, 148, 152 – 63, 166 – 75, 177 – 85, 188 – 89, 191, 196 – 97, 200, 210, 213, 230; (aerial view), 168; (infrastructure; stores), 154, 156, 162
Falan, H., 11, 197
faluw (Yap men's house), 50, 84, 90 – 91, 117, 120, 132, 134, 153, 203, 206 – 8, 210
family structure, 37, 119, 123 – 24
Farraulap, learning styles, 199, 208, 212
Fassarai, 3, 12, 15 – 16, 21, 25, 37, 48, 51, 54, 73 – 74, 79, 90 – 92, 129, 140, 146, 195 – 96, 236 – 37
Father Nick, 56, 58
Faurang, J. J., 197
field school, 36, 47 – 52, 54 – 55, 62, 83, 90, 97, 142, 149, 239
Figirliong, J. and D., 54, 83
Fischer, A., 193
fishhooks, 59 – 60; gorges, 64 – 66, 68, 70; stick type, 64 – 65, 68; bent type, 64 – 68, 71; history of, 66; replicas, 64; at Huahine, 70
fishing, 12, 30, 36, 48, 50, 56, 58 – 61, 64, 66, 68 – 71, 73, 76 – 77, 115, 120, 130, 162, 176, 178, 184, 200
Fitzgerald, M. H., disability in Pacific, 92
flower Lei, 201
flying fish, 36, 59 – 60, 69 – 71, 239
food, 3, 12 – 14, 18, 20, 24, 30, 38, 49, 52, 59, 73, 76 – 77, 79, 81, 92 – 93, 114 – 17, 120 – 21, 127, 130, 137, 153, 162, 163, 167, 170, 172, 181, 203, 213, 217, 221, 241
food preparation, 56, 209
foreign influences, 37, 113 – 14
Fosberg, Raymond, 219 – 20
Fritz, Governor (German), 8
FSM Supreme Court, 133, 239

G

gardens on Falalop, 73, 154 – 55, 164 – 65, 169 – 71, 174, 180 – 81
gender roles, 37, 126
Ghow, 139
Giil'ab, 3
global warming, 157
Godeffroy Trading Company, 6
Goodenough, Ward, 33, 225
Gorge, 59, 65, 70
graduation ceremonies, 78, 190
Gräffe, Edward, 6
Guam, 4 – 5, 7, 26, 28 – 29, 36, 49 – 52, 54, 58, 64 – 65, 68, 71, 78 – 79, 81, 84 – 90, 94 – 95, 97, 113, 121, 123, 133, 137, 156, 158, 163, 173 – 74, 193, 196, 213, 216
Guam's Department of Mental Health, 84
Guam's Down's Syndrome Association, 87
Guam Vocational Training Center, 87
Guiormog, T., 36, 113 – 14, 121

H

Habele Outer Island Education Fund, 34
Hadhomar, Emanual, 152
Haduemog, Carmen, 144 – 46
Hagileiram, Fr. John, 35
Hanlon, D., 14, 121, 128
Haped, A. M., 197
Harui, Fernando, 130, 134, 137
Harui-Walsh, E. J., 36 – 38, 48 – 49, 58 – 59, 83 – 84, 133, 136, 139, 141 – 42, 151, 239
Hasugulayag, J. G., 36 – 37, 113, 115 – 16, 136, 176
Head Start, 79, 92, 153, 162
Hezel, Father Francis X., 14, 25 – 26, 29, 31, 35, 113 – 14, 116 – 17, 119 – 21, 123 – 24, 126 – 27, 132, 134, 173, 226
Higuchi, Wakako, 7 – 10, 12 – 13, 15 – 22
Hikotai (tokko), 23
Hinatasou, 13
Holstrum, S., 48 – 49, 56
home visits, 192, 197
house, 77
Huahine, 70
Hulu flowers, 106

I

Immanuel, 170, 171
indigenous agriculture, 216
intergenerational learning traditions, 212

J

Japanese contact and administration, 7, 9, 11, 12, 74, 170
Japanese *dekasegi* policy, 14 – 18
Japanese Mandate, 24, 216

Japanese Military Administrative Headquarters, *Minseibu*, 8, 10
Japanese Naval Guard Unit-*Keibitai*, 22
Japanese Navy, 8, 10 – 11, 14, 18 – 19, 22
Junkei, 22

K

Kaitans, 179
Kasuga, 11 – 12
Kennedy, John F., 28 – 29, 31 – 32
King Alfonso XII of Spain, 7
King Alfonso XIII of Spain, 7
King (Chief) Ueg, 21, 25, 30, 94, 236, 241
King Malefich, 31
Krause, S., 132
Kubary, Johann, 6 – 7, 66
Kung Fu Group, 191
Kurashina, H., 14, 57, 64, 71, 97 – 100, 103 – 8, 142 – 43, 147 – 48, 151, 173, 176 – 77, 237

L

Lahasudep, Y.V., 197
Laimoh, M. J., 54, 102, 194, 196 – 97
Lamaleg, P. K., 197
Lamotrek, learning styles, 205
land navigation, 37, 115
language and disability, 93
language and literacy, 193; and graphic symbolism, 195; written Ulithian language, 195
laundramat, 79
lava lava, 37, 139 – 42; varieties, 143, 150; cultural values, 149 – 50; in home, 207; preparation of threads and loom weaving, 105, 141; ceremonial use, 141 – 42
League of Nations, 8, 11, 121
learning style: Woleai; Ulithi; Lamotrek; Farraulap; themes, 198 – 99, 204, 210, 238
LeBar, F. M., 176
Legdesog, Chandra, 3, 222
Lessa, William, 4 – 6, 28 – 31, 34, 39, 58 – 59, 73 – 76, 82, 89, 130 – 33, 137, 139 – 40, 217, 228
LISA Program, 215
Litke, Fedor Petrowitsch, 5
loom weaving, 207
Lopez de Villalobos, Ruy, 4
LORAC (long range radio navigation station), 25
Lugwa, Alex Carleton, 116
Luhudull, Maria, 152
Lytico Bodig, 88

M

Macaque monkey, 14
maliel, 105, 140 – 41

Maluchmai, Maryann Rulmal and Dominic Rulmal, 104
Mangefel, John, 32 – 33
Manner, H., 13, 38, 106, 152, 162 – 63, 169 – 70, 215, 217, 230, 237, 239, 241
Map Village, 50
Maria Christine of Austria, 7
marketing, 38, 152 – 53, 155 – 56, 158 – 62, 173
Marshall Islanders, 218
material objects, 73
Mellen, N. & Hancock, J., 34, 198
Mellen, N. & Uwel, J., 198
Mendiola, E., 48, 49
micro-finance, 38, 152 – 63, 166
micro-markets, 152, 154, 156
Micro Spirit ship, 79
Micronesian Area Research Center (MARC), 48, 50, 52, 64, 95, 142 – 43, 151
migration experiences, 123
military, 8, 10 – 12, 16, 18, 20 – 22, 24 – 26, 28 – 30, 74, 78, 121, 123, 171, 183, 216
missile, 171 – 72
Mita and Anthony, 127
modernization, 56, 73, 77, 81 – 82, 139
Moglith, H., 69, 71, 83
Mogmog, 3, 6, 12, 15 – 17, 28, 30, 33, 51 – 52, 73 – 74, 90 – 92, 113, 121, 142, 145 – 46, 148, 189, 191, 196, 213
molfid, 77
Mulford, J., 140 – 42
Muscati, Padre, 4
Museum of New Zealand *(Te Papa Tongarewa)*, 38, 139, 142 – 47, 149 – 51
music group, 187
M/V Erroll, 31

N

Nabobo-Baba, U. W., 214
Nakayama, Tosiwo, 33
Nan'yo Boeki (Nanbo, South Seas Trading Company), 8 – 13, 17, 20, 22
Nan'yocho, 11, 14 – 16, 18, 22
Nan'yocho airplane *(Shirohato)*, 18
Nan'yocho Meteorological Observatory, Ulithi Sub-branch, 18
Nan'yo Gunto, 8 – 12, 15 – 17, 21
Nan'yo Gunto Gakko (kogakko), 10, 12, 21 – 22
Nelson, J., 54
Nery, P., 68, 71, 83, 97
Nery, S., 97
Neylon, Bishop, 35
Ngulu, 4, 102
Nikko Hotel, 64

O

OBEMLA (US Office of Bilingual Education and Minority Language Affairs), 184
O'Keefe, David, 6
Outer Islands High School (OIHS), 34, 52 – 53, 56, 78, 91, 122, 184, 186, 191, 197, 199, 207, 210 – 11, 213, 240
Outer Islands High School, graduation, 51, 71, 78

P

Pacific Missionary Aviation (PMA), 50 – 51, 73, 79, 167, 173, 177, 186, 196
Pacific Science Board of the National Academy of Sciences, 34
Padre Juan Antonio Cantova, 5
Padre Victor Walter, 5
Palau-Maru, 20
Palau, Palaus, 7
PALI dictionary project, 196
Palifer, Terry (of Fais), 179
palus wolfulu (land navigator), 37
Paris Peace Conference, 10
Peace Corps, 28 – 29, 32, 34, 61, 129, 139, 224
Pemadaw, Maria, 146
Phillips, Susan C., 198 – 99
phosphate mining, 8, 13, 16, 24
photography: purposes; examples, 238 – 40
Piaget, J., 198
Pineda (in Driver, 1990), 87
Piscusa Bratt, D., 36, 48, 49, 97, 215
plant species, 139, 164 – 65, 216 – 18
population, 3, 4, 9, 15, 22, 25
Portulacacae, 13
postwar, 26
proa, 175 – 76
problems in production, 152, 155, 157, 160
production marketing and crops, 152 – 53, 155 – 56, 158 – 62, 173
Project BEAM, 33, 184 – 85, 213
Purslane, 13

R

Rahoy, Fr. Nick, 35
rai (stone money), 50
Rama, L. & J., 54
Ramaliol, P. P., 197
raw resources, 38, 152, 157
reciprocity, 37, 73, 76 – 77, 93, 119 – 20, 124
recycling, 77
respect for authority, 37, 116, 126
Ridgell, R., 113 – 14, 121 – 23
Rocha, Diego da, 4
Rogoff, B., 198
role of land, 37
Rolmar, Derwin, 116, 169 – 70, 174, 176, 216, 221

Rolmar, Thomas, 68 – 71
Roosevelt, Franklin D., 26
Rose-Crossley, R., 48, 54
Rosogmar, Maria, 146 – 48
Rugulumar, 32
rules of silence, 193
Rulmal, John, Jr., 109, 135 – 36, 173
Rulmal, John, Sr., 35, 54, 81, 83, 104, 136, 169, 173

S

Sachet, Marie-Helene, 13, 219 – 20, 232
Saipan-Maru, 20
Salalu, J. J., 197
Samo, Amando, 35
sea turtles, 179
Seibu-shicho (Western District Brigade Headquarters in Palau), 22
Setsuei tai (Naval Construction Battalion), 22
Shoriki, 13, 17
Sinoto, Y. H., 36, 48 – 50, 64, 69, 239
social structure, 37
social work practice, 124, 128
socialization to literacy, 38, 185, 194 – 95, 211
Solomon, Anthony, 32
Solomon Report, 32, 233
Soren, 9
Sorlen, 3, 19, 23
Spain, 4, 7
Spanish-American war, 7
Spencer, Mary, 3, 14, 38, 135 – 36, 169, 184, 188 – 89, 193, 195, 197 – 99, 201, 203, 205, 207, 215 – 16, 221, 230, 240 – 41
stakeholder meetings, 154, 174
Stephenson, Rebecca, 3, 14, 36 – 37, 47 – 49, 57, 64, 68, 71, 81, 83 – 84, 88, 90, 97, 108 – 9, 135 – 36, 139, 141, 143, 151, 173, 176 – 77, 215, 237, 239
stores, 74 – 75, 79 – 81, 154, 156, 162, 170, 180
subsistence activities, 156, 180
suicide, 84 – 85, 179, 226

T

Tacheliol, Hilary, 32 – 33, 213
Tacheliol, Rosa, 33, 213
Taro, 20, 30 – 31, 73, 76, 115, 120 – 21, 143 – 44, 163, 169 – 72, 174 – 75, 178, 180, 215 – 18, 236, 241
taro pit, 169 – 70, 172, 181
tattooing, 6
Tawag, Joseph, 56, 59 – 62
Tawerilmang, Tony, 185, 194
Tetens, Alfred, 6, 7
Thall, Fr. Apollo, 35
Thilenius, Georg Christian, 6
Thompson, L., Guam, 65, 89

Thoulag, B. and J., 213
thur (Ulithian loom), 105, 140 – 41
Topping, D., 88
Towachi Channel, 11
travel restrictions, 28
Truk (Chuuk), 10 – 12, 14 – 15, 32 – 33, 35, 113, 121 – 22, 154 – 55, 157, 159 – 60, 163, 166, 182, 193, 223, 225
Truman, Harry S., 26, 28 – 29
Trust Territory of the Pacific Islands (TTPI), 28 – 29, 31 – 34, 37, 121, 184, 196
Typhoon Omar, 85
Typhoon Ophelia, 29 – 31, 34, 74 – 76, 143

U

Ueg, King (Chief), 21, 25, 30, 94, 236, 241
Ulithi Adventure Lodge, 81, 162, 169, 172, 177
Ulithi Airport, Falalop, 168 – 69
The 'Ulithi' Encyclopedia, 134
Ulithi Atoll: land surface; location; nearby islands, 3
Ulithi canoe house, 103
Ulithi home setting, 153
Ulithi learning styles, 204
Ulithi Men's Council, 30
Ulithi students, 212
Ulithi survey, 216
Ulithian contributions to US, 127
Ulithian dictionary, 102, 194, 197
Ulithian economics, 36
Underwood, G., 28
Underwood, R., 33, 184
United Nations, 26, 29, 32, 121, 175
University of Guam, 33, 36, 38 – 39, 47 – 49, 51 – 52, 54, 62, 64, 83, 89 – 90, 95, 97, 135, 141 – 43, 149 – 51, 154, 183 – 84, 212 – 13, 215 – 16, 222, 237, 240
University of Guam, College of Education, 184
US Army, 173
US Department of Agriculture, 173, 215
US Department of Interior, 31
USGS Climate Science Center, 218
US Navy, 25 – 26, 28, 33 – 34, 121, 134, 223 – 25; Rear Admiral Carleton H. Wright, 25, 127
USN Missasinegwa, 179

V

Von Bismarck, Otto, 7

W

Wach Micronesian district, 29
Walsh, John (Jack) A., 37, 54, 58, 83, 132, 133, 136, 139, 142, 198
Walsh, Joshua D., 36, 37, 129, 239
water catchment, 108
weaving, 37 – 38, 48, 78, 100, 105, 120, 139 – 44, 146, 149, 154, 200, 207, 209, 210, 212, 229, 239
weaving: preparation of threads, 105
wedding, 118, 136, 176 – 80, 182, 239
Wees, Marshall P., 21 – 22, 25, 137, 236, 241
Western Caroline Company, 9
western education, 37
Western Pacific Association of the Disabled, 85 – 87, 89
Woleai, Woleaian, 8 – 9, 11, 17, 19, 24 – 25, 92, 145, 167, 199 – 202, 209, 212, 217, 237
women's roles, 30, 56, 75
World War II history and impacts, 121
World War II, Japanese and US after effects on Falalop, 170, 175, 178 – 79
written word, 194

Y

Yaaor, 3
Yach (Chief), 169, 174
Yamano Yukichi, 20
Yami Tribe, Taiwan, 65, 71
Yangerluo, Robert, 237, 241
Yap, 3 – 4, 6, 8 – 24, 29, 31 – 35, 38, 47, 49 – 52, 54 – 55, 58, 60, 75, 78, 90 – 92, 102, 104, 113 – 17, 121 – 22, 127, 132, 137, 139, 142, 152 – 60, 162 – 63, 166 – 69, 173, 175 – 76, 184, 186, 188, 191, 194 – 95, 197, 199 – 201, 210, 212 – 13, 215 – 17, 220, 223, 237 – 38, 240 – 41
Yap Airport, 50, 167 – 68
Yap Department of Education, 184
Yap Visitor's Bureau, 113, 121
Yatchdar, Juanita, 212 – 13
Yatoi (Japanese government employee), 22
Ydwechog, Lourdes, 145
Ylmareg, Linda, 141, 147 – 48
Yothog, Clare, 212 – 13
young child group, 191

Milton Keynes UK
Ingram Content Group UK Ltd.
UKHW020826160324
439499UK00004BA/47